John Ford

THE OKLAHOMA WESTERN BIOGRAPHIES
RICHARD W. ETULAIN, GENERAL EDITOR

John Ford

HOLLYWOOD'S OLD MASTER

By Ronald L. Davis

UNIVERSITY OF OKLAHOMA PRESS : NORMAN AND LONDON

Also by Ronald L. Davis

A History of Opera in the American West (New York, 1965)
Opera in Chicago (New York, 1966)
The Social and Cultural Life of the 1920s (New York, 1972)
A History of Music in American Life (New York, 1980–82)
(with Paul Boller) *Hollywood Anecdotes* (New York, 1988)
Hollywood Beauty: Linda Darnell and the American Dream (Norman, 1991)
The Glamour Factory: Inside Hollywood's Big Studio System (Dallas, 1993)

Davis, Ronald L.
    John Ford : Hollywood's old master / by Ronald L. Davis.
        p.   cm. — (The Oklahoma western biographies ; v. 10)
    Includes bibliographical references and index.
    ISBN 0-8061-2708-2
    1. Ford, John, 1894–1973.   2. Motion picture producers and direc-
tors — United States — Biography.   I. Title.   II. Series.
    PN1998.3.F65D38   1995
    791.43'0233'092 — dc20   94-25178
                                                                    CIP

Book design by Bill Cason

John Ford: Hollywood's Old Master is Volume 10 in *The Oklahoma Western Biographies*.

The paper in this book meets the guidelines for permanence and durability of the Committee on Production Guidelines for Book Longevity of the Council on Library Resources. ∞

1   2   3   4   5   6   7   8   9   10

For Eleanor,
friend and colleague over many years,
with love and appreciation

Contents

Illustrations

Following page 123
John Ford during the early period of sound movies
Gorham's Corner in Portland, Maine
John Ford with his mother, Barbara Curran Feeney
Harry Carey, John Ford's first Western star
The joining of the rails in *The Iron Horse*
A Ford family portrait
John Ford's yacht, *The Araner*
Actor Ward Bond

Series Editor's Foreword

BY RICHARD W. ETULAIN

RONALD L. Davis's new biography of movie director John Ford is particularly satisfying because it does so many things exceedingly well. A thorough, well-researched life story, it is also a comprehensive discussion of Ford's mammoth influence on Hollywood's version of American history, especially of the American West. In addition, Davis's work thoroughly explains the tangled webs of Ford's troubled relationships with family, friends, and fellow professionals.

Davis's study of Ford's life is based on wide and deep research. Utilizing numerous collections of correspondence, movie records, and dozens of oral histories, he fashions a probing story of Ford's remarkable five-decade career in movie-making. In evaluating Ford's intense ties to his Irish heritage, his complex family background, and his American patriotism, Davis discusses at length how these influences shaped Ford's mythic vision of his country's history.

Davis's Ford is a complex person, with the sunshine and clouds so skillfully shaded that a multihued and contradictory figure emerges. Ford's love-hate relationships with his parents, his wife, and his children, and yet lifelong friendships with John Wayne, Ward Bond, Hoot Gibson, and Harry Carey, Sr. and Jr., illustrate the conflicting sides of his personality. Often waylaid by battles with depression and alcoholism, Ford was driven by a desire for close attachment and yet intensely ambivalent about his religious faith and his sexual identity. As a result of these conflicts, he increasingly wavered between triumph and near despair.

Equally illuminating is Davis's treatment of John Ford,

director par excellence. Often unorthodox in his directing methods, frequently dictating spur of the moment changes in scripts, and periodically flashing his blatant biases and prejudices, Ford nonetheless maintained a poetic sense of scene and action, coaxed actors into their best work, and brillantly captured mythic notions of the American West. Yet he so often alienated his underlings that they abandoned his sets and refused to work with him thereafter. To Davis's credit, he balances these achievements and failures and in doing so produces a valuable, probing life story of a major American cultural figure.

Ronald L. Davis furnishes a comprehensive biography of John Ford, simultaneously demonstrating how this monumental figure was both a product of Hollywood values and an innovator of them. Altogether, then, this important volume fulfills the goals of The Oklahoma Western Biographies series: to treat the lives of notable Westerners and to illustrate the larger world that influenced them and that they, in turn, influenced.

Preface

SINCE motion pictures consist merely of shadows projected onto a screen, they depend on movement to create a sense of reality. Action-packed Western movies are therefore ideally suited to the medium. Throughout the golden era of Hollywood, Westerns—ranging from grand spectacles to inexpensive oaters—remained popular with audiences. John Ford emerged as the undisputed master of the Western genre, unmatched as a visual storyteller with an instinct for keeping the screen alive with moving images and conflict.

Ford arrived in California just months before D. W. Griffith made his classic *The Birth of a Nation,* was there for the rise of the big studio system, and lasted as a major director until Hollywood's golden age was finished. As a craftsman he was without peer, his composition equal to the Renaissance masterpieces. Not content merely to photograph scenes, Ford painted with a camera, capturing nuances that were invisible to the naked eye. He rose to the pinnacle of his profession, becoming Hollywood's most famous director. But he also ranks among the twentieth century's most famous mythmakers. Through his individualized reading of westward expansion, and despite prejudices and misconceptions, Ford has exerted more influence on the way the world views America's past than have colleges of historians.

"In his greatest pictures," said Darcy O'Brien, son of screen actor George O'Brien, "Ford used each character to ignite and to illustrate a mythology, as Yeats did. This is very Irish. Ford had that Irish sense of the puniness of the individual before the Great Myth, yet the love of the odd, defiant individual who creates the myth. With Ford, it was the lonely soul—Lincoln, for example, creating a nation. Or Ford creating a medium."

The director's Western heroes are loners, yet Ford idealizes the community and demonstrates respect for traditional values. It is his mythic hero, outside the system and wary of society's restraits, who rights wrongs, puts an end to demons, and makes civilization possible. Ford's myths are full of sentiment and human insight; they teach lessons for the ages and, despite their flaws and heavyhanded humor, reveal the work of a visual stylist who understood his popular art form.

Privately John Ford was an elusive figure, his true identity perhaps a mystery even to himself. To survive the folderol of Hollywood, he created for himself an image of the tough iconoclast and played the legend so convincingly that the sensitive individual inside grew bereft, sequestered from family and intimate friends. Ford's life was one of loneliness and inner turmoil, but he turned his pain into cinematic masterworks, finding solace mainly in his craft.

When Richard Etulain suggested a film biography for The Oklahoma Western Biography series, we first thought of actors—William S. Hart, Tom Mix, John Wayne, so many possibilities. Yet no one seemed to represent the development of Hollywood as an industry. Quite apart from these conversations, I had planned to take a side trip to Monument Valley on my way to Los Angeles to interview for the Southern Methodist University Oral History Collection, a program I founded and continue to direct. Like John Ford decades earlier, I became captivated by the valley's rugged beauty and quickly sensed that I had found in Ford an appropriate subject for a Western film biography. Preliminary research in California showed that my instincts were correct.

With a sabbatical leave from teaching, I spent the entire fall of 1991 retracing the John Ford trail, an adventure to be sure. My sincere thanks go to the administration of Southern Methodist University for making that leave possible. On my journey I encountered a plethora of rabid John Ford fans; in each case they went out of their way to encourage my project and offer whatever assistance they could. As a result, my debts are many.

Gratitude must first be expressed to members of the John Ford stock company who shared experiences with me: Harry

Carey, Jr., Ben Johnson, Anna Lee, Joanne Dru, Robert Parrish, Mildred Natwick, Dorris Bowdon, Charles FitzSimons, Hank Worden, and Dean Smith. Eddie Albert, James Bellah, Jr., Linda Cristal, Gene Fowler, Jr., Martin Jurow, Andrew McLaglen, Winston Miller, George Peppard, Stefanie Powers, Claire Trevor, and Robert Wagner proved extremely helpful in delineating Ford as an artist and as a person. Through years of oral history work numerous interviewees have contributed stories and comments about Ford, most notably Leon Ames, Ralph Bellamy, Pandro S. Berman, Budd Boetticher, Donald Curtis, Edward Dmytryk, Philip Dunne, Bonita Granville, Henry Hathaway, Helen Hayes, John Ireland, Shirley Jones, Burt Kennedy, Otto Lang, Mary Anita Loos, James Lydon, Ken Murray, Pat O'Brien, Gil Perkins, Cesar Romero, Joseph Silver, James Stewart, Milburn Stone, Marshall Thompson, and William Wyler. Special acknowledgment must be made to Michael and Patrick Wayne, who recalled John Ford for me at length, and to Darcy O'Brien, who not only told me his observations of Ford, but allowed me access to the diary and papers of his father.

Dan Ford, the director's grandson, gave generously of his time and insights, which had the benefit of his own research for his book *Pappy: The Life of John Ford* (1979). Through Dan I was able to contact Mary McPhillips, Ford's niece in Maine, as well as Portland historian Don MacWilliams, who guided me on a tour of the town's old Irish section.

On a repeat trip to Monument Valley I was fortunate enough to talk with Leone "Mike" Goulding, wife of the Navajo trading post operator who arranged facilities for Ford's companies during many months of location work in the valley. Another never-to-be-forgotten experience was my interview with Billy Yellow, a Navajo extra who worked on Ford's Westerns; his daughter, Evelyn Nelson, translated, while Evelyn's young son looked on with polite curiosity.

Sincere thanks must be extended to the efficient staffs at the Margaret Herrick Library of the Motion Picture Academy of Arts and Sciences, the special collections division of the Doheny Library at the University of Southern California, the

Mayer Library of the American Film Institute, the oral history collection of Columbia University, the Utah State Historical Society, the special collections libraries of the University of Utah and Brigham Young University, the Arizona State Historical Society, the Hoblitzelle Theater Collection at the University of Texas, the Wisconsin Center for Film and Theater Research, the Los Angeles County Museum of Natural History, the Portland Public Library, the library at the University of Maine, the Maine Historical Society, the interlibrary loan office of Fondren Library at Southern Methodist University, and, most particularly, the staff of the Lilly Library at Indiana University, where the John Ford papers are housed. The latter made my weeks in Bloomington a productive joy.

Since I was told in interview after interview that I could never truly understand John Ford without understanding the Irish, I determined early that a trip to Ireland was essential. Before leaving for Dublin I contacted Lord Michael Killanin, who had known Ford most of his life and later worked with him as a producer. Killanin and his wife, Sheila, happened to be on the west coast of Ireland when my letter arrived, so they received my request for an interview late. On the third day of my visit I arrived in Spiddal, where Ford's ancestors had lived, and after strolling around the village decided to stop in a pharmacy for film. While waiting for change I casually asked the proprietor if any Feeneys still lived in the area. I was promptly sent across the street to John Feeney's butcher shop, and sure enough Feeney proved to be a distant cousin of John Ford's. We had no more than begun talking when the butcher informed me matter-of-factly that Lord Killanin wanted me to call him, whereupon I was handed a telephone number in Dublin. Killanin, it seems, had left messages all over western Ireland, anticipating the stops I would make.

The day I spent with the Killanins was a delight, one that deepened my understanding of Ford immeasurably. We spent the morning talking about the director, ate a leisurely lunch, then devoted a long afternoon to going through Killanin's stack of Ford correspondence. My time in Ireland was running short, and I discovered that the Irish lord is not only a gentleman and a scholar, but an energetic research assistant when the occasion demands. It was an honor to spend time in his company.

On a more personal level I must thank my long-time associate Eleanor Solon, to whom this book is rightly dedicated, Jane Elder, Craig Schoenfeld, Judy Bland, Mildred Pinkston, my colleagues David J. Weber (who never forgets my birthday), R. Hal Williams, Daniel Orlovsky, and Luis Martin. John Drayton at the University of Oklahoma Press and Richard Etulain, editor of The Oklahoma Western Biography series, were a pleasure to work with and offered intelligent suggestions throughout the months of research and writing. James Terrell shared the trip to Ireland with me and in Galway introduced me to Kay Naughton; my conversation with Kay alone made that trip worthwhile. Film historian Scott Eyman shared relevant interviews he had taped, and Ann Early added to my understanding of the Irish experience in America through in-depth conversations. Peter and Jan DeLisle, Effie Hanover, and Gideon Ong have provided emotional support, and I welcome this opportunity to thank them. My friends are an understanding lot; they accept that when my word processor is on, communication is out. I respect their patience as they seem to respect my compulsive work habits. In that regard I identify with John Ford. From him I learned what to avoid as well as where to achieve—not a bad lesson, but then Ford was a master.

RONALD L. DAVIS

Dallas, Texas

John Ford

CHAPTER I

Genius with a Camera

WHEN boy-wonder Orson Welles first visited a Hollywood studio in the mid-1930s, he couldn't conceal his excitement. "This," he exclaimed, "is the biggest electric train any boy ever had!" When asked later to name the American directors who most appealed to him, Welles answered, "I like the old masters, by which I mean John Ford, John Ford, and John Ford." Frank Capra, who won almost as many Oscars, once referred to his friend as the "king of directors," whereas Ingmar Bergman, the great Swedish filmmaker, pronounced Ford "the best director in the world."

Ford remains the most honored director in Hollywood history, having won six Academy Awards and four New York Film Critics Awards for his work. He was the recipient of the American Film Institute's first Life Achievement Award and continues to be a cult figure among movie enthusiasts around the world, revered by professionals as Hollywood's foremost film poet. During a career that spanned over fifty years Ford made 136 pictures, fifty-four of them Westerns. While he became most closely identified with the American frontier, none of his Academy Awards was for a Western movie. Instead, his Oscars for *The Informer* (1935), *The Grapes of Wrath* (1940), *How Green Was My Valley* (1941), and *The Quiet Man* (1952), plus two for wartime documentaries, reflect Ford's versatility and dimension as a cinematic artist.

Almost half of his movies were released before 1930, and nearly half of those were made before 1920. By 1940 Ford was recognized as the dean of American directors, a genius with the camera who told his stories visually, keeping dialogue to a minimum. He has been compared to Walt Whitman, Mark Twain, William Faulkner, and Charles Ives for, like them, he stands as an American original. Yet Frank Capra went further: "A megaphone has been to John Ford what the chisel was to Michelangelo: his life, his passion, his cross."

Like Capra, Ford was a first-generation American. He grew up in an Irish enclave on the New England coast, his people scorned by the Protestant power structure surrounding them. While Ford preserved his Irish identity, he loved America and struggled to prove himself in terms acceptable to the cultural majority. Despite his early success as a filmmaker, he continued to feel excluded from the mainstream, a tension that haunted him all his life. Ford overcame his background, his lack of formal training, and personal insecurities to triumph as the American cinema's most decorated director. Yet he seldom mingled in Hollywood circles, accepted none of his Oscars in person, and preferred the company of his own crowd, the hard-drinking, macho acquaintances he caroused with over many years and trusted.

On the surface Ford's work resulted in simple, uncluttered films that somehow possess great sophistication. The director liked to pose as a folksy anti-intellectual who merely did "a job of work" and saw no need to analyze how it was accomplished. Difficult to interview, Ford proved consistently evasive about his craft, which he refused to call art, and safeguarded himself behind sarcasm, lies, and even a guise of illiteracy.

To a large degree he worked by instinct. "There is no secret about directing," he said, "except good common sense and a belief in what you are doing." Like most filmmakers of his day, he started at the bottom and learned his skills through trial and error. Later directors, Ford felt, became too preoccupied with the camera, treating it like some new toy. "Instead of looking at their people," he said, "they look at the camera. The camera obsesses them, and they think that is the secret. It isn't. The secret is in people's faces, their eye expression, their movements."

As many artists have, Ford considered the mystery of what he achieved part of his creativity. He possessed the ability to reduce complexities to an essence without diminishing meaning or power, enhancing the impact of scenes through his uncomplicated approach. "Great artists work with great simplicity," actress Katharine Hepburn once reflected, and Ford understood that early in his career. While his images are breathtaking, the pictures he directed are about people and human dignity. At his best Ford's dramatic sense and timing were flawless, although his work seldom seems theatrical. His was a cinematic approach—realistic and rooted in movement. He often said that a story is a story whether it's *Two Gentlemen from Verona* or *Stagecoach;* what matters is that it "works." On projects that he personally selected, Ford honed his scripts with writers until they suited his purpose, allowing sufficient latitude for him to develop ideas with the camera.

"Don't be afraid of sentiment," Ford said, "play it honestly." His films are filled with emotion, yet they only occasionally become mawkish. When admirers attempted to read motivation into his work, he tended to grow bored and mumble something like "No kidding! Is that so?" With Ford, what you saw was what you got; to discuss allusive meaning was to him superfluous. Well-read and informed on whatever subject he was photographing, he chose to pose as a man of action—a rugged, two-fisted man's man, for whom too much talk was an affectation.

Although he worked within a commercial system, John Ford earned sufficient freedom within the movie industry to perfect a personal style. He balanced studio assignments with productions he selected himself, always keeping in mind that the making of motion pictures was a business. "I've got a whole lot of respect for the people who go to see movies," he said. "I think we ought to make pictures in their language." He saw movies not as art, but as commercial entertainment, some examples better than others. Ford's favorite posture was that of a simple teller of tales who occasionally blundered into masterworks. He insisted that it is fatal for a director to consider only the aesthetic side of his craft, just as it is fatal to become preoccupied with theories about technique. What is important is to make films that please the public, yet at the same time reflect the personality of the director.

Since Ford hated authority, he battled with studio heads, who respected his talent but found him difficult. "You don't handle Ford," one Hollywood producer said. "You turn the reins loose and you try to hang on." Within the old studios, however, he was known as a craftsman who stayed within assigned budgets and finished pictures on schedule. While working, he demanded total control. When he failed to get it, he either became bored or ran amuck, as he did with *Mr. Roberts,* when he was expected to transfer a successful Broadway play to film and felt stifled. Like other great directors of his time, Ford might spend six months preparing a movie, then shoot it in four or five weeks, sometimes less. "It is wrong to liken a director to an author," he argued. "He is more like an architect." If the director is creative, he puts "a predesigned composition on film."

Although Ford developed a reputation for making films inexpensively, he was no assembly-line director. By the time his pictures went into production, he had the story so firmly in mind that he was free to improvise as shooting progressed. He liked to keep the entire cast on hand at all times, in case he should need someone unexpectedly. If he thought of a last-minute wardrobe or prop change, there might be a flurry of activity while he altered his approach or gave actors additional pieces of business. In Ford's view an element of spontaneity, even a degree of uncertainty, was necessary to assure the freshness he wanted on film; otherwise actors simply mouthed dialogue.

He often decided at the last minute that a scene was too wordy and would eliminate lines; Ford never lost the conviction that he was working in an essentially visual medium. "When a motion picture tells its story and reveals its characters in a series of simple, beautiful, active pictures," he said, "and does it with as little talk as possible, then the medium is being used to its fullest advantage. The director must be able to take printed words and transmute them into images." For Ford the script, with rare exceptions, became what a libretto is for composers of opera—a text to focus, enhance, and add dramatic power not to music in Ford's case, but to visual imagery.

"The main thing about motion pictures is to photograph the people's eyes," he insisted. "Look at their faces." Ford didn't shoot through ashtrays or down skylights, nor did he use complicated dolly shots or moving cranes. He stationed the camera at eye level and let it tell the story. Still, his compositions are those of a painter. Ford has been called the greatest stylist in American films, but the essence of his style remained simplicity. For him less truly became more. "I try to make people forget they're in a theater," he said. "I don't want them to be conscious of a camera or a screen. I want them to feel that what they're seeing is real."

Ford boasted that he was the best cinematographer in the business, which in certain regards may have been true. Yet according to his Oscar-winning cameraman Winton Hoch, "Ford never worried about anything technical. The camera was just a box capturing an image to him. The mechanics were not important unless they became unwieldy." Fortunately Ford worked with excellent cinematographers, who knew how to carry out his intent. He often claimed that he cut his pictures with the camera, giving the editing room minimum footage to work with. Film editor Gene Fowler, Jr., denied the contention, but admired the filmmaker's straightforward approach. "I always said that if anybody wanted to direct, they should look at about six John Ford pictures," Fowler declared, "because his techniques of shooting were so simple, yet so obviously effective."

Visualist though he was, Ford also won the respect of moviemakers more oriented toward language. Screenwriter Joseph L. Mankiewicz, who later turned director and won Academy Awards for both two years in a row, is a prime example. In 1948, approaching the height of his celebrity, Mankiewicz wrote Ford, "Not so long ago I ran across an old diary of mine in which, after seeing one of your films, I commented rather unhappily upon the likelihood that I could ever come within even hailing distance of you as a director. It was a possibility about which I still have very little optimism."

Ford took all of his honors and praise with a grain of salt, rejecting the notion that moviemaking owed much to genius or profound theories on art. He told his friend Robert Parrish that his six Oscars meant nothing. "The only thing that's

important," said Ford, "is to keep working." Although picturemaking was his life, the director found taking his profession seriously difficult and claimed he never thought he was
doing anything important. The son of proletarian parents,
Ford continued to view the world through proletarian eyes.
While he respected art, he could never accept himself as an
artist. He hid his sensitivity beneath a blustery facade and
attempted to cloak his creativity in workaday jargon, fearing
that to do otherwise would appear unmanly.

Although John Ford's work is filled with conflict between the
individual and society, he seldom deals with inner turmoil. It's
the public person that Ford is concerned with, the individual
who will contribute to society or will fail. Yet Ford himself was
a mass of inner turmoil that stemmed in no small measure from
his Irish background. What Hollywood projected was the
work-oriented Irish director, gaining acclaim and self-esteem
through a job well done. Less public was Ford's Gaelic penchant toward despondency during idleness and his abuse of
alcohol. What the pub offered his kinsmen in malebonding and
social solidarity, Ford found on location in Monument Valley
and with his cronies in Hollywood.

    But the tensions went deeper, as a study of his films will
reveal. Ford was squeamish about sex, while the characters in
his movies seem incapable of accepting mature love. "I cannot
recall one of his films in which the man-woman relationship
came off with any feeling or profundity," Ford's long-time
screenwriter Dudley Nichols maintained. "Like many fine
artists—Herman Melville for instance—his true feeling was
for the man-man or man-men relationship." Sexual attraction
in Ford's hands was sublimated in courtship and gallantry,
while love between the sexes acquired value only when linked
to marriage and family.

    In the villages of Ireland's western coast, from which Ford's
parents emigrated, sexual division was traditionally sharp—
women worked in the farmhouse and kitchen, men in the barn
and fields. Male celibacy remained high, while bachelors tended
to be awkward around women other than their family. Mar-

riage frequently came late and was between members of the same village or parish. Even after marriage the sexes congregated with their own kind.

Irish Catholicism, social anthropologist Nancy Scheper-Hughes points out in her study of mental illness in rural Ireland (*Saints, Scholars, and Schizophrenia*), has been steeped in sexual repression, while its priests have glorified ascetic virtues. The personality of the Irish rural male tended to revolve around feelings of masculine inadequacy and alternate dependency and hostility toward women, a conflict that originated in a strong mother-son relationship. That Ford's male-female love interests on the screen seem deficient in sexual vitality (as was his own marriage after a brief while) reflects the repressed turn-of-the-century Irish village attitudes that he learned from his parents. Although he spent most of his life in Hollywood (notoriously libidinous if one believes the scandal sheets), he opted to stand apart. Fearful of intimacy, mistrustful of love, ashamed of sex, Ford was most comfortable with a celibate life, which he could view in traditional Irish fashion as martyrdom.

In a different age Ford might have turned to homosexuality, but had he done so in the first half of this century, guilt would have overwhelmed him. Without question he preferred the company of men, and male bonding reached inordinate proportions. He may have been physically attracted to men on occasion, but there is no indication that he gratified his appetites homosexually. The director's unquenchable need to dominate might be construed as a subconscious desire to ravish, but it is unlikely that the impulse became overtly sexual. Whether Ford harbored doubts about his sexuality is a matter of conjecture. His discomfort with behavior that smacked of effeminacy suggests that he was not secure in his masculinity. But his was neither an age nor a society that prized sensitivity in males, and to be labeled an artist made a man suspect in all but the most sophisticated circles. Ford resolved his dilemma by dwelling in a masculine world, enjoying male companionship and post-adolescent horseplay and desexualizing situations he wasn't comfortable with or that harbored potential danger.

It has been said that while Americans are in love with love, the Irish are in love with death. Modern psychiatry has linked sexual repression with morbidity and a preoccupation with death — characteristics rampant in American popular culture throughout most of the nineteenth century. John Ford had a morose side, particularly evident when he wasn't working and, like traditional Irish villagers, he dwelt in a secretive, privatized world. But while Ford flaunted his Irish heritage, he was also an ardent American — pragmatic, aggressive, a man of action. His screen images, although full of Irish undercurrents, more directly establish his vision of America and embody the immigrant's dream of a new world.

"Westerns," said Ford, "are typically American," but he lifted this popular genre on the screen to epic proportions. Until late in his career inexpensive Westerns were the financial mainstay of the American movie industry, but Ford did more: he captured the nation's creation myth on film. Movies and the frontier saga were ideally suited to one another, but it took Ford's genius to raise the Western to its full potential. "A running horse remains the finest subject for a motion picture camera," he once said. "Is there anything more beautiful than a long shot of a man riding a horse well, or a horse racing free across a plain?" As the screen's greatest action director, Ford filled his canvas with the West. Yet his West went beyond historical fact to incorporate legend as well.

In myth the hero often matures psychologically by devouring monsters; in Western movies the frontier hero may not develop emotionally, but he triumphs by slaying whatever demon impedes civilization's progress. Even in Ford's masterful hands, the anima, as Carl Jung called the male's inner feminine side, is almost never explored. The Western hero is all male — one sided, emotionally underdeveloped, fearful of delicate undercurrents, and ultimately afraid of women. Ford's superstar John Wayne, the quintessential American male, admitted late in his life, "Women scare the hell out of me. . . . I've always been afraid of them." Jung argued that while the anima can be destructive, it is also potentially creative. The maturing

male must conquer the dangerous side and release its creative
force. That is what Ford's heroes were incapable of doing, and
what Ford himself struggled with, so that his screen heroes
remained emotionally limited, unable to sustain mature relationships with the opposite sex, bonding among themselves,
preferring adolescence to full maturity. Although Ford har-
nessed the creative force within himself, he was frightened by a
residue he had slight capacity to understand.

The frontier had officially closed a quarter of a century
before John Ford arrived in Hollywood, but unemployed
cowhands were still drifting across the western mountain
ranges, awaiting their call as wranglers and stunt performers
outside studio casting offices. Ford fell in love with the West
and found companionship among the movie cowboys, who in
many instances were as emotionally repressed as he was. In a
curious way Irish Catholicism and frontier individualism meshed
in what proved to be lasting friendships for Ford, and resulted
in celluloid images comparable to the paintings of Frederic
Remington and Charles Russell.

"I have been a cowboy and I punched cows for a while," Ford
once claimed. "The boss's daughter, believe it or not, fell in love
with me. She was six-foot-two and weighed about 210 pounds,
so I stole a horse and rode away . . . and came to California.
But I have been a cowboy, and I know the West pretty well."
Ford initially learned about the West from Harry Carey, his
first cowboy star, and his claim of having been a cowboy is pure
fabrication. To say that Ford was prone to extending the truth
would be putting it kindly; he was a confirmed liar. Prevarica-
tion was integral to his persona and at times part of his charm.

Since Ford was incapable of dealing with the more disturbing
aspects of his inner self, he invented and perfected an exterior
to camouflage the side he most feared. The combination of
sensitive artist and public curmudgeon tallied up to a complex
personality that perplexed even Ford's closest friends. Those
who saw through the ruse generally loved him all the more, but
others found him an unbending tyrant. One longtime colleague commented, "The John Ford we know is a legend, a

living legend who was created by John Ford himself to protect the other John Ford, the sympathetic, sentimental, soft John Ford." Translated into his own imagery, Ford's gruff exterior guarded an inner tenderness much as the cavalry protected women and children from attack on the untamed frontier.

Part of the confusion stemmed from Ford's own acceptance of the role he had created for himself; at times he mistook his histrionic self for reality. Since he was promiscuous with truth and performed the part he'd fashioned with grandeur, his life became as fictional as his films. Occasionally the text shifted, amusing close friends and misleading acquaintances. At film editor Robert Parrish's wedding, for instance, Ford met the bride's aunt, bestselling novelist Kathleen Norris. During the reception Norris and Ford spoke bad Gaelic to one another and she, a devout Catholic, was enchanted with him. A short time later in Washington, D.C., during World War II, Parrish encountered Ford one evening walking past the Washington Monument, looking bored. They stopped to talk, and Ford eventually asked Parrish about his wife's aunt. "She's wonderful," Parrish assured. "I spoke to her, and she enjoyed talking to you at the wedding. She said she thought it was a shame that you didn't continue to study for the priesthood, as you started." Ford took off his glasses, pulled out his handkerchief, dabbed his eyes, and said, "I've always regretted it." Parrish recognized Ford at his most theatrical; the director had no more studied for the priesthood than he'd been a cowboy.

Katharine Hepburn, who was once in love with Ford, accused him of having a split personality. But his persona was less fractured than clouded. Hollywood found the image good copy and enlarged it to suit the needs of studio publicists. Throughout his career Ford played the ogre, brutalizing interviewers and mocking attempts to praise. He seldom talked about movies except in nuts-and-bolts terms, maintaining that he was just a "hard-nosed, hardworking, run-of-the-mill director." When someone called him the greatest poet of the Western saga, he replied, "I am not a poet, and I don't know what a Western saga is. I would say that is horseshit."

Yet his thinking ran far deeper than he liked to admit. Even in his action classics, Ford's characters and relationships are skillfully drawn. *Stagecoach* may be a small story, but Ford was genius enough to film it against a big background. As a director, he knew every facet of moviemaking, much of it second nature to him. Still, he had intellectualized his craft more than he wanted outsiders to know. When actor George O'Brien's son told Ford that he was considering a career as a novelist, the director said, "Well, you ought to start by reading Fielding, so you'll know how to tell a story." Young O'Brien was amazed that Ford knew Fielding and Thackeray and other British novelists backwards and forwards and could analyze their works in detail.

The heroes and legacy of the Old West were passing into mythology before the historical evolution of the American frontier was complete. While literature, painting, and sculpture captured parts of the Western epic, its most sweeping expression awaited the twentieth century and the arrival of the motion picture as a popular art form. John Ford stands at the apex of Western moviemakers, blending reality and myth. On the locations where his Western films were shot, Ford recreated life on the frontier. In part because raw outdoors fulfilled his need to demonstrate a tough, masculine image, Ford loved working in remote areas and tried to bring authenticity to Hollywood's depiction of the American West. "It is probable that the Westerns have been most inaccurate in overglamorizing the heroes and villains of the period, and in playing up the gunfights," he said. "We could do without such stock characters as the hero who leaps from two stories onto his horse, fires twenty shots at a time from his six-shooter, and has a comical, bearded rascal for his sidekick." But Ford considered action-filled Westerns to be ideally suited to the motion picture medium, utilizing its strength by emphasizing the visual. When critics failed to take the genre seriously he dismissed them as snobs.

Ford clung to certain clichés, but they were largely of his invention. Director Leo McCarey once made Ford angry by telling him, "John, you're slipping." Ford demanded to know why. "Because," said McCarey, "you didn't let that bartender take the mirror down off the wall before those fellows started shooting." McCarey referred to a humorous touch that Ford used time and again before saloon brawls.

But the director knew how to capture the sense of the West. He possessed an eye for composition, color, and action and demonstrated an exceptional talent for storytelling. He was able to fuse legend, historical reconstruction, frontier attitudes, and psychological truth to create cinematic masterpieces that bore his unmistakable signature. "Ford always saw things with that crazy Irish slant he had," said screenwriter Winston Miller, "but he was one of the few directors whose pictures you could see and, without screening the credits, know that you were watching a John Ford picture, because of his pacing and attitude." Ford's men of the West spoke his language, and he identified with their outlook and values. "They had a warm, rugged, natural good humor," he said. "Strong people have always been able to laugh at their own hardships and discomforts." Ford considered humor the strength of his pictures, although critics often disagreed. But few could deny that he caught the spirit of the frontier with grandeur and eloquence. "When I pass on," he remarked two years before his death, "I want to be remembered as 'John Ford—a guy that made Westerns.'"

It is easy to think of John Ford as strictly a Western director, and if he had made nothing else, his place in Hollywood history would be secure. Yet one need only recall Gypo Nolan swaggering through the streets of Dublin in *The Informer,* the Joads rattling down Route 66 on their way to an empty stewpot in *The Grapes of Wrath,* young Huw Morgan searching for his father through a caved-in Welsh coal mine in *How Green Was My Valley,* or Sean Thornton and Mary Kate Danaher in an Irish battle of the sexes in *The Quiet Man* for the filmmaker's versatility to come into focus.

Although Ford accepted the fact that he was making commercial entertainment, material rewards were never his major concern. Nor did he accept Hollywood's self-satisfaction or internalize its ballyhoo. It was always the world beyond Sunset Boulevard that commanded his respect, and he was sincere when he claimed that his admiral's stripe meant more to him than all six of his Academy Awards. What counted most to Ford were life's basics—the land, family, justice, traditional morality, personal integrity, sacrifice, work well done. He had nothing but contempt for the hypocrisy of pseudointellectuals, phony sophisticates, and self-serving moralists, even though he lived amid his share, and he increasingly came to view the world as bleak and undisciplined. Strong-minded, irascible, opinionated, sensitive, and above all, gifted, John Ford remains an enigma, yet he created motion pictures for the ages.

CHAPTER 2

Outsider

"JOHN Ford had one great emotional tragedy in his life," said Dublin-born producer Charles FitzSimons, brother of actress Maureen O'Hara. "That was that he hadn't been born in Ireland. He wanted to be as Irish as anybody could be, so he wore an Irish tweed jacket with the collar turned up and either a cap or a hat. If he wore a hat, it would have the brim turned down all around, and he would often tie his slacks up around his ankles. The reason for that was that he was trying to be a native Irishman. In Ireland the grass is long and wet, and we will very often tie up the legs of our pants to save them from getting wet. Of course we wear Irish tweed jackets and always wear the brim of our hat down and the collar of our coat up, so the rain runs off the brim of the hat and over the collar of the coat. Ford didn't really know that, but he was adopting what he thought was native Irish garb. He was a deliberately self-directed character, determined to make himself a native Irishman."

Although Ford was born in Cape Elizabeth, Maine, just south of Portland, emotionally he remained an immigrant, outside the mainstream of American life, yet with a consuming need to belong. His parents were the actual immigrants, both from the Galway area. John A. Feeney, Ford's father, came from Spiddal, a small fishing village on the Galway coast, across the bay from the rugged Aran Islands. Feeney, an intelligent, outgoing man, was born in 1854, less than a decade after the potato famine. His family lived in a cottage on the estate of the Morris family. Tall and big-boned, John Feeney enjoyed boasting in later years about his prowess as a youth, such as the time he lifted a boulder out of the water or how he swam Galway Bay. Like his illustrious son, Feeney was not above manufacturing the truth, and his tales added conviviality to gatherings of his children and friends.

The Great Famine of the 1840s killed a million people, one-eighth of Ireland's population, and its aftershocks launched an exodus that would continue through successive generations. Almost one and a half million Irish emigrated to the United States during the decade after 1845, and by 1921 another three million had followed. The first to leave brought relatives and friends from home as quickly as possible, while those who stayed saved their coins until they had enough to send a son or a daughter to America, hoping he or she would become wealthy and bring the rest of the family over one by one. Still, devastating economic conditions added to the Irish sense of melancholy, while drink became the opium and social bond of the people.

Spiddal stood as a final gateway before the Atlantic Ocean. John Feeney had a cousin who sailed for America in 1862, served in the Union Army during the Civil War, and later laid track for the Union Pacific Railroad. Sponsored by his cousin, Michael Connolly, red-headed Feeney at eighteen determined to seek his fortune in the New World. In the late spring of 1872 he visited his parish priest, kissed his mother good-bye, and, with landowner George Morris, a great-uncle of John Ford's friend and later producer Michael Killanin, walked down the narrow road to Queenstown, where Feeney boarded a Cunard ship for Boston.

He arrived to find no jobs. Since his cousin's family then lived in Portland, Maine, Feeney decided to join them, taking work with the gas company. Portland in the 1870s was a thriving seaport, bustling with loggers and sailors, but in need of strong laborers eager to prove their worth. The Irish flocked to the city, by the close of the century comprising more than 15 percent of the town's population. While the Irish looked up to the frame houses and shaded streets on Portland's hills with hope, their nostalgia for home deepened. They were a rural folk transplanted to an urban setting, cut off from the land and villages their kinsmen had known for centuries. "When the

Irish went to America," Connemara resident Kay Naughton observed decades later, "they went for life." Treated with suspicion by the Protestant majority in New England, the Irish Catholics pulled into their own clannish communities, where they eased the rejection they felt with memories of their beloved Emerald Isle.

Shortly after arriving in Portland, nineteen-year-old John Feeney met Barbara Curran, who hailed from the next village over the hill from Spiddal. Although John and Barbara had never met in Ireland, they rejoiced in their similiar background. A year younger than John, Barbara was a stylish blond who knew how to select clothes. Otherwise she was conservative and practical. Perceptive and intelligent in a quiet way, Barbara could neither read nor write English. Her parents had sent her to America when she was sixteen, along with a younger sister. She and John Feeney married in 1875 and became naturalized citizens three years later.

Before their wedding John had worked as a dockhand, living beside the railroad tracks in Portland, but his spirited, green-eyed bride would have none of that. The couple initially boarded with his Aunt Mary Kilmartin; then they lived for a time over a saloon on Center Street. Barbara, who hated liquor, objected to the boisterous laughter and singing and fistfights that persisted below well into the night. For a decade they moved from flat to flat, each bigger than the last to accommodate the couple's expanding family.

For a time John Feeney operated a grocery store on Center Street, but in 1889 he decided to move his brood to a two hundred–acre farm on nearby Cape Elizabeth. It was there, close to Two Lights, in an old farmhouse on Charles Jordan Road, with a midwife in attendance, that John Martin Feeney (known to his family as Jack) was born on February 1, 1894, the youngest of thirteen children. He later gave his birth date as 1895, but an insurance policy and baptismal records support the earlier year. He also claimed his name was originally Sean Aloysius O'Feeney, a more Irish-sounding name, but that is incorrect according to parish records at St. Dominic's Church in Portland. As an adult he insisted that his kin were low Irish, when in reality they stood midway between lace-curtain and shanty Irish on the social scale. "The truth about my life is nobody's damn business but my own," the director stated when pressed on such matters.

John Ford liked to picture his parents as part of the great westward migration, coming to the New World with little but family pride and determination, which helped forge a mighty democracy as well as a fresh start for themselves. "I am of the proletariat," he told a university symposium in 1964. "My people were peasants. They came here, were educated, and served this country well."

But Cape Elizabeth, inhabited mostly by farmers, had its share of bigotry where Irish Catholics were concerned. Making a living and keeping personal dignity was not easy for them. John Feeney, by birth a man of the soil, worked his farm but also ran a saloon in town, using the farm as an economic buffer against times when prohibitionists forced his business to close. John Ford later claimed that he grew up "pinching poverty," but his family more accurately lived in modest comfort.

Two other Feeney children, Edward and Josephine, had been born in Cape Elizabeth. Patrick, Jack's oldest brother, had been born in Portland, as had Mary and Francis. The other seven children died during birth or infancy. The remaining six grew up in a supportive circle, insulated to a degree from the hostile Protestant world around them. John Ford remembered his childhood as happy, yet insisted that he was "a fresh kid at the table." He was often mischievous, with a fondness for mystery and secrecy.

In 1897 the Feeneys sold their farm on Cape Elizabeth and moved back into Portland so that the older children could attend better schools. They settled on Danforth Street, and John Feeney opened a restaurant and saloon at the corner of Fore and Center streets, in a downtown section known as Gorham's Corner, a junction where five streets come together. Located a few yards from the waterfront, Gorham's Corner was adjacent to Portland's maritime activity. Its residents were poor, the area tough, its reputation unsavory. The city's first Irish immigrants settled there during the 1840s, staying until they had prospered enough to move out. Gorham's Corner was the hub of a wheel, down the spokes of which ran wooden and brick tenements for a substantial segment of the city's Irish population. During evenings workers poured out of crowded dwellings, eager to forget their poverty after a fourteen-hour work day, filling nearby saloons where they could relax, meet friends, and escape the anguish of their toil.

Portland rapidly grew into a major seaport, connected directly to Liverpool by ocean steamer, while its waterfront became busy with longshoremen and sailors who frequented the saloons of Gorham's Corner. Since the city was then the terminus for the Grand Trunk Railroad, ships from Europe and Africa docked at Portland and unloaded their cargo on its wharves, from which goods were reloaded onto the Grand Trunk and taken by rail to Montreal and Detroit. Those cities in return sent goods via railroad back to Portland, where they were loaded on boats and shipped abroad. By the close of the century Portland had become one of the busiest harbors on the East Coast, third in tonnage behind New York and Boston.

The saloons near Portland's docks were viewed as oases by workers and did a thriving business. Would-be entrepreneurs who couldn't afford to open a saloon settled for a kitchen bar, selling drinks from the back of their homes at cheaper prices, to the disgust of prohibitionists. Fights broke out frequently in Gorham's Corner, especially on Saturday nights, often sparked by clan rivalry or competition for a colleen's attention. But John Feeney's establishment made money, enough that his son Patrick, a staunch teetotaler, was conscripted to help his father. Slowly the family climbed its way into Portland's middle class.

In 1902 the Feeneys moved to Monument Street and four years later into a green-shingled triplex at 23 Sheridan Street with the Mahoney and Myers families. Sheridan Street, located on Portland's Munjoy Hill, is near downtown, but then was in the midst of a more affluent Irish neighborhood on the edge of what was predominantly Yankee territory. The Feeneys were advancing into the lace-curtain category (those Irish with enough means to flaunt their success and worry about what the neighbors thought of them).

The atmosphere on Munjoy Hill was solidly Irish. The Feeney children grew up speaking both English and Gaelic, while social life revolved around St. Dominic's Church and the family. Pat and Jack shared a room, while Eddie, more of a loner, had his own quarters. Jack reached adolescence with only a dim recollection of his brother Francis, who was absent most of the time and spoken of in hushed voices by his mother and father. Josephine, who would eventually become a school-teacher, was the studious member of the family, while Mame, the oldest, was more domestic.

John Ford later suggested that his home environment was much like what he depicted in *How Green Was My Valley*. His mother occupied the central role, always a devoted homemaker and a strict disciplinarian with her children. "The boys never came in or went out without stopping to kiss her," Josephine Feeney remembered. While her gregarious husband worked long hours in his saloon, Barbara emerged as the dominant force in the Feeney household. If one of the children asked something of her, she typically responded, "You'll have to see your father about that," but in family matters, John deferred to her. "One word from her and that was it," Josephine said of her mother's discipline. "Barbara had complete control over Jack," Cecil de Prida, Ford's niece, maintained. "She had control over all of them. Her children never thought of talking back. Barbara was a lovable authoritarian, as was Jack. He was more like her than were any of the others, less like his father. Jack was authoritative, shrewd, forceful."

Barbara Feeney also possessed an artistic temperament, although she had few ways of expressing it aside from her cooking, at which she excelled. Barbara, whom her husband called Abby, made marvelous baked beans and brisket, and codfish that tasted like chicken. She showed an aristocratic strain at times and insisted that her children receive the education she lacked herself. She was proud of her husband's success, yet refused to go inside his saloon, ashamed that her family owed its middle-class status to the despised liquor trade. Her idea of handling money was either to put it in a trunk, which she dug into from time to time, or to deposit larger amounts in a bank. It was a proud day for Barbara when she could afford to hire a woman to help with household chores.

John Feeney read a great deal, and the family subscribed to a Gaelic paper printed in Boston, along with several other newspapers and magazines. One of the children read the English papers and translated the news into Gaelic for Barbara, while she sewed. Since John and Barbara spoke different dialects, constant spats occurred over the pronunciation of Irish words. Still, in varying ways both parents kept abreast of what was happening in Ireland and in American politics.

John became a minor power in the local Democratic machine. He would meet ships and encourage arriving immigrants to register for citizenship, then help them find jobs and involve them in local politics as swiftly as possible. He became a ward boss, and party caucuses were held at his saloon. John never ran for office, but he worked diligently behind the scenes to strengthen the Democratic party in Portland.

A man named O'Keefe ran a saloon on the corner opposite from Feeney's, but the two men were never friendly. When O'Keefe ran for alderman, some of his supporters came to ask John Feeney to vote for his fellow Irishman despite their differences. As a faithful Democrat John promised he would, but added "so help me God only once!"

The Feeney children grew up surrounded by kinfolk. Aunt Mary Kilmartin owned a saloon on Forrest Street, a few houses down from John Feeney's establishment, while John's sister, Hannah O'Toole, owned a saloon on Pleasant Street, just a couple of buildings away from her brother's. Since he was the baby of the family, young Jack reached school age nurtured by hovering relatives. "All of Ford's people, except for one girl, eventually migrated to Gorham Corner," Portland historian Don MacWilliams remarked. "It was a case of yelling out the back door and speaking to your sister." The congenial Irish world was self-contained. Outside, the Yankee Protestants waited with distrust, ready to vent their anger on a Catholic enclave they considered threatening. Jack witnessed this antagonism, despite the protection of his own kin. Like other boys, he lost himself in childhood fantasies, but his lingered into adulthood.

On Cape Elizabeth Jack had adored romping with animals and playing in the snow during the long Maine winters. In Portland he spent hours on the third floor of the house on Munjoy Hill gazing over the bay. He loved the sea and told himself that one day he would be an admiral and sail the mighty oceans. Although his eyesight was poor and he wore thick glasses, Jack became a voracious reader. At Emerson Grammar School, an easy walk from Sheridan Street, he drew Indians and cowboys and developed a deep fascination with the American Civil War, an interest that continued throughout his life. "I had four uncles in the Civil War," he later bragged. "I used to ask my Uncle Mike to tell me about the battle of Gettysburg. All Uncle Mike would say was, 'It was horrible. I went six whole days without a drink.'"

Although the Irish clustered into clannish communities, they developed a dual identity—fiercely loyal to Ireland, yet also American superpatriots. John Ford remembered watching as a boy a Fourth of July parade with his father. "When the flag passes take off your cap," John Feeney told his son. "I don't have a cap," young Jack answered. "Well, then cross yourself," his father said.

Even though the youngest Feeney was no better than a fair student in grammar school, and downright poor in arithmetic, it was clear that he possessed a creative mind. When he was eight an attack of diphtheria put him a year behind in school. Mary, Jack's oldest sister, took him in hand and introduced him to good books. The year at home seemed to deepen his sensitivity. William Mahoney, later a Portland attorney, who grew up with the Feeney children, recalled that Jack would "do things in writing compositions that showed artistry, but at the time we didn't think much about it. They were just things which were funny." Barbara Feeney often remarked, "All the children are normal, except the youngest, Johnny."

Young Jack showed strong religious tendencies and was fascinated with the drama of the Catholic Church. A devout

Catholic always, he nonetheless grew up with Irish superstitions and a belief in fairies and "little people." Present, too, was the Irish penchant for fatalism, guilt, and doom, with laughter sometimes masking melancholy. The rigid sexual segregation of rural Ireland continued to a lesser degree in American surroundings. A devotion to Mariolatry caused traditional Irish to view women as saints, so that wives and mothers were placed beyond sensuality, reinforcing a puritanical attitude toward sex within Irish-American strongholds. Mothers and wives became matriarchs, their control of the home absolute, to such an extent that men either yielded or fled. Sons sought male bonding in the priesthood, the military, the police force, politics, or the saloon. John Ford would find it among his actors and wranglers.

Ford retained fond memories of his years in Portland long after he went to Hollywood. "I have kept from my childhood a liking for good people," he said, "simple people, people who go on doing their job in the middle of cheats and crooks." Some of his happiest times as a child were spent on Peaks Island, a resort community off the Maine coast, where the Feeneys purchased a summer cottage. The vacation house was fairly large, with a porch that swept around the side. John Feeney liked gardening, and on Peaks Island he raised vegetables and became known for his strawberries. Before dinner he would ask his wife, "Abby, what would you like tonight for vegetables?" She would name five or six choices, and her husband would go to his garden and gather them. "We grew everything," John Ford remembered. "We dragged seaweed up from the shore to use as fertilizer."

But Jack spent most of his time on Peaks Island running through fields and watching ships pass by in Casco Bay. Occasionally he was allowed to accompany his father to the county fair, where the elder Feeney bet on horse races. Barbara usually tagged along to handle the money. "One dollar per race — no more!" she insisted.

Jack's favorite pastime was going to the nickelodeons, and he and the movies matured together. "Anytime I had a nickel or a dime I went," he said later. The flickers arrived in Portland in 1908, first shown at the Dreamland Theater on Congress Street. "As a kid I was fascinated by the nickelodeons," John Ford declared. "I loved the glamour of the movies." His father's saloon was only two blocks from the theater, so it was easy for the Feeney children to attend shows there. Later Jack became an usher at the Gem Theater on Peaks Island, which was built during the 1880s as a skating rink and eventually was converted into a theater for movies.

Jack also ushered at the Jefferson Theater in Portland, a venue for visiting road companies. After the second night of a drama he could repeat most of the lines and sometimes acted out all the parts when he came home. "I loved to watch plays," he later maintained, "but I never thought of going to New York."

When DeWolf Hopper played Portland, Jack supplied him with a bottle of ale each evening. "He'd give me a dollar," John Ford recalled. The youth also caught a private glimpse of Ethel Barrymore. As a boy Jack served the 6:00 A.M. mass at St. Dominic's. One cold morning he got up at 5:30, threw on some clothes, and ran to the church. A woman was sitting midway back. She wore a fur coat and a blue cloche hat with a veil. As the sunlight poured through the window, the coat began to shine. When she came to the rail to receive communion, the woman lifted her veil, and Jack saw tears in her eyes. "I recognized her," he later remembered, "because I'd seen her when ushering in the theater, but I never knew what made her so sad."

In 1910 Jack entered Portland High School, still within walking distance of the Feeney home on Sheridan Street. His consuming interest was football. At six foot two inches and 175 pounds, he was big enough to play halfback, fullback, and defensive tackle, and earned himself the nickname "Bull." Oscar Vanier, a teammate, later recalled, "He couldn't see too well. We'd yell 'off tackle,' and he'd put his head down and charge. It didn't matter if there was a stone wall there, he'd drive right for it." Hot-tempered, Jack took penalties during games and was frequently in trouble with his coach, John

Clifford. Once Jack picked up the team captain and carried him across the scrimmage line, only to be thrown out of the game. Football toughened him, added to his competitive spirit, and earned him three football letters during his high school years.

He also played baseball and, since he was the fastest runner in school, made the track team. Basketball at the time was considered a WASP game, which the Irish boys thought was for sissies. Football remained Jack's favorite sport, serving as an outlet for his adolescent energy and a means for an Irish youth to win acceptance by the Yankee majority.

Assimilation did not come easily, and there were constant fights among the boys at Portland High. By the time Jack enrolled, the Italians, Poles, Russians, Greeks, and Jews had moved into Portland. The Irish had become established and moved into white-collar jobs, while manual labor fell to the recent arrivals. The Italians had their own church and at first lived in the downtown flats, but they eventually began moving up Munjoy Hill. Since homes were crowded, children escaped into the streets. Soon gangs formed and street fights broke out. Adolescent status depended on a boy's bravado. Jack proved a tough, aggressive youth, ready for a scrap and capable of handling himself in a fight. "We overpowered everybody," he later boasted.

"You learned how to protect yourself," historian Don Mac-Williams said of his own adolescence in Portland. "You became toughened and you learned how to run away if you were not a good fighter, because you were assailed by various forces." While it could get rowdy, brawling supplied adventure, fun, and a sense of power to otherwise powerless minorities. Interference from local authorities was minimal.

Meanwhile Jack Feeney remained an indifferent student. For a time he worked two hours before school driving a fish wagon and later served as a delivery boy for a shoe company. He once played hookey from school for ten days. He left town on a tugboat and when he returned, dirty and salt-stained, his schoolmaster, William Jack, was waiting for him on the dock beside John Feeney. John Ford later credited William Jack with being a major influence in his life. They had long talks together in which the teacher encouraged the boy in his artwork. "He was the greatest man I ever met," declared Ford. "He set the pattern for my life."

Such insight came later. During his school years Jack remained a discipline case. He seldom took books home and got into fights on his way up Munjoy Hill. Robert Albion, a classmate who later became a professor of maritime history at Harvard, said, "He seemed about as unintellectual a person as you could imagine. In one class Jack was told he had no imagination. But at our fiftieth reunion in 1964 he surprised us all by saying he had always had a love affair with Eleanor of Aquitaine."

Jack secretly loved history, especially American history, and possessed a retentive memory. He later claimed that he got through school by listening, since he had no time to study, but he read a great deal more than his teammates realized. Only Oscar Vanier recalled his friend as an avid reader. "Every time you'd see him he'd have a book in his hand, Shakespeare or something," said Vanier. "He'd fight at the drop of a hat, but he had a great mind and a great sense of humor. Someone would tell him a funny story, and the next day Bull would retell it, adding all kinds of new touches to it."

A retired Portland language teacher remembered Jack Feeney as "a very good looking, dark-haired boy who always had the nicest smile." Jack was a senior when the teacher arrived fresh out of Wellesley. She had trouble maintaining order during her study hall period. Jack gathered his gang together and told the class, "Let's give this young lady a break, because our principal, William Jack, will never let her stay if she can't keep discipline." He and his pals maintained order for the rest of the year.

Besides football and reading, Jack enjoyed shooting pool with his friends. Although he eventually had a part-time job unloading trucks at the Casco Bay Lines Terminal, he and his teammates frequented the poolroom by the Strand Theater, where they challenged all comers. Since they were skillful players, more times than not they won. "We'd take our winnings and head for the dance hall that was on Pitt Street at the time and find some girls," Oscar Vanier recalled.

But Jack Feeney was never the womanizer his brother Francis was. In high school he was shy and self-conscious around girls, although he may have had a crush on his young language teacher. "I wasn't interested in girls," Ford said later. "The only girl I was ever close to was from one of the first familes in Maine." While there was never a romance between them, Jack respected the girl because she was willing to dance with an Irish Catholic.

Rugged lad though he was, Jack had internalized traditional Irish notions about separation of the sexes, celibacy before marriage, and exaltation of women, and the belief that sexual activity for pleasure is a religious offense. He entered manhood sexually repressed, needing to prove his masculinity with no counterpoint. More than anything, he needed to belong, for he suffered tremendous insecurities and developed a lifelong inferiority complex. Despite his success on the gridiron, Jack Feeney viewed himself as an outcast—born to an immigrant family, the son of a saloon keeper, a follower of a despised faith, in love with a land that lauded equality yet practiced discrimination.

Time and again the boy had seen the phrase "Irish need not apply" in newspapers where jobs were advertised. He knew that such attitudes explained why his father had operated a saloon despite the growing prohibition movement. He understood that his people had worked their way out of the ghetto by seizing political power, and he saw that by winning a slice of the American dream the Irish had grown more threatening to the Protestant majority. Underneath the football hero was a sensitive disposition, more artistic than Jack Feeney wanted to admit. He grew up angry, rebellious, resentful, anxious to prove himself, yet determined to justify his Irish heritage.

Young Jack graduated from Portland High School in June 1914, hoping to enter the Naval College at Annapolis. Those ambitions were thwarted when he failed the academy's entrance examination. Instead he planned to attend the University of Maine on a football and track scholarship. The summer after graduation he worked in a shoe factory, then left to enroll in the university at Orono. According to the registrar's records, he never did. Jack discovered that athletes at the university were expected to take courses in agriculture, which had no appeal for him. To support himself he took a job waiting tables in the campus dining hall, where he quickly experienced prejudice among the students. "Hey, shanty," a wealthy undergraduate yelled at him, "where's my dinner?" After a few days of getting up at 5:30 in the morning to arrange tables, serve breakfast, and wash dishes, Jack decided to leave Orono before fall classes began. "I was getting more and more disgusted with campus life," he said later, "so why stay?"

What fascinated teenage Jack Feeney was the movies. On the screen of the Dreamland Theater in Portland he had seen his brother Francis in a Hollywood serial. Eleven years older than Jack, Francis was a mysterious figure to the younger Feeney children. He had run away from home at age fifteen to fight in the Spanish-American War, during which he survived a cholera epidemic. He returned home only to run away again to join a circus. Soon he became a stage actor in New York City, changing his name to Francis Ford. "Every Irishman is an actor," John Ford later remarked, noting that they are among "the most natural actors in the world." Francis exhibited dramatic talent and eventually performed extensively in the theater. He worked in films for Gaston Melies, who made serials in Nepara Park, New York. When Melies moved to California in 1909, Francis went along, soon emerging as a pioneer in the movie industry. By 1914 Francis Ford was doing less acting and had begun to direct silent two-reelers.

Disillusioned with college, Jack decided to follow his brother to California, much to his friends' surprise. "You'd never even have known that his brother was in the movies," Oscar Vanier recalled. "He never mentioned it." Barbara Feeney had prayed that her youngest son would become a priest, but Jack harbored no such ambitions. He dreamed of going to Hollywood and becoming a writer. Aware that the Irish have been good with words and have produced more than their share of noteworthy writers, Jack yearned to join that tradition—not through literature or drama, but by writing for a commercial art form. "I was hooked on the notion of the movies," he declared after attaining success. "I never realized that later in life I would become a director."

The lure of a strange frontier beckoned, and Jack Feeney welcomed the challenge. His mother packed him a box of sandwiches, and he took off on his life's adventure. He boarded a train for Boston, then started his journey westward. He hoped to begin his apprenticeship working for his brother. In California he took the name Ford to associate himself with Francis; soon John Ford would become a legend.

CHAPTER 3

Silent Pictures

MOST of the giants who shaped the American motion picture industry were outsiders. Uneducated immigrants for the most part, they were nonetheless men of vision, willing to risk their future on a business not yet respectable, hoping to gain wealth and acceptance from the established order. Nearly all of the movie moguls were Jewish, and practically all came from poverty. Carl Laemmle emigrated from Germany and had been in the clothing business. Adolph Zukor, a Hungarian orphan, became a furrier's apprentice after coming to America. Samuel Goldfish (later Goldwyn) worked as an office boy in Poland, then as a blacksmith's assistant, before entering the glove business. Louis B. Mayer immigrated from Russia and set up a junk business. The father of the Warner brothers had been a cobbler in Poland, but traveled as a peddler before settling with his family in Ohio, where his son Jack worked in a meat market. What the film pioneers had in common was a determination to forge their own empire. They possessed style combined with a tough business sense, along with an uncanny ability to determine what audiences wanted in mass entertainment.

At first the movie industry was unstructured and freewheeling, much as the early frontier had been. From the outset the American West served as a source of adventure for filmmakers struggling to turn out enough product to fill the nation's theaters. With the appearance of Edwin S. Porter's *The Great Train Robbery* in 1903, the movie Western was launched. Porter's film ran a little more than eight minutes and had been shot in three days near West Orange, New Jersey. Broncho Billy Anderson, who appeared in the movie, could barely sit a horse, but overnight the demand for Westerns became so great that filmmakers couldn't supply the market.

A decade later the center of the new industry shifted to California, especially after the success of Cecil B. DeMille's *The Squaw Man* in 1913. When stage actor William S. Hart arrived in Los Angeles the year before, he found that the principal companies making Westerns were Universal in the San Fernando Valley and the New York Motion Picture Company in Santa Monica. The latter was headed by Hart's friend Thomas Ince, a brilliant organizer who had negotiated with the Miller brothers of Oklahoma for their 101 Ranch to supply the cowboys, stock, and equipment needed for making films. Sioux Indians, sixty or more at a time, were brought to the West Coast from their reservation in South Dakota for picture work. The Indians, including women and a tribal chief, pitched their tepees in Santa Ynez Canyon and made camp around the company's headquarters, which became known as Inceville. Hart remembered his introduction to Inceville well: "Tom called and took me out to the old camp. I was enraptured and told him so. The very primitiveness of the whole life out there, the cowboys and the Indians, staggered me. I loved it. They had everything to make Western pictures. The West was right there!"

If the West had been won by 1890 on the frontier, it would continue for decades on the screen and, in a restricted way, in the lives of film pioneers. William S. Hart gave up stage acting to work for Ince and become the first of Hollywood's great cowboy stars, striving for a realism in his Westerns that Broncho Billy Anderson and the earlier breed had lacked. Actress Ann Little, who made three pictures with Hart, recalled leaving her home at six o'clock in the morning seven days a week and driving by automobile to a station in Santa Monica, where she caught a streetcar, before riding the rest of the way to work on horseback. "We worked all day long, about twelve hours, and then we got on our horses and rode back to the streetcar," the actress maintained.

Ince's company went up into the hills to shoot, where Little and her fellow thespians did most of their own stunts. During free time cowhands at Inceville practiced roping, riding bulls and bucking horses, or whatever might be expected in upcoming pictures. While Hart himself was a bit of a ham, more theatrical than cinematic in his approach to acting, he was a tireless worker and supervised his productions carefully. "He was very sincere," an early movie cowboy said. "He really had no facial expression, although he had the two-gun bit down pretty good. Other than that he was the same in every picture." Still, Hart projected the mythic West on the screen more authentically than anyone had before.

While Francis Ford had vaudeville and theater experience, both in New York and in stock, his style of film acting was more natural than that of the melodramatic Hart. Besides his work for Gaston Melies, Francis had acted in movies in Fort Lee, New Jersey, and for Vitagraph after coming west. Thomas Ince hired him in 1912 as a performer and as a second-unit director. Within a year Francis became a full-fledged director, writing many of his own scripts. He continued to act now and then, doing most of his own stunts, and grew skilled in filming action sequences. John Ford later referred to his brother as "Johnny of all trades and master of all. He couldn't concentrate on one thing too long."

Francis had chosen the name Ford when he understudied a part on Broadway and had to step in at the last minute. Since Ford was the name of the actor on the bill, Francis adopted it. Although he had married in Maine, the restless Irishman separated from his wife without divorcing her, leaving behind a son. A man of great sex appeal, Francis seemed to overcome the repressions his youngest brother experienced, perhaps by going to an opposite extreme. In Hollywood he became a lady's man and playboy, living like a rajah, generous with his money but saving little. He made serials with Grace Cunard and, while still married, lived with Cunard for several years.

By the time his brother arrived in California, Francis Ford was working at Universal Studios for Carl Laemmle. "Francis was a hell of a good actor," director Allan Dwan recalled, "one of our top stars. He was an exception because we didn't have good actors in movies then. A self-respecting actor wouldn't come near us." Ford's stature at Universal was important enough that he secured his kid brother a twelve-dollar-a-week job there.

Jack started by digging ditches. He worked hard and fell in love with the picture business. "I loved the glamour," he said, "all the glitter. I even loved digging ditches."

Soon Jack was made an assistant property man, working beside Henry Hathaway, another future director. "We used to steal rugs from one another," Jack claimed. Allan Dwan remembered him as willing to do anything, excellent with props. "The reason he was a hell of a good property man," Dwan said, "was that if you wanted anything, he would go out and steal it for you."

Before long Jack was doing stunts for his brother, since they looked alike. If a double was needed to catch a speeding train on horseback, Jack was there; if someone had to jump a horse off a cliff, he volunteered—all for the sum of fifteen dollars a week. Sometimes Francis goaded reluctant actors into doing their own stunts by embarrassing them. "You call that dangerous!" he'd exclaim. "I'll have my little brother do it for you." Jack held his brother in awe, although Francis picked on him unmercifully.

Eventually Jack tried acting—nothing more than extra work and bit parts, but enough to provide experience that would prove valuable later. Oscar Vanier recalled seeing his former classmate in silent pictures and said, "Jack would always be in the barroom brawl scene; that was right up his alley."

Jack rode as one of the clansmen in *The Birth of a Nation,* the D. W. Griffith epic that in 1915 marked the beginning of American films as art. "I was the one with the glasses," he maintained. When filming the Ku Klux Klan scenes, his hood kept slipping down over his glasses as he rode. He failed to see a low-hanging branch and was knocked out of the saddle. He returned to consciousness to find Griffith standing over him. "Are you all right, son?" the great director asked, while a hundred extras awaited the answer. The youth assured Griffith that he was ready to work, but the filmmaker gave him a flask of spirits and sent him off to rest for a while.

Ford claimed he came closer to worshipping Griffith than any man in motion pictures. "I wouldn't say we stole from him," he said. "I'd say we copied from him outright." Ford credited Griffith with inventing the grammar of American cinema, insisting that he influenced the whole industry. "If it weren't for Griffith," said Ford, "we'd probably still be in the infantile phase of motion pictures. He started it all—he invented the close-up and a lot of things nobody had thought of doing before. Griffith was the one who made it an art—if you can call it an art—but at least he made it something worthwhile." Ford recalled that he attended the Hollywood premiere of *The Birth of a Nation* and "at the end I actually strained my voice yelling." He couldn't believe Griffith's skill with a camera, the subtle touches that gave individuality to his characters. "D. W. was the only one then who took the time for little details," he declared.

But Jack also learned from his brother Francis, whom Hollywood friends called Frank. Like Griffith, Francis was an experimenter, willing to try different camera angles and unusual touches. Jack admired his brother at the same time that he was jealous of him. "In everything John Ford did, I could see the reflection of Frank," said Australian filmmaker Frank Baker, who worked with Jack during his silent picture days. "I am quite sure now that John Ford suffered tremendously from a great inferiority complex, and sitting right at the foundation of that inferiority complex was his brother Frank. He realized that he was just walking in his brother's footsteps, because Frank was the most picture-wise man I've ever known. Jack knew this is where his approach came from, and he took it out on Frank for the rest of his life."

From the beginning Jack was fascinated with the camera. But he also watched how his brother applied makeup to players. If Francis felt that an actor needed a beard, he'd put one on. If the actor was playing a mountaineer, Francis put licorice on his beard to make him more realistic. Jack observed and mastered the craft, finding motion pictures as challenging as they were thrilling. He learned about timing, about breakdowns, about budgets, expanding his knowledge as the business entered its prime.

By 1916 Jack had become an assistant director at Universal, in charge of extras and cowboys, making thirty-five dollars a

week. Within another year he directed his own pictures. Ford
claimed that his big break came when Carl Laemmle visited
from New York during the opening of Universal City and a big
party was thrown on the lot. The party lasted until four in the
morning, with Ford serving as one of the bartenders. To be on
time for work the next day, he decided to sleep under the bar.
The following morning neither the director nor any of the
actors showed up. Some of the cowboys were there, but no one
else. Isadore Bernstein, the studio manager, panicked when he
realized that the studio boss was about to arrive and no
director had reported for work. "We've got to do something,"
Bernstein said.

When Laemmle appeared with his entourage, Ford told the
cowboys to go to the end of the street and ride toward the
camera fast, yelling as loud as they could. Laemmle seemed to
like what he saw, so Bernstein whispered to Jack, "Can't you
get them to do something else?" Ford thought a minute, then
told the cowboys to ride down the street again and race back.
When he fired a gun, he instructed, several of the men were to
fall off their horses. Since Laemmle's party included a number
of attractive women, the cowboys were eager to make an
impression. "When I fired my gun, not two or three but all of
them hit the dirt in all directions," Ford recalled. "Can't you do
something else?" Bernstein asked in desperation. "So we
burned the street," Ford said. Soon afterward, when Universal
needed a director for a two-reel action picture, Laemmle
suggested, "Try Ford. He yells loud."

Jack was never the man about town his brother was. He
dressed simply and even as a youth disliked formal dinners and
lavish affairs, preferring to socialize with his own group.
Hollywood at the time was an unpaved boomtown, a second
gold rush, with fortunes made virtually overnight. The Protestant establishment, the Catholic Angelenos, the recently arrived oil barons, and the native work force did not welcome the
Jewish movie producers who invaded with such a rumpus. By
association Ford was again an outsider. He quickly became
aware that to gain a foothold in such a competitive business,
resourcefulness was essential. "I definitely believe in the

American Dream," he declared. "I think if you work hard enough, you will succeed."

During his early years in Hollywood, Ford lived at the Virginia Apartments on Hollywood Boulevard, which was lined with pepper trees and supported only a couple of restaurants at the time. His roommate was Hoot Gibson, the future cowboy star, whom Universal had signed in 1915 to double Harry Carey, the studio's reigning Western star. Gibson came from Nebraska and had ridden horses since childhood; later he worked as a cowboy and for Dick Stanley's Wild West Show. When Gibson began doing stunts in movies, he received $2.50 for falling off a horse bareback and five dollars if he got shot out of the saddle. Sometimes he doubled the star; other times he played villains or Indians. "When we played Indians," Gibson explained, "we'd put a feather in our wig and wear a breech cloth. Sometimes we'd play an Indian in the morning, and after lunch we'd put our western clothes on and chase ourselves all afternoon."

Ford liked Gibson and loved associating with wranglers and cowboys. Hollywood in those days demonstrated more than a touch of the Old West, and Ford soon bought a saddle horse named Woodrow. A livery stable stood on the corner of Sunset and Gower streets, where cowboys mounted their horses for the ride over Cahuenga Pass to Universal for a day's shooting. Many of the wranglers had worked on ranches and migrated to Hollywood when the Cattle Kingdom fell into decay. They came from all over the Western states, Canada, and northern Mexico. Those from ranches were a salty bunch, viewing themselves as a breed apart, and some had been shady characters. They gathered at watering holes, whether liquor was legal or not, and formed their own social club, the Chuck Wagon Trailers. Movie producers always knew where to find experienced riders when jobs became available. Most often wranglers were instructed to wear their own clothes to work, and they could either supply their own mount or the studio would cut them one from their herd.

The Virginia Apartments, where Ford and Gibson lived, were not far from where the cowboys congregated. Landlords were reluctant to rent to movie people, but the owners of Ford's building were appeased when he announced that his parents were coming to visit and he would need to rent an adjoining apartment. The senior Feeneys made their first trip to California in 1917, sleeping in a bed that pulled down from the wall. "What's this?" John Feeney asked. "A Murphy bed," replied Jack. "The hell it is," his father snorted. "No Irishman ever built a bed like this."

The Feeneys were proud of their sons, even though Francis was still regarded as the family renegade. Barbara was pleased that Jack had joined the Knights of Columbus and relieved that his poor eyesight would probably exclude him from military service. With World War I in progress, he had threatened to enlist in the navy, but his attempt proved futile. He kept up with the war through acquaintances. "We expect to leave for overseas about the middle of September," a friend with the Canadian Expeditionary Forces wrote him in August 1916. "That means the trenches about the middle of October."

The Tornado, John Ford's first directorial credit, was released in March 1917, just a month before the United States entered the war. A two-reeler, the film (also written by Ford) centers around a cowboy (played by Ford himself) who rescues a banker's daughter from a gang of outlaws and uses the reward money to bring his mother over from Ireland. Ford dismissed the movie later as "just a bunch of stunts," claiming *The Soul Herder* as his initial effort at directing.

The Soul Herder was the first of Ford's twenty-six Westerns starring Harry Carey. Carey played a saddle-tramp, Cheyenne Harry, a man at odds with the law as the film opens. Ford got the job of director because Carey asked for him. The two had talked on the Universal lot, and the star found young Ford intelligent and responsive. Their personalities meshed from the outset. "Harry helped me immeasurably," Ford declared. "He was natural and rugged, but he had an innate modesty. He was a great, great actor, maybe the best Westerner ever."

Initially Carey was far more interested in the frontier West than Ford was. Born in the Bronx in 1878, the son of a judge,

Carey spent his boyhood reading dime novels. "I'd never been farther west than Elmira," the actor said, and "I saw my first Wild West show in a little ballpark"—a show featuring "Jim Kidd, the Wyoming Cowboy." Carey left the arena in a state of euphoria. "In that little ballpark I saw steers roped, bucking horses ridden, and the pony express. I saw Jim do 'The Race for the Bride,' and I saw him rope, drag, and hang the horse thief. The show closed with the holdup of the overland stage." Carey claimed he was "punch drunk" for weeks.

Carey attended New York University and entered law school in the class with Jimmy Walker, New York's future mayor, but kept up his interest in Western history through reading. The university asked him to leave when he and some friends got drunk and stole Madam Moran's underdrawers from her whorehouse and ran them up the school's flagpole. Carey denied that he had any interest in acting, but he soon found himself playing cowboy parts on the stage.

His relationship with the theater began shakily when his father took him to see his first play, *Old Davy Crockett* with Frank Mayo in the lead. "There was some shooting on stage," Harry recalled, "and I got scared and I hollered. The old man took me out in the lobby and walloped my tail." Later Carey wrote a Western melodrama for the stage and acted in it himself. He called the play *Montana,* raised three thousand dollars, and produced it. "I knew nothing about producing or acting," he admitted, "but I formed a company, and we toured the country presenting *Montana* in all its riproaring melodramatic glory for five years." Carey bragged that the show played five weeks in Chicago; what he failed to mention was that it played one week in five different theaters.

Back in New York, actor Henry B. Walthall introduced Carey to D. W. Griffith, who had just formed Biograph Studios. Harry's first picture for the company was *The Unseen Enemy* with Dorothy and Lillian Gish. When Griffith began making annual trips to Los Angeles for winter filming, Carey went along. "Hollywood was a cow pasture surrounded by orange groves," the actor recalled of these early visits. "I liked the country atmosphere, and it was not many years before I began

buying land at Saugus[in the San Fernando Valley, just north
of Los Angeles], adding a few hundred more acres every chance
I had."

Carey stayed with Biograph until Griffith left, then signed
with Universal. By that time he was almost forty years old, but
his tall, gangling appearance and down-to-earth approach to
acting made him ideal for Western movies. When John Ford
met him, Carey knew the motion picture business inside out.
He recognized that Ford shared his enthusiasm for realistic
Westerns with believable characters. "They started cranking
out films with dime-novel plots and tough titles like *Bare Fists,
Hell Bent,* and *Riders of Vengeance,*" said actress Olive Golden,
Carey's third wife. "The movie public went crazy over them,
and Harry Carey became Universal's number-one-box-office
star." His salary soared from $150 a week in 1917, to $1,250 a week
in 1918, and an astonishing $2,250 in 1919.

Carey's knowledge of the West came mainly from books. "I
played a cowboy on the stage for four years before I saw my
first cow horse," he confessed. "A year later in a moving picture
I roped my first steer." But Carey wanted his saddle tramp—
Cheyenne Harry, the role he played time and again—to seem
authentic. He wanted him to look like a working cowhand and
dressed for the part in an old flannel shirt, a vest, and patched
overalls, with a gun stuck in his belt and no holster. Carey never
wore makeup in his movies and seldom got the girl. He did his
own stunts and objected to winning a fight when he was
outnumbered, playing most brawls for comedy. While Cheyenne Harry was a hard-riding, fast-shooting cowboy, he was
also human and frequently looked disheveled. In contrast to
the intensity of William S. Hart's good bad-guys, Carey played
Cheyenne Harry in a lighter vein, having him perform routine
chores such as putting out rock salt and mending fences.

John Ford agreed with Carey's approach and extended it.
"Louse up your hero" became an early Ford dictum. "Get him
thrown in jail if possible. Have him arrested for stealing a horse
or something. Heroes shouldn't be holier-than-thou and namby-
pamby. Heroes shouldn't be clay statues, but they should have
feet of clay." Ford felt that Carey's depiction was not only more

acceptable to audiences, it explained why the actor had become a Western star. "All the other cowboys on the screen bored you to death with their righteousness," the director said.

Carey expanded his ranch, and most of his pictures with Ford were shot there. Although there was a three-room house on the property, the two wanted to emulate real pioneers and slept in bedrolls out in an alfalfa patch. At night they sat around the kitchen table with a wood fire in the stove, drinking and talking until the wee hours of the morning, with Ford taking notes. The next day they'd shoot what they'd discussed the night before. If they needed a leading lady, Olive Carey was recruited; otherwise she was in charge of cooking. When asked later about the magic of making silent pictures, Ollie Carey exploded, "Magic—hell! It was just a guessing game. We made it up as we went along."

Crews on the first Cheyenne Harry pictures consisted of Ford, Harry and Olive Carey, a property man, an assistant director, and a writer to put a rough continuity on paper after the movie had been shot—enough to satisfy the story department at Universal. The first pictures the team made were one and two-reelers, shot in four or five days. When they ran out of film, the director and his star informed the studio that their camera had fallen into water and said they needed more. If one of them had to drive in to Universal, they pushed out Harry's car, which usually wouldn't start. Ollie was then called upon to steer, while the rest hooked a rope to the radiator cap and pulled the vehicle with a horse until its engine turned over.

Since Carey was eighteen years older than Ford, the director looked upon him as a mentor. Ford had a keen sense of humor, and they both enjoyed harassing studio executives, particularly Carl Laemmle, Jr., an incompetent who had become the laughing stock of the industry. Junior Laemmle's father was not always pleased with his new director and Western star, and he objected to some of their earthy touches. In *Hell Bent,* Ford had Carey scramble up a cliff and be kicked at the top by the ranch foreman. "You can't kick the leading man," Laemmle complained. Not only did Ford refuse to alter the scene, in their next picture he had Harry tossed out of a saloon.

"Harry Carey tutored me in the early years," Ford later said, "sort of brought me along. The only thing I always had was an eye for composition. . . . As a kid I thought I was going to be an artist; I used to sketch and paint a great deal." Ford always credited silent pictures for his success as a filmmaker, insisting that was where he learned to tell his story with a camera. Even as a mature director he looked for the natural, the impromptu, never permitting too much dialogue.

Soon the Cheyenne Harry movies grew in length to five reels, as Carey and Ford built their reputation and put a stock company together. Robust action continued, but also natural warmth, told for the eye. Influenced by Carey, Ford's interest in the lore of the West increased, but so did his salary—from $75 a week to $150, and finally $300 before leaving Universal.

Money was never Ford's primary motivation, for he continued to live simply. His preference in clothes always would be khaki riding breeches, a hunting jacket, and boots. Most of Carey's salary—much bigger than Ford's—went into his ranch, particularly as his interest in movies dwindled. "I only make them to buy fence posts," he was fond of saying.

His ranch grew to three thousand acres and included a sprawling house with adobe walls, a Spanish tile roof, high beamed ceilings, and a massive stone fireplace. Once Harry and Ollie traveled to Ganado, Arizona, where they visited Hubbell's Trading Post and became fascinated with the Navajo. Harry returned home, set up a trading post near his property, and brought in fifty or more Navajo to live there for six-month intervals. On Sundays the Careys held barbecues, and during the evening the Navajo would dance for guests. The Indians sold blankets and jewelry to tourists, and Ollie began wearing Navajo clothing. Ford's interest in Navajo culture stemmed from his association with Carey. He may have heard the actor talk about his journey though the Navajo Reservation and describe the beauty of Monument Valley, for Ford continued to visit the Carey ranch after it became a gathering place for figures such as Charles Russell and Wyatt Earp and such Hollywood celebrities as William S. Hart and Hoot Gibson.

Olive Carey accepted her husband's fascination with the

West and dismissed his antics by saying, "Well, Harry's out playing cowboy." The couple never considered themselves part of the movie colony, and Ollie later described herself as "just a dizzy blond back then." During the 1920s Harry bought a Lincoln town car, which was the rage at the time, and it was not uncommon to see Ollie, her blond hair flying, driving the car through Hollywood with Harry in a Western hat sitting beside her and a Navajo or two riding in back.

While Carey and Ford had their share of arguments, they worked well together through three productive years. *Straight Shooting* (1917) was their first feature film, its climax almost a repeat of D. W. Griffith's gathering of the clan in *The Birth of a Nation*. *The Outcasts of Poker Flat* (1919), an adaptation of the Bret Harte story, was their most ambitious work together, while *Marked Men* (also 1919), based on Peter B. Kyne's short story "The Three Godfathers," proved among their most popular. The bulk of Ford's silent pictures have been lost, although a print of *Straight Shooting* was discovered in Czechoslovakia in 1966 and later restored to circulation by the American Film Institute.

It was during the years with Harry Carey that Ford developed many of the characteristics that would become his hallmarks — a hero uncomfortable with social responsibity, a cinematic eye for landscape, a straightforward approach to storytelling, romance combined with authenticity, artful composition with minimal movement of the camera, and above all, forceful imagery.

In *Straight Shooting* Cheyenne Harry is forced to choose between civilization and the wilderness when he has marshaled his outlaw friends and saved some homesteaders from competing ranchers. Ford's heroes are often outsiders, responsible for rescuing a society they are reluctant to join. A romantic individualist in tune with the natural order, Cheyenne Harry finds himself at odds with a collective system, yet is drawn to the support offered by an idealized family, a theme close to Ford's heart as an Irishman. Although Ford and Carey used basic dime-novel plots, they blended action, plausible characters, and compelling situations in an artistic way. Women were marginal to their masculine world, and their male heroes were gentle and redeemable, although far from perfect.

If the filmmakers needed a gunfight, they conferred with one of the frontier characters hanging around the Carey ranch—most often Ed "Pardner" Jones, a thickset sharpshooter with a handlebar mustache who Ford claimed helped Wyatt Earp clean up Tombstone. "In those days we didn't have any tricks," the director said. "If you had to have a glass shot out of somebody's hand, Pardner would actually shoot it out—with a rifle." Jones had ridden in Buffalo Bill's Wild West Show, was supposedly related to Pat Garrett (the gunman credited with killing Billy the Kid), and as an Arizona lawman had reputedly killed the Apache Kid. According to Ford, Pardner insisted that "none of those fellows—Wild Bill Hickok, Wyatt Earp— had been great shots with a pistol." If they engaged in a gunfight, they used a rifle. "Pardner couldn't hit the ceiling with a pistol," Ford declared, "but he'd take a rifle and put a dime twenty-five yards away and hit it. So we tried to do things the way they had been done in the West—none of the so-called quick-draw stuff."

As Ford's pictures with Carey grew in popularity, studio executives showed their support. Universal issued a memo listing what producers did *not* want in their Westerns: fake wallops in fight scenes, stories about the ruin of young girls, betrayal of virtue, neglect of children, cruelty to animals, sissies, "heavy dames," preachments. Ford and Carey's realism had led the way.

Ford could be tough as a director, and there were stunt performers on the lot who wouldn't work for him. Some objected to living in the desert when he shot *Marked Men,* while others thrived on outdoor life and reveled in the company of hearty individualists.

Ford directed eight movies in 1917, seven in 1918, and fifteen in 1919—thirty films in three years. In 1921 he and Harry Carey made *Desperate Trails,* the last of their joint Westerns. A contemporary reviewer described the results: "Mr. Carey is no ladies man, no smooth-chinned Adonis of the canned drama. He has no effete marcel wave undulating from his alabaster brow. His duds are rough and ready ones. His manner careless and masculine."

But Carey was ready to move on to other roles, and Ford was soon to leave Universal for the Fox Film Corporation. Although Ford came to resent the discrepancy between his salary and Carey's, the star had given him an opportunity to experiment with a variety of filmmaking techniques. Ford learned invaluable lessons working with Carey—fundamentals about plot, story construction, handling of exposition, set organization, how to photograph with a minimum of setups, and above all, how to use the camera creatively without having the audience aware of it.

In 1920 Ford directed his first non-Western, *The Prince of Avenue A,* about the legendary boxer "Gentleman Jim" Corbett and Irish life in New York. *Hitchin' Posts,* made later that year, was a Civil War drama with Frank Mayo as a southern aristocrat turned riverboat gambler. Then Ford returned to Westerns: *Action* and *Sure Fire* (both 1921) starred his friend Hoot Gibson, featured earlier in some of the Harry Carey pictures. Ford tried to recreate with Gibson the success he had earned with Carey. *Action* was an approximation of *Marked Men,* with the director's brother Francis playing one of the outlaws. Gibson remembered the work as enjoyable but hard, sometimes lasting all night, and John Ford as a demanding director who showed no favoritism.

Universal surrounded Gibson with actual cowboys, whom the studio kept under contract. Some were genuine characters, right out of the Western myth and living the part. One studio cowboy, named Murphy, was married to an Indian, who beat him regularly. Every few mornings Murphy showed up for work at Universal with a lump on his head, a black eye, or a skinned face. Other cowboys got into fights and had to miss work.

On the Universal lot were barns and corrals and a tack room with enough gear to supply a cavalry unit. In the actors' lounge, cowboys played cards when not working, while a Western street stood ready for town scenes. Herds of horses, cattle, and sheep grazed on the studio's hills. If not busy on a film, cowboys were expected to help care for the stock. The

San Fernando Valley, still nearly as wild as when the Cahuenga Indians roamed there before the arrival of the Spanish, offered filmmakers a choice of canyons, valleys, and oak-studded rises for outdoor shooting.

By the time Hoot Gibson starred in Ford's Westerns, the director was an experienced hand at action filming; he knew about reflectors and lighting and found that a degree of uncertainty among actors resulted in realistic performances. Ted French, one of Universal's cowboys, recalled working for Ford in winter weather around a river. "Ford wanted us to chase this guy down into the river, go down into the river, and then come up the other side," French said years later. But his horse fell on a rock, so that horse and rider were unexpectedly submerged. "I didn't know what to do," French declared. "I knew I'd ruined the scene, so I just came up shooting my gun. It just tickled Ford to death. I think that's where he got the idea of changing scenes right in the middle of shooting. He appreciated anything that didn't disrupt the story—something that would carry the story on, something he didn't expect."

Ford was still rooming with Gibson in 1920 when he met Mary McBryde Smith at a St. Patrick's Day dance given at the Hollywood Hotel by director Rex Ingram. He had not dated much since coming to Hollywood, although he did have an affair with a girl named Janet Eastman, who Olive Carey claimed was the first woman he had slept with. Carey described Ford during this period as an impressive youth with a beautiful walk, arms swinging confidently.

Mary Smith was an attractive young woman with classic features, delicate bone structure, long dark hair, and beautiful legs. Ford was taken with her elegance and humor. Mary came originally from North Carolina and was a Protestant of Scotch-Irish descent. Her grandfathers had been Confederate officers, and Ford claimed she'd grown up hearing how Sherman burned her family's house. Mary had been raised in New Jersey after her father became a member of the New York Stock Exchange. During World War I she had worked as a nurse, and her family had a navy background. "I was raised with the navy," she said, "and was always around stiff white collars and black ties."

After a whirlwind romance, Jack and Mary married in a civil ceremony at the courthouse on July 3, 1920, having selected that date because he had the following day off. Actor J. Farrell MacDonald was best man at the wedding and, with his wife, accompanied the couple on a brief honeymoon to Tijuana. The newlyweds initially lived in a bungalow on Beachwood Drive in Hollywood, then bought a stucco house at 6860 Odin Street, near the Hollywood Bowl. Jack always referred to their home as "the little gray house on the hill"; unpretentious, the Odin Street residence fit their lifestyle adequately.

On Sunday afternoons the Fords' home became the setting for parties that lasted until the food was gone and the bottles were empty. "They were all hard drinkers," Mary said of their guests. Hoot Gibson was usually there—"a wonderful guy, amusing and good company." Tom Mix came with his wife, Victoria. "I adored him," said Mary. "Tom was hot tempered, and he went on drunks. Victoria went Hollywood in a big way, but she was my best friend—she and Ollie Carey." Rudolph Valentino visited the Fords' house one night and cooked spaghetti. Later, while Jack was on location, he escorted Mary to a premiere, picking her up in a limousine with silver serpents on the front that became headlights and hissed. "Valentino was the rage," Jack boasted. "He could have had any broad in town, but he took Mrs. Jack Ford."

"The whole community was so close," actor George O'Brien recalled. "We all went to the beach together and went to football games together." Those who could afford to tried to outdo one another with cars, for it was the craze to see who could buy the longest. Jack bought Mary a Stutz touring car, which she rode to luncheons in, driven by a black chauffeur. The Stutz was replaced by a Rolls Royce that Jack purchased during his lunch hour and gave Mary as a Christmas present, with a mink coat in the back seat for good measure.

On the surface theirs seemed to be the perfect marriage, but in truth it never was. Mary claimed Jack's Irish relatives never accepted her. "I was an outsider," she said. "I was a Protestant.

And I had drawn the pick of the stable." She and Jack had not been married by a priest, a fact that concerned Ford's family. Even on their way to Tijuana the couple got into a fight. Mary complained that Jack's Hollywood friends were slow to welcome her. "There were a lot of sore heads when Jack married me," she said. "He had stepped outside the fold; I was the straw that broke the camel's back."

Jack, on the other hand, was sensitive about Mary's blueblood background and claimed she felt superior to his Irish family. "She had married an immigrant," their grandson Dan said. "My grandmother was a classy lady, a member of the old Confederate aristocracy. She was a member of the Daughters of the American Revolution and the Daughters of the Confederacy. My grandfather wanted to measure up to her values and traditions." But Jack's insecurities were too great; in his mind he remained a saloon keeper's son from a seaport ghetto. To compensate, he buried himself in work. He became more inward and stubborn, mixed crossness with affection, turned on people to assert himself, and lashed out at those he loved.

In the early days of his marriage the gray house on Odin Street was the scene of much drinking, despite Prohibition. Jack had a secret den upstairs, with a sliding door that hid its entrance, where he stored his liquor. Mary relished Hollywood gossip and liked to spend money, which irritated Jack. He in turn disappointed her by ignoring Hollywood society. When the Fords were invited to spend a weekend at San Simeon, William Randolph Hearst's castle on the California coast, Jack refused to accept, insisting it was a good place to stay away from. Even before their marriage he had laid down a cardinal rule: Mary was not to visit his sets. "I never did," she declared.

The Fords' first child, Patrick, was born in 1921. A frail boy, he proved a disappointment to his father, who pushed him hard, afraid Mary would make a sissy out of him. Yet Jack was too busy and preoccupied with work to be a model father, while Mary's social schedule limited what she gave of herself. As the Feeneys began to migrate to California, Patrick was surrounded by cousins and uncles, from whom he learned discipline and masculine behavior.

In November 1921, seven months after Patrick's birth, Jack made his first trip to Ireland. He spent most of his time crossing the Atlantic in the bar of the S.S. *Baltic.* He wrote Mary, "The clouds and fog lifted and three miles away we could see the shores of our beloved fatherland — 'the Emerald Isle,' as green and fresh as dew on the down." The ship docked at Liverpool and Jack left for Wales to catch a boat for Dublin. At Galway he rented a car and drove to Spiddal, where he "had a deuce of a time finding Dad's folks. There are so many Feeneys out there that to find our part of the family was a problem." He discovered Spiddal in a confused state. "Most of the houses have been burned down by the Black and Tans," he wrote, "and all of the young men had been hiding in the hills." Jack arrived during a period of truce, but said in exaggerated Fordian fashion, "I naturally was followed about and watched by the B & T fraternity."

He wired Christmas greetings to Mary and Pat from London and returned home on the S.S. *Olympic.* After spending a few days in New York City on studio business, he came back to Hollywood feeling rested and eager for work.

Before leaving for Europe, Ford had signed a long-term contract with the Fox Film Corporation. He had directed twenty-nine features for Universal in less than four years, all but three of them Westerns. He had made his first picture for Fox on a loan-out in 1920, a Buck Jones vehicle entitled *Just Pals,* which combined homespun Americana with Western action. By 1921 both Harry Carey and Francis Ford had left Universal, and Jack decided to sign with William Fox because Fox agreed to pay him a great deal more money.

In 1922 Ford made *The Village Blacksmith* for Fox, based on the poem by Henry Wadsworth Longfellow, who had also grown up in Portland, Maine. While the film was melodramatic and sentimental, it possessed a simplicity that audiences found pleasing. Then in 1923 Ford made two pictures with Tom Mix: *Three Jumps Ahead* and *North of Hudson Bay.* Mix was a flashier Western hero than was Harry Carey. He dressed in tight white pants, embroidered shirts, and silk

neckerchiefs, but his characters were clean-cut and appealed
to young audiences. Mix was long on action, hard riding, and
show business tricks, which he had learned working on the
101 Ranch in Oklahoma and in various Wild West shows.
Three Jumps Ahead was advertised as "a tale of the Western
Plains where the best man wins." Mix's approach was unrealistic, but it started a trend that continued throughout the
1920s. "Tom had an image," Ford remarked. "He was the
well-dressed cowboy—and that's all he could do. I toned him
down a little bit."

For a time Mix was Fox's leading star. Mixville, the studio's
sixty-acre backlot in the Fox Hills, where most of Mix's Westerns were shot, included bunkhouses where cowboys working
on Fox pictures slept, barns, corrals stocked with horses, and a
western town. Location shooting meant a fifteen-mile ride to
Newhall (near Harry Carey's ranch) on horseback, traveling
single file along the roadside. William Clothier, who worked
later as Ford's cameraman, remembered making Westerns for
Vitagraph around 1923 and going for a day's filming to Newhall. He would put a camera in his car, drive into Hollywood
and pick up a couple of cowboys, stop on his way across
Cahuenga Pass to buy lunches for the crew, and continue on to
Newhall, where the company shot in the streets. The town had
a blacksmith shop, jail, and railroad depot; movie companies
used townspeople as extras, not bothering with makeup.
"Newhall was a western town," Clothier said. "We ran horses
up the street."

Jack Ford adjusted to current vogues in Westerns, even
though Francis could not and was forced to work for his
brother. Francis began drinking heavily after he and Grace
Cunard parted, and for some time he and Jack weren't on
speaking terms. But the younger Ford showed an adaptability
Francis lacked, and while Jack was handed many assignments
at Fox he disliked, he accepted them and did the best he could.
Since Fox was a larger studio than Universal and made more
sophisticated pictures, Jack had an opportunity to film different kinds of stories. He added to his reputation, and in 1923 his
income was $45,000.

The Fords' daughter, Barbara, was born in 1922, and she became the apple of her father's eye. Named after Jack's mother, Barbara was a healthy, intelligent child; as an adult she developed a keen wit and had a firm grasp of the movie business. Mary was a nervous mother, full of fears about her children's safety, and interfered more than was wholesome. Barbara accepted her mother's complexes and, according to Jack's niece Cecil de Prida, "played the little princess." Mary showered the children with clothes, parties, and the best schools available. Barbara later told her friend Joanne Dru about attending a birthday party for Tom Mix's daughter Vicky, at which the cowboy star rode a horse into the entryway of his Beverly Hills mansion and shot out the lights in the chandelier, to the delight of Vicky and her playmates. "Barbara said it was the most exciting, wonderful thing," Dru recalled.

But underneath the glitter were serious problems. Liquor had already become a menace for both Mary and Jack, and Barbara and Pat would suffer from alcoholism once they reached drinking age. While Jack remained a workaholic, between pictures he went on destructive binges that took days to recover from. On April 26, 1923, he signed a pledge at the Church of the Blessed Sacrament in Hollywood: "This is to certify that on this date I have firmly resolved to abstain from all alcoholic beverages." It was a pledge he took time and again without success.

Meanwhile Ford continued to mature as a director. *Cameo Kirby* (1923) demonstrated how far he had come. Based on a play by Harry Leon Wilson and Booth Tarkington, the film was the first to win Ford great critical acclaim. Silent screen idol John Gilbert played the title role, a southern aristocrat driven by an accidental killing to become a Mississippi riverboat gambler. Among the picture's highlights was a duel that revealed Ford's mastery of the camera. From *Cameo Kirby* on, he would be billed as John Ford in film credits rather than Jack.

Ford still hesitated to call movies an art and denied that he was an artist. He studied the great German and Swedish films that appeared after World War I and borrowed from their expressionist style, modifying their excesses to create a more realistic mood. Yet while Ford developed his craft, he continued to see himself as a laborer. "I love Hollywood," he said. "I mean the lower echelons and the grips, the technicians." For most Hollywood celebrities he voiced little but contempt.

In 1924 Ford was catapulted to the top of his profession. That year he made *The Iron Horse,* regarded as his silent masterpiece, an epic that chronicles the building of the nation's first transcontinental railroad. The year before Paramount had released *The Covered Wagon,* a Western spectacle directed by James Cruze, which earned millions at the box office. William Fox asked Ford to make a rival spectacle, awarding him the largest budget of any Fox picture to date, $450,000. Ford approached the project with enthusiasm, viewing the story as a symbol of American progress; through the wonders of technology, the United States had reached its inevitable destiny. *The Iron Horse* became a silent classic and established John Ford's reputation permanently.

For the star of his picture Ford chose George O'Brien, an athlete and former property boy who had worked at Fox as a stuntman and assistant cameraman. A body builder who lived at the Hollywood Athletic Club, O'Brien had made a habit of walking up and down Hollywood Boulevard in the hope of meeting a director who would cast him in an important role. When *The Iron Horse* was made he was twenty-four, weighed 180 pounds, had been a boxer, and knew how to handle horses. When O'Brien tested for the part, Ford had him change into his costume in his office. The director recognized that O'Brien was perfect for the lead. O'Brien was tanned from his job as a lifeguard, and had a gentle personality and flawless manners. "George was poetic, he was beautiful," actress Joanne Dru remarked. O'Brien's son, Darcy, remembered his father's saying that he thought he'd won the role in *The Iron Horse* "when he demonstrated he was able to pick up a hat off the ground at full gallop."

Since *The Covered Wagon* had been made on location, William Fox decided to send his company to Wadsworth, Nevada, near Reno, for most of the filming on *The Iron Horse*. They worked in haste, since Paramount was preparing another Western epic, *North of 36,* to be shot in Texas. The location chosen by Fox had no housing facilities, so production manager Sol Wurtzel hired a train with sleeping cars from the A. G. Barnes Circus. A company of two hundred gathered on New Year's Eve 1923 at Union Station in Los Angeles, where a circus train of fifty cars stood waiting. Cowboys, actors, actresses, and crew piled on for the all-night journey into Nevada, while the elephant car was loaded with groceries. There was singing, dancing, and drinking on board all evening. "It was raining like hell the night we left, and everybody was getting drunk," property man Lefty Hough declared.

The company arrived in Wadsworth the next morning to find that the temperature had plummeted to twenty below zero and the ground was covered with snow. Many of the extras had come inappropriately dressed for the weather in white knickers, which were in vogue at the time. Most of the women stayed aboard, even though the cars weren't heated. Ford told the wardrobe department to issue costumes to his actors, since the costumes were warmer than the clothes they were wearing. Most of the crew went to bed that night fully dressed, only to discover that the aged circus train was infested with fleas.

Ford began filming the following morning in the snow, which made for atmosphere, but the actors' nostrils showed the cold. The studio had built a railroad construction town for the picture, and some of the company moved into the shacks built as sets and slept there. "We all lived exactly like real railroad tracklaying crews did fifty years earlier," wrote Native American actor Iron Eyes Cody. "We slept in tents and ate out of tins and had a wonderful, miserable time of it."

The site became known as Camp Ford. A team of cooks arose around three o'clock in the morning to start preparing meals. Sleeping in wooden bunks was uncomfortable and water ran short, but the biggest problems were getting washing done and finding an empty toilet. "On the train those toilets were going all the time," Lefty Hough recalled. An outhouse built for the women lasted until a wagon and some horses knocked it down; the men took to going out behind a bush. A schedule was worked out for baths—men one day, women the next.

Nightlife ranged from colorful to rambunctious. A prostitute named Blossom set up a brothel in a nearby tent, and hookers and gamblers from Reno drove out in automobiles on Sundays. The company had its bootlegger, who operated at night, and a daily newsletter, which reported such happenings as the wedding of a couple who fell in love during production, the birth of an Indian baby, and the death of the steward who ran the commissary.

Most of the forty Chinese used in the film (a fraction of what Fox publicists claimed) lived in tents outside of town. Some were retired laborers from the Central Pacific Railroad, still wearing queues, and the oldest had helped build the original line. Real Irish tracklayers were hired, most of whom did their own cooking on board the train. "Those bastards were full of flit," Lefty Hough remembered, "drank all the time and fought. Jesus Christ, they would fight a buzz saw!"

Since the scenario called for "the largest band of Indians you can gather riding into view over the rise of ground," Sioux, Pawnee, Cheyenne, and nearby Paiute were brought in and told to wear traditional tribal dress for the picture. Most of the Indians camped outside the town, toward the mountains. During the filming of crowd scenes Indians played Chinese and Chinese played Indians. While Ford described Native Americans as "a very dignified people," he also said, "The audience likes to see Indians get killed. They don't consider them as human beings." He regretted that statement in later years.

Ford was making *The Iron Horse* at the same time that Charlie Chaplin was preparing *The Gold Rush,* also in the Sierra Nevada. Near Lake Tahoe Ford located a railroad engine from the first transcontinental train and planned to run it over the mountains. His crew arrived to find the engine frozen in ice. "They got about forty head of horses and tried to pull it," Lefty Hough recalled, "but the only way we could made it look like it was moving was to make a dolly shot alongside of it."

For the joining of the rails at Promontory Point, the Central

Pacific lent Ford the original "Jupiter" locomotive, while the Union Pacific lent him "Old 119," a twin engine used by the first transcontinental line. On February 10, 1924, the location newsletter reported the recreation: "We stood watching these two ancient engines move slowly toward each other and finally touch over the last tie and the golden spike. This ceremony, though only the motion picture revival of the original, took on a greater significance than is usually felt during the filming of scenes that are inspired by a lesser theme."

To add to the film's authenticity, Ford cast Frances Teague in the role of Polka Dot. Teague's great-grandfather had supplied teams for grading on the Sacramento end of the Central Pacific construction, her grandfather had worked on the line as a fireman, and her father at eighteen had begun as a mechanic for the railroad. The director also took advantage of impromptu shots. When a Portuguese herdsman approached his set with a flock of sheep, Ford photographed them, using the scene to open his picture. "It was a great shot," the director said, "a great stroke of luck." He wanted to film a buffalo stampede so audiences would feel they were part of the action. He ordered a pit dug six feet deep, and three of his crew, along with Ford himself, crawled into the hole as two thousand animals lumbered toward them. Their only protection was a roof of planks flush against the ground. The director stood peering out a hole for the camera when the planks gave way; he sustained minor injuries about his face and hands.

The four-week shooting schedule proved inadequate and the production ran over budget. Lefty Hough stated that he saw no script while they were shooting *The Iron Horse*. "I would go up to the train every night where Ford was staying to find out what the hell we were going to do the next day," he said. The director often sat up late at night in his parlor car making changes. "In those days he'd bleed you dry," Frank Baker said. "He'd talk to you and talk to you, and suddenly you'd find half of what you'd said in the picture he was making." Studio executives liked the early rushes the company sent back to Los Angeles and urged Ford to keep up the good work. Sol Wurtzel telegraphed Ford shortly after filming on *The Iron*

Horse began: "After you review scenes on screen you will feel that all trouble of present location was worthwhile."

Later Wurtzel grew nervous about the prolonged schedule and additional budget and notified Ford that he must speed things up. The director called for Pardner Jones, telling him to step back forty paces. "I have a message here from Wurtzel," Ford told the sharpshooter. "I'm going to fold it up, and I want you to shoot a hole right through the name." The director held the wire in his right hand, while Jones put a rifle to his shoulder and fired. Ford never moved. He unfolded the telegram and lifted it for all to see. The bullet had gone right through Wurtzel's name. The crew cheered, then went back to work.

George O'Brien became more comfortable with his role as filming progressed, more natural in his expressions. He spent most of his time between scenes doing push-ups. In one sequence he was to catch a moving train on horseback. During filming the horse slipped on some snow beside the tracks and fell. O'Brien was thrown, but then caught the train on foot, much to Ford's delight. "That's my boy," the director yelled. O'Brien and Ford became close friends during the making of *The Iron Horse* and would work together many times afterwards. The athletic actor was Irish, and near enough to Ford's age to share many interests. O'Brien exuded the masculine image Ford would have liked to have projected himself, much as John Wayne did later.

Already the director had begun selecting a professional family that would remain with him through many years, a substitute perhaps for the problematic family at home. Sometimes the two overlapped. Jack's brother Eddie O'Fearna (Gaelic for Feeney) became his first assistant, although the two fought bitterly. Eddie had moved to California in 1917 after he married, soon becoming Jack's right-hand man. Eddie battled with studios, battled with actors, and argued with Jack. "I'm not going to make this picture if my people have to live in these cars," he told a Fox representative when the company of *The Iron Horse* arrived on location in Nevada. Unpopular though he was, Eddie served his brother faithfully throughout most of Jack's career, looking after details and keeping sets organized.

Ford finished location shooting on *The Iron Horse* in mid-March 1924 with a better understanding of the pioneer experience. He felt he had lived some of the hardships his uncle, Michael Connolly, had endured laying track for the Union Pacific. "Uncle Mike . . . told me stories about it," he claimed, "and taught me the songs they had sung."

Ford turned thirty while he was on location and soon found himself thrust into the front rank of American filmmakers. Although he later belittled *The Iron Horse,* referring to it as "The Metallic Mustang," the film proved an unqalified success and contained features that became Ford's hallmarks. Shot at an unprecedented cost and running twelve reels, two longer than *The Covered Wagon,* the epic grossed more than $3 million.

The picture opened in Los Angeles on August 24, 1924, the first movie to play Sid Grauman's new Egyptian Theater. Fifteen Indians were brought from the Blackfoot Reservation for the premiere, and Colonel Tim McCoy appeared as master of ceremonies. Fanchon and Marco staged a Hoop Shirt Dance, and a locomotive ran up Hollywood Boulevard with Indians on it, dressed in ceremonial regalia. "That was a great moment in my life," Ford acknowledged.

The New York opening was preceded by the most extensive promotional campaign for any film in years. Posters dotted the city, while billboards were plastered with lurid advertisements to intrigue the public. For weeks the New York newspapers were full of publicity, and thirty skywriters spelled out the name Iron Horse in huge letters over the city. At night thousands of people on Broadway watched an aerial daredevil somersault above Manhattan with flaming letters across the bottom of his plane calling attention to *The Iron Horse.*

The picture opened at the Lyric Theater in New York, with a special score composed by Erno Rapee; it ran there for almost ten months. Film celebrities, as well as leaders from the railroad world, attended the premiere. "Grayed-haired men, whose fathers had constructed railroads in the pioneer days, were much moved by the spectacle in shadows that passed before their eyes," the *New York Times* reported. "And some of them wept." The *Times* reviewer felt that John Ford had "done his share of the work with thoroughness and with pleasing imagination," but concluded that George O'Brien dominated the show too much at certain points, "especially where he heaves his manly chest." The critic stated that O'Brien seemed preoccupied with what a fine specimen of manhood he was, and complained that the actor's shirt sleeves were repeatedly "tucked up high enough to give one a good view of his biceps."

Despite its melodramatic plot, *The Iron Horse* exhibited effective dramatic composition and characteristics that Ford became famous for later: broad humor, Irish references, adoration of Lincoln, Indians grouped along the crest of a hill, dogs barking beside intense action. Perhaps the greatest shot in the film comes with the Indian attack on the train, when Ford captures their shadows against the cars, poetry in motion achieved with a second camera.

Ford punctuates his story with heroic images. His saga tells of a grand accomplishment that made America the land of promise, with no hint of the capitalist motives behind railroad building. The film's first subtitle caught its spirit: "It [the transcontinental railroad] links the shores of a continent and the aspirations of a great nation." To Ford the story was inspiring, one that should make every American proud; workers labored in the face of danger, sickness, and fatigue to link the nation's shores. The Native American was viewed as a hazard, standing in the way of civilization's progress. Immigrants, on the other hand, banded together, overcame deficiencies, and were transformed in the service of their adopted country.

The success of *The Iron Horse,* however, did not relieve Ford from directing his share of program pictures essential to the studio's financial health. He next drew a series of routine assignments that he handled effectively, but failed to give his personal stamp. *Lightnin'* (1925) contains no breathtaking climaxes, but has its share of folksy humanity. *Kentucky Pride* (also 1925) is a fragile and comic story about horse racing, in which the Irish are contrasted with Italians. *The Fighting Heart* (again 1925) deals with prizefighting and features Victor

McLaglen in his first Ford film. *The Shamrock Handicap* (1926), for which cinematographer George Schneiderman photographed the Irish landscape through gauze to achieve a misty effect, is a nostalgic portrait of Ireland.

Not until *Three Bad Men* (later in 1926) did Ford return to the American West, in what may be the finest Western of the silent era, one that mixed courage with greed. George O'Brien again starred, and a land rush provided the film's climax — 150 wagons dashing into unsettled territory. The company began shooting the picture in late September near Jackson Hole, Wyoming, while snow was falling on the Grand Tetons. They lived in tents, four to a unit, bathed in the Snake River, and ate from a chuck wagon. A recreation hall was built, where dances were held for the actors, crew, and visitors. "We drowned a horse up there," Lefty Hough remembered. "You could see this poor bastard going to the bottom all the way down."

The land rush was shot on a dry lake bed outside Victorville, California. Ford wanted a baby placed on the ground, with wagons racing past at a terrific speed. The wife of one of the stuntmen came to visit her husband and brought their baby along. Ford talked her into letting him use the infant in his picture, with the money earned going into a fund for the child's education. Four cameras were grinding as the baby's father rode by and snatched the child up, rescuing it from an oncoming wagon. "Several of the company had been in the actual land rush," Ford claimed. "They'd been kids and rode with their parents. So I talked to them about it. The incident of snatching the baby from under the wheels of a wagon actually happened."

Three Bad Men possessed a vigor that lifted it above such melodramas and sentimental comedies as *Upstream* (1927) and *Mother Machree* (1928), which Ford directed next. By contrast, *Four Sons* (also 1928) stands as one of his major silent pictures and proved an enormous financial success. Ford traveled to Germany to shoot background scenes for the movie in the Bavarian countryside. While there he met F. W. Murnau, the great expressionist director, and fell under his spell, so that

Four Sons abounds in shadows and expressionist techniques. Ford later called the film his "first really good story" and continued to profess pride in his work. Fox executives were pleased, too. "If the proper care, analysis, and thought is given to the editing and titling of this picture," Fox production chief Winfield Sheehan wrote in a studio memo, "I am of the opinion that it will register as the greatest picture ever made."

Silent movies had taken giant strides forward by 1928, evolving into an aesthetic medium that many pioneer filmmakers considered more poetic than were sound features. John Ford had matured with the industry, mastered the craft, and never completely abandoned silent principles, finding in movies a release for his creative energy and some of his personal fantasies.

As a veteran director, Ford would play down his early accomplishments, claiming that he remembered none of his silent pictures "with any warmth—they were all hard work." Yet his approach to filmmaking had been shaped during those formative years. As the industry became more solidified, the freewheeling practices of the pioneers came to be replaced by assembly-line procedures. Ford, the outsider from Maine, continued to be an iconoclast in the picture business. He not only accepted the fact, but flaunted that image, exaggerating his eccentricities. While other Hollywood pioneers vanished, Ford survived, sometimes employing outlaw tactics to protect his artistry.

"Every kid is in love with the West," the director said. Through Harry Carey, Ford himself had fallen in love with the West and begun to understand the values of its people. He recognized that the conquest of the frontier was the American epic, the nation's creation myth, established through dime novels, Wild West shows, and scores of one- and two-reel silent films. Ford lifted the myth to grander proportions, adding spectacle, dramatic sweep, realistic characters, conflict, and honest sentiment, presenting his stories with personal involvement and visual poetry. "I have an eye," Ford told his Irish friend Michael Killanin. At his best he also had enough heart to humanize his sagas for mass audiences.

CHAPTER 4

The Sound Revolution

PANIC struck Hollywood when sound was introduced. Many silent stars failed to make the transition; either they possessed too strong a foreign accent or their voices did not record well on the primitive equipment. Just as often melodramatic silent screen acting seemed ludicrous when sound was added, making torrid lovers such as John Gilbert appear overstated and downright silly. Having acquired a voice, films for a time tended toward garrulousness, as movies became little more than filmed plays. With sound the mobile camera was temporarily restricted, since recording devices required enclosing cameras in heavy, cumbersome, sound-proof boxes. The Broadway stage meanwhile was raided for actors who could speak lines and directors who knew how to handle dialogue.

The small independent studios were swallowed up by larger ones, until by 1936 the industry was dominated by five major companies: Metro-Goldwyn-Mayer, Paramount, Warner Bros., 20th Century-Fox, and Radio-Keith-Orpheum. These five studios, as well as such smaller ones as Universal and Columbia, produced movies on an assembly line to supply the nation's cinema chains, which studios either owned or controlled.

Gone was the casualness of the early flickers, which had focused on lives of ordinary people and allowed a wide latitude for innovation. With the appearance of the big studios and their theater chains, Hollywood moguls sought to capture the entertainment dollars of the American middle class, giving more sophisticated audiences romance, glamour, and beautiful stars dressed in designer clothes. Producers took care to balance expensive films with budget pictures certain to make money, since it was essential for companies to show a profit at the end of the year.

Like other early filmmakers, John Ford viewed the coming of sound with suspicion. "I fear that the art of telling stories by motion pictures is becoming lost," he said shortly after the introduction of sound. "It is too simple to take the easier way of telling the story through dialogue, and thus lose the most vital factor of the motion picture, the motion." While studio workers all around him were fired, Ford continued at Fox, operating in much the renegade vein that he had during the silent era. *Napoleon's Barber* (1928), a three-reeler, was his first talkie. "It was the first time anyone ever went outside with a sound system," Ford declared. "They said it couldn't be done." With a Western Electric sound expert on the set, Ford mastered the new technology faster than most of his contemporaries. "This is another talking film that may win converts for this new type of entertainment," the *New York Times* said of *Napoleon's Barber*.

Soon studios realized that most of the directors they had brought in from the theater knew nothing about the camera. "We had schedules of three or four weeks in those days," Ford said, "and after eight weeks, these fellows had about a half reel of picture, and the stuff was terrible." So the silent directors came back into favor, often paired with a dialogue coach from the stage. Ford tolerated no such union, although he accepted the advantages of sound so long as dialogue was kept short and crisp.

The Black Watch (1929), Ford's first feature-length talkie, was an adventure yarn set in India, with several wordy scenes added by British stage director Lumsden Hare after Ford left for another project. The film starred Victor McLaglen and Myrna Loy and was remade by director Henry King as *King of the Khyber Rifles* in 1954. Ford took pains to give the picture atmosphere and expressionistic lighting, but Hare's additional dialogue seems interminable. Winfield Sheehan felt the movie needed more love scenes between McLaglen and Loy, who played an Indian seductress. "They were really horrible — long, talky things," Ford said of Hare's scenes. "I wanted to vomit when I saw them."

Loy found Ford a sensitive director despite his macho facade. After the picture was finished, he invited her to a party at his house. She arrived to discover Ford and his guests—all men—in the library. "That son of a gun was having a stag party," Loy recalled, "and he'd invited me." She eventually realized what a compliment he had paid her. Ford played tricks only on people he liked, and he liked Myrna Loy a great deal. "I stayed and had a wonderful time with the boys," the actress wrote.

Among Ford's gang that night was a young football player from the University of Southern California; his name was Marion Michael Morrison, soon to be changed to John Wayne, but he was called Duke by his friends. He had worked as a property boy on Ford's *Mother Machree* while still in college, and the two had become friends. The director enjoyed talking football with Morrison and assigned him a bit part in *Hangman's House* (1928), his last silent feature. Soon a father-son relationship developed between them. Myrna Loy remembered seeing Morrison around the set of *The Black Watch*, but thought him shy. It was evident to her that Ford was grooming him for something bigger.

Soon Fox assigned the director a football picture, *Salute* (1929), which centered on the rivalry between the army and navy teams and would be filmed at the United States Naval Academy in Annapolis. Ford asked Duke Morrison to hire players from the University of Southern California's Trojan squad to go to Annapolis for action sequences. Just as those selected were about to leave by train from the Los Angeles station, an uninvited player named Ward Bond appeared, luggage in hand. Bond and Morrison had been teammates, but they disliked each other. Bond, a 220-pound tackle eager to escape the classroom, shoved his way onto the train and insisted that he was going to Annapolis, too. Impressed by his gall, Ford agreed to take him along, and Bond proved as natural before the camera as Morrison later would. "When I needed a couple of fellows to speak some lines," the director recalled, "I picked them out, and they ended up with parts."

Ward Bond became a permanent member of Ford's stock company, as well as a personal friend. Since Bond revealed a

giant ego and often spoke before he thought, he was an easy
foil for Ford's sarcasm and practical jokes. Through the decades the director rode him unmercifully, but Bond's hide was
so thick he seemed not to notice. As one regular in Ford's films
put it, "Ward was fairly high on himself, so old Ford would put
the needle in and let a little of the air out." Poking fun at Bond
was a sport the director's inner circle enjoyed, and one that
made Bond feel important, since he was the center of attention.
"Ward was a terrific snob," said Ford. "Actually he was very
unsophisticated, but he wanted to be a man of the world."

During the trip to Annapolis, Morrison and Bond became
friends. Since both were hard drinkers, they fit into Ford's
crowd. The director shared a compartment on the train with
Salute's star, George O'Brien. Ford and O'Brien had become
best friends and spent hours in each other's homes. "My
mother used to make great chili," O'Brien said, "and Jack used
to appear from nowhere, sometimes on weekends." The actor
had served in the navy during World War I and was as obsessed
with the military as Ford was, giving them plenty to talk about.

The superintendent of Annapolis was from Peak's Island,
where Ford and his family still spent part of every summer, so
the director was given the freedom to film anywhere he wanted
at the Academy. Ford didn't believe in excessive closeups,
preferring to let the action swirl past the lens. To achieve
performances he found it desirable to know his actors off the
set as well as on. "Jack was a hypnotist," director Allan Dwan
remarked. "He could do anything with an actor if he liked him.
He could be pretty brusque if he didn't. Duke Wayne was just a
stick of wood when he came away from USC. Jack gave him
character."

Duke Morrison hadn't planned to become an actor when he
entered the movie business. "I wanted to be a director," he
said, "and naturally I studied Ford like a hawk." Ford liked
Morrison and Ward Bond from the start, in part because they
stood up to him, treating him as an equal. One evening in
Annapolis, Ford was in the bathtub shaving when Bond entered his room and ambled over to the dresser where Ford had
lain his wallet, keys, and money. "Listen, Jack," the future actor

yelled through the door, "I'm taking about twenty bucks. I'm going into town drinking tonight. You can go with us if you want to come." Before Ford could stop him, Bond was gone. While the director complained about such brash behavior, he loved being treated as part of the gang. "That's the reason he drank," John Wayne later maintained, "—to be one of the boys."

Salute proved a solid success at the box office and contained some of the most stirring football sequences yet put on film. Ford argued that he had no difficulty making the transition from silent pictures to talkies, but the early years of sound did constitute a transitional period in his career and a temporary decline in his standing. His first three sound pictures were financial failures, and he needed *The Black Watch* and *Salute* to bolster his prestige within the industry.

Ford continued to argue that the spoken word was for the stage; movies should concentrate on movement and the visual. "It's still a silent medium," he vowed. "There's no such thing as a good script, really. Scripts are dialogue, and I don't like all that *talk*." Ford thought of himself first as a cameraman, then as a director. He learned to move narrative along swiftly and not to pack too many ideas into a single scene. Movies were at their best when they told their story through "a series of simple, beautiful, active pictures." That's when "the motion picture medium is being used to its fullest advantage," he said.

Ford felt that Westerns—with their action and outdoor settings—brought out the best of the medium, but throughout the 1930s Western films were out of favor with the Hollywood establishment. Budget Westerns were made in abundance, the specialty of smaller studios such as Republic and Columbia. With sound the singing cowboy came into vogue among the poverty-row companies, which aimed their movies at rural and Saturday-matinee audiences. But the major studios avoided Westerns, so that Ford's pictures for a decade took a different turn, focusing on dramas, adventure tales, comedies, and masculine subjects with modern settings. Most of these projects were selected by the studio, and many of them the

director despised. Scripts "were thrown at you," Ford said,
"and you did the best you could with them." He would be told
to report at a specified time on a certain set for a picture that
might not have a title yet. "You didn't know what the hell you
were doing, you never got a week's rest to prepare anything,
and you never knew who the hell was in it," the director
recalled.

Men Without Women (1930), a story about sailors trapped in a
crippled submarine, marked the beginning of Ford's long
collaboration with screenwriter Dudley Nichols. Whereas other New York writers concocted dialogue that was static and
dull, Nichols made every word count. *Men Without Women*
had the benefit of an actual submarine, and was filmed in part
off Catalina Island with the cooperation of the navy. Despite a
tragic plot, the movie skillfully balanced pathos and humor.
Duke Morrison, working as a prop boy and stuntman, appeared in a small role, spoke a few lines, and was even awarded a
closeup as a navy lieutenant. "There was something special
about Duke even then," Ford told Pilar Wayne, the actor's third
wife. "Sure—he was callow and untutored, but he had something that jumped right off the screen at me. I guess you could
call it star power."

Although *Men Without Women* was not a commercial success, the picture won praise for its realism. The *Film Spectator*
declared, "John Ford is a great motion picture director, because he has an inborn sense of dramatic values, because there
is a strong human streak in him, because at heart he is a
sentimentalist with a tender, poetical, and whimsical outlook
on life. *Men Without Women* is a truly great motion picture. It
shatters all our highly respected screen traditions."

A true artist, Ford paid little attention to the assessment of
critics, determined to tread his own path. He collaborated with
Dudley Nichols on thirteen films, offering suggestions without ever sitting down with pen in hand. Whereas Ford burst
with energy and enthusiasm, Nichols proved more subtle and
controlled. Both were consummate craftsmen, yet Ford en-
hanced the writer's words with added emotion during filming.

It was easier for Ford to express feelings through his work

than privately. He continued to treat his wife with reverence, yet rarely spent much time with her. "I don't think he had the capacity to be a friend to a woman, to be relaxed with her," actress Joanne Dru remarked. Mary Ford enjoyed her privileged life, yet was something of a snob and tended to look down on Hollywood. Despite her husband's success in the industry, she refused to be impressed with movie-making, regarding Jack's career as superficial and "low Irish," tinsel in a business of glitter. Mary remained the loyal wife, taking the course of least resistence in her relationship with Jack, sometimes appearing indifferent. Yet it was obvious that she loved him dearly.

While Mary delighted in spending money, Jack was notoriously frugal, living simply by choice. His family ties were more theory than fact, since he spent most of his leisure hours with his cronies or alone in his bedroom reading. He was often irascible and uncommunicative at home, caustic and witty in public. He was never an open man and seemed to feel that the test of friendship was a companion's capacity to weather his shifts in mood and even personal humiliation. "I know people like him in Ireland," Charles FitzSimons declared, "that same contradictory type—the macho surface, the terrific sensitivity, the creative, artistic strains, and yet very simple. Ford was complex and simple; it was an amazing combination." Darcy O'Brien, George's son, observed that the Irish temperament tends to join romanticism and realism in a unique fashion. "They're a very hard-headed, tough people," the younger O'Brien said, "and yet there's this alternate, romantic and lyrical side. Ford had both strains. It comes through in his movies, but it also came through in the way he was able to survive in Hollywood and end up doing exactly what he wanted. He was as tough as they come."

On a set Ford would gnaw the corners of a crumpled handkerchief and, particularly on location, look slovenly. He preferred baggy pants, a safari jacket, a weathered cap, and boots, usually with a day's stubble covering his face. He tended to be courteous to little people, crusty with friends and equals. In either case there was an aloofness even toward his inner circle. Those who knew him best recognized this as a defense mechanism. In preparing scenes, Ford gave little actual direction, but when he did make a suggestion, he went straight to the point. Some accepted him as a bellicose Irishman, but others resented what they saw as outright cruelty.

Up the River (1930), a comedy about two convicts who don't mind prison since they escape with regularity, featured Spencer Tracy and Humphrey Bogart, both of whom became Ford's friends, although not part of his inner circle. Like the director, Tracy was Irish—erratic, volatile—and an alcoholic. Neither took Hollywood seriously, and both disliked the ballyhoo that went with promoting films and stars. Tracy hated phonies as much as Ford did and had little truck with ostentation or pretense. While both harbored deep artistic impulses, they avoided talking about their craft in aesthetic terms. "American artists claim to be tinkerers rather than geniuses," Joseph W. Reed declares in his book *Three American Originals*, in which he compares John Ford, William Faulkner, and Charles Ives. In that sense Ford and Tracy were thoroughly American, since they both preferred to work in an informal vocabulary.

Up the River was followed by *Seas Beneath* (1931), a World War I story starring George O'Brien and again filmed mainly off Catalina Island. Fox at the time wanted its action pictures centered around modern technology rather than the American West—airplanes, submarines, blimps, but not horses. Ford turned again to a navy picture, filling it with as much excitement as possible. "We did the actual refueling at sea," the director said. "That stuff was good and so was the battle stuff, but the story was bad."

Screenwriter Philip Dunne remembered meeting Ford on an indoor set for *Seas Beneath* at the old Fox studio on Western Avenue. "At the time," Dunne said, "he was a lordly director and I was a lowly reader, but he let no such social distinctions stand between us. We were both Irish history buffs, and we reveled in the legendary exploits of Finn MacCool and Cuchulainn, the darker realities inflicted on Ireland by the injustices and cruelties of Cromwell and Castlereagh, and the heroics of Robert Emmet and Michael Collins." A large portion of

Ford's library consisted of books on Irish subjects by Irish authors. While he was suspicious of intellectually pretentious college graduates, he liked bright people who could discuss issues in down-to-earth terms. Philip Dunne was as sophisticated as he was genuine, and Ford paid him the compliment of inviting him home for drinks and conversation. The screenwriter recalled evenings that "were damp inside and out—fog without and Irish whiskey within." Later Dunne wrote a masterful script for *How Green Was My Valley*, which won the director his third Academy Award.

Bored with studio assignments and fearful that his life was becoming routine, Ford decided to make a trip to East Asia via the Philippines in January 1931, inviting George O'Brien to come along. Delighted by his Hollywood success, yet resisting the social expectations that went with it, Ford savored romantic notions of himself as an adventurer, a man of action, as he remembered his youth in Portland. He fantasized that a trip to Asia by freighter would offer excitement and a chance to prove that he was still athletic and vital.

O'Brien met Ford at the dock in San Pedro. Mary and the Ford children were on hand to see them off. When Mary started weeping, George shouted to her from the boat: "Why are you crying so, Mary? We'll be back before long." Mary stifled her sobs enough to reply, "You'd cry, too. You've got my ticket!"

Ford and O'Brien left on their adolescent romp aboard the *Tai Yang* with one other passenger, a man from Singapore. After the first day they referred to the freighter as "Outward Bound." They discussed Asian women, read books, and Ford drank. Then they ran into a typhoon. For twelve days they weathered severe rain, wind, and dark, menacing clouds. "Jack and myself have been sleeping on our heads most every night," O'Brien wrote in his diary. Ford described the storm more graphically in a letter to Mary: "The ship has been under water all the time. Mountainous waves which broke over the bridge." But he insisted they were having a good time—sleeping twelve hours a night and eating four meals.

After five days Ford had read all the books he had brought along and became restless. While he liked O'Brien, the actor didn't talk much, and Ford showed little respect for his mind, calling him "Muscles" in a derisive way. "Yesterday we passed a live volcano fifteen miles away," Ford wrote Mary. "It was thrilling to see land after nineteen days at sea." He went on to say that he had never felt or looked better in his life. "Even O'Brien looks at me admiringly. I look and feel twelve years younger."

Later the weather turned hot, and Ford and O'Brien spent a lot of time sunbathing, followed by a salt-water shower. "George and I go around in shorts and khaki shirts," the director wrote home. But as his boredom grew, Ford started to drink more heavily. Since O'Brien was not much of a drinker, Ford turned surly and obnoxious. When he drank, his Irish melancholy rose to the surface. He became morbid and fatalistic, eventually drinking so much that he couldn't get out of bed. O'Brien discovered bottles under Ford's bunk and even in bed with him, while their relationship became strained to the breaking point. They celebrated Ford's thirty-seventh birthday aboard ship by shaving and playing records on an old victrola, but the arguments between them grew vicious.

The two celebrities from Hollywood were greeted in Manila by local dignitaries who feted them royally. They traveled on to Hong Kong, where Ford continued drinking, and in February O'Brien left for Shanghai alone. "Shanghai was the Paris of the Orient in those days," the actor said. "White tie and tails and all that sort of thing." He never revealed what happened between Ford and himself, but the director shunned O'Brien for more than fifteen years. Not until *Fort Apache* (1948) did the actor appear in another John Ford film. He worked in budget Westerns to earn a living, then was reduced to character parts.

When Ford returned from East Asia, Samuel Goldwyn borrowed him for the director's first movie away from the Fox lot in a decade. The picture was *Arrowsmith* (1931), based on the Sinclair Lewis novel, a prestigious asssignment that resulted in a box-office and critical triumph. Ford described his pictures between *Three Bad Men* (his last silent Western) and *Arrow-smith* as potboilers. *Arrowsmith*, which starred Ronald Colman and stage actress Helen Hayes, helped pull him out of his professional stalemate. Ford liked the story and added forceful imagery to Sidney Howard's wordy script. Again the influence of German director F. W. Murnau is evident, particularly in the film's expressionistic lighting.

Ford found Sam Goldwyn meddlesome about insignificant details, and they clashed severely. Before the picture began Goldwyn secured Ford's promise in writing that he wouldn't drink during the production, but abstaining grew difficult as the project wore on. Ford and Helen Hayes disagreed over the director's habit of trimming dialogue. When Hayes objected to a lengthy cut, Ford showed his disdain for stage technique by demanding, "Who's directing this picture, you or me? You go out on that set and do what I tell you to do." The actress sped to her chair beside the camera devastated and sat there rigidly. Within a few minutes Ford came over to her and asked, "What's the matter, honey, did I make you mad?" Hayes drew herself up and, with the whole company looking on, said with great dignity, "I'm not accustomed to being *speaken* to in that manner!" The set broke into laughter, and even Hayes and Ford had to join in. "It was the longest and loudest laugh I ever had in my life," the actress declared. "The electricians and the lighting crew nearly fell off the parallel. Jack had a very brusque way and he was an Irish bully, but a loving one. I'm Irish, so I understood. Ford was a fine director; he knew how to get a performance out of you. He got stuck on me a little, to use an old-fashioned phrase, and took to calling me all the time."

Toward the end of the picture Ford got into a major hassle with the stubborn Sam Goldwyn and bolted from the lot, leaving retakes unfinished. He started drinking and soon boarded the S.S. *Wilhelmina* with Mary for a vacation trip beginning in Hawaii. The intent was to restore marital harmony, but the effort failed miserably. The couple continued on to Manila, but Ford went on alone to Bali and Singapore, drinking all the way. Mary resigned herself to the fact that life with Jack would be lonely and emotionally draining.

In March 1932 Ford agreed to return to Universal to direct a picture for Carl Laemmle, Jr. As the Great Depression approached its nadir, the financial situation at Fox became unsettled and ultimately ruinous. Drastic changes in policy were issued, and everyone under contract to the studio took a cut in salary of between 10 and 25 percent. Desperate for money, Ford agreed to direct *Air Mail* (1932) at Universal, an aviation story written by Lieutenant Commander Frank "Spig" Wead, a pioneer navy aviator whose career Ford would film in *The Wings of Eagles* (1957).

Air Mail, one of the first big aviation pictures, featured Pat O'Brien and Ralph Bellamy. Both actors found Ford difficult to work with, and agreed he was a perfectionist. "He would incorporate tiny things into a picture that sounded like nothing when he told you," O'Brien said. "Then when you saw the dailies, something came off the screen that was revelatory, something you weren't cognizant of while you were shooting." Ford added a humorous sequence that wasn't in the script, in which actor Slim Summerville sweeps the floor. "In those days," the director said, "when a script was dull, the best you could do was to try and get some comedy into it."

Next on Ford's agenda was *Flesh* (1932), with Wallace Beery playing a waiter in a German beer garden who amuses patrons by wrestling, then emigrates to America. Broadway playwright Moss Hart wrote the dialogue, but the static film bore few of Ford's distinguishing traits and was judged no more than competent by critics. *Pilgrimage* (1933) found the director back at Fox, after the studio had declared bankrupty and was placed in receivership. The picture portrayed motherhood in highly sentimental terms, but audiences at the time liked sentimentality and the film proved a box-office success.

In September 1934 Ford signed another long-term contract with Fox, which offered him financial security but immediate frustrations. The director pleaded against making *The World Moves On* (1934) and threatened to quit, but in the end was forced to do the studio's bidding. "I did the best I could, but I hated the damn thing," Ford insisted. "You were getting paid big money and there was very little income tax, so you swallowed your pride and went out there and did it."

Happier assignments were three pictures with Fox's reigning superstar, Will Rogers: *Doctor Bull* (1933), *Judge Priest* (1934), and *Steamboat Round the Bend* (1935), all brimming with homey Americana. In the first Rogers played a small-town physician, in the second a folksy Kentucky judge. Ford enjoyed working with him and liked the nostalgic stories they filmed together. To Ford, Rogers's attitude was symbolic of traditional America. "The men of the West were like Will Rogers," the director said. "They were rugged and imperfect men, but many were basically gentle, and most were basically moral and religious, like most people who live with the land. . . . Strong people have always been able to laugh at their own hardships and discomforts." Ford allowed the Oklahoma humorist to use his natural speech and maintained that no writer could create dialogue for Will Rogers. Ford advised him, "This is the script, but just learn the sense of it and say it in your own words." Otherwise the phrasing would sound false. "Some of the lines he'd speak from the script," Ford said, "but most of the time he'd make up his own."

The three pictures Ford directed with Rogers are trivial, yet they contain enchanting evocations of America's past. Exteriors for *Steamboat Round the Bend* were shot near Sacramento, mainly on the American River, with part of the company living on board an actual steamboat. The film found Will Rogers at his homespun best, but Rogers was not to experience its public reception; the film premiered at Radio City Music Hall one month after the actor's death in a plane crash in Alaska.

The year before, Ford had made his first picture at RKO, a masculine drama entitled *The Lost Patrol* (1934) about a group of British cavalry troops lost in the Mesopotamian desert. Victor McLaglen starred, and Max Steiner's music won an Academy Award for best dramatic score. A few months later Columbia engaged Ford to direct *The Whole Town's Talking* (1935), a riotous script about a gangster that burlesqued the current public-enemy theme, with Edward G. Robinson giving a dual performance. Robinson stated that he knew he was in the hands of a consummate professional from his first meeting with Ford. "I felt safe and secure with him," the actor wrote. Ford remembered the picture as "all right," but claimed he never saw it.

By then Ford's pattern was to finish an assignment and quickly put to sea on the *Araner*, the 110-foot yacht he'd purchased in June 1934. Named for the Aran Islands off the coast of western Ireland, the two-masted vessel became his most prized possession. According to Darcy O'Brien, the *Araner* was "a classic example of the Irish American's not wanting to lose touch with the old country, but announcing a new prosperity at the same time. There was never a boat like that in the Aran Islands." The yacht was painted green and white, and had polished wood staterooms and a central salon with a huge poker table. Rip Yeager served as the *Araner*'s skipper, overseeing a crew of six.

Earlier it had been Jack's practice to complete a project and come home and tell Mary, "I've filmed the picture, I've cut the picture, music has okayed it, the producer has okayed it, now call the bootlegger." From the mid-1930s on, much of his drinking was done aboard the *Araner*. He drank to escape; it became his way of turning off his mind while keeping the euphoria of creativity alive until the next assignment. Once the pressures of making a picture were over, he wanted to surround himself with friends, sail into oblivion, and forget the pressures he had been under. When working, he would sometimes drive down to San Pedro to have a drink or two on the *Araner*, play cards, and then drive back home. During summers he kept the yacht moored off Catalina Island, spending as much time there as possible.

In December 1934 Ford made a cruise to Mazatlán with Henry Fonda, Duke Wayne, and Ward Bond, purportedly for marlin fishing. A Christmas tree was set up in the *Araner*'s salon, and liquor flowed from the time they left San Pedro. Mazatlán was not the tourist attraction then that it would become later, and few Americans were around. Ford and his cohorts enjoyed sitting in the bar of the Belmar Hotel, looking out over the ocean and watching sunsets. They'd go back to

Ford's yacht at night, but Wayne and Fonda often slipped ashore and spent the night in a whorehouse. The *Araner*'s skipper's log for December 31, 1934, gives a vivid account of their New Year's celebration:

> 1:18 P.M. Went ashore—got the owner, Fonda, Wayne, and Bond out of jail. Put up a bond for their behavior.

> 9:30 P.M. Got the owner, Fonda, Wayne, and Bond out of jail again. Invited by Mexican officials to leave town.

The January 1, 1935, entry continues in the same vein:

> Owner went to Mass—brought priest to *Araner*— purpose to sign pledge [to give up drinking]: pledge signed—celebrated signing of pledge with champagne, later augmented with brandy.
> Arrived Muertos—great time, 14 hours-35 minutes. This would never have been possible without the advice and help from Mr. Bond, a great navigator who is sneaking drinks. Gave lessons on fishing to Mr. Fonda.
> Mr. Bond started telling Mr. Ford, owner, how to fish from the *Araner*.

> Mr. Ford coins new expression. Told Mr. Bond to go fuck himself.
> Mr. Bond gets fish line tangled in propellor. We drift for 3 hours.

By January 4 screenwriter Dudley Nichols had come aboard to work with Ford on the script for *The Informer*. Nichols loved to talk politics and fish, but planned to devote evenings to the script. Since the story dealt with the Irish Rebellion, Ford promised to fill him in on the background of the Black and Tan War. By ten o'clock on the evening of Nichols's arrival, the writer was so inebriated he fell down the hatch. His remaining days aboard ship, fortunately, proved more productive and resulted in a script that would win both Nichols and Ford Academy Awards.

With the acquisition of the *Araner* the three major themes in Ford's life had come into focus: Ireland, the American West, and the sea. During the late 1930s he made annual cruises down the West Coast into the Gulf of California. Having recently made a series of navy films, on September 12, 1934, he was appointed a lieutenant commander in the Naval Reserve, a commission that Ford felt gave him the status of a gentleman. Filled with self-doubts and needing to prove his worth to Mary, he looked upon the military as a means of elevating himself in the social order. In his mind the navy offered far more prestige than did Hollywood. Whereas he dressed sloppily for his movie work, his navy uniforms were carefully tailored and neatly pressed. Since Mary came from a military family, he was determined to augment his limited background by proving himself on his wife's terms.

Meanwhile *The Informer* (1935) earned Ford the highest praise he had yet enjoyed as a director, winning for him both an Academy Award and a New York Film Critics Award. He had tried unsuccessfully for four years to interest studios in the picture. Set in Dublin against the political strife of 1922, *The Informer* deals with a betrayal to the Irish cause. Its director sought to lift its simple story into an arty, expressionistic film. After Fox, Warner Bros., Paramount, Columbia, and Metro had turned the project down, Merian C. Cooper at RKO agreed to let Ford make the picture, so long as his budget did not exceed $220,000. Most of the RKO executives considered the story depressing and were convinced that the picture would be a failure. Ford was assigned an antiquated sound-stage across Melrose Avenue from the main studio; the stage was so dusty that the cinematographer had to mask the sets with fog. The Dublin slums were no more than painted canvas, but the studio left the director alone to make his film. The result was a John Ford classic that was sparse in dialogue, yet full of imagery, symbolism, and Irish mysticism.

Victor McLaglen, who was cast in the pivotal role of Gypo Nolan, also won an Oscar for his performance. McLaglen had been a professional fighter and played to perfection the Irish bruiser who betrays a friend. Ford treated him like an overgrown child, kept him off balance with erratic behavior, but pulled from McLaglen the performance of a lifetime. "I've seen big Victor McLaglen stand there and cry like a child," Frank Baker said of Ford's treatment, but what came out of the screen was brilliant. Several of the supporting players in the picture came from the Abbey Theatre, adding a realism that Hollywood actors could not provide. The film was completed under budget in less than three weeks; Ford knew that he had done an exceptional piece of work.

When the preview was held in Hollywood, however, a number of people walked out. "I was treated like a leper," Ford said. The picture opened at Radio City Music Hall and was poorly attended at first. Then critics gave the film favorable notices, and attendance picked up. "It's a pleasure to congratulate you on *The Informer*," director Frank Capra telegraphed Ford. "I am going to get sappy and say it was inspiring." Jean Renoir saw the film and arrived at his friend George Seaton's house afterward full of excitement. "I learned so much today," Renoir told Seaton. "I learned how not to move my camera." Before long the press heaped praise on the picture, turning it into a popular success. "It is an excellent piece," a fan wrote from Newburgh, New York. "Here the cinema has approached its height in making people feel and think along worthwhile lines."

Overnight Ford was hailed as an artist and suddenly found himself able to dictate terms. *The Informer* became his first unqualified masterpiece, and as Hollywood entered its golden age, John Ford emerged as a major talent. Although he continued to film his share of program pictures, Ford would tolerate no interference from studio executives. "Now get a good look at this guy," he was fond of telling his cast and crew at the start of a picture. "He is the producer. Look at him now, because you will not see him again on this set until the movie is finished."

He made enemies in Hollywood, and there were those who hated him. "I worked with Ford only twice," RKO head Pandro Berman declared, "and I found him about the meanest man I ever met. He was nice to me because I was running the studio. But, God! he could be a mean man when he wanted to." Stuntman Gil Perkins couldn't tolerate him. "I thought Ford was an overbearing, arrogant, professional Catholic," Perkins said. "He would pick on people who couldn't fight back. If he got on somebody and they were the patsy, he would crucify them."

All through his success Ford alternated between not taking Hollywood seriously and standing above it—refusing to attend premieres and awards ceremonies, leaving town whenever he could on the *Araner*. At home he spent hours in seclusion, demanding that Mary ask permission before entering his bedroom, or drinking and playing poker with Wayne and his gang.

Ford matured into a man of contradictions—rough and tough, yet artistic and sensitive. He was ambivalent about even his religion. Devout Catholic though he professed to be, he seldom attended mass, referring to his neighborhood church as "Our Lady of the Cadillacs." He kept a rosary on the back of his bed, but as his friend Michael Killanin remarked, "It needed dusting." Ford's religion seemed more social than spiritual. While he was well read in literature and history, he bordered on anti-intellectualism, snorting displeasure at any hint of academics. And while his respect for the family was evident time and again in his work, his own family ties were tenuous. Mary was kept at a distance; Patrick was enrolled in Black-Foxe Military Institute, then Bancroft School; and Barbara, although she remained his pet, saw little of her father. Ford's parents visited California during the winter months, but Barbara Feeney died in 1933 and her husband five years later.

Even with the prestige that *The Informer* brought him, Ford found making pictures with a social content difficult under the old Hollywood system, remarking that "the whole financial set-up is against it. What you'll get is an isolated courageous effort here and there." But the situation changed in 1935 when the old Fox studio merged with 20th Century Productions. Darryl F. Zanuck was appointed the new company's production head and proved an intelligent filmmaker with an eye for socially relevant dramas. Zanuck was determined to turn 20th Century-Fox into a progressive studio, and while he didn't like Ford much personally, he recognized his monumental talent.

The Prisoner of Shark Island (1936) marked the beginning of Ford's ten-picture collaboration with Zanuck. The film, which starred Warner Baxter and featured Harry Carey, was based on the life of Dr. Samuel Mudd, the Maryland physician who set John Wilkes Booth's fractured leg after the actor shot Lincoln. Mudd was subsequently convicted as a conspirator in the assassination plot. Ford and Zanuck were two forceful personalities, and it was inevitable that they would clash. The director resented any interference during the shooting of his films, and a confrontation occurred when the studio head complained to him about Warner Baxter's southern accent. Ford characteristically replied, "If you're not satisfied with the way I'm directing this, you can get somebody else!" Zanuck bellowed, "Are you threatening me?" Ford attempted to explain. "Don't ever threaten me," Zanuck warned. "I throw fellas off my sets. They don't quit on me." It was a showdown between giants, even though Ford outweighed Zanuck by at least forty pounds. While each harbored reservations about the other, from that point on they worked together satisfactorily and even came to respect one another.

Zanuck was a skillful administrator, demonstrated amazing story sense, was knowledgeable about film construction, and understood marketing. He wrote Raymond Griffith regarding Griffith's synopsis of *The Life of Dr. Mudd*: "I like your idea of having the colored regiment at the prison, but I believe they should be commanded by white officers so that when we want to go into brutality, such as the swell incident of feeding the sharks dogs and cats as a lesson to the prisoners—that this dirty work can be done by white men, as otherwise we would find ourselves in too much hot water with the Dixie theatre patronage." Nunnally Johnson, one of the studio's most talented screenwriters, was assigned to the script and later insisted that Ford had followed his text to the letter. "It was on the set that John made all of his contributions to the picture," said Johnson. "These were in the staging of the scenes, the shaping of the characters, and his wonderful use of the camera." On the three pictures Johnson scripted for Ford, the writer certified that the director showed far more respect for his dialogue than had many lesser filmmakers—a compliment to Johnson's writing, but an indication that Ford had nothing against the spoken word, so long as it was honest and well paced.

Ford tended to lose interest in a film once principal photography was completed, allowing the editing department to shape the footage into its final form. That was particularly true at 20th Century-Fox, where Darryl Zanuck kept a watchful eye over postproduction and worked closely with his editors. It is not true, however, that Ford never looked at rushes. He did, but in private or with the cutter and an assistant cutter. "If anyone else walked into the projection room," Robert Parrish maintained, "he would stop the screening and asked the intruder to leave." As a director schooled exclusively in motion pictures, Ford had high regard for the editing process. "If you want to be a director," he told Parrish, "stay in the cutting room. That's the best place to learn."

Ford's health by the mid-1930s was not the best; he often complained of feeling listless, nervous, and tired. He went to see Dr. Harley J. Gunderson, who found him too heavy, with a prominent abdomen and an enlarged liver. Dr. Gunderson's advise was to imbibe "no alcohol, especially beer, which accounts for the enlarged abdomen and liver." Ford lived at a time when drinking was an accepted part of sophisticated social life. He drank to relax, to escape, and to project a facade time tended to erase. Drinking was heavy among his cronies, while drunken pranks leaned toward the outrageous. Although Ford and his circle were dedicated workers, they found routine stifling. His renewal lay in his imagination, and liquor offered a route into fantasy once the pressure of picturemaking was over.

"Poor old Pappy had his alcoholism problem," Ford's friend Charles FitzSimons declared. "Once he got started, he would keep going until he would be a slobbering, helpless drunk. It was tragic. You would look at him and you couldn't believe it was the same man. You'd see the fastidious Ford—despite his eccentric clothing—and then you'd see this slobbering drunk with his head hanging and the drool going down his chin. It was heartbreaking." Unable to share his personal fears and anxieties with anyone who might understand and comfort, Ford became racked with pain, locked in his private cell, suffering loneliness and guilt.

In early 1936 RKO asked the director to make a film version of
Maxwell Anderson's play *Mary of Scotland*, which the studio
intended as one of its most important productions of that year.
The picture would star Katharine Hepburn as Mary Stuart,
with Fredric March as Bothwell, and March's wife, Florence
Eldridge, as Elizabeth Tudor. Hepburn didn't relate to the
character, thought Mary was "a bit of an ass," and felt she was
too modern an actress for the part. The script followed Anderson's play closely and proved too talky for the cinema. Ford
thought the plot was weak and lost interest midway through.
The picture was advertised as "History's greatest love story,"
and posters brandished the caption "Mary . . . born to
rule . . . yet helpless in the arms of love!" But the film proved
dull and failed at the box office.

Hepburn was a stronger actress than movie audiences were
used to at the time, and she maintained that she was "probably
the worst choice in the world for Mary of Scotland." Ford
retorted that she was no worse than he was as the project's
director. The two got along from the start and admired each
other's talent. Hepburn claimed that Ford's major gift as a
director was an ability to make action on the screen look "as if
it had just happened." She recognized that he was fiercely
independent and that it didn't pay to cross him. Yet Hepburn
could be as opinionated as Ford, and they bickered during the
making of the picture. Still, they were attracted to one another.

By the time *Mary of Scotland* was completed, they had fallen
in love, meeting at Hepburn's Laurel Canyon home and stealing away for weekends on the *Araner*. In the spring of 1936 they
spent a month together at Hepburn's home in Connecticut.
Friends had no doubt that Jack loved Hepburn, but knew that
he was equally reluctant to break up his home. Hepburn found
him mysterious, yet understood him and respected his privacy.
She experienced how difficult Jack could be, but attributed
that to his Irish background. "To be truly Irish," she said, "you
have to play a joke on someone and never wait to see what the
outcome is. This used to drive me absolutely insane." She could
never be sure how he was going to react and never fully
understood him. The key, she suspected, lay in his Irish mysti-

cism—the combination of his religious beliefs, his imagination, and his artistic gift. "I'm not sure you even understand yourself entirely," she told him in later years.

Ford found Hepburn mysterious, too. "You're a remarkable woman," he told her. "You're half pagan, half Puritan." They talked about marriage, but decided against it. Divorce posed problems for both of them. "I can only say that I am facing (and have been for a time) the first crisis in my life," Hepburn wrote Ford at the Hollywood Athletic Club in March, 1937. "You have given me strength and understanding, and I count you my dearest friend. . . . I would give a lot to talk to you and know what you think—of me and . . . a lot of things."

"Jack wanted out," his niece Cecil de Prida said. "He admired Hepburn for her talent and her intellectual qualities." Yet whenever they spoke of divorce, Jack would smile and appear uncertain. Finally Hepburn made the decision. "I have come to the conclusion that to do anything (and particularly where human relations are involved) one must say yes or no—but not maybe," she wrote him on April 10, 1937. "Maybe is a feeble way of saying no. . . . Clarity is a necessity as everyone gets so mixed up they don't know what is important to them. I used to be a great exponent of clarity, and I shall try to be again."

Another girlfriend later said, "Jack has bragged to me about all the women that he has had affairs with, but I don't believe him. I think he just talks big. I believe that Jack has been absolutely faithful." Yet Ford loved Hepburn as she did him. "Oh, Sean," she wrote in 1937, "it will be heavenly to see you again if I may, and if I may not, I can drive by Odin Street in an open Ford and think a thousand things. In my mind and heart your place is everlasting."

They settled for a lifelong friendship. "Men and women are so different," Hepburn said, "that they're almost not fit to live in the same house." She recognized that Ford's main interests were masculine, knew that he was of an era when one was expected to be dominantly one sex. She understood that he was happiest with his macho friends, and saw that he had no patience with dependent people. "He really blazed his own trail," she remarked later. "Most people don't. They don't hit their own trail at all, and he hacked his way through life in the most individual way."

Hepburn understood that Ford was sensitive, that he came by peace of mind with difficulty, and that he was probably better off staying with Mary. "Had he been happy, he never would have been the artist that he is today," a friend observed. Yet with Hepburn he was relaxed; she quite possibly was the one woman who could have made him content.

Mary had been fond of Hepburn until she discovered that her husband was in love with the actress; then she thought Hepburn had double crossed her. "Mary threatened to take Barbara, the apple of his eye," Cecil de Prida declared. "He stayed because of the kids, particularly Barb."

Ford's relationship with Hepburn ended any pretense of monogamy. After that Mary gave Jack unspoken permission to go his own way, so long as his affairs didn't become public. "Jack is very religious, he'll never divorce me," she told John Wayne's first wife, Josephine. "He'll never have any grounds to divorce me on. I'm going to be Mrs. John Ford until I die."

Ford was not a womanizer; in reality he felt most comfortable with celibacy. He drew love and support from people he trusted, those he could predict or control. When working and not on the *Araner*, he would stop by the Hollywood Athletic Club for a steam bath and a massage, talking with the crowd that hung out there. Besides his immediate circle, he enjoyed professional friends — Boris Karloff, C. Aubrey Smith, Barry Fitzgerald, and Arthur Shields, among others. With strangers he was insecure, needing unqualified affection to bolster his confidence. He constantly sought to prove himself, yet berated himself when he fell short of the demands he placed on himself. His sensitivity was enormous, his pain excruciating, his walls a defense. He found work a haven, then needed drink to relax.

In the summer of 1936 Ford directed *The Plough and the Stars* for RKO, an attempt to repeat the triumph he and screenwriter Dudley Nichols had enjoyed with *The Informer*. Based on Sean O'Casey's play, *The Plough and the Stars* came nowhere near the earlier success. Ford said the studio ruined the picture by attempting to turn it into a love story. But critics claimed that Ford had misinterpreted O'Casey's work by attempting to glorify the Easter Rebellion of 1916.

Five players from the Abbey Theatre, including Barry Fitzgerald, appeared in the picture, although Barbara Stanwyck and Preston Foster starred. Child actress Bonita Granville was cast as a consumptive girl, and was expected to speak with an Irish brogue. "John Ford's direction was very casual," said Granville, "and he never really tried to form a performance with me. It was the feel, the mood, that he was interested in. He would never tell me anything specifically that I should do. He would let me start out and ramble and feel the part, then he would bring it into shape."

After finishing *The Plough and the Stars*, the director signed another long-term contract with 20th Century-Fox, although by then he knew the limitations of the big studio system and refused to grant Darryl Zanuck exclusive rights to his services. "It's a constant battle to do something fresh," Ford remarked in 1936. "First they want you to repeat your last picture. . . . Then they want you to continue whatever vein you succeeded with in the last picture. You're a comedy director, or a spectacle director, or a melodrama director." Zanuck was prone to duplicate winning formulas, although he permitted Ford as much freedom as any director on the lot.

Ford did not look forward to his next Fox assignment, *Wee Willie Winkie* (1937), a vehicle for the studio's top moneymaker, child star Shirley Temple. Zanuck wanted to disregard the approach taken in earlier Temple pictures and therefore selected Ford to direct her. Based on Rudyard Kipling's poem, with the central character changed from a boy to a girl, *Wee Willie Winkie* was shot mainly around Chatsworth, about forty miles from Los Angeles. Ford anticipated working with a child star with horror and was distant toward Temple at first, considering her a nuisance. He started to soften when the moppet marched around like a soldier, and he mellowed even more when she bolted across a path of stampeding horses and leaped onto some boulders just in the nick of time. "I could see he was smiling," Temple wrote in her autobiography, "finger and thumb circled in the traditional gesture of approval."

The director permitted no profanity on the set during the making of the Shirley Temple picture and seemed easier on his cast and crew than usual. Ford liked the military theme of the film and inserted plenty of action. He drew an outstanding cameraman, Arthur C. Miller, who recreated the feel of the Khyber Pass out of the parched terrain around Chatsworth. "After working with Ford for some time," said Miller, "I realized what an impossible task it was to describe his work, because when John Ford made a picture, he could not be compared even to himself from one day to the next. He was 100 percent unpredictable and had no special method or formula for proceeding."

The director believed that the best moments in movies happened by accident. What seemed a mishap could result in effective realism. Sometimes he made use of a happenstance to add humor. One morning the *Wee Willie Winkie* crew left the studio with the sun shining, but by the time they arrived in Chatsworth, dark clouds had gathered and a strong wind whipped nearby eucalyptus trees. No one expected to work until the weather had cleared. As Ford and Miller stood drinking coffee together, the director asked the cameraman if he didn't think it would be a good time to shoot a burial sequence. Miller couldn't remember any burial in the scrip, but to take advantage of the weather, Ford improvised one for Victor McLaglen's character and blended it into the story. "A casket draped with a British Union Jack, resting on the flat bed of an army vehicle, drawn by four black horses and with an honor guard marching in slow step, and the wind whipping back and forth as though in protest against the menacing black clouds in the sky was one of the most dramatic and effective sequences in the picture," Miller declared. Even McLaglen, playing the corpse, was touched. When the camera stopped rolling, the actor raised up on his elbow, placed a hand on Shirley Temple's, and said, "If I wasn't already dead, I'd be crying too."

It was during the making of *Wee Willie Winkie* that one of the most famous Ford anecdotes took place. An executive from Fox appeared on the set after the company had moved to the backlot. Ford, sitting with the script on his lap, noticed the fellow and beckoned him over. As the executive approached, Ford asked what he had on his mind. The man explained how there had been a production meeting, during which it was pointed out that the director was four days behind schedule on the picture. With no change of expression, Ford looked at him, then casually opened his script, tore out some pages, and handed them over. "Now we're on schedule," he said. "Beat it."

Later in 1937, when Hollywood directors seeking protection from studio interference formed the Screen Directors Guild (renamed the Directors Guild of America), Ford played a conspicuous role in its organization. "We feel that the guild fills a very great need," he wrote. "The producers have associations; every other division of the industry is organized. Why not us?" He became one of the firebrands of the guild, along with Frank Capra, George Stevens, William Wellman, George Marshall, and others who argued that screen directors should have more rights and a greater voice in artistic matters. Since studio executives and producers opposed the notion, as they did the creation of the Screen Actors Guild, Hollywood stood on the verge of labor strife.

Basically apolitical, Ford claimed to be "a rock-ribbed Republican from the state of Maine." The 1930s, however, were a period of political activism; influenced by Dudley Nichols, a liberal Democrat who had reported the Sacco-Vanzetti trial for the *New York World*, Ford's politics swung temporarily to the left. With the outbreak of the Spanish Civil War in 1936, many Hollywood intellectuals supported the Spanish Loyalists. Ford donated an ambulance to aid the liberals' cause. He had a nephew in the Abraham Lincoln Brigade, and he wrote the young man in September 1937 praising him for volunteering to fight against totalitarian forces: "I am glad you got the good part of the O'Feeney blood. Some of it is sure God-damned awful. We are liars, weaklings, and selfish drunkards, but there has always been a stout rebel quality in the family and a peculiar passion for justice. I am glad you inherited the good strain." He went on to say, "Politically, I am a definite socialistic democrat—*always* left. Communism to my mind is not the remedy this sick world is seeking." A decade later his position would swing to the right.

With *The Informer*'s success, Ford had become a power in the motion picture industry, although he was considered eccentric and unreliable in terms of box office. Producer David O. Selznick was eager to borrow his services, either for a film version of Eugene O'Neill's *Anna Christie* or Jack London's *The Sea Wolf*, and willing to pay him five thousand dollars a week. Still, Selznick cautioned his backers: "We must select the story and sell it to John Ford, instead of having Ford select some uncommercial pet of his that we would be making only because of Ford's enthusiasm. . . . I see no justification for making any story just because it is liked by a man who, I am willing to concede, is one of the greatest directors in the world, but whose record commercially is far from good." Ford resented Selznick's attitude and refused to work for him, leaving the producer wounded. "None of us can figure out what is in John Ford's mind," Selznick wrote. "The man is hard to figure out."

Samuel Goldwyn also found Ford baffling, but knew from experience that the director could deliver the quality Goldwyn demanded. When the producer asked Ford to direct his version of Charles Bernard Nordhoff and James N. Hall's novel *Hurricane*, Ford agreed. Part of the lure was that Goldwyn promised Ford he could make the film in the South Seas and wait for an actual hurricane. With Ford's insistence on realism, and his love for the sea, the assignment seemed ideal. Soon after Ford agreed to make the picture, Goldwyn said, "To hell with the South Seas. We'll put a wind machine on the backlot, and we'll shoot it there." So *The Hurricane* was filmed with studio sets and wind machines. Ford lost interest in the assignment and became bitter toward Goldwyn. "He didn't give a damn about the picture," writer Ben Hecht said. "I was working for Goldwyn at the time and looked at the picture, and it wasn't any good." Goldwyn asked Hecht if he could improve it. The writer said that he "wrote nine reels in two days" and handed them to Ford, who "shot them without reading them."

One of the few bright spots during the filming was that Ford used the *Araner* in some scenes shot off Catalina Island. Also, the male lead was played by Jon Hall, the muscular nephew of the book's coauthor. Hall had never acted before, but he possessed a strong voice and a natural ability. He and Ford became friends, although they never worked together again.

Dorothy Lamour, Hall's costar, was lent to Goldwyn by Paramount; *The Hurricane* established her in sarong roles. Lamour remembered that truckloads of gardenias and other Hawaiian flowers were delivered to the set each morning for a luau scene that took days to complete. She also recalled Ford's temper rising to a boil in a discussion with Goldwyn and the producer's walking away, muttering to himself. The storm alone took five weeks to shoot, with airplane propellers hurling sand and water against the actors' faces, and lasted twenty minutes on the screen. Ford ordered a second camera to cover the sequence and told his cinematographer, "If the roof blows off or a sarong blows off or somebody falls down, get it."

On a Ford set workers had to accept his ribbing or leave. The director customarily had a patsy he picked on, sometimes to the point of abuse. Mary Astor was the victim on *The Hurricane*, although she accepted Ford's barbs with good spirits and understood his complex disposition. "I think 'laconic' is a good word for John Ford and for his technique of direction," the actress wrote. "No big deal about communication with John. Terse, pithy, to the point. Very Irish, a dark personality, a sensitivity which he did everything to conceal."

The Hurricane was released on November 9, 1938, and opened to mixed reviews, but the public received it enthusiastically. The *Hollywood Reporter* said the movie approached greatness—a "supreme spectacle" and "the most masterly and moving marriage of music and picture ever achieved." Other critics dismissed it as a potboiler.

Earlier in the year Ford had returned to 20th Century-Fox for two program pictures. The first was *Four Men and a Prayer*

(1938), which he hated. "I just didn't like the story or anything else about it," he declared, "so it was a job of work." Loretta Young starred in the film, an improbable melodrama that Zanuck's story department could never straighten out. Ford enjoyed making the second assignment, *Submarine Patrol* (also 1938). "Of course, all the comedy in it wasn't in the script," he said. "We put it in as we went along." Zanuck cautioned that there should not be too much warfare in the picture, arguing that it wouldn't appeal to women unless gunfire were kept to a minimum. "We must be as clever as we can in keeping the war out of the picture," the Fox production head insisted.

When *Submarine Patrol* opened to good notices, Zanuck and his wife Virginia gave a party for Ford at their home in Santa Monica, but the guest of honor failed to appear. He told the studio head later that he had been on the *Araner* and couldn't get ashore because of engine trouble. Actually Ford was furious with Zanuck over a statement the Fox publicity department had issued requesting that reviewers not judge newcomer Nancy Kelly by her performance in *Submarine Patrol*, but wait until the studio's upcoming *Jesse James*. "Naturally this coming out in print is an adverse criticism from my own studio of my direction," Ford wrote a Fox executive. "I presume I am no longer wanted at 20th Century-Fox to direct pictures, especially pictures with women. I am terribly sorry that the studio should have to take this means of protecting their stars, but perhaps they know best. Naturally this affair . . . has caused me much humiliation."

Ford hated studio politics and anything that interfered with his artistic freedom. This would not be the last time he and Zanuck quarreled, although they did some of their best work together. "I argued and fought, and that was how I got the reputation of being a tough guy—which I'm not," Ford said. "I can be tough with an executive producer . . . but never with my people." His people were the stock company of actors and crew he used time and again. Ford could be vindictive and possessed a long memory for slights or insults, yet he remained loyal to those he liked and respected.

The motion picture business required compromise, although Ford made as little as possible. His position with Zanuck was that he would direct a picture the studio wanted made in exchange for one he considered a personal statement. On those of his own choosing, he worked closely with the writer and involved himself with every detail. On the others he let Zanuck have a major input.

Thoughout the 1930s Ford worked on a variety of projects, but he established a consistent, recognizable style. He maintained that he could become involved in "any good story with a colorful locale that's about human beings, anything with interesting characters—and some humor." His films most often dealt with common people struggling to survive in a harsh world. Ford had the capacity to create a grand vista without losing the simplicity of his characters. After a decade of working with sound, he had made the necessary adjustments and was ready to take his place as a master craftsman, an Irish-American original working in a commercial art form.

CHAPTER 5

Americana

THE film that Ford wanted to make for David Selznick, the one Selznick dismissed as an "uncommercial pet," was *Stagecoach*. During the summer of 1937 the director had bought the screen rights to a short story that had appeared a few months before in *Collier's* magazine, written by Ernest Haycox, entitled "Stage to Lordsburg." The story was filled with Bret Harte-like characters who journey across Arizona by stagecoach toward New Mexico amid an Apache uprising. Westerns during the late 1930s were still out of favor with the Hollywood studios, except for inexpensive oaters churned out by Republic, Columbia, and Monogram for double bills. Ford had not made a Western since *Three Bad Men* in 1926, but he liked the characters in "Stage to Lordsburg" and continued to view the Western genre, with its emphasis on action, as ideal for motion pictures. When sound came in, producers insisted that rugged outdoor pictures were finished, since recording techniques required enclosed sets for proper pickup.

Ford approached studio after studio with the notion of filming Haycox's story, only to be told that big Westerns were dead. Selznick International, Columbia, and RKO all turned the project down. Finally the director went to Walter Wanger, an independent producer with a commitment to make a picture for United Artists, who was searching for a property to film inexpensively. Wanger read "Stage to Lordsburg" and agreed to let Ford photograph the Western on condition that he stay within a limited budget.

Dudley Nichols wrote the script in close consultation with Ford. The writer agreed that a Western script should be intelligent, entertaining, and contain a basic moral quality. "The people who coined that awful term 'horse opera' are

snobs," Ford said. He urged Nichols to write the way people
speak and to keep dialogue to a minimum. It was the characters
in "Stage to Lordsburg" that fascinated the filmmakers
most—a drunken doctor, a pregnant southern aristocrat, a
chivalrous gambler, a timid whiskey drummer, an embezzling
banker, a prostitute, and a young gunslinger called the Ringo
Kid in the film.

Wanger had wanted to cast Gary Cooper in the role of the
Ringo Kid, but Cooper's fee proved too high for the producer's
budget. Bruce Cabot, who had just starred in *King Kong*, was
tested for the part, but Ford had someone else in mind. On
board the *Araner* he asked his buddy and surrogate son, John
Wayne, to read the script. When Wayne finished it, Ford asked
him, "Who can I get to play the Ringo Kid?" Wayne had
recently seen Lloyd Nolan in *The Texas Rangers* and suggested
him. Ford shook his head. "You idiot," he snorted, "couldn't
you play it?"

Stagecoach, as Ford's film was called, not only prompted a
resurgence of the big Western, but catapulted John Wayne into
major stardom. Since leaving college he had worked at Fox,
shuffled from studio to studio, and finally ended up under
contract to Republic Pictures, where he starred in cheap Westerns turned out in eight days. Wayne's success in *Stagecoach*
lifted him into another stratum, and he soon became the
quintessential Western hero. "The cowboy is the hero of American folklore," Michael Wayne, his son, declared, "as knight-
hood and chivalry are in England. My father became the
symbol of that cowboy." Wayne was aware of the space he
occupied, yet never forgot that he owed his celebrity to John
Ford.

"I don't like to do books or plays," Ford said. "I prefer to
take a short story and expand it, rather than take a novel and try
to condense." With "Stage to Lordsburg" he had an ideal
property, not only for an excellent script, but for elevating the
Western landscape into a panorama of beauty and symbolic
importance. During the 1930s most movies were shot in the
studios rather than on location. Crews making Westerns might
travel a few miles outside Los Angeles, but nearby Vasquez

Rocks was about as far as companies went on budget oaters. *Stagecoach* was the first sound film to use as its principal location Monument Valley, on the Arizona-Utah border, a wonderland of cathedrallike buttes and mesas in a remote section of the Navajo Reservation, a site Ford returned to six more times.

How Ford first discovered Monument Valley is uncertain. Harry and Olive Carey had traveled through the area and probably told him about it. George O'Brien had made a Western for Fox in nearby Kayenta, Arizona, where he heard about the valley, drove through it, and returned to Hollywood raving about the beauty he'd seen. Ford later claimed he had traveled through Monument Valley himself on his way to Santa Fe and had been impressed with its rugged terrain. But in all likelihood *Stagecoach* was filmed there because Harry Goulding and his wife, Leone (whom he called Mike), who ran a trading post midway between Kayenta and Mexican Hat, Utah, made a trip to Los Angeles with photographs of Monument Valley's formations, having heard that an important Western was in the planning stage.

When the Great Depression hit, the Navajo suffered impoverishment. Monument Valley had experienced a series of harsh winters, and the Indians stood on the verge of starvation. The Gouldings' own business had fallen to nothing. When Harry heard on the radio that John Ford was planning to make a Western movie, he decided the time had come for action. Harry and Mike took the only sixty dollars they had, piled into their car, and headed for Hollywood. Mike had a brother living in Burbank who knew his way around the studios. The brother directed Harry to United Artists, where Ford was preparing *Stagecoach*. Harry went armed with a stack of photographs showing the monoliths of Monument Valley, taken by Joe Muench and others who had visited them through the years.

Goulding arrived at the studio wearing faded Levis, a weatherbeaten Stetson, and scuffed boots. He was greeted by a blond receptionist seated behind a glass partition. Goulding explained that he wanted to see whoever was in charge of selecting locations for movies. The receptionist insisted that he had to have an appointment. Goulding heaved a sigh. "I can wait," he said. "I've lived among the Navajo so long that I don't get so busy that I can't wait. I've got a bedroll. I've got plenty of time, so I'll just stay right here."

Realizing he was serious, the receptionist dialed Danny Keith, the location director on Ford's picture. Goulding showed him the photographs of Monument Valley, and Keith looked impressed. "I've got a friend upstairs," the location director said. "Would you mind if I brought him down to take a look at these?" Harry shook his head and prepared for another wait. "Down he came," Goulding remembered, "and that was John Ford."

They spent hours examining the photographs, spreading them out over the room for a better look. Ford grew excited and asked endless questions. Eventually Walter Wanger was called in. Three more hours went by, as the discussion continued. Logistics would pose problems in Monument Valley, and the weather could be an obstacle. Then came the big question: Could Goulding prepare in three days for the arrival of the one hundred people needed to film the movie?

A check was made out and handed to Harry. He returned to Mike and said, "Let's go home quick." They stopped in Flagstaff to order supplies at a general store; United Artists had wired money ahead to pay for the goods. Then the Gouldings drove back to their trading post to await the invasion.

For a motion picture company to travel that distance in 1938 was unusual, the mark of an important film. George B. Seitz's epic *The Vanishing American* had been shot in part around Monument Valley in 1925, but the remote area was still unknown to the outside world. A photographer or a band of vacationers had occasionally come through, hiring Harry Goulding to escort them on a tour. Zane Grey had visited the valley by 1913, and Norman Nevills in nearby Mexican Hat had made a successful business of river trips. But the valley's dramatic monuments—the Mittens, the Big Hogan, the Three Sisters—had not been fully exploited until John Ford shot portions of *Stagecoach* there, turning Monument Valley into a symbol of the American West.

Since the Gouldings had only a few guest cabins at that time, they could house no more than twenty-six people at their trading post, although meals for most of the company would be served there. Wanger Productions paid seventy-five cents for each breakfast and a dollar for every dinner. Rooms at the Gouldings' were three dollars a day. Forty-five members of the company were lodged in a hotel in Tuba City, while fifteen more, including Ford, stayed at Weatherill's Hotel in Kayenta. The rest were assigned bunks in a nearby camp built for the Civilian Conservation Corps, in exchange for the installation of electric lights and a shower. Since the barracks had been abandoned by the CCC, Navajo had been living there, and a representative of Wanger Productions hired two Indian youths to scrub the floors and clean up. "I certainly don't want our boys to be full of lice," he wrote. Weatherill permitted the crew staying at the CCC camp to use the lobby of his hotel for evening recreation so those who wanted to retire early in the barracks weren't disturbed.

Roads were still dirt, but the western-style meals of steak and barbequed ribs were worth the commute. Film talk was banned after work, but games—particularly pitch, dominoes, and poker—were encouraged. From the outset the director was awed by the remoteness and grandeur of the valley and loved the freedom he experienced there—no studio executives interfering, no telephones, and few family pressures to contend with. On location Ford became a patriarchal figure, sur-rounded by people he trusted. In a world apart, they formed a family unit, sharing the creative experience amid matchless beauty. "Monument Valley in 1938 was heaven," John Wayne later declared.

Navajo from the reservation were employed to play maraud-ing Apache in the film. Lee Bradley served as the contact man with the Indians and worked as interpreter once the produc-tion commenced, since 90 percent of the Navajo did not speak English. Native Americans working on the film lived in their own camp; Bradley bought supplies for them at the Gouldings' trading post under the supervision of a Wanger representative. The movie company supplied hay for the Indians' horses, and

Navajo laborers received three dollars per day, paid each evening.

Shooting on *Stagecoach* began in Monument Valley in October 1938. Among Ford's major concerns had been the weather, since climatic conditions could be disastrous for outdoor schedules. Soon after Ford arrived in the valley, he met Hosteen Tso, a Navajo shaman of local renown. Harry Goulding assured the director that the Indian, whose name translates into English as Old Fat or Fatso, could produce whatever weather was needed for the day's shooting. Ford laughed, not taking Hosteen Tso seriously until the Navajo on repeated occasions reportedly delivered the exact cloud formations the filmmaker requested. Old Fat came to hold an honored place among Ford's location personnel.

There were surprises, however. One morning the director was awakened by Wingate Smith, his brother-in-law and assistant director, who rushed into his room and announced, "Jack, it snowed last night! What are we going to do?" Ford remained calm and said, "Don't worry about it. I'll think of something." The company went to work that morning as usual, and Ford instructed Andy Devine (playing the stagecoach driver) to remark once the camera started rolling that he'd taken a mountain road rather than the usual route. "I'm using my head," Devine's character said. "Those breach-clothed Apaches don't like snow." With that Ford explained the abrupt change in weather.

Although the director planned his days carefully, he improvised constantly, taking advantage of the landscape and incidents he happened to notice among his players. "He was the only one who knew from day to day what we were going to do," Andy Devine declared. "He'd reach in and pull out these sheets and hand them to us, maybe in the morning. But we never got a script to see whether we liked it or not." Cast members sometimes grew so frustrated with Ford that they refused to speak to him off the set. "But everybody that ever worked for him really loved him," Devine assured. "We all understood him."

Veterans in the Ford stock company knew better than to

make suggestions to the director. If they did, Ford would bark, "Have you got a director's card? Do you belong to the Directors Guild?" Andy Devine made the mistake of offering an opinion one day during the shooting of *Stagecoach*. Ford shouted out so everyone could hear, "Mr. Devine's going to direct this scene now." Actors learned quickly that Ford demanded total control.

Like any artist, Ford had a vision of what he was attempting to create and resented compromises. In working with actors he was forced to deal with limitations and interpretations that conflicted with his own. Yet he had various ways of keeping actors compliant—sometimes through fear, sometimes out of loyalty, sometimes from embarrassment. During the making of *Stagecoach* Thomas Mitchell, who played the drunken doctor, was the object of Ford's needling. Practically everybody who worked for the director, including his closest friends, spent time "in the barrel." "We'd all get our turn," Andy Devine said.

Actors tolerated Ford's abuse because they loved him, understood him, or knew he could draw a better performance from them than could any other director in Hollywood. Thomas Mitchell, for example, won an Academy Award for best supporting actor in *Stagecoach*. Some argued that Ford treated actors badly because he was a sadistic son of a bitch; others claimed he was a supreme psychologist, pulling what he needed from performers by whatever means were necessary to achieve the results he knew they were capable of delivering. There is truth in both viewpoints. Ford was an artist determined to mold his components into the design he had fixed in his imagination.

"He never let the picture out of his mind for one minute," Lefty Hough remarked. Most performers agreed that Ford showed more skill manipulating actors than did any director they'd experienced, although with actresses he seemed to want to get the job done as quickly as possible. He worked with everyone differently, but wanted his entire cast on the set at all times. "If he'd get a feeling for a particular scene, and he felt people were in the mood, he'd grab that rather than do what he had set up," John Wayne said. He worked by instinct and saw everything through the eye of the camera. "John Ford has gone back damn near to the [D.W.] Griffith days," director George Seaton observed, "because he finds the perfect place to put his camera and works the people toward it. You get the feeling of motion, but you're continually wondering who the hell is moving and why it's moving. I believe, and I think most directors believe, that you have to have a reason to move your camera. You have to move with the character, because just an arbitrary movement of the camera is often disturbing." Director Billy Wilder commented on Ford's lack of complicated camera angles in *Stagecoach*; there was only one panning shot, said Wilder, "when he took the camera around about fifteen degrees."

John Wayne realized during the shooting of the film that Ford was "probably the finest artist I'd ever known." Although Wayne had a decade of movie experience by the time he starred in *Stagecoach*, the director treated him as a novice. Ford often took hold of his chin, shook his face, and shouted, "In pictures you don't act with your mouth, you act with your eyes. The camera sees your whole soul through the eyes!" More screen personality than actor, Wayne demonstrated a naturalness that would make him a star, and Ford had great faith in him. Wayne took Harry Carey as his role model, imitating Carey's stance and locked arms. "Harry Carey possessed a quality that we like to think of in men of the West," Wayne said. Ford even dressed Wayne the way Carey had dressed in silent Westerns, having him wear suspenders rather than a belt.

Carey's son claimed that Ford created in Wayne's screen persona what Ford would have liked to have been himself. "Ford was a tender, loving man," Harry "Dobe" Carey, Jr., said, "and he was a delicate, artistic man. You could see that his hands and eyes were so gentle. Yet he was intrigued with machoism. He wanted to be a two-fisted, brawling, heavy-drinking Irishman. He wanted to do what John Wayne did on the screen and clean up a barroom all by himself, which Ford couldn't do. There was a part of him that Wayne exemplified physically, something he always wanted to be. So he created that on the screen. No one had a presence on the screen like

John Wayne did. Physically he was overpowering." Ford once commented, "I myself am a pretty ugly fellow. The public wouldn't pay to see me on film." But John Wayne, as had George O'Brien earlier, became an alter ego.

Shooting on *Stagecoach* had no sooner started than Ford began ridiculing Wayne in front of the company. He'd call him a big oaf, a dumb bastard, and make remarks such as, "Can't you walk normal instead of skipping around like a goddamned fairy?" Although Wayne knew that Ford had deep affection for him, the actor seemed to be scared to death of him on the set. Wayne remembered his first days in Monument Valley as the toughest of his career. For years Ford had complimented Wayne on his athleticism; suddenly everything he did seemed wrong. "If I didn't do anything else, I moved well," the actor said later. Yet Ford kept shouting at him, "Can't you even walk? Put your feet down like you're a man!" Wayne took the abuse, although Ford pushed him to the limit. "I don't think anybody who observes acting as such would say that John Wayne is an actor," screen star Dana Andrews remarked. "He's John Wayne, a big hulk of a man who has learned how to walk in a very masculine way with high boots." Under Ford's direction, the Ringo Kid became a believable, multidimensional character — manly and tough, yet vulnerable and innocent.

Wayne was only paid $3,700 for *Stagecoach*, whereas Claire Trevor, his leading lady, received $15,000, still not a huge amount. (John Ford's fee was $50,000.) Film editor Robert Parrish, a close friend, once asked Ford how he managed to pull better performances from Wayne than did other directors. "Count the times Wayne talks," Ford replied. "That's the answer. Don't let him talk unless you have something that needs to be said."

During his first visit to Monument Valley, the director developed a deep respect for the Navajo. The Indians not only were grateful for the jobs he gave them, but returned his affection. Ford employed some of them, such as Son of Many Mules and the Stanley brothers, time and again in his pictures. He came to understand that the Navajo did not consider themselves part of a larger Indian community, but viewed

themselves as "the people." For only one scene in *Stagecoach*
did the director use a non-Navajo in a Native American role;
that was the shot in which he panned up from the valley to the
face of Geronimo. There Ford used an Apache, whom the
director claimed was a descendent of the famous chief.

Ford's company left Monument Valley having paid the Navajo $48,000 in wages. The director had hired hundreds of
Indians as extras, bit players, and laborers, insisting that they
be paid on the Hollywood scale. That employment saved a
number of them from starvation and served as a tremendous
boost to business at the Gouldings' trading post. Ford and the
Gouldings became lifelong friends, for he returned time and
again to scout locations and film Westerns.

Not only did *Stagecoach* offer memorable characters, but it
contained stunning movement, paced superbly. The climactic
chase, where the coach is pursued by Apache, was shot on a dry
lake bed outside Victorville, California. The company arrived
there near Christmas, and the weather was freezing. "I've never
been as cold in my life," Andy Devine said. "It was so cold
sitting on top of the stagecoach that I couldn't move my hands;
the lines actually locked on them. I don't know how those poor
guys in breech clouts stood it." John Wayne's memories were
equally vivid: "In my life I've never been any colder than I was
up there that two or three days working on that dry lake. The
wind was blowing, and there was a fine silt dust. My lungs
became raw, and my vocal pipes were shot."

The famous stunt during which an Indian jumps from his
pony onto a horse pulling the stagecoach and attempts to seize
the reins was performed by veteran stuntman Yakima Canutt, a
former rodeo performer. The Ringo Kid shoots the Indian,
who drops to the tongue of the stagecoach, drags a while, then
lets go, as the horses and coach pound over him. Canutt had
first done the trick for a serial at Republic and had repeated it
two or three times in budget Westerns, but *Stagecoach* introduced it to a broader audience. The stunt was great showman-
ship and has been imitated many times, including in the
remake of *Stagecoach* (1966) and *Raiders of the Lost Ark* (1981).
"The hardest thing I had to learn in the picture business,"

Canutt declared, "was to forget reality sometimes and figure that you're making entertainment." Ford adopted the same principle.

After Christmas the company moved to the Kern River to film the scenes in which the stagecoach is ferried across a stream. After returning to Hollywood, Ford used the Western town at Republic and shot interiors at the Samuel Goldwyn studio. The cost of the picture totaled $531,374.

Walter Wanger previewed *Stagecoach* at the Village Theater in Westwood, where an audience of mainly college students loved it. When Claire Trevor saw the movie for the first time she became so caught up in the characters and action, she forgot she was in it. "I was just stunned," she said. When the film opened at Radio City Music Hall in March 1939 it did fantastic business and received rave notices. "In one superbly expansive gesture," Frank Nugent wrote in the *New York Times*, "John Ford has swept aside ten years of artifice and talkie compromise and has made a motion picture that sings a song of camera. It moves, and how beautifully it moves." Ford won the New York Film Critics Award for best director of 1939, and reviewers from coast to coast hailed the movie as a director's achievement par excellence. Overnight the sophisticated Western was back in vogue, lifted to a level of respect.

What made the film work was the interaction of its striking characters, played against Ford's visual panorama. The story was constructed so that it moves with increasing tension toward the thrilling chase. In the beginning the stagecoach leisurely winds its way across Monument Valley, giving the sense of having entered an eternal wilderness, grand yet savage. Ford used the landscape as a dramatic device for thrusting his Western into the realm of legend. "I think you can say that the real star of my Westerns has always been the land," he said. The Native American is portrayed as the untamed child of Ford's mythic wilderness, not so much bad as angry at invaders. The Indians who terrorize the band journeying to Lordsburg are seldom individualized; they remain part of the land. Only Geronimo emerges briefly from the background, and while he is seen as a menace, he is also a leader with dignity.

Ford's focus is a theme he would return to time and again — society's outcasts in time of danger mustering the strength to slay the monster that threatens the community that rejects them. While *Stagecoach* is populated with misfits, its central characters are the Ringo Kid (a good bad-guy of classic proportions) and Dallas (a prostitute cast out of Tonto by the town's law-and-order league). Ringo has broken out of jail to avenge his father and brother's murder by the Plummer Gang. Hero and heroine are strong, young, eager for a fresh start. Ringo is a primitive individualist, a loner from necessity, who demonstrates courage and nobility in the face of crisis, rescuing a vicious society and restoring it to order. Dallas realizes that the bigoted society that banished her could be "worse than Apaches." Yet when Lucy Mallory gives birth to her baby, Dallas proves to be a pillar of strength and wins the aristocratic lady's respect. In the end Dallas and Ringo turn to one another for love and a sense of belonging. They ride off to the Kid's ranch south of the border to start a new life, while the imbibing doctor expresses relief that they have been "saved from the blessings of civilization."

Ford's ambivalence toward society was close to the surface in *Stagecoach*. As did historian Frederick Jackson Turner, the director imbued the wilderness with regenerative powers. If the West in its natural state was spiritual and pure, urbanity brought corruption; cleansing came through the healing effects of nature. And like Ralph Waldo Emerson, Ford worried that the human race might die from too much civilization. Yet he continued to idealize the family and community values, depicting them with affecting sentiment. The tension between these two viewpoints permeates his work, constituting a central issue that he never resolved. Time and again Ford's camera peers through doors, windows, gates, porches, and canopies, contrasting indoors and outdoors, refuge and danger, civilization and wilderness, but the opposites are never reconciled. Despite his love for the natural, Ford's Irish upbringing remained too strong for him to dismiss human society. At the same time his identification with the outsider as a creative force made him antagonistic toward a collective order.

"We all have an escape complex," Ford said. "We all want to leave the troubles of our civilized world behind us. We envy those who can live the most natural way of life, with nature, bravely and simply. . . . We all picture ourselves doing heroic things." Ford would agree with historians who look upon the conquest of the frontier as America's creation myth. He felt that Western movies, like earlier myth, probed fundamental moral issues. Film director Fritz Lang once stated that the Western was to the United States what the Niebelungen saga was to Germany, and Ford would doubtless have concurred, at least in instances where the Western explored the question of social harmony. Ford lamented the passing of the Old West, which for him had finalized around 1940 with the death of Tom Mix. He regretted the loss of the traditional American hero and welcomed as his second assignment from Darryl Zanuck *Young Mr. Lincoln*, a film version of the early life of Abraham Lincoln, Ford's political idol.

Artists during the Great Depression rediscovered the American heartland, and regionalism returned to vogue in literature and drama. Painters emphasized simplicity, the forgotten segments of society, and old-fashioned virtues, while composers wrote accessible music on basic American themes. While the nation's heroes had been debunked during the more sophisticated 1920s, they were restored during the desperate 1930s. Ford tended to agree with Hegel, who argued that the purpose of a hero is "to bring a new world into existence." The filmmaker felt that Abraham Lincoln had done that; he had abandoned his law practice to alter the course of American history. Lincoln emerged the great democrat, responsible for the modern American state.

Paralleling his reservations about the established order was Ford's nostalgia about simpler times and a moral fiber he felt past generations had demonstrated. His reading of history mingled truth with dreams. He invented an American past that restored faith and taught lessons, and he laced history with poetry and myth to glorify the American character and illustrate a superior existence. He viewed ritual and formalized behavior as anchors that stabilized society in the face of sweeping change. Without intellectualizing his work, Ford created images on multiple levels, many of which supported the ideals he believed were being lost.

He read a great many biographies over the years and was a lifelong student of the Civil War. "I like to study people," said Ford, "not just famous people, but the rank and file. The most interesting people are the down-to-earth people." His heroes were mainly commoners. He recognized that Lamar Trotti's script for *Young Mr. Lincoln* was largely imaginative; Trotti presented Lincoln as a populist hero from the outset, a view that coincided with Ford's own concept. Besides being the Great Emancipator and the Savior of the Union, Lincoln to Ford was the idealized American—quiet, self-reliant, resourceful, pragmatic, honorable.

Henry Fonda, soon to be under contract to 20th Century-Fox, read Trotti's script, and while the actor found it a beautiful story, he could not imagine himself playing Lincoln. "It would be like playing God," he said. Zanuck sent Fonda to see Ford. The director was sitting behind a desk when the actor walked in; he had a slouch hat on and clothes that looked like they came from the Salvation Army. He had a pipe in his hand, which he kept filling. "What's all this shit about your not wanting to play in this picture?" the director growled. Fonda attempted to explain. "This isn't the President of the United States," Ford barked, "this is a jackleg lawyer in Springfield."

The actor gave in and spent three hours in the makeup room, where his nose and hair were made to look like those of young Lincoln. For the test he wore shoe lifts. The next day he viewed the rushes with Trotti and producer Kenneth Macgowan. "When I first saw this man on the screen," Fonda remembered, "I thought Jesus Chirst, this big tall son of a bitch is Lincoln! Then he started to talk and my voice came out."

Together Fonda and Ford recreated Lincoln as a living, breathing human being—clean-cut, full of folksy tales, but the incarnation of American justice. Rather than a remote figure in history, their Lincoln was real, torn by indecision, devastated by the death of Ann Rutledge, his first love. Ford took liberties with his narrative, convinced that drama need not reproduce the past exactly. "There have to be some compromises with historical fact and accuracy in all movies," he said. "The public will simply not accept certain things which seem strange to them, true as they may be." *Young Mr. Lincoln* focused on heroic ideals rather than on Lincoln's politics and compromises.

Shooting on the film began in February 1939. From the beginning the project was special to Ford and resulted in one of his favorite pictures. He and Fonda developed a rapport that grew over successive pictures. The actor respected the director's instincts, his ability to delineate character without expansive dialogue, his pacing and atmosphere, and his avoidance of cinematic tricks. "Ford was old-fashioned," said Fonda, "so he hated dolly shots. He'd do them, reluctantly, but he loved it if the camera was on a tripod."

Like most performers, Fonda was in awe of Ford's ability to pull more from his performers than they thought possible. "Ford was so inventive and imaginative with things that were not in the script," the actor said. The director rarely analyzed characters with actors ahead of time, nor did he delve into the emotions of a scene. He'd simply indicate movements, keeping rehearsals to a minimum. "Ford can't talk without using the worst profanity that exists," Fonda declared, "and you get the impression he doesn't like actors. He treats them badly. He has a perverse sense of humor—sadistic as can be—even with the people he likes."

Actress Dorris Bowdon, who made three pictures with Ford before marrying screenwriter Nunnally Johnson, played Hannah Clay in *Young Mr. Lincoln* and found the experience delightful. "I was John's pet on the Lincoln picture," the actress said. "He was darling to me." Bowdon was fresh from drama school and recognized that she had been thrust into the major league working on a Ford film. "John resented the fact that I had been in a drama school," she said. "He wanted to feel that he had raw material that he could totally mold to his liking. Ford hadn't had much schooling, and he feared the patina of education. He didn't want to see any evidence of poise or correct speech, the things I considered most attractive in people. But I thought he was the best director with actors that I had worked with."

Bowdon's part was small, but she reported to the set more days than necessary to watch Ford work. "Every once in a while," she recalled, "he'd take my chin and move my face and say, 'You look like my daughter, Barbara.' I guess maybe he was making something up to Barbara. He probably felt he had failed as a father." But Bowdon also observed Ford's cruel side. "John had a way of choosing some individual in every picture that he needled endlessly," she said. "It was an unfortunate characteristic, and I even think he suffered from it. Whenever people start telling stories about John Ford, they always get around to saying that he was a Jekyll-Hyde character in his behavior with people."

Milburn Stone, who played Stephen A. Douglas in the picture, remembered Ford as a great director, but fearsome and hateful. "He was a very selfish guy, and he could be a tyrant," said Stone, "yet he got tremendous performances out of people. On *Young Mr. Lincoln* I saw him break an old actor's heart, someone who had been a friend. Ford jumped on him all of a sudden and just destroyed the guy."

The director prided himself on his knowledge of the Civil War. One day Stone and Fonda were talking on the set when Ford suddenly appeared and asked, "Who held Lincoln's hat when he was inaugurated?" Stone replied, "Stephen A. Douglas." Ford nodded and walked away. Soon he was back: "Who was the first man President Lincoln sent for when Fort Sumter was fired on?" the director asked. "Stephen A. Douglas," said Stone. Again Ford nodded, satisfied that the actor had done his homework, but peeved that he hadn't been able to best him.

Ford called a break each afternoon around four o'clock for tea to be served on the set. That's when his sense of humor was likely to show. During work his mind spun like a whirlpool, turning up fresh ideas. "On the set you forget everything else," he said. "As a director I must help actors as much as I can. I think a director can help an actor or an actress, and he can also help the cameraman, the electricians, and everybody else." No one on a John Ford set ever forgot who was in charge, for Ford never faltered in making decisions. If a performer offered a contrary opinion, the director likely threw the script to the floor and shouted, "Some goddamned actor has been reading the script!" That was enough to silence opposition. Yet he established a reputation for staying within budgets and finishing pictures on schedule. "I found out the first take had more sparkle to it," the director insisted. "The longer you did it, the deader it became."

Ford's scenes are so rich in humanity that they burn themselves into the memory of audiences. In *Young Mr. Lincoln* he has a white-haired old man, a boy beating a drum, and a youth playing a fife march down a street in a Fourth of July parade, a recreation of the familiar print "The Spirit of '76." The director loved graveyard scenes and has Lincoln come to the grave of Ann Rutledge alone and talk of his hopes and dreams. Near the end of the picture, after Lincoln has saved the lives of two young clients, he leaves the courtroom and stands mute before a throng of cheering admirers. Then, looking tall and thin in his stovepipe hat and black suit, he walks up a hill, against black clouds and a menacing sky, to face his destiny. "Everybody knows Lincoln was a great man," the director said, "but the idea of the picture was to give the feeling that even as a young man you could sense there was going to be something great about this man."

Although *Young Mr. Lincoln* was a product of the 20th Century-Fox assembly line, Ford was able to shape it into a personal statement. Once a script was approved, Zanuck granted the director enough freedom to shoot it the way he saw fit, without major changes in dialogue. To some degree Ford cut his pictures with the camera, shooting only the footage he wanted editors to use, sometimes putting his hand over the lens to eliminate what he didn't want on the screen.

Although Ford knew the necessity of a solid script, he came as close to being an *auteur* director as did any the old studio system produced. He knew he was creative, yet never liked to talk about himself in artistic terms, preferring to appear workaday. "I take a script and I just do it," he told critic Lindsay

Anderson. There was no ostentation about Ford's work, and he made filmmaking look deceptively simple. Yet nothing in a Ford picture was arbitrary; everything contributed to the whole. His pose as a practical moviemaker was part of the disguise to hide a sensitive personality. Ford's blustery exterior was largely a ruse, his aggressiveness a shield, to protect his delicate nature. He described himself as an entertainer who tried to please mass audiences and make money, but that was a superficial response to students who analyzed his composition and noted the beauty with which he framed his pictures. Despite all protests to the contrary, by the time *Young Mr. Lincoln* was made, John Ford had developed into a mature artist.

The director's admiration for Darryl Zanuck grew with the passage of time. Ford respected Zanuck's story sense, his administrative flair, and his eye for film construction. "Darryl knew the business," Ford said. "When I'd finish a picture, I could go off to Catalina on my boat and fish. I didn't have to hang around. I could leave the editing to him. He never hurt a picture; he always helped it." Yet Ford kept his relationship with the Fox production chief on a professional level, never becoming part of Zanuck's inner circle. The director's contract with the studio was nonexclusive, earning him $75,000 a picture. In theory he had no choice over the material assigned him; it was up to Zanuck to choose. In reality Ford held veto power, for the studio head was wise enough not to force him to take projects that didn't suit him. Their quarrels came mainly over pacing. Ford liked his films to meander, stopping occasionally to focus on something inconsequential; Zanuck wanted pictures to move. But if Ford slowed Zanuck down, Zanuck speeded Ford up.

Young Mr. Lincoln was completed on April 15, 1939. As usual, Ford sailed off on the *Araner*, leaving Zanuck to oversee postproduction. The director did not like too much music in his pictures and showed a fondness for folk tunes, played unobtrusively. He also liked silent passages, which he used effectively to reenforce the simplicity of his story.

Most critics considered *Young Mr. Lincoln* to be among the

most human of the Lincoln portraits, and the consensus was
that Henry Fonda had not only delivered a believable characterization, but had never before been so well cast. What
impressed columnist Louella Parsons was the "simple dignity"
of the picture, whereas Peter Bogdanavich later wrote that it
was more like Ford was telling a story about an old friend than
an exhalted public figure.

Within weeks after finishing *Young Mr. Lincoln*, Ford began
shooting *Drums Along the Mohawk* (1939), again for Zanuck and
with Henry Fonda as his star. Based on Walter Edmonds's
novel, *Drums Along the Mohawk*, Ford's first picture in Technicolor, was filmed partly in the Wasatch Mountains of Utah.
The director said he found working in color easier, but that he
preferred black and white, where cinematographers had to
take greater precautions to create shadows and achieve the
proper perspective. "It's all a matter of taste," Ford said. "But
anybody can shoot color; you can get a guy out of the street
and he can shoot a picture in color. But it takes a real artist to do
a black-and-white picture."

Ford and Zanuck had disagreed during story conferences,
with Zanuck insisting that *Drums Along the Mohawk* not become strictly an epic. "The only epics that are successful today
are the simple, human epics where the personal story is so vital
and emotional that the picture becomes great because the
characters are great," the production head argued. "I feel we
must discard completely all of the episodes dealing with war
campaigns, revolutionary politics, and everything that does
not directly include and have intimate bearing on our two
leading characters." Ford wanted to humanize the story
through humor, often broad humor that Zanuck found objectionable. Both envisioned an entertaining picture, not a depressing story of massacres and defeat. "[W]e should see the
personal struggle of two people to conquer the land and make a
home for themselves," Zanuck declared, "and we should see
what they have to go through to accomplish this."

Lamar Trotti again wrote the script, and Claudette Colbert
starred opposite Fonda, playing a well-born wife married to a

pioneer farmer at the time of the American Revolution. Ford
devised rituals that fit the period yet bore his signature—
dances, family meals, military drills, a wedding, a birth, a
death, moments of communal suffering and joy. Throughout,
home and wilderness were depicted in images that were pure
Ford. The farmers of the Mohawk Valley became representa-
tives of the agrarian myth, examples of what frontier scholar
Henry Nash Smith called "the yeoman ideal."

The Indians in the picture are seen as devilish marauders, a
threat to white settlers, yet they rarely come into the foreground enough to become believable characters. When one
does step forward, he is usually played for laughs. Blue Back, a
Christian Indian, acted by Chief Big Tree, remains loyal to the
film's hero, but the Iroquois are depicted as bloodthirsty
enemies who burn homes and fields and attack forts.

The picture focuses on the determination of preindustrial
farmers to hold the Mohawk Valley. Gil and Lana Martin
(Fonda and Colbert) see their wheat and cabin destroyed, but
they survive their loss and keep on pioneering. The tribulations
of the Mohawk settlers become tests for American democracy,
but an agrarian utopia triumphs in the end. *Drums Along the
Mohawk* leaves no doubt that the American dream is intact;
God and nature are on the side of the small farmers, who have
rejected Eastern artifice and dedicated themselves to tilling the
soil of an expanding America.

Despite its optimistic theme, *Drums Along the Mohawk* was
not an easy picture to make. Claudette Colbert did not feel
comfortable in her role, and Ford, rarely patient with women,
resented having to pamper her. He took his frustrations out on
Dorris Bowdon, whom he had favored during the making of
Young Mr. Lincoln. "John tormented me all through that
second film," Bowdon recalled. "He was a demon, I was his
victim. He would be very sharp with me in front of the cast for
no rational reason." When the actress came on the set, Ford
would complain, "Your hair is sloppy. Why didn't you get it
checked before you came out and held us up?" If she was in her
dressing room, he'd shout, "Well, let's everybody wait. Miss
Bowdon is holding us up at $15,000 a day." Nothing she did

pleased him. "I don't think he was trying to get an attitude for the film," Bowdon declared. "He wanted to needle me, because he had learned that I was going with Nunnally [Johnson] and he didn't approve."

Ford had begun shooting the picture with Linda Darnell in the part Bowdon ultimately played. Darnell had gone to Utah with the company, and her scenes were never reshot once Bowdon took over the role. Only distance shots from the location work could be used once the film was edited. Ford averaged eighteen hours a day working on the picture in Utah, since Zanuck kept urging him to speed the production along. "This is a terrific task up here," the director wrote in July, "and despite Technicolor and some adverse weather, I believe we will be ahead of our schedule." Ford prided himself on being a dedicated craftsman and resented interference from studio executives. "Your letters and wires about tempo frighten me," he wrote Zanuck. "Both the script and the story call for a placid, pastoral, simple movement, which suddenly breaks into quick, heavy, dramatic overtones. All this requires care."

Although the company was filming on location during the summer, a fire was built in their camp at night and huge logs were placed around it for watching entertainment after dinner. Danny Borzage, a fixture on Ford's sets, played the accordion, while members of the company sang three-part harmony. The evenings ended with a bugler's playing taps from the woods, while cast and crew hovered around the fire, some with tears in their eyes.

When *Drums Along the Mohawk* opened in November 1939, the *Hollywood Reporter* proclaimed it "a triumph of color and beauty. Rarely, since color came into pictures, has its use had such opportunities as in this production, and 20th Century-Fox has gone the limit." The movie had romance, adventure, humor, sentiment, and above all blood and thunder; audiences loved it.

Ford and Zanuck were on a definite winning streak, filling the screen with vignettes from America's past. The stories they fashioned were entertaining, their characters consistently strong, their craftsmanship unparalleled. The films Ford made

at 20th Century-Fox were unpretentious, full of human dignity, yet highly commercial.

Director and studio head shared a preference for scripts
about believable people, and while Ford respected tradition,
he also had a penchant for anarchy, evident both in his films
and in his personal life. His favorite characters were refugees
from a restrictive society (Europe or urban America) who
fashioned a better world through fortitude and adherence to
personal ideals. By the close of 1939 Ford had secured his
reputation as Hollywood's foremost director, but greater
achievements lay just ahead.

While Ford was on location in Utah for *Drums Along the
Mohawk*, Zanuck offered him *The Grapes of Wrath* (1940) as his
next project. The director read Nunnally Johnson's script,
based on Steinbeck's novel, and was delighted. He was intrigued by the similarities between the dispossessed Okies
during the Dust Bowl of the 1930s and the Irish peasants
evicted by landowners and left to wander and starve during the
famine in Ireland during the nineteenth century. "I was reared
in poverty," said Ford, "so the picture appealed to me." He
could understand the breakdown of the family and their
mourning the loss of the land they had worked for generations.
The Grapes of Wrath would stand as Ford's masterpiece of
contemporary history.

While Zanuck was enthusiastic about pictures with social
impact, he was uneasy about John Steinbeck's novel. Winthrop
Aldrich, one of the biggest bankers at Chase Manhattan, was
chairman of the board of 20th Century-Fox, and Zanuck
worried about how the studio's financial backers would react
to such a hard-hitting story of poverty and exploitation. The
Fox production head sensed that Ford, with his love of common people and his special feel for Americana, could make the
subject powerful yet still acceptable to the moneyed interests
backing the studio.

Ford later claimed that he was interested in *The Grapes of
Wrath* only as a good story with well-drawn characters, not as
social commentary. He recognized that the subject was timely,

but was attracted to it for its dramatic potential. At the time he was sympathetic with Franklin Roosevelt and the New Deal, and it was easy for him to transfer his belief in the traditional family's relationship to home and the soil to the Okies' attachment to sharecropped land. He had no difficulty in updating the westward movement to include the Okies' migration to California in search of a promised land. With his affinity for the outsider, he could identify with Tom Joad as he lashes out at an unjust system and strikes out to forge a new social order.

Ford agreed to direct the picture on condition that he have a month's rest after completing *Drums Along the Mohawk*. Zanuck agreed to postpone *The Grapes of Wrath* until September, giving the director time to rest on the *Araner*. The vacation was interrupted when art director Richard Day came aboard to discuss sets for the upcoming production. Day and Ford decided to follow the paintings of Thomas Hart Benton in their recreation of the American heartland. When cinematographer Gregg Toland was assigned to the project, he agreed to strive for a documentary look in photographing the Joad family's dying America. Henry Fonda was selected for the role of Tom Joad, his third picture in a row for Ford, while character actress Jane Darwell was cast as Ma Joad, the source of the family's strength.

A second unit was dispatched to the Southwest to film the Joads' jalopy as it headed west. Since many readers considered the book trashy and politically radical, Zanuck feared protests and began production under the title *Highway 66*. By the time Ford returned from his vacation, Nunnally Johnson's script had been finalized; the director would take few liberties with it. What Ford did was to add his own touches—haunting glimpses of abandoned farms and empty houses, Tom Joad's walking out of a ruined landscape against a line of telephone poles, Muley's face lighted by a match, Ma Joad's holding up a pair of cheap earrings and gazing into a broken mirror, defeated Hooverville occupants walking with fatigue in front of the Joads' truck—without destroying the screenwriter's intent.

Dorris Bowdon, who played Rose of Sharon in the picture, had come to understand what a sensitive man Ford was, yet knew his determination to hide it. "He could do very mean things to cover up his softness," the actress said. When they started filming *The Grapes of Wrath*, he remained aloof toward her, but Bowdon recognized what a wizard he was at achieving performances. The day they shot the scene where Rose of Sharon's husband has abandoned her, Bowdon awoke with a painful sore on her face. Her cheek was throbbing, so she went to Ford and begged him not to shoot her close up that day. The director took her face, studied it, and said, "Go over and take your place. I want to light it and see." Bowdon found her place on the set, and Ford sat down beside her out of camera range. He began speaking to her in a calm voice: "He's just left you; Connie walked out. It was too much for him. He couldn't face not being able to feed you and the baby. You're alone now, and although you've got Ma and Pa and Tom, you may not be able to hold on. You're lost." He continued talking in that vein until Bowdon became mesmerized by his words. Finally Ford said, "Now read those lines to me." Bowdon began saying her dialogue. Her face started moving and tears streamed, as she continued speaking her lines. When the scene was finished, Ford said, "Cut," and the actress realized that the camera had been rolling. "It was a one-take scene," she recalled, "and that's the scene that's in the film. He wanted this, he wanted my face distorted. It was all right if a starving, pregnant girl was getting hickies on her face, showing the rawness of life. If he had thought of it, he probably would have had makeup put one on me."

But Bowdon again experienced Ford's vicious side. They were shooting the Saturday-night dance at the government camp, where Ma and Rose of Sharon are sitting on the edge of the dance floor and Tom walks up behind them in a playful mood. Tom pulls Ma onto the floor, and they begin to dance. It was a touching scene, but Jane Darwell, a warm, friendly lady, was self-conscious about her size and felt she looked ridiculous dancing. When the scene was over, Darwell laughed as she started back toward Bowdon, expecting a second take. She smiled at Bowdon, happy the scene had gone well, whereupon Bowdon clapped. Through a microphone Ford shouted, "Who did that?" A hundred and fifty extras fell into absolute silence. The young actress didn't know that in picturemaking it is considered bad luck to clap. Bowdon admitted that she was the guilty party. In front of everybody Ford shouted, "You amateur! You foolish amateur!" Bowdon was devastated. "It was the most painful thing he could have called me," she said. "This was the third film I had done with him, but I knew I was an amateur. It hurt so badly to be exposed before this very professional cast. But John had the fixed attention of a large crew and a large cast, and he excoriated me it seemed for hours. I went back to my dressing room, and as soon as I'd closed the door I burst into sobs. I had never experienced such painful humiliation."

The actor that Ford needled most on the picture was John Carradine, who played Casey, the preacher-turned-labor agitator who is eventually martyred. Ford loathed Carradine, although he often cast him because he was such a fine actor. "Carradine had an ego which was about three times John Ford's," screenwriter Nunnally Johnson remarked, "and Ford could not put him down in any way." The director would bawl Carradine out or try to make him look ridiculous, but the actor seemed impervious to insult, which infuriated Ford all the more. "Carradine had an armor of ego," Dorris Bowdon said, "yet he added something to that role in timing, body language, and the sensitivity of his face. He went from a man of God to being a man of purpose, determined to see that justice was meted out."

Most of the footage Ford shot on *The Grapes of Wrath* was filmed in the studio. The Colorado River, outside Needles, California, where the Joad men take a baptismal bath, was the farthest the actors traveled. Henry Fonda remembered how Ford kept performances fresh, not wanting to dilute them through too much rehearsal. Before shooting Tom Joad's farewell to Ma, the director found excuses for not letting Fonda and Darwell rehearse their lines. He kept stopping them before they got to the final moment. By the time Ford was ready to shoot the scene, Fonda recalled, "Jane Darwell and I were like racehorses that wanted to go." When the camera rolled, they'd never said the dialogue out loud; Ford wanted the scene done in a single take. "After we finished Pappy didn't say a word," said Fonda. "He just stood up and walked away. He got what he wanted." On the screen it was brilliant.

Zanuck was convinced that Ford was turning out a great picture, but insisted on an upbeat ending. After Ford left town Nunnally Johnson wrote and Darryl Zanuck directed the final scene, a coda in which Ma Joad talks about how women handle change better than men and praises the indestructibility of common people. Ford accepted the scene as satisfactory.

By November 1939 *The Grapes of Wrath* was ready for editing, after forty-three days of shooting. The director finished the picture under budget and requested a musical score consisting of American folk songs, featuring "Red River Valley." The simple tunes established a sense of time and place, but also underlined the populist theme.

When the picture opened on January 24, 1940 at the Rivoli Theater in New York 12,917 people jammed the theater the first day. "In the vast library where the celluloid literature of the screen is stored," the *New York Times* declared, "there is one small, uncrowded shelf devoted to the cinema's masterworks, those films which by dignity of theme and excellence of treatment seem to be of enduring artistry, seem destined to be recalled not merely at the end of their particular year but whenever great motion pictures are mentioned. To that shelf of screen classics 20th Century-Fox yesterday added its version of John Steinbeck's *The Grapes of Wrath*." The reviewer stated that the film "is just about as good as any picture has a right to be."

Despite right-wing criticism, the film was hailed by critics as a masterpiece. John Ford won his second Academy Award for the picture and the New York Film Critics Award. Jane Darwell also won an Oscar as that year's best supporting actress. Most observers agreed that the political radicalism of Steinbeck's novel had been muted, yet felt that Ford's picture made a strong social statement. Dancer-choreographer Gene Kelly declared later that, despite their different approaches, John Ford was his idol. "Here was a man who, like myself, was making pictures for a mass audience," said Kelly. "But *The*

Grapes of Wrath stands as one of the most powerful political-sociological documents in the history of the cinema. The end of the frontier was in that picture."

Ford typically claimed that making *The Grapes of Wrath* was just another job, done to the best of his ability. "I didn't wave any magic wand or look into a crystal ball," he said. "I just went out and did it. It was a lot of fun because I was back working again with Henry Fonda, really one of my favorite actors."

The night that shooting on the picture finished Ford boarded the *Araner* and set sail for Mexico, where he was joined a few days later by Fonda. Ford loved mariachis and had a group on board the yacht when the actor arrived in Mazatlán. "He was always drinking on those trips," recalled Fonda, "and the first week or two he was a good companion to be with. You'd go ashore with him and do the rounds. Sometimes they were the rounds of the whorehouses, not just for sex, but because they were colorful and had drinks in them." Ford's drinking had become more destructive. During this trip with Fonda down the Mexican coast, Ford went on a bender and had to be hospitalized at Guaymas to dry out. That became a pattern.

A controlled alcoholic, Ford would abstain from drink during the making of a picture, limiting his social life to the Hollywood Athletic Club and playing cards with John Wayne, Ward Bond and a few others. He rarely attended parties, never went to nightclubs, seldom accepted dinner invitations, and almost never appeared at film previews, voicing scorn for the Hollywood social circuit. At home he spent most of his time reading, frequently late into the night. His relationship with Mary had become increasingly estranged, although they shared the same house, and contact with his teenage children grew sporadic. Patrick and Barbara found being John Ford's children difficult, in part because of the expectation heaped upon them, but also because of their father's erratic personality.

As the years went by Ford became more of an enigma. He realized that he had a good life and was grateful for it, yet he viewed life as a tragedy. Despite his honors and financial success, his Irish pessimism remained unequivocal. He built walls around himself, but was torn apart by his sensitivity. Katharine Hepburn felt that Ford was much like Spencer Tracy; both had the Irish gift for drama, yet found living difficult. "The easiest thing Spence did was act," Hepburn said. "I'm sure the easiest thing John did was to direct."

Loner that he was, Ford hated analyzing his work and proved evasive when interviewed. What he had to say he said in his films, not by intellectualizing his craft. He grew impatient with reporters, finding their questions stupid and often answering them with lies or humorous vagaries. Even fellow filmmakers found him elusive and contentious. When he said nothing, his attack was most dangerous.

At the studio Ford might find time to loiter outside a soundstage for gossip. But on the set those who worked with him knew better than to interrupt when he was chewing his handkerchief, since that was an indication he was thinking. Ford was democratic in his relationships and respected only those who would level with him. He admired loyalty and creativity in others, yet could rarely express his appreciation to the people nearest to him. "It's strange and sad," Charles FitzSimons said, "because I think he could have had a better life if he hadn't had all of these foibles."

Ford was born with poor eyesight, but by the late 1930s his vision had grown far worse. He wore tinted glasses for years, then added a black patch over his left eye, which in part was an affectation. Although he would never admit to being ambitious, he possessed tremendous drive and excessive energy. A big man, with a pale face that grew craggy with age, Ford had thin legs and slender hands that didn't fit his frame. His baggy clothes, which were not washed any too often, smelled of tobacco, since he was constantly fiddling with his pipe and spilling some of its contents.

When not working on a picture, Ford drank and waited for the next project. On the *Araner* he lived like a member of the crew and surrounded himself with intimate friends. He seemed thoroughly alive only when involved with a movie. He spent most of the spring of 1940 at sea, learning that he had won the Academy Award for *The Grapes of Wrath* on the *Araner*'s radio. Asked by the press why he hadn't attended the Oscars ceremony, Ford replied, "Why should I? I don't like those things." Ford pursued his course in Hollywood in an individual way, compromising as little as possible in an industry built on compromise.

Ford's contract with 20th Century-Fox granted him the right to make one feature a year away from the studio. Having done three big pictures consecutively for Zanuck, he was eager to turn to a smaller, more personal project. He chose *The Long Voyage Home* (1940), based on four one-act plays by American dramatist Eugene O'Neill. Dudley Nichols wrote the script, and Walter Wanger produced. Ford collaborated with Nichols, developing sequences by talking and arguing back and forth. Once their script was complete, they went to San Francisco to meet with O'Neill, who approved the job they'd done.

Gregg Toland, chosen as the film's cinematographer, agreed that the script should be shot in an expressionistic style with few close-ups. "When *The Long Voyage Home* was made," Ford remarked, "I wanted it very, very sharp, as a razor, and it was. I wanted to see everything. I didn't want any tricks. It's a story of character." Ford gave John Wayne the role of Ole Olsen, a part requiring more dramatic skill than Wayne had previously shown. The star worked hard at creating a believable character and turned out a strong performance, although Thomas Mitchell played the actual lead. Ward Bond, John Qualen, and Jack Pennick were in the picture, all regulars in the Ford stock company. "I've always relied on my old standbys," the director said, because "I know they'll come through without any fuss."

On any John Ford film much of the strength lay in the character actors. *The Long Voyage Home* was Mildred Natwick's first movie, and the actress remembered the experience fondly. "Ford was a wonderful director," said Natwick, "and I think he knew how nervous I was. He really told me everything to do; it was marvelous coaching. When I had to make my entrance, I remember he said, 'Why don't you have your sweater down and sort of be pulling it up over your shoulder?' And then he would put in lines. The line in the script I think was, 'A drop of gin, Joe.' But Ford added 'and with a beer chaser.' He just made me so comfortable. He took a lot of time and nurtured me along."

The Long Voyage Home was filmed during the summer of 1940, as the shadow of World War II was lengthening over Europe. Ford wanted a sense of the sea in the picture and achieved it. Yet the story was as tough as it was profound, dealing with contemporary humanity's odyssey over the oceans of the world in search of inner peace. Dudley Nichols saw the film's rushes and was ecstatic. "I know you're going to get a magnificent picture," he wrote Ford, "and I think you know it too. Another sixteen-inch shell into the MGM glamour empire."

Reviewers praised the movie for its authenticity and dark realism and agreed that Ford had delivered another powerful screen drama. *The Long Voyage Home* won the director his third New York Film Critics Award and made many lists of 1940's ten best pictures. Producer Walter Wanger was so enthusiastic about the final results that he commissioned artists to paint scenes from the film. Commercially, however, *The Long Voyage Home* failed to recover its costs.

Darryl Zanuck next assigned Ford to the screen version of Erskine Caldwell's *Tobacco Road*, hoping to repeat the success they'd enjoyed with *The Grapes of Wrath*. Whereas Steinbeck's book had dealt with dispossessed farmers forced to seek a new way of life, the emphasis in Caldwell's novel (and its long-running Broadway adaptation) was on comedy. *Tobacco Road* depicted poor whites in Georgia who had grown shiftless as the sharecrop system reached its end. It, like *The Grapes of Wrath*, dealt with the decline of American agrarianism, as machine agriculture replaced the tenant farmer and put an end to the sharecropper's dream of land ownership. The Jeffersonian ideal of a democracy based on yeomen farmers had given way to industrial capitalism. But where Steinbeck extolled the nobility of the evicted poor, Caldwell and Jack Kirkland, who adapted *Tobacco Road* for the stage, exploited the ignorance and eccentricities of poor southern whites.

Ford claimed that he had never read Caldwell's book or seen the play. He accepted the film during the fall of 1940, after scriptwriter Nunnally Johnson had scouted locations. The picture would not rank among the director's best efforts, mainly because his broad comedy led him into excesses that seem clumsy and fake. Both Caldwell and Johnson hated his handling of the film. "I thought I knew Tobacco Road and Tobacco Road people backwards and forwards," said the screenwriter, who came from Georgia. "At least I knew something about them, and I could follow their reasoning, and I think my script was written that way. But Ford did a lousy job on *Tobacco Road*." Johnson claimed that Ford twisted the indolent Southerners of Tobacco Road into shanty Irish.

The screenwriter remembered sitting in the projection room with Ford watching a test of William Tracy, who played Dude in the film. Dude was shouting and screaming like an imbecile, and the writer turned to Ford in dismay and asked, "Is that the way you're going to play this fellow?" Ford grew defensive and snapped, "Who's being tested, the director or the actor?" Johnson realized that Ford was too arrogant and powerful a man for him to levy an effective protest. "To Ford a low, illiterate cracker and a low, illiterate Irishman were identical," the screenwriter declared. "Since he didn't know anything about crackers and he did know about the Irish, he simply changed them all into crazy Irishmen." Johnson liked the story and thought his script was better than the picture, remaining convinced that Ford had misinterpreted its characters. "When you send the thing in red and it comes out green," the writer said, "that's a disappointment. But I didn't have any control."

The project also suffered from questionable casting. Over Ford's objection, Zanuck selected Gene Tierney, one of his favorite contract stars and an excellent actress in society roles, for the mentally deficient Ellie May. Tierney was too sophisticated for the role and made the part a caricature. Her seduction of the Ward Bond character became a mating of two simpletons. Bond, who would work in twenty-two pictures with Ford and had recently gotten married on board the *Araner*, was the director's choice for the role of Lov. Excellent actor though Bond became, he was never a romantic lead, and *Tobacco Road* did nothing to change that.

While the film proved a sour note in a stanza of Ford triumphs, cameraman Arthur C. Miller liked working with the director better than anyone else in the business. Miller vowed that he might say only fifty words to Ford in a day, but their communication was so great that he could sense what the director wanted. "Ford knew nothing of lighting," the cinematographer declared. "He never once looked in the camera when we worked together. The man had bad eyes as long as I knew him, but he was a man whose veins ran with the business. He had a tremendous memory. He could come up with an idea from some picture he had made thirty years before and suggest you do that."

After *Tobacco Road* was photographed, the film was turned over to Barbara McLean, Zanuck's favorite editor, who found cutting a John Ford movie easy. "He never did bother too much about the cutting of his pictures," said McLean, "because everything he wanted was on the film. You couldn't hurt a Ford picture." McLean liked the director and came to feel close to him. "He was sort of like Zanuck," she said. "If he liked you, it was great. But if he didn't, God help you."

Despite the technical skill that went into the picture, it was evident from the preview that *Tobacco Road* was in trouble. Zanuck remained hopeful, writing Ford in January 1941: "The last half of the picture was magnificent, but the first half was long and drawn out and full of a lot of gags that failed to register. However, the cutting problem will remedy all of this and you need have no worry on this score."

When the movie was released a month later, the response was negative. The picture bore slight resemblance to either the novel or the stage play. "As a matter of fact," Bosley Crowther wrote, "it barely resembles a believable slice of life, and just comes under the wire as an amusing but pointless film." Most reviewers found *Tobacco Road* a perversion of the longest-running play in theatrical history to date. Some blamed the failure on censorship; others pointed an accusing finger at

John Ford, arguing that the director had not concentrated on
anything vital or solid.

Ford claimed he enjoyed making the picture and took pleasure in watching it. "I don't consider *Tobacco Road* a failure," he
said. "There was sheer vileness in the original play. We cleaned
it up, made it presentable. It was not a good play, but I made it
into a good picture." Not many agreed.

Ford's instincts, normally so good, had let him down. But his
record during the two years before America's entry into World
War II was astonishing by any standard. His populist views fit
the national temperament. Despite indications that technology and the continuing urban influx were undermining traditional values and a society based on agriculture, Americans
during the Great Depression looked wistfully at images of
their disappearing heartland. Ford paid homage to an American past in pictures rich in nostalgia, yet avoided attitudes of
defeat. The director's sympathy for the downtrodden may well
have stemmed from his Irish background, but he shaped it into
mature dramas that catapulted him to the top of his profession.
Ford admired the rare individual angry enough to fight
against society's wrongs, yet his films never preached. He
denied that he ever intended to produce messages of lasting
value. He simply presented his stories cinematically and let
audiences draw their own conclusions.

"I am of the proletariat," the director said. "My people were
peasants. They came here, were educated. They served this
country well. I love America." He proved his love time and
again. Like Walt Whitman, Ford saw dignity and pride in the
common people, "the lifeblood of democracy," as he saw them.
He miscarried with *Tobacco Road* mainly because it dealt with a
segment of American life he hadn't experienced and didn't
understand. At the time he made the film, he was distracted by
more important considerations; making movies seemed almost trivial. The spring of 1940 saw clouds of war gather over
Europe and Far East Asia. As Ford watched the storm grow
darker, his hidden agenda took shape. Even before America
was involved, he became determined to participate in the
conflict.

John Ford during the early period of sound movies. (Courtesy of the Lilly Library)

Gorham's Corner in Portland, Maine, where Ford's father operated a saloon around the turn of the century. (Courtesy of the Maine Historic Preservation Commission)

John Ford with his mother, Barbara Curran Feeney, who frequently wore this lace shawl. (Courtesy of the Lilly Library)

Harry Carey (on left), Ford's first Western star, in their silent version of *The Outcasts of Poker Flat*. (Courtesy of the Lilly Library)

The joining of the rails in *The Iron Horse*. (Courtesy of the DeGolyer Library Southern Methodist University)

A Ford family portrait: Patrick, John, Barbara, and Mary. (Courtesy of the Lilly Library)

Ford's yacht, *The Araner*, a vacation retreat and the scene of heavy drinking. (Courtesy of the Lilly Library)

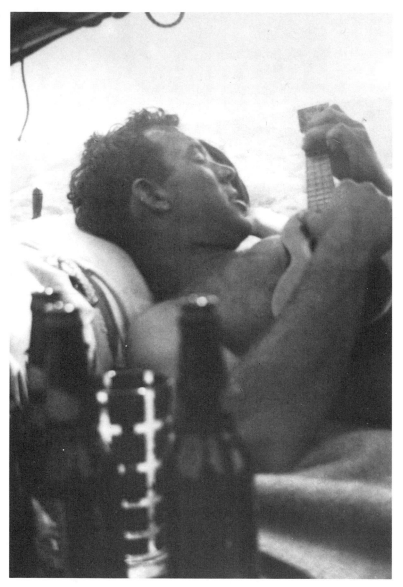

Actor Ward Bond relaxing aboard *The Araner*. (Courtesy of the Lilly
Library)

A scene from *The Informer*, the film that won Academy Awards for Ford and acto
Victor McLaglen. (Courtesy of the Lilly Library)

ohn Wayne riding to major stardom in *Stagecoach*. (Courtesy of the Lilly Library)

Ford on the set of *The Grapes of Wrath* with Henry Fonda, a visitor, and Jane Darwe
(Courtesy of the Lilly Library)

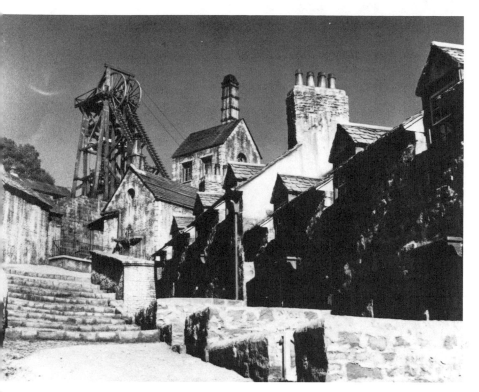

The set 20th Century-Fox built in the hills behind Malibu for *How Green Was My Valley*. (Courtesy of the Lilly Library)

John Ford during World War II with the Field Photographic Unit. (Courtesy of the Lilly Library)

Joanne Dru and Chief Big Tree on the set of *She Wore a Yellow Ribbon*. (Courtesy of the Lilly Library)

Director Ford at work on location. (Courtesy of the Lilly Library)

Harry Carey, Jr., Ben Johnson, Maureen O'Hara, and John Wayne enjoying lunch on the set of *Rio Grande*. (Courtesy of the Lilly Library)

Actor and horseman Ben Johnson. (Courtesy of the Lilly Library)

Maureen O'Hara, Ford's favorite leading lady. (Courtesy of the Lilly Library)

At the height of the action in *Rio Grande*, the final segment of Ford's cavalry trilogy. (Courtesy of the Lilly Library)

John Ford attempting a Duke Wayne pose during location work.
(Courtesy of the Lilly Library)

ord on location in Ireland for *The Quiet Man*. (Courtesy of the Lilly Library)

John Wayne and Maureen O'Hara in *The Quiet Man*. (Courtesy of the Lilly Library)

Ford on the set of *The Sun Shines Bright*, one of his favorite films. (Courtesy of the Lilly Library)

Henry Fonda re-creating his role in *Mr. Roberts*. (Courtesy of the Lilly Library)

Ford's son-in-law Ken Curtis and Vera Miles in *The Searchers*. (Courtesy of the Lilly Library)

John Wayne, John Ford, and friend during a Christmas celebration at the Field Photo Farm. (Courtesy of the Lilly Library)

Lee Marvin and John Wayne tangle in *The Man Who Shot Liberty Valance*.
(Courtesy of the Lilly Library)

Ford directing Jane Wyman in one of his rare television shows, "The Bamboo
Cross" for *Fireside Theatre*. (Courtesy of the Lilly Library)

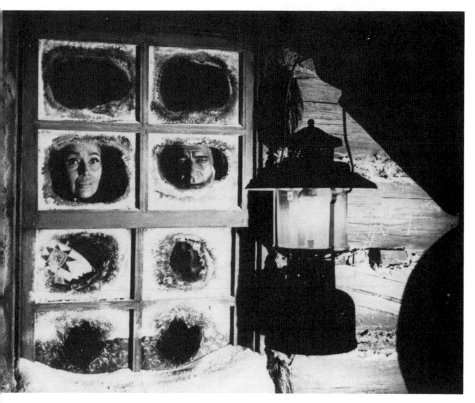

Dolores Del Rio and Gilbert Roland, dramatically framed, in *Cheyenne Autumn*. (Courtesy of the Lilly Library)

A scene from *Seven Women*, Ford's final film. (Courtesy of the Lilly Library)

John Ford in later years. (Courtesy of the Lilly Library)

CHAPTER 6

War

BETWEEN 1936 and 1939 Ford had made periodic cruises down the coast of Baja California, attempting to gather information for the U.S. Navy. Convinced that Japan was concealing spies amid its fishing fleet off the Mexican coast, Ford used his rank in the Naval Reserve to engage in secret service activity he considered necessary to national defense. "I wish to extend to you my sincere personal thanks for the good work lately performed by you on your southern trip in the yacht *Araner*," Lieutenant Commander A. A. Hopkins wrote Ford on June 21, 1936. Hopkins assured that Ford's report, together with the chart and photographs he'd provided, had gone to the proper authorities and that the filmmaker's efforts had been of vital importance. "For your own personal information," Hopkins continued, "of the six yachts who have been requested to make observations during the past two years the *Araner*, its owner and commander are the only ones who have made entrance to the area you explored and who have brought back the data wanted."

Disregarding his success in Hollywood, Ford dreamed of becoming a naval hero. Not content with his role as an artist of the cinema, he sought recognition in a world of masculine valor and adventure. He hoped that by becoming a military paladin he would prove himself to Mary, who had steered him toward the navy during the early years of their marriage. He also hoped that his espionage work would bolster his flagging sense of manhood. Uncomfortable with his artistic temperament, afraid that the sensitivity he tried to camouflage might suggest darker ramifications, Ford hid his delicate nature behind a blustery facade and an unkempt lifestyle, yet dreamed of a chance to prove himself heroic and brave. World War II provided him with opportunities to demonstrate physical boldness — "his last chance to be a boy," as Theodore Roosevelt might have said.

By 1939 Ford was convinced that the United States would soon be drawn into the war and began taking his reconnaissance activities seriously, earning praise from the naval hierarchy for his "unselfish and patriotic work." When he finished *The Grapes of Wrath* in the fall of 1939, Ford again went to Mexico at the request of Captain Ellis Zacharias, chief intelligence officer of the Eleventh Naval District, who asked him to make a detailed report on Japanese movements. Ford accepted Zacharias's invitation, eager to advance his standing in the Naval Reserve. He loved secrecy, being on the inside of confidential operations, and thirsted for adventure.

On December 16 the *Araner* sailed into Guaymas Harbor (where Ford was eventually hospitalized), where dozens of Japanese fishing boats were anchored. Ford studied the vessels through binoculars and became convinced that they were more than fishing trawlers. He took notes on their size and made detailed charts of their location, certain the Japanese crews were spying. He went ashore and mixed with the fishermen, again taking notes for his report to Zacharias. Mary Ford was aboard the *Araner* with her husband, and she asked a Japanese sailor to row her over to his boat so she could make a call from the ship-to-shore telephone the vessel had on board. Once there she saw "all kinds of photographic equipment" and navy credentials on the wall of the ship. "They let me use the phone and were very polite," said Mary, but "when we woke up the next morning, they were all gone." Like Jack, she became convinced that the Japanese boats had been putting on an act with their fishing nets.

Ford's report to Zacharias read like a movie script. "The Japanese shrimp fleet was lying at anchor," he recorded upon their arrival in Guaymas. "It is my belief that the crews and officers of this shrimp fleet belong to the Imperial Navy or Reserve. The crews are not the same class of fishermen that I have seen so many times in Japan." He speculated that the Japanese knew every bay, cove, and inlet of the Gulf of California, "a bay which is so full of islands and so close to our Arizona borderline that they constitute a real menace."

Whether Jack was fantasizing, inebriated, or trying to advance his position with the navy is difficult to judge. He was eager for promotion and hoped to win respectability in the eyes of Mary and her family. Also, his friend and later partner Merian C. Cooper walked away from a vice-presidency at RKO, where he was earning $100,000 a year, to help the American aviator Claire Chennault organize the Flying Tigers, a group of mercenaries who flew missions for Chiang Kai-shek. Cooper's daring impressed Ford, but he was impatient even before that to enter the war in a significant way.

In April 1940 Ford created, without offical sanction, a Naval Reserve unit made up of professional filmmakers, which he called the Naval Field Photographic Unit. Among his recruits were cinematographer Gregg Toland, writer Budd Schulberg, writer-director Garson Kanin, and film editor Robert Parrish. From a military standpoint the unit more closely resembled extras from a Mack Sennett comedy than a serious fighting force. Uniforms were rented from Western Costume, weapons were borrowed from the 20th Century-Fox property department, and drills were held on a studio soundstage. But Ford loved the pageantry of military life and was in his element playing warrior.

By this time Ford was well connected in the Naval Reserve and planned to mold his recruits into an effective wartime unit and present them as a trained auxiliary, ready to photograph front-line combat. He had no doubt that the United States would become involved in the war and wanted his group to be ready when the time came.

The navy recognized the advantage of having a major Hollywood director as a reserve officer, since newsreel divisions of motion picture studios were the prime visual news coverage at the time. Fox's Movietone News ranked among the best, almost an equivalent of CNN in television coverage later. Since Ford had clout with the studios, his outfit could move into areas where the navy wanted photographic coverage that would be difficult for others.

Throughout the latter part of 1940 the Field Photographic Unit trained in anticipation of naval authorization while Ford made trips to Washington, D.C. On September 5 Captain Felix Gygax wrote Ford: "The Bureau of Navigation is issuing instructions to the Commandant of the Eleventh Naval District to recruit photographic personnel for the Naval Reserve somewhat along the lines we discussed when you were in my office on your recent trip to the East." A few weeks later Ford met Jack Bolton, an officer serving as liaison between the navy and the Hollywood studios. Bolton knew how the bureaucracy worked; he traveled to Washington and within record time the Field Photographic Unit received official sanction.

Among the group's assignments was a thirty-minute documentary for the Signal Corps on sex hygiene. Ford prepared the film at 20th Century-Fox, with Darryl Zanuck lending his name as producer. *Sex Hygiene* became the official antivenereal disease training film of the war years. Its message was that the only sure way to avoid disease is sexual abstinence. "It didn't make much sense to the soldiers," said Gene Fowler, Jr., who edited the documentary, "but this was the time when if a fellow got a venereal disease in the service, he went to the guardhouse and didn't get paid for that time." Ford arranged for the head surgeon at Fort McArthur to serve as technical director for the film, and the doctor soon caught the acting bug. "He became the biggest ham who ever was," Fowler said. "Ford had one shot of him where he was injecting mercury into a guy—this was before penicillin and before sulfa. But the doctor looked like someone right out of science fiction, with this needle he was filling up. He'd squeeze the needle and stuff would squirt out; the look in his eye was just evil. Ford lit him—I think from a perverse sense of humor—from the bottom, so that he looked like a terrible man. I guess that was supposed to scare the bejesus out of the soldiers."

The film concentrated on syphilis, the effects of which were awful. "Ford just loved it!" said Fowler. "The army would send these guys up under guard for him to photograph, and I think he took a perverse pleasure in showing this shocking stuff." The documentary was finished in the summer of 1941, just as the army was gearing up for war, and taken down to Fort McArthur and shown to some draftees. "They had guys running out and throwing up," Fowler remembered. "They kept a record of the kids, and apparently for a week nobody went out. The picture affected them that much. But after the week was up, the whole camp went out and got laid."

Ford made one more feature film before the bombing of Pearl Harbor, another masterpiece about poverty—*How Green Was My Valley*, based on Richard Llewellyn's bestselling novel of 1939. The script had been in preparation for a full year at 20th Century-Fox, with William Wyler borrowed from Samuel Goldwyn to direct. When Wyler had to return to Goldwyn for another project, Darryl Zanuck assigned *How Green Was My Valley* to Ford. Although Wyler had worked on the script for weeks with screenwriter Philip Dunne, helped select the cast, approved sets, and done everything except shoot the picture, Ford was delighted to take over, making only minor changes. He liked the bittersweet story of a Welsh coal-mining family and found Dunne's script reminiscent of his own family background. With the passage of time the land in the valley becomes ugly from smoke, while its people sink deeper into poverty. As the family disintegrates, two of the brothers in the story decide to emigrate to America.

The picture went before the cameras on June 9, 1941. As with *The Grapes of Wrath*, the studio's financial backers in New York disliked the script, thought its emphasis on the exploitation of labor alarming, considered the subject dour, and objected to the dearth of stars in the cast. Philip Dunne, however, had fashioned a dramatic script that was poignant and hard-hitting without becoming depressing. Despite a limited budget, a realistic set depicting a Welsh village was constructed in the hills behind Malibu, less than an hour's drive from the studio. Originally the intention had been to shoot the film in Technicolor in Wales, but Hitler's Luftwaffe put an end to those plans.

The role of Huw went to twelve-year-old Roddy McDowall, already a veteran of twenty British films. Young Huw's part was initially brief, with Tyrone Power scheduled to play him as an adult, but Dunne decided to center his script on the child. McDowall recalled that Ford was able to connect with him in conversation and transmitted a feeling about the movie he'd seldom experienced. "A child actor wants to be treated like an adult," McDowall said. "The thing that sticks out about *How Green Was My Valley* is that I never remember being directed. It just all happened. Ford played me like a harp."

The director created a harmonious atmosphere on the set that contained excitement at the same time. "I was scared to death of him," McDowall declared. "To me he was sort of like Moses. But I feared him in a good way. He was religion to me in a certain sense, which touched me and released me and did not inhibit me. Ford could be just terrible. If he chose to, he could destroy you in a minute. But he was marvelous to me." There was no confusion on the set, for Ford remained precise about what he wanted. "There were extraordinary accidents that happened," McDowall remembered, "like planning a whole crowd coming down that hill of the Welsh mining town, and they'd start the smokestacks going. All of a sudden when the cameras would be rolling, the wind would shift, and the smoke would do the most amazing things, and the sun would shine through it. The most incredible accidents happened to make that film just a little bit better than if they hadn't occurred."

Zanuck wanted to give Gene Tierney the part of Angharad, Huw's older sister, but Ford insisted on Maureen O'Hara. An Irish spitfire, O'Hara was strong and opinionated, with a determination to achieve major stardom. She would become Ford's favorite leading lady, as well as a close friend. The two sat with their heads together on the set, speaking Gaelic. The actress loved Ford, recognizing that he was "very sentimental and a terrible prevaricator." While O'Hara spent her time "in the barrel" during the making of Ford's pictures, she was capable of giving his salty language back to him, which endeared her to him all the more.

British actress Anna Lee had been chosen for the role of

Bronwen when Wyler was still scheduled to direct the picture. After she learned that Ford was taking over, friends told her she was in trouble. "Ford hates the English," Lee heard. "He likes only Irish actors." So the actress made up a story about an Irish grandfather, Thomas Michael O'Connell. Ford accepted her tale and didn't know until years later that it was total fabrication. By then he liked Anna Lee enormously and used her often in his pictures.

"Ford was a great manipulator of emotions and a great psychologist," the British actress said. On the *How Green Was My Valley* set he would discuss with her something entirely unrelated to the scene they were about to shoot, but Lee sensed that he was telling her something. In the take that followed she found herself doing things she knew she hadn't planned, "as if there was some kind of thought transference. It was a magic that he had that I have never found in any other director," Lee said. "Ford knew what he wanted and was able to convey that without saying it."

The actress realized how much Ford liked her when he started teasing her, calling her Limey. She came to respect him as a master craftsman and marveled at his composition. She discovered there were no stars on a John Ford set; he detested the word. "I would far rather have worked for Ford than become a so-called star," Lee said. "To me that was the greatest compliment anybody could have."

The actress remembered her emotional scene in *How Green Was My Valley* after Bronwen's husband has been killed. "I am lonely without him," her lines read. "I put his boots and clothes ready every night, but they are there still in the morning. It is lonely I am." Then Bronwen walks out the door with her baby. Ford didn't give Lee any specific direction. "He took this grubby handkerchief that he carried," she recalled, "which he chewed the corners of, and he tucked it in my apron. I knew that was his mark of approval, a sort of good luck token. In all the things I've done for him, I've had that handkerchief tied around me in so many strange places."

Lee was so intimidated by Ford when she began *How Green Was My Valley* that she failed to mention that she was pregnant with twins. "I'd heard all those stories about how rough he was," the actress said, "but he was charming to me." The only exception came when he found her putting on lipstick one day, which he thought spoiled her looks. "Ford bawled me out for that in front of everybody," she remembered, "which is the way he would always do it."

After Bronwen's husband, Ivor, is killed in the mine, there is a scene in which she walks up the hill, struggling against the crowd to see her dead husband. Bronwen, who is pregnant, goes into a doorway, screams "Ivor," and falls. Lee did the fall and that night had a miscarriage, losing one of her twins. Ford was devastated, blaming himself for not knowing she was pregnant. He insisted that Lee have his doctor and came to visit her in the hospital during the five days she missed work. "He was so sweet about it," the actress said. "But I paid for it later, because every picture I did for him after that, he would wait until all the actors were on the set and all the crew was lined up. Then he'd call me in and say, 'Anna, I have to ask you a question, and I want a truthful answer. Are you pregnant?' He never let me forget."

Ford claimed he patterned the Welsh household in *How Green Was My Valley* on his own family. "I was right at home," he said. "A Welsh family is very close to an Irish. The mother, Sara Allgood, looked like my mother, and I made her act like my mother." Ford's niece, Mary McPhillips, happened to be visiting California during the making of the film and was on the set the day her Uncle Jack shot the wedding scene. "I remember meeting Sara Allgood," McPhillips said. "She almost looked like my grandmother." The similarity is interesting, since Ford gave Allgood a hard time during the making of the picture. Roddy McDowall and Anna Lee both recalled how tough he was on the actress. "He had a big beef on with Sara Allgood," said Lee. "She loved to argue and that was one thing you could never do with Jack Ford." He complained that Allgood didn't know how to cut bread and fought with her on petty matters throughout the production. Ford's hostility toward an actress fashioned after his mother raises questions about his true attitude toward Barbara. Underneath his docile exterior there may have been a resentment toward his mother he never allowed to surface. On the other hand, he may have felt that Allgood was an imposter who could never be an authentic Barbara.

Donald Crisp's performance as the Welsh father was patterned on Ford's memory of John Feeney. Crisp goes out to get drunk in the picture, and Ford acknowledged "that's a throwback to my father." At Angharad's wedding celebration Ford had Crisp sing an Irish drinking song. When scriptwriter Philip Dunne visited the set and complained that the actor should be singing something Welsh, Ford said, "Ah, go on! The Welsh are just another lot of micks and biddies, only Protestants."

Crisp was excellent in his role—stern and proud, loving and warm—and won an Academy Award as best supporting actor for his portrayal. Ford modeled the three older boys after his own brothers, Patrick, Francis, and Eddie, leading to the assumption that he himself identified with Huw, who, like Jack, was the baby of the family.

Not only does *How Green Was My Valley* possess a domestic glow, but the actors involved with the picture became emotionally connected in lasting ways. Roddy McDowall said that he adored Donald Crisp and came to look upon Maureen O'Hara as a true sister. O'Hara and Anna Lee became friends, and O'Hara named her daugher Bronwen. Forty years later McDowall telephoned Lee on the anniversary of the picture's completion and still called her Bronwen. "I think it's a very fine film," McDowall said, "but I'm so nostalgically and subjectively associated with it that I can't look at it objectively. Ford created such an extraordinary sense of being together; he was an authority figure, but in the best possible sense of the word."

How Green Was My Valley was filmed in eight weeks, a short schedule for a major production. "There was hardly ever a retake," McDowall declared. "I can't ever remember a scene running more than four or five takes." Cameraman Arthur C. Miller, who won an Oscar for his work, claimed that he scarcely used a foot of film that wasn't in the final print. "Ford would make the best picture for less money than anyone I knew," he said. "He concentrated on the entire picture at all times — never on a single day's work." Miller insisted that Ford was the fastest director he had ever worked with. "I've had people offer me money to give them the formula that Jack Ford used to direct," Miller declared. "But he had no formula."

Philip Dunne confirmed that Ford had shot the exact script that Wyler had helped prepare, yet still managed to put his stamp on the finished film. "His prints are all over it," said Dunne. "It is shot in his inimitable style, and he contributed at least one of the touches that made the picture memorable — in the final sequence having Huw sing his father's name as he searches for him in the flooded mine."

Ford admired Dunne, and the writer was insightful enough to realize that the director's insults meant approval. "Jack's courtesy to any individual was always in inverse ratio to his affection," wrote Dunne. "I knew Jack liked me, because in all the years I knew him intimately he never said a polite word to me, not one." Whenever the writer appeared on the set, Ford had his cast and crew line up and sing, to the tune of "The Farmer in the Dell":

> We haven't changed a line,
> We haven't changed a line,
> It's just the way you wrote it,
> We haven't changed a line.

Ford admitted that he added a few flourishes of his own. "That's what a director is for," he said. "You can't just have people stand up and say their lines. There has to be a little movement, a little action, little bits of business." What he did was extend Dunne's portait of family unity, seen through the eyes of a boy learning about life and love. While the director was fearful of showing sensitivity in private, he had no such reluctance in his art. *How Green Was My Valley* is full of sentiment, tenderness, and sorrow, all honestly played. What is missing, and is missing in all of Ford's films, is a sense of realistic sexual relationships.

In Ford's world the male led, the female followed, and important aspects of life, outside the home, were seen in masculine terms. "Jack always preferred to make pictures about men," Philip Dunne wrote, "if possible two strong men who are either friendly enemies or inimical friends. In studio shorthand, we called these stories 'love stories between men,' implying nothing homosexual by the phrase, but merely describing a muscular, masculine story."

Having spent weekends aboard the *Araner*, Dunne understood that Ford was most comfortable in a masculine setting. Anchored off Catalina Island, the Irish writer and director often bored Ford's other guests on the yacht, "assuming they were sober enough to notice, by delving, over a bottle, into the mysteries of Irish folklore," Dunne said. "We tended to grow more Irish as the level in the bottle sank."

How Green Was My Valley was finished in August 1941, and the recently promoted Commander Ford was ordered to Washington, D.C., a few days later. The film was edited and prepared for release by Darryl Zanuck. The studio's editors were stunned by the picture's impact (one claimed he cried every time he watched certain scenes), while Philip Dunne remained in awe of Ford's treatment of his script. "The warp and woof of comedy and tragedy were expertly knit into a single glowing tapestry of drama," the writer said. Alfred Newman composed the picture's score, music that was masterly by itself. "Congratulations on what I hear, through latrine gossip, is one of your best musical scores to date," Ford wrote the composer from Washington.

The film premiered at the Rivoli Theater in New York on October 28, 1941, as a benefit for the Navy Relief Society, with Ford in attendance. Critics hailed its poetic charm and dignity, acclaiming it one of the outstanding pictures of the year. In February *How Green Was My Valley* won the Academy Award for best movie of 1941, beating Orson Welles's *Citizen Kane*, and earned Ford his third Oscar for best direction. Ford also won the New York Film Critics Award, his fourth, placing him at the apex of his profession. *How Green Was My Valley* established Maureen O'Hara as the definitive Ford heroine, much as *Stagecoach* had established John Wayne as a male hero. After the war the director would pair the two on the screen; their exceptional rapport was the closest Ford ever came to achieving a believable sexual combination.

The fall of 1941 found Ford in Washington, D.C., staying at the Carlton Hotel and strutting his navy uniform. With the support of Merian Cooper, Ford's Field Photographic Unit had been accepted intact into the Office of Strategic Services (the OSS, forerunner of the CIA), a newly formed intelligence organization headed by Colonel William J. "Wild Bill" Donovan. On the assumption that film could be an effective propaganda tool, the unit was assigned an operating budget of $5 million for its first year. Ford was accountable to Bill Donovan, who in turn reported to the president of the United States. The task of the unit was to make photographic reports, including combat photography, outside the United States. "Our job," Ford told a reporter, "was to photograph, both for the record and for intelligence assessment, the work of guerrillas, saboteurs, resistance outfits. . . . Besides this, there were special assignments."

Ford broke every rule, but loved playing navy. He seldom hesitated to exploit his status as a Hollywood dignitary to achieve his ends, and he delighted in running his own movies for the navy brass and other distinguished personnel. He accepted an invitation to dine with President and Mrs. Roosevelt at the White House the evening after *How Green Was My Valley* opened in New York. He used his influence to get his friend Jack Pennick assigned to his unit, despite the actor's advanced age and physical shortcomings.

Meanwhile Mary stayed in Hollywood, telephoning her husband frequently, until he objected. "Honey," Jack wrote on October 2, "it was swell hearing from you last night, but, Ma, you can't call up long distance just when you're blue and lonesome. It's just too damned expensive. We've really got to adjust—not financially necessarily, but mentally."

Ford spent time in Washington with Helen Hayes when the actress opened there in Maxwell Anderson's potboiler *Candle in the Wind*. "It was my habit when I played in Washington," Hayes recalled, "to go out and take a look at the Lincoln

Memorial." Ford came to see her play and invited Hayes out to dinner afterwards. She suggested instead, "Come over to the Lincoln Memorial with me, because the moon is out and I'd love to look at it." The two drove to the famous memorial and sat on its steps. "We had been so calmed by this beautiful, peaceful sight," Hayes remembered, "but I finally said, 'Now, Jack, tell me about the performance.'" Ford looked at her with affection, but said, "Baby, do you stink!" Hayes laughed at the memory, then added, "Well, that was Jack."

With war approaching, friends contacted Ford about enlisting in his photographic unit. George O'Brien, already in the California National Guard, asked for a transfer to Ford's outfit, but authorities denied the request. O'Brien ended up teaching boxing to recruits. Stuntman Yakima Canutt wrote Ford on October 17: "If you decide to put a Running W [horse fall] on either Hitler, Mussolini, or some of the Japs, I will do the job for a very reasonable adjustment."

In November Jack met Mary in Portland, since their son, Patrick, had enrolled at the University of Maine. Jack, in uniform and wearing tinted glasses, announced to hometown friends, "I'm in the navy now." Interviewed by a local newspaper, he turned lyrical. "What is the heart of Maine?" he asked. "The sea. The sea washes right up to our doorsills here."

Later that month Colonel Donovan gave Ford his first assignment. Ford was ordered to make a filmed report on the strength of the fleet escorting convoys between the United States and Iceland, an assignment he promptly completed. Shortly after the bombing of Pearl Harbor, he was instructed to fly to Miami and proceed to the Panama Canal Zone. Over the New Year's holiday Ford and a Field Photographic camera team filmed the Canal Zone's major installations for President Roosevelt. "Somebody had to be assigned to go down there and bring back an accurate account of what the hell was going on," said film editor Robert Parrish, a member of Ford's outfit. "It was better that it wasn't an army unit or a navy unit, because the fear was that they would cover things up." Ford was instructed not to report to the military brass in Panama, but to return to Washington with up-to-the-minute information on the armaments protecting the canal.

In February 1942 Ford turned the *Araner* over to the U.S. Navy for the duration of the war. For the next three years the yacht was used as an antisubmarine patrol vessel off the coast of California. Mary Ford meanwhile kept busy at the Hollywood Canteen, while John Wayne and Ward Bond served as air raid wardens in Los Angeles. "How does Uncle Ward look with a tin hat and a pair of binoculars?" Ford wrote Wayne in January. Four months later Wayne, eager to enlist, asked Ford by letter, "Have you any suggestions on how I should get in? Can I get assigned to your outfit, and if I could, would you want me?"

By February 24 Ford was in Hawaii, requested by the president to take pictures of the war in the Pacific. "Well, here we are in Honolulu," he wrote Mary from the Moana Hotel, two months after the attack, "and 'my gawd' you'd never recognize it. . . . The trip over was uneventful but very exciting. Our gang had to stand watches, and they made me very proud and happy."

Ford and Gregg Toland filmed footage for a documentary on the December 7th bombing. When Japanese messages were intercepted revealing that the next strike would come at the American base on Midway, the OSS asked Ford to fly to the island and photograph the attack. Every plane and vessel the United States could muster was sent to the central Pacific. Although heavy casualties were expected, Jack wrote Mary from Midway on June 1: "This is some place, really fascinating. . . . The morale here is extremely high and the food is really delicious—best I've had in the Navy."

Three days later, early in the morning, before Ford was dressed, the Japanese struck. Wave after wave of aircraft bombed and strafed the island. From atop a tower, Ford filmed the battle with a hand camera, his sense of drama intact under fire. All around him bombs were dropping, while a fuel dump belched smoke and flames. He photographed the faces of marines fighting near him, capturing their excitement as well as their fear. He filmed an American flag being raised in the midst of combat. "I photographed that from the tower," said Ford. "It actually happened—eight o'clock, time for the colors to go up, and despite the bombs and everything, these kids ran up and raised the flag." The colors traveled up the pole and hung limply at the top. Then, as if on cue, the flag billowed out.

As Ford descended from the tower, a close hit knocked him unconscious. He revived and continued photographing the surrounding fury until his upper left forearm was splintered with shrapnel. He was forced to seek medical attention before resuming his duties. The siege lasted until June 6, with the Japanese task force suffering a critical defeat. The victory had been costly for the United States, but by holding Midway the United States had secured control of the central Pacific and gained vital time. Ford spent days photographing the damage to American naval installations and hospitals. On June 8 he sent a terse telegram to Mary. "OK," he wired. "Love, John Ford."

Ten days later he was back in Los Angeles. "Commander John Ford of the United States Navy is Hollywood's own personal hero," Louella Parsons announced in her column. "John got back from Midway Island Tuesday night with a shrapnel wound in his arm, which was swollen to twice its natural size." He flew on to Washington, D.C., but told reporters that he was under strict orders not to discuss the recent American victory.

Ford showed up at OSS headquarters with his left arm bandaged, needing a shave, and looking as though he hadn't slept in a week. In Hollywood he had obtained a rush print of the footage taken on Midway—eight cans of color film. "He summoned me to the projection room," Robert Parrish recalled, "locked the door, and put an armed guard outside while we viewed the film." When they finished, Ford asked the editor if he thought he could make a twenty-minute documentary from the material at hand. Parrish asked if he wanted a factual account or a propaganda film. "It's for the mothers of America," Ford replied. "It's to let them know that we're in a war and that we've been getting the shit kicked out of us for five months, and now we're starting to hit back."

Parrish found some of the shots thrilling. There were touching scenes of American boys being buried at sea, as well as American pilots taking off from Midway airstrips to bomb the Japanese fleet. The editor saw no reason why he couldn't assemble a moving film. Ford insisted he not work in Washington. "As soon as it's discovered in Honolulu that I've smuggled the film past the navy censors," said Ford, "they'll come snooping around with enough brass to take it away from us." He told Parrish to take the film back to Hollywood. "Don't report to anyone," he said. "Go to your mother's house and hide until you hear from me."

Parrish did as he was ordered, and was joined a few days later by Ford. They ran the film in California for screenwriter Dudley Nichols, who agreed to furnish a narration. "Get a sleeping bag," Ford told Parrish, "and lock yourself in your cutting room. I'll have some sandwiches sent in to you." For forty-eight hours Nichols wrote day and night on a text, while Parrish and a sound editor worked with an armed guard outside their editing room. When a rough cut was ready, they screened it for Ford in a locked room with a marine standing watch. Henry Fonda, Jane Darwell, and Donald Crisp recorded the narration, and Ford rushed the film to President Roosevelt, who approved it. Five hundred prints were made and sent to theaters across the country.

The Battle of Midway opened in New York at Radio City Music Hall on September 14, 1942. Critics were enthusiastic, finding the eighteen-minute film realistic but moving. Although Ford's footage was more propaganda than documentary, it was the first cinematic evidence that American forces might win the war in the Pacific. Not only was the picture well received, but it served to boost morale on the home front. At the Academy Awards ceremony the following spring, *The Battle of Midway* won an Oscar for best documentary short subject of 1942.

A month before his Midway picture reached the theaters, Ford returned to Maine to attend the wedding of his son, Patrick. While at the university there, Pat had met and fallen in love with Jane Mulvany, a fellow student. "Jane is really pretty and adores our Pat," Mary had written Jack earlier. "The first Maine girl I've met who thinks a 'diamond' is crap."

Soon after his son's marriage, Ford departed for England with his unit's executive officer, Ray Kellogg. "Well, here we are safe and sound," he wrote Mary from Claridge's in London. "Had a wonderful trip over." Before leaving Washington he had asked Bob Parrish to bring a print of *The Battle of Midway* to England as soon as one was available, since the OSS had asked Ford to show the British Admiralty that the United States was in the war, too. Parrish recalled screening the film for top British officers. Afterwards, when one of the admirals commented that the victory at Midway could hardly be compared with the British triumph at Cape Trafalgar, Ford became indignant. He turned to Parrish and commanded, "Get the film and let's go." It was an embarrassing moment. "Ford wasn't afraid to speak up in front of anyone," Parrish declared. "He was a man with a considerable ego, but also he had made a movie that showed Americans being killed in the Pacific. For the British to make a joke of that was offensive to him."

Ford's mission in England was to prepare camera crews to photograph the upcoming invasion of North Africa. The OSS had established headquarters in London on Baker Street, and during the period Ford was there he often met his Irish friend Michael Killanin for dinner. Ford claimed he was imbibing in the Coach and Horses Pub on Bruton Street when the buildings next to it were bombed. He drank a great deal while he was overseas, and there were occasions when his alcoholism got out of control. Junior officers tried to hide bottles from him, but he had stashed them all over. Rumors drifted back to Hollywood that Ford had been discovered crawling in bramble bushes one night in search of booze he had hidden. Still his wartime associates attested that he took his duties with the Field Photographic Unit seriously. Mark Armistead, who had owned a camera company in Hollywood, recalled that Ford's first words to him in the navy were "Square that hat, sailor." Ford didn't always follow military regulations; he insisted that the important thing was to get the job done, which sometimes meant cutting through red tape. He told his men during training, "One thing I'll promise you. I'll never send any of you on a job I wouldn't tackle myself." He proved that in time.

On November 8, 1942, Field Photographic camera crews covered all three prongs of the North African invasion. Ford waited on Gibraltar during the initial landing, but entered the combat zone as soon as permission was granted. Accompanied by Jack Pennick and Ray Kellogg, he moved inland with an American tank battalion. They advanced to the front with a cinematographer and photographed an aerial dogfight. Three members of Ford's unit were killed during the campaign, and he himself saw a great deal of combat during the six weeks he was in the field.

Toward the end of November Ford was promoted from Commander to Captain in the Naval Reserve. The following January he was back in Washington, D.C., attending to administrative details for the Field Photographic Unit. He remained there until August 1943, spending much of his time with senators, congress members, and top-ranking military officers. But he grew bored. After *The Battle of Midway* won an Academy Award, Ford decided to resurrect footage he and Gregg Toland had taken of the Pearl Harbor disaster. Toland had acquired film that navy photographers had shot during the actual attack, along with coverage of the salvage operation. After Ford sent Toland to South America on OSS duties, their Pearl Harbor footage had been confiscated by the government and locked in a vault, since portions of it were thought to be controversial. In the spring of 1943 Ford found a negative of the film in his unit's offices, had a print made, and ran it.

The assembled footage was too long for a documentary, so Ford asked Bob Parrish to cut it down to a half hour, using only the navy material. He assigned Budd Schulberg to write a narration and asked Alfred Newman to compose a score. The result, entitled *December 7th*, was not released to theaters, but was shown in defense plants with the intent of inspiring workers to increase production and avoid strikes and absenteeism. In April producer Walter Wanger wired Ford: "Just had extreme pleasure of seeing your great picture on Pearl Harbor.

I think it is a triumph and exactly what people want to see."
While later generations would brand the film racist, since it
implied that Japanese Americans in all walks of life had acted as
spies, *December 7th* won Ford another Academy Award, for best
documentary of 1943.

In June, Jack and Mary became grandparents when Patrick's
wife Jane gave birth to their first son, Timothy. A few months
earlier the Fords' daughter Barbara had been tested by 20th
Century-Fox for the studio's forthcoming production *The Song
of Bernadette*, although she didn't win the part. Later Barbara
worked in Fox's editing department, where she earned a reputation as a knowledgeable film cutter.

In August 1943 Jack flew to New Delhi to oversee the filming
of *Victory in Burma*. From there he went to China to take
photographs that would prove valuable in coping with Japanese air attacks along China's coast. "There was a great deal of
hazard involved," said Albert Coady Wedemeyer, who accompanied Ford on the mission. "The Japs were all along the area,
and if we flew down low, naturally their antiaircraft would take
our planes in. We had fighter escorts most of the time for
Ford's aerial photography; he photographed two or three air
raids in Burma and China."

For months in advance of the Normandy invasion, Mark
Armistead and an OSS crew compiled photographs, postcards,
and eye-witness accounts of the European coast from Norway
south. Early in April 1944 Ford returned to England to supervise his outfit's coverage of the D-Day landing. The Field
Photographic Unit had been placed in charge of Allied photography, and Ford arranged to draw one of the toughest
positions himself on the day of the invasion. "Ford claimed to
have virtually liberated Normandy," Michael Killanin declared,
"but he had a great imagination."

Two weeks after the D-Day invasion, the bulk of the Field
Photographic Unit sailed back to the United States. After
months of vacillation, Ford had agreed to direct *They Were
Expendable*, a feature film for Metro-Goldwyn-Mayer. He had
read William L. White's stirring book about America's loss of

the Philippines and found it powerful. But he was reluctant to abandon his Field Photographic Unit for a commercial venture so long as the war still raged. His friend Frank "Spig" Wead, who had written the script for *They Were Expendable*, prevailed upon him, while the navy, eager to have the story filmed, agreed to release Ford from active duty while the picture was shot. Since Ford dreamed of creating a recreation center and retirement community—the Field Photo Farm—for his unit after the war, he told Metro head Louis B. Mayer, "I'll direct *They Were Expendable* if you'll pay me the highest price ever paid a director. I'll contribute it all to the Field Photo Farm, and I want you to contribute an equal amount." Mayer accepted his terms, agreeing to pay the director $250,000, which Ford used to establish a retreat for his unit.

Ford later claimed that he was ordered by the navy to make *They Were Expendable* and wouldn't have done it otherwise. But he had found the project attractive even before the Normandy landing. "Been thinking a lot about the story," Ford wrote from England, "and if the Channel job goes well, would like to come back and do it. Would like to get that dough to build a club house for the kids when the War is over. I frankly admit that I am getting as enthusiastic as hell about *They Were Expendable*."

Ford went on detached duty from the navy in October 1944 and began working with Spig Wead on a final script. Although the picture dealt with the overrunning of the Philippines by the Japanese, it focused on the American torpedo boats. Since Ford was a great admirer of Douglas MacArthur, he magnified the general's image in the film to messianic proportions. But his emphasis was on the men of the PT boats who evacuated army and navy officers during the fall of Bataan and Corregidor against heavy odds. While *They Were Expendable* showed a crushing defeat, the battle had intrinsic glory. "This is a fascinating story which would make any audience thrill with pride and excitement at the exploits of these lads who didn't seem to know what danger was," an MGM reader wrote in reviewing an early treatment.

Shooting on the picture began in Key Biscayne on Ford's

fifty-first birthday, February 1, 1945. Robert Montgomery and John Wayne headed the cast, with Donna Reed playing Wayne's love interest. Marshall Thompson, a young Metro contract player who was given a small role as an ensign, remembered how frightened he was of Ford. "He was a saga unto himself," said Thompson, "the most terrifying man I ever met in my life. He was a captain in the navy, and we had a lot of actual high-ranking personnel involved in that production. Ford would take the script and thumb through it and throw it away. Of course it was all a ruse, but he'd whip through the pages and say, 'Okay, I've read it. Now we'll do it my way.' You never knew what you were going to do next. Nothing was according to the script; he'd change it around."

About three days into the production the director called Thompson aside. Ford lifted the handkerchief he'd been chewing. "You've got a smudge on your face," he told the young player, and proceeded to wipe Thompson's face. "You could never understand him," the actor said, "because he had his pipe in his mouth, and you'd have to listen very carefully. You couldn't tell whether he was really looking at you or not, because he had on these dark tinted glasses. He'd mumble and say, 'I want you to memorize this.'"

The timid player would be sitting on the set with nothing to do, when suddenly he'd hear Ford call his name. Thompson would go running, only to have the director demand, "Give me your line!" It was always the same line, time and again. The actor would enter an elevator, and there would be Ford. "What's your line, Thompson?" he'd bark. Once more the actor would say, "Gentlemen, I want to tell you that we have been awarded the Silver Star," until the words became rote.

On the last day of shooting Ford said, "It's time for your line, Thompson." The actor delivered the words in a mechanical way, then understood that was exactly what Ford wanted. "I was flabbergasted," Thompson declared. "I was telling the men that they had been awarded the Silver Star, and nobody could care less. That was the whole idea. He wanted rote. That was the way he worked with everybody; he would trick you into performing."

No one denied that Ford was a power on the set, but most found him unpredictable. Character actor Leon Ames played no more than a vignette in *They Were Expendable*, but it was a small gem of a role. When Ames appeared on the set, Ford introduced him to the cast. "New actor," he said. "Played his whole part in *Meet Me in St. Louis* a foot out of focus and damn near stole the picture." Ames thought Ford strange, but brilliant. "He was gruff and rough," the actor declared, "but he knew what he was doing."

"Ford was an enimga," said Donald Curtis, an MGM contract player who later became a minister. "You could never tell when he would turn on you. But I liked him, and we all respected him. If he wanted a startled expression from you in a scene, he wouldn't tell you what he wanted. He'd wait until you got into the scene and then shoot a gun off right in back of you. Naturally you'd jump, and he'd get what he wanted. That was his approach. If you offered any creative suggestions, he'd get furious at you."

Curtis claimed that Ford bullied John Wayne as much as the rest of the cast, making "a quivering pulp out of him." According to Marshall Thompson, "Duke just worshipped Ford," and it was clear that Ford returned his affection. Ward Bond, also in *They Were Expendable*, had been struck by an automobile a short time before shooting began and nearly lost a leg, so his movements were restricted. "Ward was just held together with baling wire," Donald Curtis said. "It was all he could do to stand."

During the making of the picture Ford enforced his rule against drinking. Every night in their hotel he'd lay down the law to the cast and crew—no booze, no women, everyone in bed early. "He was a tough taskmaster," Curtis said.

Actor Robert Montgomery, just back from a tour of duty in the Pacific, wanted to become a director and offered a suggestion one day on how a scene should be played. Ford listened attentively, then said, "Let's try it." They shot the scene and when it was over, Ford asked Montgomery, "How did it feel?" The actor replied, "It felt good." Ford said, "Did you really like it?" Montgomery assured him that he did. Ford opened the camera, took the film out, handed it to the actor, and said, "Here, take it home with you!"

Toward the end of production Ford fell off a scaffold onto a cement floor, fracturing his left leg. He was hospitalized and missed a week's work. During that time Montgomery took over the set. Ford returned with his leg in a cast.

They Were Expendable wrapped early in 1945. Ford arrived in Europe in time to cross the Rhine with the Allied forces at Remagen. Postproduction on his picture was completed at MGM, not always to the director's liking. He objected to the film's heavy scoring, which he argued was inconsistent with the documentary look he sought to achieve. Although Ford claimed that he had tried to photograph events as they actually happened, *They Were Expendable* is better mythology than history. The theme of the film is not defeat, but the courage individuals can muster when faced with disaster.

As with all of John Ford's films, *They Were Expendable* has its poetic moments, marked with the director's personal stamp. An old trader who has spent a lifetime building his business, for example, refuses to abandon the post to the Japanese. "I've worked forty years for this, son," he says. "If I leave it, they'll have to carry me out." The trader is last seen in a silent shot, waiting on the steps of his shack, a whiskey keg at his side, his shotgun across his knees. "And the film waits with him," critic Lindsay Anderson observed, "till the scene dissolves to the river, with night falling, and the image fades."

MGM delayed releasing the picture until December 1945. By then the war was over, which diminished the story's appeal. *They Were Expendable* opened to good reviews, but limited audiences. "People had seen eight million war stories by the time the picture came out," John Wayne said, "and they were tired of them. But this is the only picture I ever felt Jack put a message into." If the film had been released a year before it would probably have been a hit. Most reviewers agreed that its battle sequences were breathtaking. James Agee, writing for the *Nation*, said the picture was "so beautiful and so real" that he didn't feel "one foot of the film was wasted." Later critics would place *They Were Expendable* among Ford's most evocative films, claiming it announced the director's deepening sense of loss. Ford himself thought there were "some great things in it," but maintained he never saw the completed version.

In April 1946, with the money Mayer had paid him, Ford purchased eight acres in the San Fernando Valley, near Encino, which became the Field Photo Farm. The farm was a combination recreation center and retirement community for the 180 men who had served in the Field Photographic Unit; it also was a memorial to the thirteen men in the unit killed during the war. (Shortly after the land was purchased a sign went up at its entrance—"NO WOMEN EXCEPT ON VISITOR'S DAY." Ford's vision was that the farm should be an extension of the navy—and exclusively male.)

The property contained white wooden buildings, including a six-bedroom colonial house, a barn that became an interdenominational chapel, and a tack room. Ford's youngest grandson, Dan, recalled the Field Photo Farm as a child's paradise. "I remember the barn, the smells of the tack room, all the bridles and collars, the oats, and the smell of the hayloft," Dan said. "There was a parade ground with an old cannon on it, and my brother Tim and I would fight a million battles with that cannon." There were horses, corrals, tennis courts, a baseball field, a swimming pool, and a clubhouse with a bar and pool tables.

On Memorial Day the families of the Field Photographic Unit, along with Ford's friends, would gather at the farm for a ceremony beside the flagpole. The names of the thirteen men killed in battle were called out, and after each name the men in formation responded, "Died for his country." Through the years the list grew to include others Ford liked or admired, such people as Harry Carey and John F. Kennedy. After each name read, the Memorial Day participants still would respond, "Died for his country."

Every year there was an afternoon Christmas party at the farm, during which Santa Claus arrived for the children in a stagecoach. There were weddings and funerals in the chapel, which had a bell on its roof and a hitching post out front. There

was a Founder's Day party, which became an excuse to cele-
brate Ford's birthday. Other gatherings were held regularly at
the farm, including meetings of Alcoholics Anonymous, although Ford didn't attend those. The farm was managed by a
board of directors.

The Field Photo Farm reached its peak during the early 1950s.
After that some of the land was sold to pay for upkeep. The farm
broke up in 1966, when the chapel was moved to the Motion
Picture Home. Some of Ford's memorabilia soon went up for
auction, and the money raised and the $300,000 received from
the sale of the property went to the Motion Picture Home.
"What happened was that people drifted off," Dan Ford declared, "drifted out of the business, as the motion picture business got smaller. People went on with their lives and started
raising families and forgot about the war—except John Ford."

When Ford returned to Hollywood in October 1945 he found
adjusting to civilian life difficult. He had received the Purple
Heart and the Legion of Merit, served his country honorably,
and realized that he was leaving behind the most rewarding
period of his life. "These men were the finest and bravest I ever
knew," Ford said of his Field Photographic Unit. He loved the
ritual and structure of the military world and felt accpted there.
After the war his obsession with the military tradition continued, and the cavalry became a fundamental order in Ford's
postwar films. Although his years attached to the navy had
meant financial sacrifices, since he was away from commercial
filmmaking, he had made scores of friends and proven himself
in a male-dominated world. The Field Photographic Unit was
Ford's middle-age adventure, permitting him opportunities to
be the John Wayne hero he had helped create for the camera.
His war experiences permanently modified his outlook. Ford's
postwar films are filled with nostalgia for military glory, male
camaraderie, and a sense of purpose. The changing society he
came back to seemed empty, lost, crumbling. Ford, the Hollywood iconoclast, returned home a far more cynical man; no
longer was he the populist crusader. He felt older, more out of
step with Hollywood than ever, demanding even greater independence and looking for answers in traditions from the past.

CHAPTER 7

Back to Monument Valley

IN 1946 the Hollywood studios reached their zenith; that year ninety million people went to the movies each week. John Ford had come home from the war with a commitment to 20th Century-Fox and was prepared to accept a commercial assignment. "Why don't you do a nice easy Western?" Darryl Zanuck suggested, cognizant that the mythic West still held undiminished fascination for moviegoers. "I can round up a good cast for you," he said. Ford and the Fox production head decided on *My Darling Clementine*, based loosely on the career of Wyatt Earp, mainly because Ford saw dramatic possibilities in the climactic gunfight at O.K. Corral. *My Darling Clementine* would be the director's first Western since *Stagecoach* and only his second in twenty years, but he was entering his most productive period in the genre.

Ford liked the concept of *Clementine*, especially after Zanuck agreed that the picture could be filmed in Monument Valley. The isolation and tranquility of Harry and Mike Goulding's trading post would be an ideal place for Ford to forget the war and readjust to civilian life. Besides, the director claimed to have known Wyatt Earp personally. "In the very early silent days," said Ford, "a couple of times a year, Earp would come up to visit pals, cowboys he knew in Tombstone; a lot of them were in my company. I think I was an assistant prop boy then and I used to give him a chair and a cup of coffee, and he told me about the fight at the O.K. Corral."

Earp did live in Pasadena during his last years and occasionally served as a consultant on Western movies, despite failing health. As Ford remembered, "He married a schoolteacher in Tombstone, and she was the boss of the family. . . . His wife was a great churchgoer. Every so often she

would go on these meetings and into Arizona, Utah, and New
Mexico, and Wyatt would sneak into town and get together
with the boys, have a few nips." According to Ford, Earp knew
Pardner Jones; the sharpshooter had been Earp's chief deputy
in Tombstone. The director said he liked for Earp to visit his
set, even though his appearance held up shooting. He and
Jones would leave at noon to find a bootlegger and come back
"swacked to the gills." Ford claimed to have had several conversations with Earp during those occasions. "I asked him about
the O.K. Corral," the director said, "and he pinpointed it for
me, drew it out on paper exactly how it happened." Ford vowed
that was the way he filmed the shoot-out in *My Darling
Clementine*.

Wyatt Earp became a close friend of Western star William S.
Hart and often visited Hart's Horseshoe Ranch outside Newhall. With the passing years the legendary frontier marshal
grew concerned about his image and wanted to correct the
"many wrong impressions of the early days of Tombstone and
myself [that] have been created by writers who are not informed." Earp wrote Hart on July 7, 1923: "I realize that I am
not going to live to the age of Methuselah, and any wrong
impression I want made right before I go away. The screen
could do all this."

His alarm continued as inaccuracies spread. "It does beat the
band how the truth will be warped and misstated over a period
of years," Earp wrote in 1924. He began working with a writer
to put his story straight, hoping it might be turned into a
screenplay. "Two of the original coaches, used on the old stage
line between Tombstone and Benton, have been located," he
wrote Hart. "I thought you might be interested to know this."
In 1928, with his health deteriorating, Earp received a letter
from author Stuart Lake, asking permission to write his biography. The writer came to Los Angeles to talk with Earp, by
then a balding, white-moustached old man. "[W]e had a very
enjoyable visit," the frontiersman reported, telling Hart that
he found the author "a nice, modest young fellow. Somehow,
when he went away, there was a feeling of assurance that he left
with me; I like him very much. He is anxious to write the story,

wants to begin right away. . . . He writes in a modest and unassuming manner."

Stuart Lake's *Wyatt Earp: Frontier Marshal*, published in 1931, two years after Earp's death, proved to be a further distortion of the facts. Earp had grown disgusted with the film business before his passing, although two of his pallbearers were William S. Hart and Tom Mix. Whenever Hollywood filmmakers sought Earp's advice on silent Westerns, they paid little attention to what he told them. Colonel Tim McCoy recalled Earp's admitting to producers that he had never been a U.S. marshal and had "spent most of his days happily engaged in his profession, which was gambling." Once Earp realized that movie people weren't listening to the facts, he began regaling them with yarns that he had read in fictionalized accounts. "To his amazement," his wife wrote, "they swallowed these tall tales hook, line, and sinker, but were always skeptical of the truth." At that point Earp refused to have any more to do with those "damn fool dudes."

That John Ford gleaned anything useful from Wyatt Earp is doubtful. If he did, little of it found its way into *My Darling Clementine*, Western classic though the film became. Winston Miller, who wrote the script, admitted, "We made the whole thing up as we went along." All Miller and Ford knew when they started was that they were going to make a picture about Wyatt Earp and that it would end at the O.K. Corral. "I wasn't interested in how the West really was," said Miller. "I was writing a movie."

Miller had just gotten out of the service himself and was vacationing at the Coronado Hotel when he received a call from 20th Century-Fox, asking if he'd be interested in writing a picture for John Ford. "I'll be there in two hours," Miller told the studio representative. "The only thing I knew about Wyatt Earp was a book by Stuart Lake that I'd read," the screenwriter declared, "but we didn't use any of it in the picture. The reason that Lake got credit on the screen was that he had in his contract, when he sold Fox his book to make *Frontier Marshal*, that he had to get credit for anything made about Wyatt Earp."

Zanuck thrived on sequels and remakes. If a story was

successful once, it was worth telling again, and from the box office standpoint Zanuck's premise was valid. *Frontier Marshal*, directed by Allan Dwan, had been made in 1939 with Randolph Scott as Wyatt Earp and Cesar Romero as Doc Holliday. When Stuart Lake discovered that 20th Century-Fox was planning another Earp picture he contacted the studio, maintaining that he hadn't told the whole story in his book. "The key to one whale of a dramatic situation I left out for very sound reasons," he said. "With the deaths of several persons since that time, I know that I am the only living person who knows about it." The Fox script department forwarded Lake's letter to Ford with a memo: "Wasn't sure the crazy bastard was still ticking. . . . He knows more about that Earp than any living mortal and might do you some good, so use your own judgment."

Ford decided to ignore the writer. "Some of Lake's book was interesting," Winston Miller said. "I wish I had been able to use some of it. The story had been made before at 20th, but we didn't even look at the picture. We didn't want to be influenced. We made up our own story out of whole cloth." Ford had his approach, his own pacing, and there wasn't room for extraneous material if he was to have time for his visual moments. "I didn't go in for subplots," Miller said. "That wasn't my field. I just followed the two main characters and concentrated on what happened to them."

Miller had worked for Ford before, not as a writer, but as an actor. In his youth he had played George O'Brien's character as a boy in *The Iron Horse*. After discussing *My Darling Clementine* in the director's office for four weeks, he saw Ford in a completely different light. "We both kicked ideas around," said Miller. "It was really a collaboration." They talked over every scene until Ford was certain that his signature was on each one. "He saw things through his own prism," Miller declared, "and nobody else had that prism." The writer experienced Ford's volatile side, too. "He could be the nicest guy in the world," Miller recalled, "and he could be the meanest. You never knew which was going to happen. Ford was a fascinating man because he played a cat-and-mouse game. Sooner or later he wanted to dominate you. He would try to maneuver you into an unfortunate position." The director put Miller on the defensive, set traps for him, only to humiliate him. "Ford had a mean streak," the screenwriter said, "there's no doubt about it. He was the boss and made a dictatorship look like a weak democracy, as far as his authority was concerned. But he was exciting to work with on a script."

Ford thought in terms of scenes. One day he was seated across from Miller, chewing his dirty handkerchief, when he said, "I always wanted to do a scene of a whore's funeral in a small western town. The casket is on a wagon, and it starts down the street on the way to the cemetery. Only the madam and the other girls are following it. As the casket goes down the street, different men look out of their store windows and their consciences get the better of them. Finally they fall in behind the wagon. Pretty soon all the men in town are following the casket." Miller answered, "That's fantastic. I love it." Ford repeated, "I always wanted to do a scene like that." They planned the scene for Chihuahua, the Linda Darnell character in the picture, then Miller decided it wouldn't work because Chihuahua wasn't a whore with a heart of gold. Ford kept the idea in mind and used it in *The Sun Shines Bright* (1953).

Once the director and his scriptwriter had talked the story through, Ford began working with the art director on the design for a street to represent Tombstone, with the O.K. Corral at the end. Meanwhile Miller started writing the script. He and Ford met occasionally, but by then Miller understood Ford's style. "I knew that he liked lean dialogue, and that's the way I liked to write," the screenwriter declared. Ford suggested *My Darling Clementine* as the title, simply because he liked the song.

Darryl Zanuck supervised the finished script and during story conferences showed that he understood Ford and knew how to maneuver him. Once Zanuck suggested an incidental touch that Ford thought was corny. "Jack, if anybody but you were directing, I wouldn't have made the suggestion. But when I visualized it, I was thinking of the way you'd shoot it." Ford decided the notion had merit after all.

"Ford had a command personality like a general," Miller said. "He created a legend of himself, and he was great at playing the role he'd created. For a guy that chewed a dirty handkerchief all the time, he had the soul of an artist. It was well covered with an outer crust, but it was there. He had great taste and a great visual sense. Monument Valley was his territory; he had an artist's eye for that bleak desert terrain and shot it simply, no trick photography."

With the script of *My Darling Clementine* ready in March 1946, a bevy of carpenters, masons, and painters appeared among the pinnacles of Monument Valley to reconstruct Tombstone as the Arizona town supposedly looked in 1881. "I saw Tombstone pop up out of the desert like a rabbit from its hole," Harry Goulding said. "There, right in the middle of the driest spot on earth, were half a dozen big machines — bulldozers they were — ripping around through the soapweed and rabbitbrush." Lumber, including seven thousand cedar poles for corrals, was trucked in from Flagstaff. Instead of putting up fronts only, the carpenters built real buildings — but on just one side of the street. "The buildings looked fresh and raw when they were done," Goulding remembered, "until painters came swooping in. Then, in a few hours, you'd have sworn those houses were eighty years old." Among the structures in evidence were the Bird Cage Theatre, the Mansion House Hotel, and a reconstruction of saloons that had thrived in the "town too tough to die." All together the set cost $250,000.

The Navajo were paid to supply fifteen hundred head of cattle. "There must have been four hundred Indians setting up shelters all around the place," Goulding recalled. "They'd come from fifty miles in every direction." In May buses, cars, and station wagons brought in actors, seven hundred of them before the picture was finished. "To hear them try to talk to the Navajo was really something," Goulding said.

Since the making of *Stagecoach*, parts of other Hollywood films had been shot in Monument Valley: *Kit Carson* (1940), *Billy the Kid* (1941), and *The Harvey Girls* (1944). Movie work was a stimulant for the local economy. "You'll have the whole Hollywood gang here permanently at the rate you're going!"

Mexican Hat trading-post operator Norm Nevills wrote in 1943. "And that's what we want!" The Gouldings' post particularly had benefitted from the movie companies and groups of tourists headquartered there. The road into the valley was still just two wheel-tracks. "We'd have one of our cloudbursts, and that would wash it out," Mike Goulding said.

During the shooting of *My Darling Clementine* eighty people stayed in the red-rock buildings at the Gouldings' trading post, including Ford and his stars. The other six hundred or more were quartered in tents on the flat below. Breakfast and dinner were served either in the camp or at the Gouldings', whereas lunch was catered near the day's set.

The picture starred Henry Fonda as Wyatt Earp, Victor Mature as Doc Holliday, and Linda Darnell as Doc's Mexican girlfriend, with Walter Brennan playing Old Man Clanton. Darryl Zanuck had considered Douglas Fairbanks, Jr., for Doc Holliday, then thought of Mark Stevens, but chose Mature after the actor agreed to diet and stay on the wagon. To Ford's surprise Mature turned in a solid performance, although the director embarrassed him on numerous occasions for no particular reason. Jeanne Crain had been announced for the title role, but was eliminated when Zanuck decided the part was too small for a star of her current popularity. "We would be crucified by both the public and critics for putting her in it," the production head wrote Ford. "She is the biggest box-office attraction on the lot today." Ford replied that he wasn't concerned much with who played Clementine, "providing she doesn't look like an actress." They finally agreed on an unknown, Cathy Downs. Ford wanted black actor Stepin Fetchit for the role of Buttons, a night clerk at the Tombstone hotel, who brings a chair out for the marshal when the stagecoach arrives. Zanuck vetoed the idea. "To put him on the screen at this time," he contended, "would, I am afraid, raise terrible objections from the colored people."

Ford liked working with Henry Fonda because Fonda's pace was compatible with his. The director could hold a camera on Fonda, and although the actor's face didn't move, audiences knew what he was thinking. Ford liked Fonda's walk, which was unique since he didn't swing his arms. The actor enjoyed working in Monument Valley and remembered *My Darling Clementine* as an exceptionally happy film. "It was Ford at his best," Fonda said.

The director wanted Wyatt Earp played in a restrained, dignified manner that contrasted with the brusqueness of the Clantons. Linda Darnell was made up to look like Hollywood's concept of a Mexican dance-hall girl, with her part expanded to accomodate Darnell's star status. During location shooting Ford rode Walter Brennan to the point that the veteran actor claimed he'd never work for the director again. He never did, even though the three-time Academy Award winner's performance in *Clementine* was outstanding. "Everything in film acting is thinking," Brennan declared. "The camera picks up what you think and not what you say or do." Ford couldn't have agreed with him more.

Ford brought with him to Monument Valley a cluster of his regulars: Ward Bond, Jane Darwell, Russell Simpson, his brother Francis, J. Farrell McDonald, and Jack Pennick, as well as cowboys and technicians who loved and feared him. "Ford was always surrounded by a lot of his group," Fox screenwriter Nunnally Johnson said. "John would chew on his handkerchief and tell some corny joke, and they'd all roll on the ground laughing." The Ford stock company was essential to the camaraderie the filmmaker was trying to achieve.

Each evening after the dining room at the Gouldings' lodge was cleared, the director and a half dozen of his gang would spend the evening playing pitch at an old table. Ford arrived on location with 150 silver dollars in a bag for their games. "He loved the sound of clinking money," Henry Fonda said, "particularly when he won. Ford cast his stuntmen and small-part character actors for their ability to play pitch." Every night the camp heard shouts and carrying on from the dining hall; quarrels there sometimes erupted into fights, although mostly verbal ones. "It was part of the fun of playing the game to argue and fight," said Fonda. The feuding was seldom as serious as it sounded, and rarely did blood spill. "That was just an outlet for those guys," Mike Goulding declared.

One night Ford, Fonda, and some of the rest were playing pitch in a hogan up on the side of a butte close to the post. Actor Tim Holt had developed a crush on Cathy Downs during the production, and the pair went walking in the moonlight down through the valley. "The dialogue from our pitch game hit those buttes and echoed back and forth," Henry Fonda said. "If somebody said 'shit,' you would hear it eight times in echoes. We didn't know that until the next day when Tim told us."

In the tents below the lodge, actors and crew members played cards at night. Victor Mature and John Ireland, who played Billy Clanton, shared a tent and ran around together. "Ford found out we were staying up until one in the morning playing cards," Ireland recalled. "After that, by ten-thirty or eleven o'clock they turned all the lights out so we couldn't play anymore."

Having the lights off didn't bother the Navajo, many of whom danced into the night, but showed up the next morning ready to work. In 1946 most of them were dependent on wage labor and welcomed the money movie companies brought into the reservation. Out of gratitude they adopted Ford as a tribal member, giving him the name Natani Nez, meaning "Tall Soldier."

The director arrived on the set each morning like a Titan surveying his territory. Harry Goulding drove him to the day's location, always calling him Mr. John. Ford was surrounded by ex-servicemen during the filming of *Clementine*, men like himself just back from active duty. Fonda had been in the navy; Victor Mature had served in the Coast Guard. *My Darling Clementine* was the first picture for all three since the war ended, so there was added bonding. Ford would arrive on the set, grab his finder (an optical device that showed the area visible through the camera's lens), and be ready to go to work. He drove his company hard, made demands that were unreasonable, yet commanded the respect of his cast and crew. "I think they loved him," Mike Goulding declared, "and they certainly recognized his knowledge. Mr. John knew how to bring out the best in everyone who worked for him."

During one scene the actors playing the Clanton boys were

to ride through town shooting guns near their horses' ears. Ford had a wind machine blowing to simulate a dust storm. Between the gunfire and the propeller stirring up dust, the horses became spooked and handled nervously. Since John Ireland was fresh from the New York stage and Grant Withers was uncomfortable in the saddle, the actors breathed a sigh of relief when the scene was over. With the take finished, they dismounted and handed their horses over to the wranglers. No sooner had they done that than Ford shouted, "Mount up boys. We're going to shoot it again." None of the actors looked happy, but Withers hung back from the rest. "Come on, Grant damn it, hurry up," Ford bellowed. "Which is your horse?" Withers gave the director a wary look and said, "The one with shit in the saddle."

Film students have dissected virtually every frame of *My Darling Clementine*, pointing out the tension between the community and the individual. Critics have interpreted the scene on the hotel porch in which Wyatt Earp, the outsider, balances himself on one foot, then the other, while tipped back in a chair as showing Earp's tentative position within Tombstone society. "If you told Jack Ford that, he'd have punched you in the nose," Iron Eyes Cody declared. The script called for Earp to sit on the porch, but to make the scene more interesting Ford told Fonda, "Lean your chair back and brace yourself with your feet." Fonda did what he was told. "Play with that a little bit," Ford instructed. "Pappy caught my movements with the camera," said Fonda. "There were things that he'd put in at the moment, little pieces of business, sometimes little pieces of dialogue, that were so right."

Earp's slow walk with Clementine down the street to the unfinished church has been viewed by critics as the marshal's gradual acceptance of organized society, while his awkward dance with her (the picture's civilizing influence) — a dance that grows in speed and grace as the marshal becomes more comfortable — has been construed as Earp's reluctant union with the community. "Without quite realizing what he has done," Joseph McBride and Michael Wilmington wrote, "Wyatt Earp has hewn a garden out of the wilderness."

Screenwriter Winston Miller took issue with this interpretation. Fonda had done the same dance in *Young Mr. Lincoln*, a funny hop waltz, and Ford loved it. "We wrote that church-social scene," said Miller, "so Fonda could do his dance. There was no secondary motive; Ford simply thought it made a good shot. He shot the long scene with the two of them walking because he liked to watch Fonda walk."

Each evening at sunset the company returned to the Gouldings' trading post, washed up, and waited outside the dining hall until Ford arrived and the dinner bell rang. Then those eating in the hall followed him inside, where ten people sat at each table after going through the line for food. The rest of the company ate in the camp below. Steak was served every night, although the vegetables changed. After dinner it was not unusual for Wingate Smith, Ford's assistant, to help out in the kitchen. Talking about work was forbidden during dinner, and no one was permitted to drink anything alcoholic. The director sat at the head of the third table from the door, with his bone-handled jackknife next to him, presiding over the company like a biblical patriarch. While they ate he told jokes, played pranks, and bragged about his athletic exploits. He could be as warm and caring in casual moments as he'd been stern and frightening on the set. Henry Hathaway, who also earned a reputation as a tyrant on the set, felt that an intimidating personality was a requisite for the job. "Look at the big directors," he said, "all of them are bastards." There were plenty who thought John Ford headed the list.

Yet a family spirit developed among the cast and crew of *My Darling Clementine*, which included the Gouldings and their staff. If Ward Bond (who played Morgan Earp) wasn't needed on the set, he'd help Mike Goulding out in the trading post. "When we needed a case of coffee, he'd bring it in and help stack the shelves," she recalled. Linda Darnell worked in the trading post, too. "I'm part Indian," she told Mike, "and I'd like to see how these Navajo are." The Gouldings found the actress a sweet, unaffected person. "Any day that Linda didn't have to work on the set, she was with me at the trading post," Mike said. "She was as pretty as could be and slept in our front bedroom."

Fonda seemed more reserved, a real gentleman. "I couldn't get close to him the way I did with John Wayne," Mike said, "but he was just as polite and dear as he could be." She felt that he was Wyatt Earp the entire time he was in Monument Valley, even at dinner. "We had a nice visit the day he was through with his part and ready to go home," she recalled. "He told me about his daughter Jane and his home life. I always thought he was trying to tell me, 'I have been somebody else all this time; now this is me.'"

The day Ford was scheduled to shoot the gunfight at O.K. Corral, he informed Mike that she should be on hand to watch. "So I made every effort to get there," she said. "That was all new to me." Although Ford claimed he depicted the shootout "exactly the way it had been," his was a cinematic version. The real Doc Holliday was not killed at the corral, but died of tuberculosis four years later in Colorado. Furthermore, James Earp was the eldest, not the youngest, brother; none of the Earps was killed in a rustling incident; the brothers had no cattle in Tombstone; and Doc Holliday was a dentist, not a surgeon. Since so many discrepancies exist between the actual Earp story and Ford's account, it is doubtful that the gunfight was enacted with much concern for accuracy. Old Man Clanton had died before October 1881, when the showdown at the corral took place, and none of the Earp brothers had yet been killed. "I'm sure Ford shot the O.K. Corral sequence the way he thought it worked best for the movie," Winston Miller declared.

By early June exterior filming on *My Darling Clementine* was completed, and Monument Valley returned to normal. "The troopers climbed into cars and rolled away in a cloud of dust," Harry Goulding said. "The Indians rubbed out their fires and scattered with the wind." Only the reconstructed town of Tombstone remained, an anachronism on the valley floor that disconcerted visitors who came to see the monoliths. The set was left intact and rented by the Navajo tribal council to other Hollywood studios who wanted to make motion pictures there, but after five years it was sold for salvage and dismantled. "You can still see scars of it," Mike Goulding said almost a half century later.

Ford and his company returned to 20th Century-Fox for interior work. The director remained enthusiastic about the picture, even though he made minor changes. When a rough cut was shown to Darryl Zanuck, he found Ford's pace too slow. "I authorized the expenditure of more than two million dollars," Zanuck wrote the director. "I authorized the number of shooting days that you requested, and I am sure that you will be the first to admit that I gave you every actor that you asked for, regardless of whether it was a bit or an important role. You have in the film a great number of outstanding individual episodes and sequences. You have a certain Western magnificence and a number of character touches that rival your best work, but to me the picture as a whole in its present state is a disappointment. . . . It is my opinion that in this picture we have to be *big time* all the way."

Zanuck ordered further alterations in the editing room, to which the director objected, claiming that he no longer felt the picture was his. In Ford's cut Earp had reached out and shaken Clementine's hand in the final scene. When a preview audience laughed, Zanuck ordered that scene reshot, so that Earp leaned over and kissed her on the cheek. "There was quite a sour note over Darryl's editing," Winston Miller said. "I never saw Ford's initial cut, so I don't know what Zanuck did. But Ford liked a deliberate pace; Zanuck liked a fast pace. I think John felt that Zanuck had destroyed the rhythm that was one of his trademarks."

"If anybody really analyzed that script," Miller said, "it violated all the rules. Earp comes to Tombstone, decides not to be sheriff, his brother is killed, and he stays to find the killer. It's the only reason he stays. For five reels he doesn't do a damn thing about it. He sits on the porch with his feet up, and you have John Ford vignettes. You have interesting scenes, but there's no urgency, just a lot of shambling around. It's not until toward the end that you get the clue that motivates the final part of the picture." Yet Ford and Zanuck made the story work, turning Western lore into a film classic.

The ingredients of *My Darling Clementine* fit the Ford mold to perfection. The story's simplicity allowed the director plenty of opportunities to digress. "Time after time," film critic Lindsay Anderson wrote, "he will halt the progress of a film to concentrate on a face or an attitude, not with the glancing stroke of one who makes an apt marginal observation, but with a deliberate enlargement of the detail until it seems to carry for that moment the whole weight and intention of the picture." Wyatt Earp, the mediating hero, is morally strong and fearless. His first step toward refinement is to visit Tombstone's barber, an indication of his latent impulse toward civilization. Earp possesses the Western hero's commitment to law and order, yet is reluctant to bind himself to an established community. He accepts the job of sheriff and makes decency and social progress possible in an untamed land. He sees the commitment through to a conclusion, then returns to the wilderness, preferring to live apart. But there are darker implications to his accomplishment; the name of the town is Tombstone, which symbolizes death.

For all of his lip service to community, family, and organized religion, Ford championed the loner who was free of society's shackles. He feared that communal pressures would weaken the outsider's power and independence. Wyatt Earp, as presented in *My Darling Clementine*, is the classic mythic hero, from whom something has been taken and who becomes involved in extraordinary adventures, yet reverts back to his original status in the end. Earp rescued civilization from primitive forces through superior frontier skills, aided by Doc Holliday, a renegade from culture with a death wish. An element of legend exists in all of Ford's Westerns, but *My Darling Clementine*, despite its deceptive simplicity, is among his most complex, open to interpretation. As the conquest of the West became the nation's creation myth, the saga incorporated elements of the American dream: equality, freedom, democracy, individuality, social harmony, open land, economic gain, change, rebirth—ideals that contain conflicts and contradictions among themselves. *My Darling Clementine* mirrors the stress within American civilization, pitting freedom against social responsibility.

This same conflict existed within Ford himself. As the son of

Irish immigrants, he continued to see himself as an outsider, who fit less into Hollywood society than he had into Portland's establishment as a boy. He demanded independence, yet functioned within the studio system, always resenting corporate dictates. While he rose to the top of his profession, Ford remained an iconoclast, fleeing on the *Araner* once the activity of his current picture was behind him. He could identify with the Ringo Kid and Wyatt Earp and his other Western heroes. While he became a force in Hollywood and set new standards of excellence, Tinseltown for him might just as well have been named Tombstone. In his view the big studio system spelled death to the creative spirit. Rebellion was the only way to achieve quality. So Ford remained ambivalent, professing respect for stability and orthodoxy, yet championing autonomy and insurrection—values so at odds that they could be reconciled only by a mythic hero, himself.

"Men like Wyatt Earp had real nerve," said Ford. "They didn't have to use their guns. They overpowered the opposition with their reputations and personalities. They faced them down." The director minimized violence in his Westerns, but recognized that those were violent times, when even the powerful couldn't survive by ordinary means. He also had learned that one didn't survive in the Hollywood jungle by normal procedures.

My Darling Clementine opened at the Centre Theatre in Salt Lake City on November 7, 1946, and at the Rivoli in New York a month later. It was hailed as a worthy successor to *Stagecoach*. Reviews noted the sensitivity of Ford's eye and his ability to create captivating moods, finding beauty among rugged people living in a rugged world. *Time* called the movie "horse opera for the carriage trade" and acknowledged that Ford had accomplished more than "an intelligent retelling of a hoary yarn." Walter Wanger, who had produced *Stagecoach*, wrote Ford: "Just saw *My Darling Clementine*, which made me sick because you didn't make it with me. I think it is wonderful. I haven't seen any picture I liked as much in years. You are still my favorite."

With his commitment to 20th Century-Fox out of the way, Ford eagerly turned to his own projects. Before the war he and producer Merian C. Cooper had talked about forming their own production company. Once Ford returned from the navy he and Cooper resumed their plans, creating Argosy Pictures in April 1946, shortly before Ford left for Monument Valley to begin *My Darling Clementine*.

By the close of World War II the film industry was no longer the freewheeling business it had been when Ford arrived in California. The frontier atmosphere of Hollywood had given way to a rigid corporate approach governed by profit motives. As contemporary life became saddled with bureaucracy, legalism, and urban sprawl, Hollywood's major studios evolved into factories, standardized to turn out enough product to fill the world's theaters.

Outstanding directors were not only eager for an increased share of the profits, but they wanted the independence to work on projects of their own choosing. To achieve this, William Wyler, George Stevens, and Frank Capra formed Liberty Films in 1945; Enterprise Pictures was launched by Lewis Milestone and others in 1946. When Ford and Cooper incorporated Argosy Pictures, they were following a trend that would result in a new Hollywood, one in which independent filmmakers predominated.

While Ford had little use for producers and often claimed that he had yet to discover what a producer did, he respected Cooper. The director demanded total control over artistic matters, yet sought to be free of financial worries; Cooper allowed him to have his way. Although the partners were opposite personalities, they got along with minimal friction. Cooper was well connected with moneyed people and took care of finances, while Ford directed and was the creative head of their company. "Cooper went along with whatever Ford wanted," said Bea Benjamin, who worked for years in the Argosy office. "Ford, on the other hand, was never involved with deals. He never even read contracts. I read them."

During World War I Cooper had been an aviator, flying with Eddie Rickenbacker. His plane was shot down, and Cooper was captured behind enemy lines and sent to a German prison camp. During World War II he served as chief-of-staff for the Flying Tigers under Claire Chennault, then as head of Douglas MacArthur's advanced echelon for aircraft in the South Pacific. When Cooper returned from active duty, he brought Ford a Japanese sword that he had picked up the day MacArthur landed in Japan. "Ford had respect for Coop's integrity, decency, and social position," John Wayne said. "Pappy liked that a lot more than he pretended. And he had great respect for what Coop had done in the war."

Cooper became president of Argosy Pictures, while Ford was chairman of the board. Initially the company had offices at Pathe Studios in Culver City. Ford later characterized Cooper as "a promoter and a hustler" and complained that he was a "glory hunter" and spent too much money. "My main quarrel with Coop, although we had few," the director said, "was that he had telephonitis. He'd get on the long distance phone and talk to Paris or Budapest and stay on the line for hours. He couldn't resist a phone." Others maintained that Cooper was a worrier and "a fussbudget," but all agreed that he had nerve. That's what it took to launch a successful film company in Hollywood.

"I think Ford envied Coop his incredible military record," Charles FitzSimons declared. "Ford was very much in love with the fact that he became a rear admiral in the navy reserve, because that put him into competition with his partner. Coop was a brilliant military man, so it was hard to compete. Here was a man who had lived the John Wayne life, and here was a man who was directing the John Wayne life. I think Ford would loved to have been born a military hero."

Ford unwisely decided to launch Argosy Pictures with *The Fugitive*, an artistic film consistent with his Catholic faith. Based on Graham Greene's novel *The Power and the Glory*, the story dealt with a priest hunted during the anticlerical phase of the Mexican Revolution. Dudley Nichols wrote the script, his last for Ford. "The war ended," Nichols remembered, "and I dropped my other work to script *The Fugitive*. We had talked about this project for years, but no studio would back it."

Disgusted with Darryl Zanuck's reaction to *My Darling Clementine*, Ford went into St. Vincent's Hospital in July 1946 for minor surgery, then spent a few weeks aboard the *Araner* convalescing. Meanwhile Nichols made progress on *The Fugitive*, following their earlier discussions. Henry Fonda recalled Ford's talking about the picture before the war and, at the director's request, had read Greene's book. Fonda told Ford that he didn't think he was right for the lead and suggested José Ferrer. Ferrer was set for the role, but by the time the film went into production, the actor had succeeded on Broadway in *Cyrano de Bergerac* and was unavailable. Ford then persuaded Fonda to take the part, although Zanuck balked at releasing the star from a commitment to 20th Century-Fox. "If you cannot hold your picture until February for him," Zanuck wrote Ford, "then you can do me a favor. Do not tempt Henry any farther." After much dickering the Fox production head agreed to delay his project and let Fonda make *The Fugitive* for Argosy.

Then came censorship problems. Dudley Nichols realized that it was impossible to follow the novel in his script, since the book deals with a priest who, involved with a prostitute, waivers between his holy mission and sins of the flesh. The Hollywood censorship office would tolerate no such characterization. "I suggested writing an allegory of the Passion Play in modern terms, laid in Mexico, using as much of Greene's story as we dared," said Nichols. "Ford liked the idea." So the priest became a disguised Christ figure, with Ford concentrating on the mystical aspects of the story. The director argued that the role was "one of the greatest parts ever offered to an actor." He liked the simple story, yet admitted to Zanuck, "It is really not a sound commercial gamble, but my heart and my faith compel me to do it."

In September 1946 Ford and Cooper left for Mexico by train to select locations. Shooting on *The Fugitive* began on November 4, 1946, at Churubusco Studio in Mexico City. Ford arrived with a script, no equipment, a half dozen actors, a production manager, and two assistants. The cinematographer, sound technicians, additional players, crew, and lab technicians he recruited from the budding Mexican film industry, and acquired sets, props, wardrobe, cameras, and sound equipment in Mexico. Among those hired were director Emilio Fernandez, who became Ford's associate producer, cameraman Gabriel Figueroa, actor Pedro Armendariz, and actress Dolores del Rio (all of whom had worked with Fernandez earlier). The picture was shot entirely in Mexico, with the cooperation of the Mexican government. Work was far from easy. "I am here in the wilds of Mexico directing a picture," Ford wrote Michael Killanin in January 1947, "and believe me when I say that it has been very, very difficult."

Back in Hollywood, right-wing gossip columnist Hedda Hopper heard that Mexican labor unions had forced Ford to employ Communists to work on *The Fugitive*, but Ford denied the charge. "All you have to do is to remember the theme of the picture," he said, "and you'd know that a Communist wouldn't touch it with a ten-foot pole. . . . The picture is anti any political party that forbade the complete freedom of worship."

Fonda continued to feel uncomfortable in the part of the priest. "I didn't like *The Fugitive*," he later declared. "Ford put those images in, the door open and the crucifixion poses," turning the film into a stylized, expressionistic art movie. Any disagreement with his approach turned into a fight. Fonda had reservations about one particular scene and mentioned his concerns. Ford heard him out and said, "Okay, we'll shoot it both ways—your way and my way." Fonda felt triumphant. They shot Ford's way first, whereupon he walked away. "I never did get to do it my way," said Fonda.

J. Carroll Naish, who played a police spy in the picture, was an actor who needed to dissect his character, but Ford refused to discuss motivation, which frustrated Naish. Throughout the filming the director continued to feel that he was making an important picture. "I honestly think we are making great progress," he wrote Dudley Nichols in December 1946, "and I also honestly think that the story is greater than even you and I first believed."

"I liked the script of *The Fugitive* enormously," said Nichols. "I don't know what happened in Mexico; I didn't go down with [Ford]. Perhaps he ran into insuperable difficulties. I saw

Henry Fonda when he returned, and he was unhappy and perplexed. He said he didn't know what had happened to Ford down there. To me, he seemed to throw away the script."

The picture was finished on January 27, 1947, and released through RKO. It opened in New York City on Christmas Day almost a year later. Bosley Crowther, writing for the *New York Times*, called *The Fugitive* "a strange and haunting picture," but one of "monolithic beauty," comparing it with *The Informer*. Critic James Agee listed *The Fugitive* among the ten best motion pictures released in the United States during 1947, yet the picture was not a commercial success.

Already the domestic market for Hollywood pictures was declining, and American audiences found the tempo of *The Fugitive* too slow. Producer Walter Wanger, on the other hand, told Ford that he thought it was the greatest picture he had ever directed, judging it "magnificent in every department." Wanger declared, "I haven't seen anything in years to touch it." Other filmmakers claimed Ford had indulged himself with religious symbolism and a turgid development of atmosphere.

The financial loss on *The Fugitive* meant that Argosy Pictures had to deliver a series of box office successes fast. Having thumbed his nose at convention, Ford settled on three safe, commercial Westerns—*Fort Apache* (1948), a remake of *Three Godfathers* (1948), and *She Wore a Yellow Ribbon* (1949). Meanwhile Merian Cooper concentrated on a project he hoped would equal his success with *King Kong* (1933), another special-effects yarn that Argosy entitled *Mighty Joe Young* (1949).

"When Cooper and I were starting our own company," Ford said, "I made four or five Westerns in order to make some money. They were potboilers, but they served a purpose." The films in Ford's legendary cavalry trilogy, which came out of that period, were far from potboilers, but neither were they the consciously arty films the director had intended *The Fugitive* to be.

If Ford didn't realize how much he needed Zanuck's fast-paced editing, Merian Cooper did and prevailed upon the director to turn loose of his films once principal photography was over. "Ford doesn't really understand scripts," screenwriter Philip Dunne once commented. "He has no story sense. He has a great sense of scenes. But Ford should never be the producer of his pictures." Without question he benefitted from a producer with Zanuck's story instincts and astute sense of construction.

Between directing and planning future Argosy projects Ford had little time for home and family. Mary had grown used to his absences, but Patrick and Barbara suffered from lack of their father's attention. By the end of the war Patrick had his own family, and Mary and Barbara spent time with Jack on the *Araner*. But he might also take along John Wayne, Ward Bond, Grant Withers, or other members of what they called the Young Men's Purity, Total Abstinence, and Yachting Association. The abstinence applied in name only, since the members spent weekdays in the steamroom at the Hollywood Athletic Club sweating out their liquor intake from the weekend before. Despite Jack's romantic notions of family, he gave little of himself to either his wife or children. "He wasn't able to," said Barbara's friend Joanne Dru. "Papa was not a nurturer."

Patrick entered adulthood lacking self-esteem, overshadowed by his father's accomplishments. He wanted to be like his father, yet didn't possess the talent. "I loved Pat, but always thought he was very inhibited," said Dru. "He didn't have the brain that his father did. He wasn't stupid, but Barbara should have been the son. She was brilliant." Barbara was also witty and attractive and adored her father. "It was sad," Dru declared, "because the family never really communicated."

Mary was an interesting conversationalist and a great storyteller. She and Jack occasionally gave dinner parties, but neither led a conspicuous social life during their middle years. Mary enjoyed her wealth and loved the racetrack, although Jack refused to go with her. She was fond of baseball and became an ardent Dodgers fan. Mary turned into a family person in later life, and although she had vowed she would never become a Catholic, she ultimately did. Aboard the *Araner* she played the role of the submissive wife. As Jack grew more volatile and quick-tempered, she became more gentle and diplomatic. "Mary was complex," Joanne Dru said. "I always felt she seemed rather bitter. She kind of did her own thing. Of course, alcoholism was very strong in that family."

"I would compare Ford's marriage to an old shoe," Charles FitzSimons declared. "I think they were comfortable with each other and that communication was there, but not necessarily in the sense that the average person knows it. There was understanding, yet they treated each other like an old shoe." Jack and Mary stayed in the same house for decades and were content to live without pretense. "After being in pictures so long," Jack told Hedda Hopper, "I consider myself lucky to have a house at all."

The Fords employed a black chauffeur until he died. By the end of the war Mary had given up driving, while Jack drove himself in a filthy car. The older he got, the more contemptuous he became of formal attire. He sometimes showed up for work with an old necktie around his waist as a belt. Even at his best he looked rumpled, and rumor had it that Mary resorted to stealing his coat to have it cleaned. On the rare occasions when he wore a tuxedo, it was old enough to have green on it. Pilar Wayne was introduced to Ford at a formal dinner. "He was tall," Duke's third wife said, and "wore glasses and a black patch over his left eye, reminding me of an aging, debauched pirate."

In public Jack's attitude toward Mary and Barbara was cold to brusk. He'd frown at Mary and tell her to shut up, asserting that women were suited best to cleaning windows and floors and raising children. "Don't speak unless I tell you to," he'd bark at her. In the time Pilar Wayne knew him, he treated other women as badly, although he could also be the epitome of Irish charm. "He had a strange, old-world quality with women," said Frank Baker, who worked with Ford often. "He was always very courteous with them. If you used bad language in front of women, he'd throw you right off the set."

Ford's friendship with Katharine Hepburn continued through the years on a platonic level. "We have fundamental respect for each other," Hepburn said, yet she continued to find Ford mysterious. "He has the most remarkable group of qualities that I ever met in anyone," Hepburn told his grandson Dan. "He's terribly tough and arrogant, but he's truly sensitive. You can see the sensitivity in his hands." The actress admired Ford for never concerning himself with what others thought. "Nobody has a career that lasts with the distinction of his who hasn't traveled his own trail," said Hepburn. "Most people have about a fifteen-year product that is of any interest; they never refill the reservoir." She recognized that Ford's navy experiences pleased him most. "He has taken an enormously distinguished artistic career absolutely for granted," she said. "He has the artistic point of view of an old Renaissance craftsman. He just could do it, without a lot of conversation. He had great faith in his work, and he had marvelous general knowledge of what was thrilling, what was beautiful, what was original, and what moved. Instinctively he had a gift for the picture business."

Once the work was done, Ford had difficulty keeping in touch with himself, and so he drank, partly to shut off his mind, partly to keep the euphoria of creativity going, partly from boredom. In his younger days, he could handle alcohol fairly well; after the war his binge drinking became a serious problem. "Mainly he drank around people he knew and could trust," his grandson Dan said. "He did it around Duke Wayne and Ward Bond. They'd all go off on a toot, and they all did it for the same reason. They couldn't drink and work; it had to be one or the other."

When Ford wasn't directing a picture, he'd occasionally play golf, although Katharine Hepburn claimed she beat him regularly. "We both belonged to the Lakeside Golf Club," screenwriter Winston Miller said. "I'd see him on the driving range with a patch over one eye hacking away." But most of his leisure hours were spent in private, reading and smoking nickel cigars he'd cut in half. Ford had a tremendous library, and there were always books stacked on either side of his armchair. Few who knew him doubted that behind his bucolic facade was a shrewd and sophisticated man, with no tolerance for foolishness.

Ford often acknowledged that he was blessed, that he had an

instinctive talent for filmmaking. "Yet he seldom talked about making movies," Charles FitzSimons said. Ford was not an analytical man and saw no need to verbalize what came to him naturally. He held no consistent political philosophy, voting through the years for Franklin Roosevelt, Barry Goldwater, and Richard Nixon.

While he was a dedicated Catholic in principle, in practice he remained a lax one. Ford went to mass only sporadically, and in conversations might make a sarcastic remark about the Church for effect. Yet he was charitable and had a number of friends who were priests. "I would say that Ford was a dyed in the wool, sentimental, spiritual Catholic, but not a practitioner in the everyday sense," Charles FitzSimons declared. "If you'd ever questioned his Catholicism, he'd probably have chopped you down." FitzSimons maintained that Ford had a need to oppose any form of establishment. "Had he been in the military on a permanent basis," FitzSimons said, "he would have resisted authority there. He would have ended up in the brig, no question about it."

Most of Ford's friends accepted that he was one of the world's great prevaricators. "Subconsciously he was always aware of the fact that he was lying," said FitzSimons, "and he would develop a tic. So you'd be talking to Ford and he would be exaggerating about something, and his eye would begin twitching. You knew immediately that he was lying. He wasn't lying in the vicious sense; he was lying in the daydreaming sense. He wanted what he was telling you to be true, yet he knew it wasn't, and the eye would give him away."

"Ford was an enigma," declared Robert Wagner, who met the director before he became an actor. As a youth Wagner had crewed on Humphrey Bogart's *Santana* and spent much of his time around boats. He remembered baseball games after the war with Ford, Bond, Wayne, and other Hollywood celebrities playing, most of them owners of yachts. "I had an opportunity to be around Mr. Ford," Wagner recalled. "I was a young kid, but Ford used to stay on his boat with those guys around and get loaded. He was a strange man. I don't think he had much of a life."

In June 1947, with *The Fugitive* awaiting release and *Fort Apache* about to go before the cameras, Ford received an honorary degree from Bowdoin College in Maine. The University of Maine had already awarded him an honorary doctorate, but the Bowdoin commencement gave him an opportunity to visit relatives in Portland and catch some shows in New York.

He wrote his friend Michael Killanin in Ireland, asking for snapshots of Spiddal. As early as 1946 Ford had planned to make a picture about Ireland called *The Quiet Man*, based on a Maurice Walsh script he had purchased and originally intended to film for Alexander Korda. "We will wander all around, shooting it in color, all over Ireland," the director wrote Killanin, "but with the stress laid on Spiddal. I will bring the principals there from America and pick up the incidental parts and bits in England and Ireland." Those plans would germinate for another six years.

Argosy Pictures must first be placed on a solid financial footing. In the years after World War II Westerns still had an assured popularity, and despite his success with other genres, Ford had become most closely identified as a Western director. "You can't knock a Western," he said. "They have kept the industry going." Ford thought to belittle Westerns as entertainment for illiterates was nonsense. "It's time those of us who make Westerns, or go to them, or enjoy them in any way, stopped ducking into dark alleys when the subject is brought up," he said. Through the decades he had developed an interest in the folklore of the West and had come to believe that, since motion pictures are served best by movement, a Western with action and sweep was a perfect vehicle for cinematic art. "There are no more clichés in Westerns than in anything else," declared Ford. "I don't think there is any aspect of our history that has been as well or completely portrayed on the screen . . . as the Old West."

Although his focus on Westerns in Argosy's early years was dictated by finances, the director lifted what had been dismissed as "horse operas" to epic heights. His portrayals were idealizations of the West, more myth than history, personalized views to teach moral lessons. "Fewer and fewer persons today are exposed to farm, open land, animals, nature," said Ford. "We bring the land to them. They escape to it through us." He felt that Western heroes had continued appeal because of the simplicity of their lives. "We all wish to leave behind us the civilized world," he told a French critic.

Fort Apache, Argosy's first Western, introduced Ford's cavalry trilogy. Far from being the potboilers he labeled them later, the trilogy stands close to the center of Ford's greatness. More than grand action entertainment, wrote film historian Michael Goodwin, "Ford invites us to join the men and women of the 7th Cavalry, to share their time and place in history, to dance with them, drink with them, die with them." The trilogy, seasoned with Irish humor and prototypes, reflects Ford's war experiences, his love for the military, and the sense of community he felt exists among fighting men and military families.

The cavalry pictures were based on short stories by James Warner Bellah that appeared in the *Saturday Evening Post*. Bellah believed that while the public was tired of modern warfare, they fundamentally liked war. What he created was a romantic struggle against an enemy that couldn't fight back politically or economically—the American Indians, whom Bellah depicted as killers, rapists, and thieves. "My father was an absolute military snob," said Bellah's son James Jr. "His politics were just a little right of Attila. He was a fascist, a racist, and a world-class bigot. I think my father had great contempt for Ford, not as an artist but from the social standpoint. He referred to Ford as a shanty Irishman and considered him a tyrant. But my father liked money. He disliked Hollywood; it was full of Jews and crass commoners, but there was money to be made in movie work."

Bellah wrote terse, forceful dialogue that could easily be adapted to films, while his language lent an authenticity to the Old West. *Fort Apache*, filmed under the title "War Party," was based on Bellah's "Massacre." Ford had read the story aboard the *Lurline* on his way to Hawaii. He told his daughter to wire Merian Cooper and instruct him to buy the movie rights. Although the names and setting were changed, *Fort Apache* became Ford's version of the George A. Custer legend.

New York Times movie critic Frank S. Nugent was hired to write the script, beginning an eleven-picture collaboration. When Nugent accepted the assignment, Ford handed him a list of fifty books to read—novels, memoirs, everything he could think of about the period. He sent the writer on a trip into Apache country to get the feel of the land. Nugent hired an anthropology student from the University of Arizona as his guide and drove to various sites. When the writer returned to Hollywood, Ford asked him if he thought he'd done enough research. Nugent answered yes. "Good," said Ford. "Now forget everything you've read and we'll start writing a movie."

Nugent proved a tireless worker and had his share of battles with Ford. According to James Bellah, Sr., "That was one of Ford's methods—to make people mad so they'd work harder." Nugent's approach was to write a rough scene, then send it to the director for comments. The writer usually sensed that Ford had an idea in mind, but didn't know how to develop it. "I've had the feeling often in story conferences that he's like a kid whistling a bar of music and faltering," said Nugent. "Then if I come up with the next notes and they're what he wanted, he beams and says that's right, that's what he was trying to get over." The screenwriter focused mainly on character development, aware that Ford detested exposition and would furnish much of his own dialogue. "He made me do something that had never occurred to me before," Nugent declared, "but something I've practiced ever since: write out complete biographies of every character in the picture—where born; educated; politics; drinking habits, if any; quirks." Ford didn't establish the close personal relationship with Frank Nugent that he had with Dudley Nichols, nor did he have the same respect for his talent. "Once the script is finished," Nugent said, "the writer had better keep out of his way. The finished picture is always Ford's, never the writer's."

While Nugent worked on the script for *Fort Apache*, Ford made a visit to Monument Valley to scout locations. He had developed an almost spiritual attitude toward the desert area that was becoming the definitive Western location. "I wouldn't make a Western on the backlot," Ford said. "I think you can say that the real star of my Westerns has always been the land." The image of cavalry soldiers fighting and dying amid Monument Valley's formations, with billowing clouds dwarfing the human drama, had an almost mystical appeal for him, suggesting a higher reality. "Jack lived in a dreamland," Charles Fitz-Simons said, "or rather he lived in Fordland."

When Ford was ready to hunt for sites, Harry Goulding met him at the train station in Flagstaff and drove him to the trading post, where he stayed in the guest room. Ford had grown fond of Harry and Mike and considered them true friends. Mike claimed that she never saw Ford's complexity, but admitted that she never looked for any. "I'm sure he knew that," she said. "We couldn't be anything but ourselves out here in the valley." When Harry was asked his opinion of John Ford, he said simply, "There was a human being."

Although Ford never became a serious student of the Navajo's culture, he respected their ways. His arrival on the reservation meant easy money for the Indians, and they were eager to work for him. "Mr. John would tell the Bradley brothers what he wanted the Navajo to do, and they'd get it done," Mike Goulding recalled. "The Navajo loved it when there was a movie coming. They'd travel in their wagons from a long way off. They wanted jobs, and they got a big lunch when they worked for Mr. John. He always said the Navajo were natural-born actors."

"When I come back from making a Western on location," Ford declared, "I feel a better man for it." He found peace in Monument Valley. "I like to get in the desert and smell the fresh clean air," he said. "You get up early in the morning and go out on location and work hard all day and then you get home and you go to bed early. It's a great life." Ford claimed that he remembered his Westerns with great affection because he enjoyed the outdoor life so much. "My grandfather's macho image was part of his time," Dan Ford remarked. "He was a Hemingway type of guy, a Bogart type of guy. He was a man's man—hard drinking, carousing—and he enjoyed the company of men over women. That's the way men were supposed to be in his day. The people associated with him were the same."

Much of the power of Ford's films stemmed from his attention to detail. Barbara Ford said that her father once told her that the director's hardest work was done before he arrived on the set, in planning. Ford made certain that several Irish characters appeared in *Fort Apache*, and he continued them throughout the cavalry series. "A lot of the Irish went west after the Civil War," he wrote movie censor Joseph Breen. "I'm quite enthused about [this] as a bit of Americana."

Upon reading Nugent's script Breen cautioned Ford about a scene with men working at a manure pile, urging him to photograph their work carefully "in order to give no offense." Breen also insisted that the scene showing two dead troupers spread-eagled should be shot so as not to be unduly gruesome. No toilet was to be shown on the screen, and scenes of drinking were to be kept to a minimum. Ford was instructed to stay in touch with Mel Morse, the western regional director of the American Humane Society, when scenes involving horses or other animals were filmed.

The Running W stunt technique—in which a horse's front legs were wired and the wire was attached to a stake driven into the ground, causing the animal to fall when it ran to the end of the wire, sometimes breaking a leg or tearing one loose—had recently been outlawed for horse falls in movies. A number of horses were killed as a result of the stunt. Later horses were trained to fall. "Those wranglers were tough cookies," stuntman Hubie Kerns declared.

Shooting on *Fort Apache* began in Monument Valley late in July 1947. Among the stunt performers Ford had hired was Ben Johnson, who doubled for Henry Fonda. Johnson had grown up on a ranch in Oklahoma and worked as a rodeo rider before entering movies. "I've been able to ride a horse ever since I could walk," said Johnson. "It's second nature to me. Riding is like dancing; it's all timing."

The horseman sat mounted behind the camera one day watching Ford film a speeding munitions wagon. When the wagon with three actors and a driver went around a sharp bend to the left, it turned over, dragging the men toward a rock wall. "If they had hit that wall, it would have cleaned them all out,"

Johnson recalled. "I saw what was happening, and I galloped in and stacked up the runaway." Ford came off the parallel from which he'd been watching the scene, walked over to the wreckage, and turned to Johnson. "Ben, you'll be well rewarded for that," he said. Two weeks later the stuntman received a seven-year contract with Argosy Pictures, his salary escalating to five thousand dollars a week. "Ford wasn't capable of being a Westerner," Johnson said, "but he was sharp enough to surround himself with people who were."

Fort Apache starred John Wayne, Henry Fonda, and Shirley Temple, then a young adult. All three made ten thousand a week for ten weeks, while Ford received a flat fee of $150,000. Wayne called the director Coach, while Fonda and others called him Pappy. In the years after *Stagecoach* Wayne had become a major star, yet kept a sense of humor about himself. "My father knew what space he occupied," Wayne's son Michael said, "but he used to say to me, 'Michael, when you start believing your own bullshit, that's when you're in trouble.'" Co-workers found the actor part bastard, part regular fellow, depending on his mood and the pressures on him. When making a Ford picture, Wayne surrendered himself to his mentor's direction, placing complete trust in him.

"Ford had writers write the script," said Wayne, "then he'd pull out three lines he'd use, lines that encapsulated what he wanted. When he pointed that camera, he was painting with it. He didn't just point it, he painted a picture each time. He didn't believe in keeping the camera in motion; he moved his people toward the camera and away from it."

Michael Wayne accompanied his father to Monument Valley to shoot *Fort Apache* and remembered his dad's coming into the barracks, where the boy was bunking with thirty or forty other guys, to take a shower. "It was very uncomfortable there," Michael recalled. "But I think that's the way Ford liked it. Crews worked six days a week on location. The only thing people could do in Monument Valley was work; there was no other diversion. But the rougher it was, the more Ford seemed to like it." Duke decided that his son brought him luck in pitch games, so every time Michael walked into the room where they were playing, his father would "shoot the moon" and win, infuriating Ford. "Get that goddamned kid out of here," the director would shout.

"The old man could get people fighting with each other," Michael Wayne said. "He seemed to like that. You never knew how you were being used. That's how he kept people on their toes. They didn't know when he was going to snap the trap. That's the way he controlled. I think he was sadistic."

Ford attended mass only sporadicaly at Blessed Sacrament Church near his home in Hollywood, yet in Monument Valley he brought a priest eighty-six miles over a dirt road to say mass every Sunday. Everybody was expected to go—Catholics, Protestants, and Jews. "Ford would pass the hat, watching to make sure you contributed," Michael Wayne recalled.

"What I remember most about Monument Valley," Wayne's son said, "were the nights. There was not a sound. Ford would have Danny Borzage play the accordion or someone would sing, maybe with no accompaniment. You'd be sitting out there listening, and there'd be lightning flashing. There you were with just a bunch of cowboys and Indians, and far off you'd hear Indians. If somebody was sick, they might be doing a sing."

Fort Apache was Henry Fonda's last picture with Ford for eight years. The actor played Colonel Owen Thursday, the self-absorbed cavalry officer who refuses to listen to advice and leads his men to defeat. Although Fonda had worked with Ford many times, he was still disturbed by the director's methods of achieving performances—sometimes being nice to actors, sometimes embarrassing them or making them mad, even causing them to cry. "I literally saw tears coming out of Henry Fonda's eyes on *Fort Apache*," Michael Wayne remembered. "He just turned and walked away."

Fonda also had qualms about Ford's foul language, and found his unwillingness to rehearse emotional scenes frustrating, but admitted that the director was responsbile for some of his best work. "Ford is a director who doesn't talk very much," Fonda declared. "If an actor came to him and wanted to talk about a scene, he would change the subject or tell him to shut up." Ford enjoyed being mysterious, liked surprises when shooting a scene, and not even his assistants knew what he was going to do next. During a scene on *Fort Apache* it began to rain, but Ford continued working. "You didn't see the rain on the screen," Fonda said, "but there was just enough moisture to highlight the leather on the harness and saddles, and it added a quality that was unusual. This was Pappy taking advantage of whatever presented itself."

The statement has been made that before meeting John Ford, Henry Fonda was a star; when they worked together, the star became an actor. Although Owen Thursday was among Fonda's least sympathetic roles, he was excellent as the tyrannical officer, stiff with gallantry and fiercely stubborn. "Henry was a real professional," declared Ford.

Shirley Temple hadn't made a picture with Ford since she was a child. In 1947 she was a married woman and pregnant. Ford adored her, allowing the young star to sit in his chair on the set, which no one else dared to do. Actress Anna Lee remembered shooting the scene in which the troupers ride off to their death while their women — Anna Lee, Irene Rich, and Shirley Temple — stand on a deck and watch them disappear. Discharge papers for Lee's husband arrive, but she doesn't call him back, knowing he'd rather die a hero. Her dialogue was "I can't see them anymore. All I can see is the flags." After the scene was shot, Temple piped up, "I don't think that's good grammar. It should be 'All I can see *are* the flags.'" Anna Lee and Irene Rich stood frozen, expecting Ford to explode. Instead he smiled and said, "Where did you go to school, Shirley? Did you graduate?" Everyone on the set had a good laugh, but the line remained unchanged.

Temple's husband, John Agar, was in the picture, too, playing his wife's love interest. *Fort Apache* was Agar's first movie, and Ford rode him unmercifully, as he tended to do with "pretty boy" actors. "He ate John Agar alive!" stuntman Gil Perkins remembered. "There was nothing this poor kid could do that was right. Ford just chewed him up one side and down the other." Whether Ford resented Agar's marriage to Temple or was testing his manliness is difficult to determine. Ben Johnson thought, "He just did it for damn meanness." Psychologists might suggest that Ford feared the feminine side of himself and lashed out at "pretty boy" types as an affirmation of male dominance. An even darker interpretation might infer that the director's need for dominance was a form of seduction.

Several of Ford's associates claimed that he was terrified of women, or held them in low regard, despite his courtly manners, expecting women to be pretty and docile. Anna Lee thought that Ford liked and respected women who were honest—no-nonsense women such as Katharine Hepburn and Maureen O'Hara. Lee herself had a warm relationship with Ford, which took the form of affectionate kidding. On *Fort Apache* the director kept her on the deck in the sun waving to vanishing troupers so long that she fainted. "I've got a bad head for sun," Lee said, "and I woke up in John Wayne's arms, which was lovely." Wayne carried the actress down from the deck, and the first thing Ford said when she came around was, "Anna, are you pregnant?" He'd never forgotten what happened on *How Green Was My Valley*.

George O'Brien and Ford were reunited on *Fort Apache*. The two hadn't been friends since their trip to the Philippines together over fifteen years before. By 1947 O'Brien's career had tumbled and his marriage was in trouble. His wife, actress Margarite Churchill, went to Ford and begged the director to give George a part in his next movie. Ford said, "I wouldn't give that son of a bitch a part if he were the last actor on earth after what he did to me in the Philippines." O'Brien's wife knew Ford well enough to reply, "Jack, if you don't do this, it will mean the ruin of a good Catholic family." Ford cast O'Brien as Captain Collingwood, a supporting role. After that the two resumed their friendship.

Ward Bond played Sergeant Major O'Rourke in the film but harbored ambitions of becoming a romantic lead, much to his friends' amusement. All through the making of the picture he kept complaining, "Duke is playing my part." Ford nicknamed him "Big and Double Ugly," which invariably brought a reaction from Bond, again to everyone else's delight. Many members of Ford's stock company were included in the cast:

Pedro Armendariz, a warm, outgoing man; Jack Pennick, an actor and Ford's assistant; Victor McLaglen, playing a sentimentalized Irishman—boozing, brawling, bragging; the director's brother Francis, always in need of money; Grant Withers, who committed suicide a short time later; and others who needed little direction, since they'd worked with Ford so many times.

The director also brought along his cadre of wardrobe people, makeup artists, and craft workers. "They were talented people," Michael Wayne said, "and had to be good, because Ford would be on their case if they weren't." He felt obligated to hire certain ones whenever he could, aware that they might not work if he didn't. Danny Borzage was a mainstay of any Ford set, playing the director's favorite tunes on his accordion to keep the excitement going between takes. "Ford would hire Danny for a picture as a bit player in order to have him around every day," Charles FitzSimons said.

Even among Ford's regulars tensions existed. Archie Stout, whose son Jay had been killed in the Field Photographic Unit during the war, served as cinematographer on *Fort Apache*. Stout argued with Ford repeatedly on the picture and even refused to shoot certain scenes the way the director wanted. The next time the cameraman worked for Ford he was reduced to second-unit work. John Wayne didn't care for Eddie O'Fearna, Ford's brother, who worked as second assistant and herded extras, but Ford and O'Fearna didn't get along too well either. "Eddie, being older, resented Jack's bossing him," Ford's nephew Phil said. "He was sarcastic about it and didn't want to work too hard. But Jack stood up for him."

Shooting on *Fort Apache* was delayed several times by high winds and desert storms, so that the picture fell behind schedule. The movie required one hundred extras as cavalry troops, two hundred Navajo as Apache warriors, and another one hundred Indians for Apache women and children. Battle sequences were shot on the Arizona side of Monument Valley, since insurance rates for stunt performers were lower than in Utah. "Battle scenes require plenty of smoke pots, plenty of firecrackers, and a lot of action on the part of stuntmen," said

Ford. "You do the stunt work separately and later cut it into the action of the scene." Junior Hudkins broke his back during the filming of *Fort Apache*, although the number of accidents that occurred while making Ford's Westerns was remarkably low. Veteran stunt performers had mastered techniques for protecting themselves; most rode their own mounts, preferring a horse they knew and trusted. Rehearsing action scenes tended to make them look phony, and it was impossible to predict when a horse might fall or something would happen unexpectedly.

The *Fort Apache* company headed back to California on August 11 and resumed shooting at the Selznick studio in Culver City two days later. The fort itself was built at the studio, and all of the interiors were filmed there. Mornings in Culver City began with the cast seated around a table, discussing whatever subject came up. Eventually Ford would interject something related to characters in the script, without addressing his comments to the actors playing those parts. But his remarks were enough to start the cast thinking. Sequences on the parade ground required two weeks at Corrigan's Ranch, with additional stunt performers hired for the comic scene in which recruits attempt to ride horses. Finally on October 2, 1947, *Fort Apache* was finished.

Convinced he had made a strong, vigorous picture, Ford sailed down the Mexican coast with Mary, joined later by John Wayne and Henry Fonda. "The first four or five days Ford came to town with us," Fonda wrote about the trip. "After that he was too drunk to leave his boat."

In the three cavalry pictures the harshness of military discipline is overshadowed by the warmth of life under that discipline. Despite the friction between Wayne's character and Fonda's, *Fort Apache* is fundamentally a love story between men. Its women are pale, little more than appendages of their men. What's important is the tight-knit community of males, bound together by military tradition and ritual—men drinking, smoking, bathing, marching, fighting, and dying together. The cavalry becomes a self-contained society, in which duty and sacrifice are essential to manliness. Honor, loyalty, and gallantry distinguish Ford's military heroes, but they are not textbook soldiers unwilling to bend the rules when necessity demands. In the cavalry Ford's outsiders, many of them Irish, have found a comfortable haven, a place where their worth is accepted, a unit in which they can contribute.

James Warner Bellah depicted the Apache as a savage, marauding enemy, but Ford gave them dignity. Cochise's people have a legitimate complaint against white encroachers; the villain is not the Apache chief, but a corrupt agent who cheated the Indians. Captain York (the Wayne character) respects Cochise and accepts the truth behind his grievances, and the two leaders are able to negotiate as equals. Unlike the Native Americans in *Stagecoach*, who serve as a counterforce to civilization, those in *Fort Apache* are seen through sympathetic eyes. Owen Thursday, the martinet played by Fonda, may view Cochise as a "breech-clouted savage, an illiterate, uncivilized murderer and treaty breaker," but Kirby York, a seasoned frontiersman, insists that the Apache warrior is behaving as any honorable man would if herded onto a reservation and abused. While Ford has been branded a racist, his position in *Fort Apache* is an argument for peaceful coexistence. Even revisionist writer Vine Deloria, Jr., himself a Native American, stated that Ford's warriors strike a commendable balance between barbarism and noble savagery.

It's the self-consumed Colonel Thursday who cannot adjust his absolute standards to a new environment, and *Fort Apache* ultimately revolves around a crisis in leadership. Thursday stupidly leads his men to their death, yet York covers up the blunder by lying to the press, insisting that "no man died more gallantly nor won more honor for his regiment." York lies, permitting Thursday to become a legend, to protect a greater truth—the loyalty of his men to their country and to each other.

"We've had a lot of people who were supposed to be great heroes, and you know damn well they weren't," Ford said. "But it's good for the country to have heroes to look up to." Joseph Campbell, who spent a lifetime studying comparative myth, maintained that "mythology is not a lie, mythology is poetry, it is metaphorical," whose function is to establish harmony. "The hero sacrifices himself for something," Campbell declared. Owen Thursday sacrificed himself for the military honor he lived by. Wrong though he was, and Ford leaves no mistake about that, military tradition outweighed the insolence and personal ambition of one foolish leader. Therefore York in the end sanctions the legend: "Correct in every detail."

Fort Apache supports the importance of myth, yet Ford's genius enabled him to create an epic of majesty and sweep and still people his saga with human beings, etched in detail. Amid his operatic style are sublime moments so subtle that only the finest lieder singer could match them. If his humor is broad, it is true to Ford's nature, as much as his sentiment.

Fort Apache was released in June 1948 and proved a commercial success despite only modestly enthusiastic reviews. The *Hollywood Reporter* judged the film "a vigorous, sweeping western adventure drama" done with an "eye for shocking dramatic effect and spectacular action sequences." But other reviewers dismissed it as just another Wild West yarn. Walter Wanger, always eager to flatter Ford, wrote, "Last night I had the pleasure of seeing *Fort Apache*. I think it is a wonderful American picture and the direction is great. I was thrilled by the picture from start to finish, and my only regret was that it wasn't in Technicolor."

Later analysis pointed out the extent to which Ford used the past to draw moral lessons, rather than recording history accurately. *My Darling Clementine* and *Fort Apache* on the surface seem so uncomplicated that they were often praised for their craftsmanship rather than any degree of depth. More recently film scholars have argued that Ford took ingenuous horse opera and transformed it into cinematic art, filling the screen with hopeful visions, melancholy for lost innocence, and dreams that were doomed in the fragmented, dislocated society the director saw on the horizon. Like his life and personality, Ford's best work is rife with tension, paradox, and contradiction.

CHAPTER 8

Troubled Times

THE autumn of 1947 found Hollywood a battleground. An aggressive House Committee on Un-American Activities, chaired by J. Parnell Thomas, launched a purge that would pit the motion picture industry against itself. Convinced that recent strikes by studio workers had been inspired by Communist leaders, Thomas's committee subpoenaed two groups of witnesses to Washington, D.C., one deemed "friendly," the other "unfriendly." Having weathered an earlier investigation, both Republicans and Democrats within the industry deplored another onslaught from Washington lawmakers. But in November 1947 the congressional committee cited the "unfriendly" witnesses for contempt, and all ten went to prison. Meanwhile studio executives, fearing punitive action from Washington, decreed that workers who would not answer questions posed by the committee or could not clear themselves of Communist charges would be fired.

John Ford opposed the House investigation and the ensuing blacklist, although he remained essentially apolitical. While his friends John Wayne and Ward Bond became spokesmen for the militant right wing, Ford stood in the shadows, reluctant to take sides in the conflict that was tearing Hollywood apart. Like many others he urged moderation in a time of growing hysteria.

Wayne claimed that the war had changed Ford; he had less edge to him, was kinder, and more sympathetic. When friends accused Ford of being tough to get along with, he voiced surprise. "I've always thought I was abrupt," he said, "but never rude." He later claimed that the postwar years, the period during which he made the cavalry trilogy and other successful Westerns, were the happiest years of his life.

If Ford had changed, so had John Wayne; at least Wayne's image had. As a result of Wayne's screen portrayals, he had become the symbol of rugged individualism. To most movie-goers he came to represent the mythic West—quiet, resource-ful, self-reliant. "I was America to them," Wayne said. He symbolized leadership—pragmatic, understanding the need for authority and consensus, yet never hesitant to act. Wayne's hero tried to keep peace, but fought valiantly when necessary. He was in control, loved and protected his own, and earned respect and loyalty from his followers. He believed in order, yet was flexible enough to bend the rules to achieve results. Ford contributed to the John Wayne persona and identified with the image Wayne projected. He admired the mythic Western he-roes for their naturalness, their individualistic spirit, and their determination to live life bravely but simply. "We all picture ourselves doing heroic things," said Ford. On the screen John Wayne became his paragon.

With *Fort Apache* behind him, Ford and his family celebrated Christmas 1947 aboard the *Araner,* off the coast of Mexico. Ford alternated between fishing and working on the script for *Three Godfathers,* his forthcoming remake of *Marked Men.* He had filmed the story in 1919 with Harry Carey, and director William Wyler had made it again ten years later under the title *Hell's Heroes.* But Ford liked the story and wanted to rework it with John Wayne in the lead.

Whenever Ford was away from the Argosy offices, his long-time script supervisor and secretary, Meta Sterne, handled routine matters and answered correspondence. Devoted and efficient, Sterne was a short, stocky woman with red hair, who protected her boss and guided him through endless paper-work. She could be counted on to read scripts intelligently and with insight. If she thought a story treatment was worthwhile, she marked it for Himself (as she referred to Ford) to consider. If the director was in his office, no one saw him without being screened first by Sterne. "She was a strange woman in a lot of ways," Anna Lee said. "If she liked you, she was wonderful. But she liked very few women; she loved men." Yet anyone

doing business with Ford realized that Meta Sterne was a force
to reckon with.

The preparation of *Three Godfathers* took on added fervor
when Harry Carey died of cancer in September 1947. Ford
went to see his old friend several times while the actor was sick,
then went out and got drunk. Harry was sedated toward the
end and talking about the old days, so Olive got word to Ford,
who was beside Harry when he died. Ollie happened to be on
the patio at the time, and remembered how Ford had come out,
put his head on her breast, and cried for fifteen minutes. Ford
arranged a memorial service in the chapel of the Field Photo
Farm. An all-night vigil was held there around a giant fire,
during which liquor was consumed and stories were spun. At
the funeral Carey's horse was tied to the hitching post in front
of the chapel, and the actor received military honors. George
O'Brien and his son were present, as were John Wayne, Ward
Bond, and hundreds more. "I'm sure they were in modern
dress," Darcy O'Brien said, "but I have fantasized in my mind
that they were in cavalry uniform. They did have a bugler."

Ford decided to dedicate *Three Godfathers* to his deceased
friend. "To the memory of Harry Carey," an opening title read,
"bright star of the early western sky." Ford told Ollie the day
Harry died that he intended to cast her son in the picture.
Harry had predicted that before his death, telling Dobe that
one day he would work for Ford. "Pop knew how Uncle Jack's
mind worked," the actor said. "He knew that because of their
early friendship Ford would want to do something for Harry
Carey's son." Not only did Dobe Carey become a member of
John Ford's stock company, his mother did, too.

Although *Three Godfathers* was an Argosy production, the picture was distributed through MGM. John Wayne was cast in the
role Harry Carey had played in Ford's silent version, while Pedro
Armendariz and Dobe Carey completed the trio of outlaws. The
director initially planned to film the picture in Mexico, then
shifted its location to the Mojave Desert. Shooting the picture in
Technicolor added almost two hundred thousand dollars to the
budget, but Metro argued that since the movie had no female
star, color was needed to ensure box office returns.

Laurence Stallings and Frank Nugent wrote the screenplay. (Robert Nathan had contributed to an earlier draft.) The story tells of three outlaws who escape into the desert only to come upon a dying mother and her baby. Ultimately they give their lives for the child. Ford turned their sacrifice into an allegory of the Three Wise Men from the Nativity. Although the story is set in the American West, Christian symbols are evident as the three outlaws win redemption through saving the child.

Three Godfathers was a difficult movie to make, involving thirty-two days of work in Death Valley beginning in May 1948. "It was a terrible location," Ben Johnson remembered, "with the sand and dirt." Argosy housed the company at the Furnace Creek ranch, and since there was no air-conditioning, Ford arranged for the swimming pool there to be open at all times. "Ford used to let us off for a couple of hours at noon when it was really hot," character actor Hank Worden recalled, "and everybody would hightail it to the pool, with its natural springwater, for a swim."

Wayne and Pedro Armendariz roomed together in one cabin, Ward Bond and Dobe Carey in another, and Worden, Ben Johnson, and two others in a third. Since Armendariz liked to eat and needed to watch his waistline, Ford called him Gordo and went out of his way to needle him. Aware that the Mexican actor wanted to project a majestic appearance on film, Ford would hang pots and pans on his saddle to irritate him. When the actor complained, Ford would say, "Well, you can take this one off; we don't need that." Meanwhile Armendariz fumed.

The director gave Dobe Carey an especially rough time. Ford told the actor before they started the picture, "You're going to hate me, but you're going to give a good performance." Carey was terrified of Ford and had trouble adjusting to the camera, yet realized later how much the director had helped shape his performance. "An untrained actor," said Carey, "will underplay because he's afraid to really get into it." Ford encouraged him to relax and taught him to understand movie acting. "You'd want to murder Ford during the course of the day," Carey declared, "and then by the end of the day you wanted to put your arms around him, because you knew you'd done a good job."

Each morning the cast sat around and talked for a while, then they walked through their first scene on the set. If an actor needed coaching, Ford read the lines in an exaggerated way to show how he envisioned them. Carey recalled that if a scene was tender, the director treated his actors with care; if it was a physical scene, "he went to work on you," often berating or humiliating the performer. When young Carey had trouble with his death sequence, Ford snapped, "I should have gotten Audie Murphy for the part. But we're too far into the picture, I can't replace you." Carey doubled his efforts, which was what Ford wanted. If the director's insults got too severe, Wayne was usually on hand to reassure newcomers. "Don't take it seriously," he told Carey. "He's kidding you." By the time *Three Godfathers* was finished, Carey had experienced Ford's sarcasm and had witnessed his cruelty and need to control, but agreed with his father, who had complained about Ford but usually added, "Of course the son of a bitch is a genius."

"I learned to love John Ford very much," Dobe Carey declared. "I feel related to him, because he was a father figure to me. I knew he loved me, and I knew he thought I had ability. When I didn't give everything, it infuriated him, and he got mean. A lot of people didn't understand that part of Ford. He didn't know how to be kind when someone wasn't giving their best. But the strange thing is that he managed to get you relaxed in front of a camera by making it seem so simple."

At night in the Mojave Desert, Ford, Wayne, Bond, Armendariz, and Carey played dominoes while the rest of the company watched. If someone wanted to go to a movie or drive into town for dinner, he had to ask Ford's permission. No drinking of alcohol was permitted, even on weekends. One Saturday afternoon Wayne, Armendariz, and Bond broke the rule and went on a spree. The following Monday the director gave his three hungover actors a hard time, forcing Wayne to eat eighteen pieces of chicken before he printed a take, during which Wayne periodically excused himself to throw up.

When the company returned to Los Angeles, they had about ten days of interior work to do. Mildred Natwick, who played the dying mother, joined the cast in the studio. Although

Natwick preferred stage work to movies, she loved working for Ford. "I just had one scene really in *Three Godfathers*," the actress said, "and I did it in one morning. But Ford was wonderful. You get things by osmosis from a great director, in this case his feeling about what that woman was thinking and feeling. Ford could bark at people, but I always thought it was for effect. He wanted to get things cracking." During the shooting of Natwick's scene, Ford said to Wayne, "You look as though you're just watching Millie act." Wayne understood what he meant and began reacting to her more naturally. "I felt such real sympathy then from John Wayne for the character I was playing," Natwick declared. "I remember having lunch afterwards with Ford and the three men in his office. I've never forgotten my glow that Ford seemed pleased with the scene and pleased that I had done it."

Photography on the picture was completed on June 9, 1948, much to the relief of the director and his exhausted cast. "I've been working very hard and am just finishing a picture which took me and my company to Death Valley," Ford wrote Michael Killanin, "a place three hundred feet below sea level and as hot a place as you can imagine." When the picture was released, most critics found all the trudging across the desert tiring and boring. The reviewer for *Family Circle* claimed to have been moved more by the hardships the director and troupe must have endured to photograph the ordeal than by the story itself. All in all *Three Godfathers* was dismissed at the time as one of Ford's lesser efforts.

In July 1948 Barbara Ford married actor Robert Walker aboard the *Araner*, in a cove off Catalina Island. Ford had hoped that his daughter would marry Dobe Carey and didn't approve of Walker. "What are you doing out with that goddamned sissy son of a bitch?" he would ask his daughter. The couple had met at Joanne Dru's house, when Dru was married to singer Dick Haymes. Divorced from actress Jennifer Jones and unhappy, Walker had developed a drinking problem that made him volatile. His marriage to Barbara lasted only five weeks. In August the actor beat his bride at their house in Pacific

Palisades, whereupon Barbara drove to her parents' home. She arrived there black and blue and in tears. Ward Bond threatened to beat Walker up, but Jack stopped him. Barbara filed for divorce on charges of extreme cruelty. She never talked about the marriage in later years; for her Robert Walker was a closed subject.

Since Ford was scheduled to leave for Monument Valley again in October to make *She Wore a Yellow Ribbon* with Joanne Dru in the feminine lead, Dru asked if she could take Barbara along as her stand-in. "You two will drive me crazy," Ford protested. "I'm not going to make a picture with Barbara on the set." But he finally gave in, and Barbara enjoyed a merry retreat with her best friend. "They had to stand her on boxes to bring her up to my height," Dru said, "but we laughed and had such a good time. Papa made everything special."

She Wore a Yellow Ribbon was Ford's first experience with photographing Monument Valley in Technicolor. He intended for his camera to capture the cavalry as Frederic Remington would have painted it, in movement and color choice. He tried to establish a format for each of his films and before shooting *Yellow Ribbon* he studied Remington's works carefully, noted the artist's groupings and composition, and recreated the painter's imagery with striking accuracy. Many of the scenes out of Remington last only a moment, but they are identifiable to the trained eye. The artist's "Cavalryman's Breakfast on the Plains" is recreated in Ford's grouping of actors around a fire in the foreground with a repeated arrangement behind.

She Wore a Yellow Ribbon marked a watershed for John Wayne as an actor, since he confirmed that he was not exclusively a leading man, but capable of playing an older character with dimension. Wayne wore a streak of silver in his hair as Nathan Brittles, a widower soon to be retired from the cavalry. The actor played a graveyard scene that could have become sentimental, but he gave it sincere emotion. In another scene the men present Brittles with an engraved watch upon his retirement. "I imagined I couldn't cope with the reaction in that scene any more than Brittles did," said Wayne, "but Pappy was very conscious of the personality of each actor he had, aware of their sensitivity." Ford suggested that Wayne take out a pair of spectacles before reading the inscription, and Wayne performed the scene simply but effectively. Nathan Brittles—fearless, gruff, yet warm and understanding, with more than a touch of sadness about him—remains one of Wayne's finest portrayals.

She Wore a Yellow Ribbon was based on James Warner Bellah's story "War Party," with a script by Frank Nugent and Laurence Stallings. Ford, ever the visual poet, made the picture his own by condensing the dialogue, adding a love interest with two young lieutenants vying for the same girl's attention, making the most of Monument Valley's color palette, and including the visual moments that had become his trademark—dogs barking beside mounted cavalry soldiers, a line of horses along the crest of a hill, vignettes that spell John Ford as clearly as does his name in the credits. From time to time Bellah complained that Ford violated historical accuracy. "On the frontier the troops didn't wear those sloppy hats on garrison duty," Bellah told the director. Ford gave him a firm look and said, "They do now." Ford created a cavalry hat that turned up in front, worn often by John Wayne in later pictures. "The main thing with a Western is hats," Ford told Ben Johnson. "If you have decent hats on people, their character will come through. If you put something on them that doesn't look right, it won't come across."

Ford's West was a cinematic West, and Monument Valley became the Valhalla of Western epics. On a Ford picture the director's word was law. Even Wayne jumped when he called. Aware that Wayne and his gang would try to sneak liquor into rooms against his orders, Ford began smelling their breath in the morning to see if they had been drinking the night before. If he found they had, he took lines away as punishment, giving their dialogue to someone else. If he discovered that an actor had a hangover, he arranged for him to stand in the sun for hours. "Here was a guy who probably had drunk enough to float a battleship," Wayne's son Michael said, "punishing people because they'd taken a drink when he couldn't."

Joanne Dru claimed that she never felt completely comfortable with Ford, even though she knew him well. "I don't know how to explain that," she said. "Maybe it was because he couldn't relax. He really didn't relate to women. I've often thought that Papa had tremendous insecurities — never regarding his talent, but as a man. He surrounded himself with these big, strong bruisers. He was an emotional man and a man of many moods."

Ford's grandson Dan realized when he grew older that his grandfather was aware of his own sensitivity and almost ashamed of it. "He was a very guarded man," said Dan Ford, "but I think he surrounded himself with John Wayne, Ward Bond, and those people because they represented the way he wanted to be." Ben Johnson agreed that Ford had created in Wayne's screen persona what he would have liked to have been, projecting himself through Wayne's macho image. "That's what he did with all of us," Johnson declared. "Ford liked to watch me ride a horse. He looked like a sack of walnuts on a horse, but he'd set the camera up and have me ride by. All of those guys were better actors than I was, but I could beat them riding a horse. We did those chases over some pretty rough terrain; you had to be tough to survive."

"I always felt that deep down Papa was not a director of women," said Joanne Dru. "He was wonderful with me, but I didn't feel that I got a lot of direction and I needed direction." Dru had made one earlier Western, *Red River* for Howard Hawks, which Ford helped edit. She was terrified of horses and considered herself an inexperienced actress. "Papa sort of left my role up to me," she recalled about her part in *Yellow Ribbon*. "He never really helped me develop a scene and would only stop me if I was wrong. I know he caught me many times being too theatrical. He wanted us to know our lines, but didn't mind if we transposed them."

Dru confided to Ford in private about her marriage, her immaturity, her choice of men, yet she still felt ill at ease around him. "I would always play the court jester with him," she said. "Actually I was frightened of him, yet I more or less adopted him, since I'd lost my own father. Papa teased me, and we laughed a lot. I think he was a compassionate man, but he had to cover that up with bravado. He was always attempting to assert his masculinity; I think he was the original male chauvinist. But there was no one quite like him. He was truly an original. I loved him."

Barbara Ford was on the set with Dru one day watching Wayne shoot a scene on horseback. "Barbara and I laughed all the time and were silly and flighty," Dru recalled. "She was one of the funniest women I've ever known." While they were observing Wayne work, Barbara suddenly said, "Joanne, why are we out here watching him ride a horse?" Dru answered, "Because he turns us on, Barbara." "Yeah," her friend agreed, "but once he dismounts — nothing." They concluded that John Wayne on horseback was the sexiest man in the world. "But once he gets off," said Barbara, "he's just Uncle Duke."

The two young women shared an adobe cabin with Mildred Natwick while they were filming in Monument Valley. "Joanne Dru was lively and full of beans," remembered Natwick, "and she was lots of fun. I adored being in Monument Valley with all the Indians around." Natwick recalled Ford's talking to Hosteen Tso during lunch and telling the Indian, "Now this afternoon I want just a few little clouds, not too many, just a few." The pot-bellied Navajo went up on a hillside, sat down, and began a ritual aimed at producing the desired sky. "I sort of giggled," said Natwick, "until Ford gave me a sharp look. But we did have just a few teeny, weeny clouds that afternoon."

The company was out working in the valley when the sky grew black and a desert thunderstorm broke. "Lightning hit this big butte right beside us," Ben Johnson remembered. Cinematographer Winton Hoch shouted, "Wrap it up," and the actors and crew prepared to take shelter. Ford yelled at Hoch, "I'll tell you when to wrap it up. I want to shoot this." Hoch argued that there wasn't enough light. The company reassembled and, over his written protest, the cinematographer shot the cavalry soldiers marching through the storm, with lightning playing havoc with his exposed film. "It was pretty scary," Ben Johnson recalled, "and everyone was mad at Ford because he was making them stay out in the rain." When the film was developed, the results were astonishing, and Hoch won an Academy Award for best color photography for that picture. The storm sequence has since become a legend in screen annals.

"John Ford understood the idea of the beauty and the beast," declared Hoch. "He tried to convey the harshness of the land as well as the beauty. In Monument Valley he avoided the temptation to shoot nothing but breathtaking scenery. He had only an occasional beauty shot. They were like diamonds, valuable because they are rare." Hoch claimed that he always determined how the camera should be set up, that Ford basically left him alone, concentrating on the actors. "John Ford is *the* auteur director," the cinematographer said, "but he knew that I knew my camera." Hoch felt that color, like sound, could add or detract from a picture. "Color used properly gives an added value," he said. "It's the abuses that are bad."

The scene in *Yellow Ribbon* in which Victor McLaglen, as a drunk Sergeant Quincannon, resists going to the guardhouse, was shot in Harry and Mike Gouldings' dining hall, and the steps that Mildred Natwick marches the brawling Irishman down are just as they were before the building was replaced. "They had to hurry up and get that dining room back in shape by dinnertime that evening," Mike Goulding recalled. Nathan Brittles's office in the picture was the trading post's potato cellar. Mike worked in the store until she heard someone outside yell, "Shoot," then she quieted everybody down, since Ford and his crew were filming nearby.

"We had an early morning setup at Goulding's," Winton Hoch remembered, "a shot right beside the cliff in the shadows. The early morning sun was on the floor of the valley and it was beautiful." Actors had to get up at the crack of dawn, but most of them loved it. Ford arrived on the set and sometimes spent ten minutes looking over the location, a cup of coffee in his hand. He once told director Elia Kazan that he got his ideas on how to stage a scene from the set. "Get out on the location early in the morning before anyone else is there," Ford advised Kazan. "Walk around and see what you've got."

Ford knew his crew—knew their names, their spouses' names, how many children they had, their religion, intimate details that made each worker want to please him. He used a lot of body language directing actors, sometimes striking grotesque poses to demonstrate what he had in mind. He was a stickler for wardrobe, threw dust on actors' uniforms to make them look more realistic, or had a prop man put dirt around their collars. Most of Ford's stock company claimed that if the Old Man was swearing, everything was all right; when he got polite, trouble was brewing.

"I'm a Protestant," Dobe Carey said. "I don't go to church on a regular basis, but when I walked onto a John Ford set, I always felt like I was walking into a sanctuary. There was a quiet, yet a controlled energy, that pervaded the set. It was like something big was happening. It was spiritual. I could cry at the drop of a hat; Ford could look at me and make me cry. But you had to make up your mind in the first few days either to play it his way or go home."

By the time he was cast in *She Wore a Yellow Ribbon,* Carey had been through his initiation rite, and Ford had decided that the young actor would be part of his group. "Duke used to talk about how much Ford wanted to be one of the guys," Carey said. "There'd be a circle of guys on the set—Ben Johnson, John Wayne, some of the stuntmen—and Ford would see them laughing and having a good time, and he'd want to be part of that. But when he'd join them, the fun would stop; everybody would start watching what they said because he was the boss. I felt that he missed the camaraderie, for there was a lot of camaraderie in a John Ford company."

Carey and Johnson became close friends on *She Wore a Yellow Ribbon,* and later frequented some of the wranglers' bars back in Los Angeles—places such as the Hitching Post near the Disney studio, where anyone looking for a brawl could find one. Ford never went to such haunts, but John Wayne did occasionally. "Duke could take care of himself," Johnson said. "But Ford was the type of person who wanted to be part of whatever was going on, and he didn't have the capacity to express himself. He absolutely couldn't, even though he wanted to. I think that was one of the reasons he was so cantankerous around us."

Johnson maintained that he purposely never got close to Ford, fearing they would quarrel if he did. "Consequently I stayed back at all times," he said. Ford knew that the horseman didn't drink and therefore trusted him. Victor McLaglen, on the other hand, nipped during a day's shooting, even though he knew Ford was watching him. On location for *Yellow Ribbon* Johnson carried McLaglen's flask. Every so often the old actor would peek around a corner, catch Johnson's eye, and call out, "Laddie!" That was the signal for Johnson to bring him a drink. "Vic was a tough character," said Johnson, "but he thought I was all right. We were a pretty wild bunch in those days."

Ford seldom referred to a script on the set, seeming to work off the top of his head. "Papa had his story in mind at all times," Joanne Dru declared. "That's why he was able to edit and cut as he went along." Wingate Smith maintained that Ford shot a picture in his mind before he ever turned a camera; consequently he was free to improvise. "He used the least amount of film of any director in the business," Smith said.

She Wore a Yellow Ribbon was a less expensive film than *Fort Apache*. Moving and handling the House Rock buffalo herd for background footage, however, cost nearly ten thousand dollars—five dollars a day for each animal. Still the picture came in under budget. After twenty-eight days on location, working at breakneck speed, the company returned to California. Ford had just arrived home when a blizzard covered Monument Valley in almost twelve feet of snow. Land travel was paralyzed for weeks. Ford arranged for food, hay, and supplies to be dropped by air for the Navajo and their livestock, a supplement to the $150,000 his company had recently spent there. "The Indians are very near to my heart," said Ford.

The plot of *She Wore a Yellow Ribbon* revolves around an attempt to avoid another Indian war after the defeat of Custer. The old chief in the picture, Pony That Walks, is as sensitive and well intentioned as Nathan Brittles, and the two have immense respect for one another. Both have lost control of their subordinates, who crave excitement; the two leaders admit that they have grown too old to fight and acknowledge the folly of continued warfare. Pony That Walks was played by John Big Tree, a Seneca from New York who had appeared in earlier Ford films. Arthur Shields, a member of the Abbey Players and a regular in John Ford's stock company, coached the Native American actor in his role, as the Irishman did other members of the cast. In Big Tree's scene with Wayne, the Indian chief emerges as a sage who's seen too much and has turned to Christianity in search of hope, but urges Brittles to get drunk with him and forget what they can no longer control. Theirs is a tender exchange between two veterans whose time is past.

She Wore a Yellow Ribbon focuses on twilight. Nathan Brittles knows the Old West is vanishing, yet as retirement approaches, he cannot bring himself to return to the restraints and pretensions of the East. He is a man of action, whose sense of community rests within the military. He is a proven leader, but his command is limited, subject to regulations that duty forces him to accept. The film's tension stems from a conflict between individual freedom and communal control, yet harmony is the issue.

Ford demonstrated far more feeling for the common soldier than did James Warner Bellah in his short stories. He seemed aware that a majority of the cavalry troops were foreign-born; over 40 percent of the enlisted men at Western posts came from Ireland. Ford lingered on the Irish component, depicting them as noisy, quick-tempered, prone to drunkenness, yet lovable and filled with community spirit. He showed unreconstructed southerners reluctantly integrating with northerners. His military wives were courageous troopers in their own right, honest and direct, although with slight hint of sexuality. To show sex on the screen, Ford said, "would be against my nature, my religion, and my natural inclinations."

Yellow Ribbon's major flaw, as with other Ford films, is in its humor. The director repeatedly sacrificed character development for cheap laughs and seldom seemed to know when he had gone too far. Victor McLaglen's brawl in the company store goes on and on, more roughhouse than humorous, almost to the point of becoming ludicrous. "I always felt that in every dramatic scene there's a chance to slip in a little comedy,"

Ford said. Yet his humor was rambunctious and too broad for sophisticated tastes. Critics objected to this overdrawn humor, but Ford continued to argue that comedy was his forte.

The strength of *She Wore a Yellow Ribbon* is in its visuals — its landscapes, its grandeur, its rhythm, Ford's faultless timing, the fluidity of his action. Still, the director was able to humanize simple realities and capture details that command attention. "Bless your heart, Pappy," James Warner Bellah wired Ford after seeing the completed film. "You sure painted a Remington this time."

Released through RKO, *She Wore a Yellow Ribbon* opened at the Capitol Theater in Manhattan on November 17, 1949. The *New York Times* pronounced it "a dilly of a cavalry picture." Bosley Crowther wrote, "No one could make a troop of soldiers riding across the western plains look more exciting and romantic than this great director does." Both *Variety* and the *Hollywood Reporter* maintained that the Western set a standard that would be hard to match.

Whenever Ford was on a set intimates knew that he was in dreamland. Friends also knew that he felt totally alive only when he was working; certainly he was happiest when making a film. "If I had my way," he said, "every morning of my life I'd be behind that camera at nine o'clock waiting for the boys to roll 'em, because that's the only thing I really like to do."

Between pictures he didn't seem to know how to occupy himself. He socialized some at John Wayne's house, showing up there for christenings and special celebrations, and, after George O'Brien divorced, he stopped by O'Brien's house in Brentwood, often depressed and looking for conviviality. "One of my best memories," said O'Brien's son Darcy, "is of sitting around with Ford and Stan Jones and Dobe Carey at my father's place and having Stan Jones sing 'Riders in the Sky.'"

Joanne Dru, a frequent visitor to the house on Odin Street, remembered Ford locked in his bedroom drinking. "Barbara and I would be squawking around outside," said Dru. "Once Barbara was showing me a little doll's house she had had as a child, when suddenly we heard this noise. We looked up and

Papa was peeing out the window. He said, 'Good afternoon, girls.'" As usual, he was quite drunk.

Jack confessed to Dobe Carey that he'd joined Alcoholics Anonymous, but his drinking continued. "Who of that bunch wasn't an alcoholic?" Joanne Dru asked. "Ford loved drunks," Carey declared. "If you didn't drink, he looked at you with a jaundiced eye, but not during a picture. When the picture was over, you could go to his house and stumble all over the place, and he didn't care." Ford did caution Carey about the actor's own drinking. "Your father couldn't drink," he said, "your mother can't drink, and my Mary can't drink. You're one of those people." John Wayne and Robert Mitchum drank twenty-two martinis each during a party at Olive Carey's house one evening, and Ford bragged about their stamina.

Jack and Mary sometimes gave Christmas parties, at which Danny Borzage played the accordion and Dobe Carey sang. Jack often played practical jokes at his parties and, after a few drinks, got flirtatious with women. "Nothing really happened," Joanne Dru said, "but he loved the ladies." Outside their home Jack and Mary were seldom seen together. Mary went to the races at Santa Anita, appearing in the Turf Club beautifully dressed. "She was a grand sort of lady," declared Andrew McLaglen, Victor's son, "but Mary had a life pretty far removed from Jack's."

Early in 1949 Ford reported to 20th Century-Fox to begin work on *Pinky,* the story of a black girl who goes north, passes for white, then returns home afraid to marry the white man she loves. Ford prepared the picture and attended story conferences with Darryl Zanuck and screenwriter Philip Dunne, but quit the film after shooting less than five days. He claimed he had shingles, but that was an excuse. "Ford was obviously miscast," said Dunne. "He was floundering. He had Ethel Waters moaning spirituals. It just wasn't his thing. He didn't understand the picture at all." Although Ethel Waters was playing an old-fashioned character, Ford had difficulty understanding black people, and Zanuck realized the problem. Dunne said that Ford recognized that he was in over his head, for he'd said little in story conferences. "He seemed puzzled by the script," the writer declared.

Elia Kazan took over for Ford, with little or no time for preparation. "Darryl was happy to junk Jack's film," wrote Kazan, "and when I saw it I understood why." The Fox production head knew that Ford wasn't sick; he simply wanted out of the assignment. Ford hated Waters and found difficulty directing her. She in turn hated him, admitting that he frightened her. When Kazan arrived on the set, he was greeted by a nervous cast. "We started from scratch," the director said, although Zanuck did use Ford's opening, where Pinky comes home.

Ford withdrew from the *Pinky* in March 1949; by June he was working at the studio again, this time on a comedy called *When Willie Comes Marching Home.* He thought the story was amusing, and Zanuck was eager to repeat the studio's recent success with *Sitting Pretty,* which had starred Clifton Webb as Mr. Belvedere. The production head was still angry with Ford for backing out of *Pinky* and out of spite had not assigned him *A Ticket to Tomahawk,* a Western Ford had asked to direct. To make the situation even more tense, the script of *When Willie Comes Marching Home* was written by Richard Sale and his wife, Mary Anita Loos, and Zanuck had chosen Sale as director of *A Ticket to Tomahawk,* leaving Loos to deal with Ford. "He scared me to death," she said. Ford tried to get even with Sale by referring to his wife as "the talented one" and demanding that Loos be present on his set. "So I'd get up about 5:30 and start to sweat," she said. "I'd have to sit there on the set, and he'd stop everything and say, 'Think of a better line.' Gaffers, electricians, cameramen, everyone would look at me. He did that just to see what I'd do. Meanwhile poor Richard was doing his first days on *A Ticket to Tomahawk* at the studio, and I'm the one who's going crazy."

After the freedom of making four pictures for his own company, Ford resented studio interference more than ever. He disliked Fred Kohlmar, the producer of *When Willie Comes Marching Home,* and refused to meet in Kohlmar's office. He mistreated French actress Corinne Calvet, referring to her as "the Frog." Actor James Lydon, who came to dislike the director as shooting progressed, said, "John Ford was a cruel, vicious, cowardly, sometimes brilliant man. It was a penance to work with Ford; he treated people like dirt."

Yet Ford got along well with Dan Dailey, the picture's star, a dancer turner actor. One day Ford asked Dailey if he had any friends who were out of work, "panics," as he called them. Dailey said that he knew several hoofers who needed jobs, and the director volunteered to hire them for the picture. The star and his friends were later sitting in a portable dressing room on the backlot, waiting for the crew to light a set, when Ford came over and sat down on the steps. The dancers invited him in, but Ford declined, listening outside while they talked. After a few minutes he said, "You know, this is a novel experience. It's the first time I've ever tried to make a picture without actors." And he got up and walked away. "That was Ford's sense of humor," Dailey declared.

Mary Loos had occasion to see the director's tender side, too. Loos had lost a baby in a premature birth and was walking through the 20th Century-Fox lot a short time afterward with her husband. Ford drove by in an open car, stopped when he noticed her, and got out. "He put his arms around me and started to cry," Loos remembered. "Ford was a sentimental Irishman."

During the editing of *When Willie Comes Marching Home* the cutter became sick, creating a quandry. Ford said, "Let the kid take over," so Joe Silver, an assistant in the Fox editing department, got the job. "*When Willie Comes Marching Home* was the first picture I cut on my own," Silver recalled. "Ford was considered a giant, and the stories you've heard about him are true. It was a nerve-racking assignment, but the way he shot the film, it was not hard to edit."

Photography on the picture finished on August 11, 1949, and it opened at the Roxy in New York the following February, proving to be a delightful comedy but no more. The *New Yorker* said, "As directed by John Ford, the picture travels along for some time in fits and starts, but when it at last does get to rolling smoothly, it is amusing stuff."

When the picture wrapped, Ford put to sea $125,000 richer. "A lovely lady from your office informed me that you have been on your boat," author Gene Fowler wrote Ford in late August, "while the rest of us were broiling on the griddle familiarly known as the City of the Angels." Aboard the *Araner* Ford worked on his next project for Argosy, a Western called *Wagonmaster,* with a script by Frank Nugent and Ford's son, Patrick. "When in doubt," the director said, "make a Western."

Small and inexpensive though it was, *Wagonmaster* proved to be one of Ford's most lyrical films. It deals with a band of Mormons who set out across the Utah desert in 1879, intending to establish a home in the San Juan Valley. Ford loved the Mormon people, admired their sense of community, and viewed them as a society of outcasts. He decided to shoot the picture near Moab, Utah, an area that had not been used before in a film. Moab in the fall of 1949 was a small town, settled by Mormons. The company arrived in mid-November and stayed until December 7. The local residents were cooperative, and entertained the movie people at night with skits and dances. Since Ford had no big-name actors in the cast, no studio executives to deal with, and few visitors on the set, he was in a relaxed mood. *Wagonmaster* proved to be one of his happiest pictures.

Ford surrounded himself with friends. He and Ward Bond pulled their customary gags on one another during the weeks on location, and Bond in his boisterous way criticized everything and everybody. "Ward was the most cantankerous man in the world," said Joanne Dru, who was featured in the picture. "He was terrible, a real pain in the behind, but I liked him. He and Papa would go at it, and we'd say, 'God, here they go.'" Anytime Ford and Bond got together they argued. Those close to the director claimed that he was hardest on the people he loved most. He certainly was never any harder on anybody than he was on Ward Bond.

"Papa had a marvelous time on that location," Joanne Dru maintained. "We used to drive out to the set together in the mornings, and he always tipped his hat to the cows as we passed by." Dobe Carey agreed that making *Wagonmaster* was a pleasant experience. "Uncle Jack was different on that than he was on any other movie I've ever worked for him on. It was like a vacation for him; he wasn't trying to outdo himself. He loved the story because it was so simple. The movie was made in black and white, and he didn't have any superstars. He enjoyed every minute of it. We looked forward to going to work every day. He never got the whip out on that picture at all."

Not only was the story simple, but its characters were the kind Ford liked best—Hank Worden playing an idiot, Jane Darwell an Earth Mother figure. Darwell, in reality a down-to-earth, loving person, had difficulty getting around in Moab because of her weight and failing legs. She was in a wheelchair much of the time. "She was a great lady," Ben Johnson said, "and wonderful to work with."

Johnson received top billing for his role of Travis Blue, the guide who leads the Mormon wagon train through the Utah desert. The former rodeo performer attributed his success in films to his ability to play himself. "If you can put something up on the screen that's honest and real," Johnson said, "it's got to be a hit. I'm not that good an actor, but I can play the hell out of Ben Johnson. All my life I've lived by honesty, realism, and respect. John Ford told me that if I'd live by those principles, life would be pretty easy for me. That's what I've done, and he was right. Ford was an education. He was a mean old scoundrel, but if you listened to him, you could learn a lot. He sort of took me under his wing."

The only person Ford rode hard during the making of *Wagonmaster* was his son, Patrick. Johnson thought it was Jack's way of showing that he wasn't giving Pat preferential treatment. Dan Ford maintained that the tension between his father and grandfather stemmed from Jack's belief that Patrick was lazy. Dan felt that his father was normal; it was his grandfather, an overachiever, who was not.

Although it won no awards, *Wagonmaster* would number among Ford's personal favorites. Argosy hired Stan Jones to compose music for the film, and the Sons of the Pioneers sang the songs he wrote. The director included a square dance sequence, as an expression of Mormon oneness, but he interrupted the dance to dramatic effect with the arrival of the heavies. The film is well paced and has engaging action, but above all it has heart. "Making Western pictures of that era has been a crusade with me since the war," said Ford. "I think *Wagonmaster* came closest to what I wanted to achieve." His choice proved financially successful, for Argosy's postwar Westerns were immensely popular, even when they didn't earn rave reviews. "I am sure," Ford wrote in 1949, "that means there are millions of people left still proud of their country, their flag, and their traditions."

When RKO released *Wagonmaster* in April 1950 the *Los Angeles Times* said, "John Wayne is all that's missing." *Variety* pronounced the picture "a hard hitting Western," while the *Hollywood Reporter* declared that Ford had brought another vivid and realistic drama to the screen, one "that will delight everyone who enjoys outdoor adventure."

Ford habitually told interviewers that his favorite film was the one coming up, and he assured them that he put everything he had into each project. But *Wagonmaster* is a more personal picture than most; its story is reminiscent of the silent movies Ford made with Harry Carey. It is a more optimistic Western than those Ford made later, after he became disturbed by a world growing more troubled and complex. *Wagonmaster* focuses on two bands of outcasts, the Mormons and some show people driven out of town for their wanton ways. The Mormon pioneers face a series of threats in their search for a Promised Land, but along the way they are forced to deal with reality. Ford still saw the American frontier as a garden where dreams and ideals could be realized, but his tone would soon shift to sadness, as his concept of America darkened.

Early in 1950 Argosy moved its offices to Republic Pictures, the smallest of the big studios, headed by businessman Herbert J. Yates. Republic specialized in budget Westerns and had a friendly, down-home atmosphere, with cowboys, a Western street, and a roster of actors and technicians who considered themselves a family. John Wayne had worked there for years; so had Gene Autry and Roy Rogers. Yates was impressed with Ford and promised him complete artistic freedom on the films he made under the Republic banner. Yates also offered Argosy a better financial arrangement than the company had had with MGM, and John Wayne urged Ford to consider the company seriously, assuring that he'd always found Yates fair, if not knowledgeable about picturemaking. Ford's relationship with the studio head proved turbulent, for Yates operated in a penny-pinching fashion and could be meddlesome and contentious. Ford tried to avoid him as much as possible and went about his business in private. Director Allan Dwan occupied an office across the hall from Ford's at Republic, but the two seldom crossed paths. "I don't think I saw that door open more than once all the time he was there," Dwan declared.

Ford hoped to launch his arrangement with Yates with *The Quiet Man*, the Irish elegy he had been planning for years. The Republic head complained that the picture would have little commercial appeal and insisted Ford direct an inexpensive Western for him first, using the same stars he would cast in the Irish picture, John Wayne and Maureen O'Hara. At Yates's urging Argosy again turned to James Warner Bellah, selecting the writer's fast-moving story "Mission with No Record" for the conclusion of its cavalry trilogy. The film was a lesser work than *Fort Apache* or *She Wore a Yellow Ribbon* and contained a bitterness not present earlier. Made under the name "Rio Bravo," but changed to *Rio Grande* when the initial title proved unavailable, the picture, like *Wagonmaster,* was shot around Moab, Utah, where the company began filming on June 15, 1950.

Wayne, whose salary of one hundred thousand dollars was twice that of Maureen O'Hara's, played a middle-aged, hardened Kirby Yorke, the same officer he had portrayed in *Fort Apache,* now on the verge of becoming a martinet himself. O'Hara played Yorke's estranged wife, a spirited daughter of the Old South. While the officer's family ties are vague and his marriage troubled, Wayne's rapport with O'Hara in *Rio Grande* and two later films for Ford make the most satisfying male-female relationship in the director's entire body of work. "The O'Hara-Wayne combination was a sensation because she was the macho woman and he was the macho man," said Maureen's

brother, Charles FitzSimons. "They were favorites of Ford,
and he had fun working with them. His relationship with
Maureen was special."

In many ways O'Hara was like Ford, a no-nonsense person,
full of Irish temperament. She was beautiful, gregarious, forceful, humorous, and a highly dependable trouper. "Maureen
was very talkative," Dobe Carey observed. "If there were a lot
of women around, she wouldn't be, but with the men she was
just like one of the guys." O'Hara loved and respected Ford, as
he did her, even though sparks flew between them. She was a
tomboy who seldom hesitated to speak her mind, and Ford
enjoyed teasing her. "She was his idea of a beautiful Irish
woman with spirit," Mary Loos maintained. "Maureen was
the sort of woman he would have invented."

O'Hara felt that her chemistry with Wayne came from an
ideal physical match; she was tall enough and strong enough to
be his partner. Wayne treated her as an equal. "He'd sit and talk
to me about his problems and his lady friends and all sorts of
things," the actress said. Somebody once asked Wayne, "What
about O'Hara?" He replied, "The greatest guy I ever knew."
Wayne's son Patrick said, "Ford saw himself as my father. He
saw himself as a Western character and identified strongly with
that. Maureen O'Hara was the perfect mate for John Wayne and
so was the perfect mate for John Ford. He was in love with
Maureen, I think, but I'm not suggesting they had an affair."

O'Hara maintained that since Ford was the absolute boss on
his set, he gave performers a feeling of security. She took her
share of hell from him, but realized that at heart he was "the
most sentimental old codger that ever was," but would die "if
he ever heard me say that." The actress drew the line with both
Ford and Wayne when their tempers got out of control. "Just
go sit down," she told Wayne on the set of *Rio Grande,*
pointing her finger at him. "And he did," Ben Johnson recalled. "I always admired her for that. Maureen knew how to
speak up for herself."

Ford and Johnson had a falling out during the making of *Rio
Grande* over something Wayne did. "Duke sat right there and
let me take the guff," said Johnson, "in front of about a

hundred and fifty people. I wasn't very smart. I told Ford what he could do with his picture. He let me finish the show, but then he didn't hire me for eleven years." As with George O'Brien earlier, the squabble was a case of Ford's Irish temperament's getting the better of him; he was easily offended and held a long grudge.

Johnson and Dobe Carey did Roman riding in the picture, a stunt they practiced for three weeks before going on location. "I knew Ben wouldn't have much trouble with it," said Dobe Carey, "but it didn't really have much to do with horsemanship. The trick had more to do with athletic ability, letting the two horses run and then standing up on them and controlling them while we rode. Ben looked different on a horse than any man I've ever seen. He just had a style all his own and was in a class by himself."

Ford sometimes gave his cadre of stunt performers lines to speak. Among his favorites were Frank McGrath, Fred Kennedy, and the two Chucks, Chuck Hayward and Chuck Roberson — "Good Chuck" and "Bad Chuck," as the director called them. Roberson, who doubled Wayne in *Rio Grande* and many other films, remembered his first day on location in Utah as much like his first day in the army. "Moab was just a little, one-horse Mormon town in the middle of nowhere," he said. "There were no motels, so we bunked in army tents with wooden-planked floors and side flaps that could be raised each day to let the sand blow through. I stashed my gear in a tent occupied by five other guys." The company arose at 5:30 every morning and ate breakfast in a school cafeteria that had been rented. "Everybody in John Ford's company was on location at seven o'clock sharp," Roberson declared, "not one minute later." The director inspected each cavalry uniform, making whatever adjustments he thought were necessary, but according to Roberson, "he was just trying to get a whiff of our breath to see if we had been drinking the night before." Since Ford liked his horse soldiers dirty, uniforms were not washed during the month the picture was in production. "Realism was Ford's motto," said Roberson.

If the director was busy with a scene involving only O'Hara

and Wayne, the stunt performers and extras were drilled on foot and horseback by Jack Pennick, who had served during the war as drill sergeant for the Field Photographic Unit and continued to take the job seriously. "Pennick drilled us in the hot sun until the sweat poured off us, and our uniforms stuck to our bodies," Roberson wrote. "And Ford loved every minute of it. We were his personal soldiers, as dirty and stinking as any army that ever chased an Indian across the desert in the middle of July."

One morning Herbert Yates showed up in Moab, complaining that the director was wasting time and money. "It's almost ten o'clock," Yates pointed out. "When are you going to start shooting?" Ford's answer was calm and succinct: "Just as soon as you get the hell off my set." Yates left with no further protest, and the company went back to work.

Since Ford wanted a spontaneous look in stunt work, he seldom gave complete instructions for what he expected. At times he even double-crossed his stuntmen to get an effect. "He would come out and talk to us," Chuck Hayward remembered, "and before he would explain quite everything, he'd dribble off his voice to where we couldn't hear. He'd head back to the camera still talking. He did that on purpose, because he didn't intend that we know exactly what we were going to do. He wanted action that wasn't rehearsed." On *Rio Grande* Hayward got his head cracked open in a fall.

The same stunt performers doubled the cavalry and the Indians on the picture, sometimes reversing sides in a single day. Harry Goulding brought fifty Navajo up from the reservation to play Apache in the film, accompanied by Lee Bradley, who again served as translator. Billy Yellow, one of the Indians selected for closeups, stated forty years later that the Navajo weren't told that they were portraying Apache, or Comanche and Cheyenne in later Ford pictures; they simply did what they were instructed to do. Billy Yellow's daughter, Evelyn Nelson, recalled that she stayed with her grandmother as a child so that her mother and father could make movies. Her father at eighty-seven lived in a hogan in Monument Valley, spoke no English, and hadn't seen any of his movies. Neither had his daughter, although she spoke fluent English and knew that some of her father's movies were available on video. She intended to watch them, but hadn't found the time. Evelyn was proud that her great-grandfather had appeared in *Stagecoach* and hoped that her young son would be in movies when he grew up, since her father had enjoyed the work and earned good money. "It was a job," Nelson declared, "and they did it." There seemed to be no sense that her people had been betrayed by the Indians hired by Ford, although Native American militants have objected to an unfavorable depiction. "At that time," Nelson said, "the Navajo didn't have much money, and they really had fun making movies. My father wanted to be recognized like those Hollywood stars."

Although *Rio Grande* was an inexpensive picture, it required fifty Indian ponies, over ninety cavalry horses hired from surrounding ranches, seventy-five extras who could ride, as well as twenty women and ten children, most of whom were recruited from the local population. Cameraman Bert Glennon remembered John Wayne's helping out with whatever needed to be done. "I've seen him put his shoulder to a location truck that was stuck," Glennon declared, "or hold a pair of shears and a comb for a hairdresser when she had to make a hurried change on one of the characters." Ford, the cinematographer assured, was "a motion picture craftsman with an unlimited photographic sense."

After the day's work the director and his cronies would settle down at their motel in Moab for an evening pitch game. Occasionally it was poker or hearts. "The Old Man was so sharp at hearts and pitch," Chuck Hayward remembered. "I liked to play poker with him because I had an even chance at that, but not at hearts and pitch. But that's when he was actually happy." Hayward claimed that Ford and Wayne both cheated at pitch, and if anyone made a mistake, "you got your ass chewed out." The stuntman confirmed that Ford enjoyed being with physical people and frequently challenged them. "One of the last things that he could do was stand in a doorway and kick the top of it," said Hayward. "He used to do that to see if he was still limber. I never could do it."

Hayward maintained that Ford commanded more respect from his crew than had any director he'd ever worked with. Ford loved having his professional family around him on isolated locations, with no place to go, so that he could rule over his own kingdom. During evenings while making *Rio Grande* Maureen O'Hara sometimes sang, as did Ken Curtis, who was then one of the Sons of the Pioneers and would soon marry Barbara Ford. "Here they were in the middle of the West," Michael Wayne said, "with bolts of lightning coming out of the sky, or beautiful cloud formations lit by the moon. It was absolutely fabulous."

All that was missing was Ward Bond, who didn't have a part in *Rio Grande,* although he visited the set. Ford and Wayne got to missing him, so they had a photographer take a picture of the two of them standing at the rear of a horse, one of them lifting its tail. They sent Bond the picture on a card that read, "Thinking of you." The gag was typical of Ford's humor.

The company returned on July 17 to Los Angeles, where *Rio Grande* was finished at the Republic studios. The arrangement that Ford and Merian Cooper had worked out with Yates stipulated that Republic and Argosy would split the cost of the three pictures made; then after the studio had deducted 15 percent for overhead, the two companies would share equally in the profits. The alliance was fragile from the outset. "I hope this is what you and Coop really want," James Warner Bellah wrote Ford when he learned of the deal with Yates. Cooper in particular had reservations, and most of those were confirmed during postproduction on *Rio Grande*. Yates charged Argosy $34,200 for the use of Republic's musicians to record the picture's score, totaling 550 hours of work. "It looks like we are taking a worse beating on the music here at Republic than we ever have at any other place that we have made pictures," Cooper complained.

Yet reviews of the film were favorable. "*Rio Grande* is filmed outdoor action at its best," said *Variety*. Direct Frank Capra screened the movie and telegraphed Ford: "Saw *Rio Grande*. It's great. After seeing the tripe that is being turned out today, it's a delightful pleasure to see a show made by the Old Master himself."

Critics noted later that the final installment of the cavalry trilogy departed from the conciliatory mood of its predecessors. In *Rio Grande* Kirby Yorke no longer proposes negotiation with the Indians and argues against the diplomatic restraints put on the cavalry to defeat aggression. The picture was released five months after President Truman committed American forces to a limited war in Korea. Ford had been an admirer of Truman, but after the president fired Douglas MacArthur for taking a position similar to Yorke's Ford took down the autographed picture of the Missouri statesman that had hung on his wall. Ford agreed with MacArthur that military effectiveness against aggression was the primary issue, even though an expanded war conflicted with Truman's policy of containment. In *Rio Grande* Yorke struggles to preserve an uneasy peace with as little bloodshed as possible for either side. To accomplish that goal, he asks permission to cross the Rio Grande (as MacArthur had sought to bomb north of the Yalu River during the Korean War), thereby stopping Apache raids into Texas by not allowing their warriors to retreat into Mexico and gather strength to strike again.

As usual, Ford's politics were ambivalent. He was a militarist, opposed to Communist aggression, but his stand on the McCarthy witch hunt then ripping Hollywood apart was unclear. His friends John Wayne and Ward Bond had become vocal right-wingers, yet Ford's position remained uncertain. The issue came to a head at a Directors Guild meeting at the Beverly Hills Hotel on the night of October 15, 1950.

Joseph L. Mankiewicz, the guild's president, a liberal but no Communist, had been in Europe. With Mankiewicz out of the country Cecil B. DeMille and a group of McCarthy sympathizers took the opportunity to draw up a mandatory loyalty oath for guild members to sign and had gotten it approved by the organization's board. When Mankiewicz returned and opposed their actions, the DeMille faction launched a campaign to oust him as president, branding him leftist and soft on communism. A meeting of the guild's membership was called, with both sides mustering support. Every prominent director in Hollywood came braced for a showdown. Mankiewicz made an hour-long speech in which he opposed the mandatory oath, the current blacklist, and an open ballot in deciding the issue at hand, all of which he claimed was un-American. Guild members hissed and booed when DeMille argued that the twenty-five directors who had signed the petition protesting his loyalty oath were affiliated with subversive organizations and pointed out that many of them were foreign-born.

For four hours the directors attacked or defended DeMille and Mankiewicz, while Ford kept silent. He sat on the aisle wearing a baseball cap and tennis shoes, sucking his pipe, and listening. Finally George Stevens summarized the charges against the board's anti-Mankiewicz faction. There was applause when Stevens sat down. A moment of silence followed before Ford raised his hand. Since a court stenographer was recording the session, everyone who spoke had to identify himself for the record. Ford stood up and turned toward the stenographer. "My name's John Ford," he said. "I make Westerns." He paused for dramatic effect. "I don't think there is anyone in this room who knows more about what the American public wants than Cecil B. DeMille—and he certainly knows how to give it to them. In that respect I admire him." Ford looked at DeMille, who was seated across the room from him. "But I don't like you, C. B. I don't like what you stand for, and I don't like what you've been saying here tonight. Joe has been vilified, and I think he needs an apology." DeMille sat motionless, staring straight ahead, while Ford waited for his words to make their impact. "Then I believe there is only one alternative," he said, "and I hereby so move: that Mr. DeMille and the entire board of directors resign and that we give Joe a vote of confidence. And then let's all go home and get some sleep. We've got some pictures to make tomorrow."

Walter Lang seconded the motion, as Ford sat down and fumbled to light his pipe. The motion carried, with four abstentions. DeMille and the board resigned, and the guild members gave Mankiewicz an overwhelming vote of confidence, whereupon the meeting was adjourned.

It had been the gunfight at O.K. Corral—with Ford entering the fray in true John Wayne fashion, setting his community straight. Although Ford was a conservative by 1950 (some thought a reactionary), he viewed the investigation of Hollywood by the House Un-American Activities Committee as a quest by bullies for media attention and power. In the shootout at the Directors Guild meeting, Ford rose in defense of individual rights and freedom of expression; his stand did little to alter his drift to the right. He was not protecting left-wing politics, but fairness and decency, values he considered basic to the American system.

CHAPTER 9

Master Filmmaker

PROFESSIONALLY Hollywood was a small town, comprised of studio workers who labored behind walls of competing factories, yet at the same time were part of a larger community aware of each other's business. Despite misgivings about the Hollywood social scene, Ford was a dedicated professional who placed art before politics. He wanted no strife in the Directors Guild and sought to heal the breach with DeMille at the earliest opportunity. In October 1950 he sent his esteemed colleague a note that passed for an apology. "Thank you for your friendly expression," DeMille replied. "Attack I am used to, kindness moves me very deeply."

Since Ford and his friend Budd Boetticher were both working at Republic at the time, Ford volunteered to help the young director with a film Boetticher had shot in Mexico entitled *The Bullfighter and the Lady* (1951). John Wayne had produced the movie, which made Ford all the more willing to help edit it. Ford quickly took charge, deleting a couple of sequences Boetticher particularly liked. Most of what he took out was forty-two minutes in which the Robert Stack and Gilbert Roland characters establish an affectionate relationship as protege and mentor. Ford referred to it as "all that chi-chi shit." Boetticher later said, "Ford figured that two men could not love each other unless there was a homosexual situation. That's a lot of baloney, but he didn't like that part and cut it from the picture. That was my pal Jack Ford." In later years the footage was restored.

The navy asked Ford to make a propaganda film about the Korean War. So the day after Christmas he left for Korea, arriving there on New Year's Day 1951. Since Ford didn't view the conflict as a heroic war, the picture he made was a somber one. James Warner Bellah worked on the script and Republic released *This Is Korea* the following August. The film was poorly received; few theater owners even booked it. Not only was the "police action" in Korea (Harry Truman's phrase) not popular with Americans, but Ford showed signs of losing touch with current reality.

He returned from Asia depressed and in need of surgery for a double hernia. "Too many hours in the air catapulting and landing on carriers, helicopters, and especially climbing mountains," he wrote Michael Killanin. "I've never climbed so many damned mountains in my life. However, I'm bright eyed and bushy tailed at the moment and working hard."

Ford was again working on *The Quiet Man,* the picture he'd been planning for fifteen years. The *Saturday Evening Post* had published Maurice Walsh's short story in 1933; Ford bought the screen rights three years later for ten dollars, although by then the story had been expanded into a book called *Green Rushes.* The film would be Ford's fairytale of Ireland, full of pastoral beauty and eccentric characters, a mixture of reality, romance, and folklore. "It's a lovely story," the director wrote Killanin, "and I think we should go all over Ireland and get a bit of scenery here and a bit of scenery there and really make the thing a beautiful travelogue, besides a really charming story."

Ford planned to integrate Irish customs into the plot, creating an endearing portrait of Irish village and family life, as well as capturing the feel of the countryside. He envisioned the picture as a robust comedy, balanced with a touching love story, a perfect vehicle for John Wayne and Maureen O'Hara. The name of Sean Thornton, Wayne's character, was a fusion of Ford's own Irish name and the surname of his cousins in Spiddal. O'Hara played Mary Kate Danaher, a village colleen every inch Thornton's match in temperament.

Herbert Yates was far from enthusiastic about the project, convinced that the film would never make a penny, and he referred to it as Ford's "phony art-house movie." Even after *The Quiet Man* was scheduled to go before the cameras, Yates called Wingate Smith into his office and said, "Wingate, you're going to Ireland to make a picture that nobody will see." While the studio head tried to scale down the budget, Ford and his cinematographer, Winton Hoch, flew to Ireland to work out final details for shooting to commence in June 1951.

The director informed Michael Killanin that he could not make the film without his friend's knowledge of the country, its people, and customs. Killanin, a large, rotund Irishman whom Ford had known for decades, was later president of the International Olympic Committee. He had connections and enough experience with moviemaking to prove useful. Ford also became acquainted with Maureen O'Hara's family and asked Maureen's brother, Charles FitzSimons, to work with unit manager Lee Lukather on selecting locations and arranging accommodations for his crew.

"Ford was a caricature more than a character," FitzSimons said. "He deliberately dressed down and deliberately drove a Buick instead of a Cadillac, not wanting to give in to the Hollywood lifestyle. Yet *The Quiet Man* is show biz. I think it's one of the greatest show biz movies ever made." Killanin felt the picture was "a Western made in Ireland," peopled by stage Irish rather than authentic types. Killanin liked Ford, although he laughed at many of his antics. "He was two different people depending on whether or not he was drinking," the Irishman declared. "He could be quite irreverent toward his Catholic background, and he had a deep suspicion of most clerics."

Meanwhile in California, Herbert Yates grew increasingly nervous. *The Quite Man* was the first picture Republic had made in Europe, and Yates fought against the $1,750,000 budget Ford wanted for the picture and resented the director's insistence on total control. Ford was adamant that *The Quiet Man* be shot in color, since he considered color vital to its dramatic value—not a garish color, but a soft, misty look. Yates knew only that the picture would be the most expensive his studio had ever produced, and he saw no way that it could be a box-office success.

Ford wanted the film to be shot in Spiddal. But since Spiddal lacked the facilities to house a major motion picture company, it was decided to shoot *The Quiet Man* in Cong, a village in

County Mayo, near the Connemara coast. Cong is located in one of the poorest sections of Ireland, but the region ranks among the country's most scenic. In 1951 the village still had no electric lights; Kay Naughton, an extra in the movie, remembered studying by candlelight as a girl. "People were poor," she said, "and the picture brought a lot of much-needed money to the area. If you were around Cong at that time, *The Quiet Man* became a fever. John Murphy's store received five pounds a day to change its name to Cohan's Bar, and they only used the exterior."

Filming in Ireland lasted eight weeks, with the cast housed at Ashford Castle. Andrew McLaglen, who assisted Ford on the movie, remembered a dinner at the castle during which Ford got up and said how happy he was to be making a picture in his ancestral homeland with all of his closest friends. Besides Wayne and O'Hara, he had Ward Bond; Victor McLaglen; Barry Fitzgerald; Fitzgerald's brother, Arthur Shields; Mildred Natwick; his brother, Francis; his son, Patrick; his daughter's fiance, Ken Curtis; much of his regular crew; plus Irish friends and members of the Abbey Theatre.

The summer of 1951 found Ireland's weather dry and with a fair amount of sunshine. Still Winton Hoch complained that many days were overcast, forcing him to use booster lights to photograph through the Irish mist. Every evening the footage filmed that day was driven to Shannon Airport and flown to Hollywood for processing. Barbara Ford, who worked as assistant editor on the picture, wrote her father on June 20: "The film is beautiful. We've received five days' work and it looks just like fairyland. They really hit it on the head when they named it the Emerald Isle." But Herb Yates thought otherwise. "Everything's all green," Yates said. "Tell the cameraman to take the green filter off."

John Wayne loved Ireland and spent much of his time there mixing with the local population. When Ford came down with a cold, Wayne directed some scenes, most notably the horse race sequence. "Ford had a love for Wayne," said Martin Jurow, who represented Wayne at the time, "as much love as Ford could give. When it came to a John Ford picture, Ford literally set the terms, the place, the location, the people. In any other movie Wayne would be the total boss. But when it came to Ford, it was best not to interfere."

While the director treated Maureen O'Hara like a star, they were also intimate friends. Since O'Hara and Ford occupied adjacent rooms in Ashford Castle, younger members of the company grew convinced they were having an affair. The two spoke Gaelic on the set, and O'Hara was not beyond taking notes and writing out script changes. She and Ford spent hours together, full of mutual admiration.

"Ford had respect for women," said Michael Wayne, who spent time on the *Quiet Man* set, "but he also had a fear of women. He dealt with them like a guy who was afraid, a little distant—except for Maureen. She was very feminine and just illegally beautiful, which she knew, but she never used that as a weapon. Maureen was a lady, yet she'd throw the overhand right if things weren't going well, just like a guy would. She could be a steamroller. I think she had the same feeling for Ford my father did—that he could be a miserable son of a bitch. But they overlooked that and saw the good side of him."

Shooting the scene where O'Hara ties her hat to a stake before the horse race, Ford placed a wind machine behind the actress, which blew her hair forward and across her eyes like a whip. O'Hara kept squinting, as Ford bellowed for her to open her eyes. Finally she rested her hand on a cart, leaned forward, and said, "What would a bald-headed old son of a bitch like you know about a woman's hair lashing across her eyeballs?" Ford roared with laughter, and everybody on the set followed suit. "That was their relationship," O'Hara's brother Charlie said. "It was a give-and-take relationship of two people who had enormous respect and affection for each other."

A major portion of Wayne's scenes dragging O'Hara across the Irish countryside was filmed at the golf course next to Ashford Castle. Andrew McLaglen pointed out that there was a great deal of fresh sheep manure on the ground and sug-gested that Ford have it cleaned up before they shot the sequence, since O'Hara would be all over the ground. "Leave it!" the director ordered, giving McLaglen his prankster's smile. But he was just as quick to take advantage of beauty he hadn't planned. As Wayne was striding across the glen to bring O'Hara back from Ballyglunin Station, Ford saw a flock of seagulls in a meadow. "Quick," he said, "get the camera and set it up. Duke, walk in there." Wayne strode into the meadow with his unique walk, and all the gulls took to the air. It became a classic shot.

Andy McLaglen remembered that his father, playing Will Danaher, O'Hara's brother in the film, was to knock everything off a table in a rage at the wedding reception. Ford told the actor to look at O'Hara before he did so. They shot the scene three or four times, but Ford wasn't satisfied, insisting that the actor look directly at O'Hara. McLaglen grew exasperated; "God damn it, Jack," he exploded, "I *am* looking at Maureen." Although the veteran performer was often lazy in playing scenes, on the next take he had so much adrenaline flowing that he almost knocked the table over. That was what Ford wanted. "I thought McLaglen would kill Ford," Charles FitzSimons said, "because Jack deliberately insulted him and insulted him in front of his son. But Ford wanted seething anger. He would almost risk a friendship to get the best out of people."

"John Ford was not a nice man," Andy McLaglen maintained. "He fabricated a lot of stories and his imagination used to run away with him. He had so many people worshipping him and quaking in his presence. I never did, but don't ask me why. I think he realized that people shook around him, and control was his middle name. He told me exactly what to do and followed the script scene by scene on *The Quiet Man*. He was king of the set, but I could tell he loved his work."

Michael Killanin coached Mildred Natwick on her British accent for the picture, but since the actress worked only twelve days during the six weeks she was in Ireland, she had plenty of time to travel. "I got to know Ireland in a way I think I never would have otherwise," said Natwick, "and Ford adored being there."

A third of the way through the filming, the director wasn't sure whether he had a movie or not, and the atmosphere on the set began to hang heavy. In Cong the director developed a reputation for being cantankerous, while Yates kept sending him telegrams, threatening to shut the picture down if Ford ran over budget.

Ford also faced personal problems during the weeks on location, particularly with Patrick, who was supervising stunt work and extras on the picture. "Pat was strange," recalled Andy McLaglen. "He was a big, blustery guy, always smoking a pipe, but Jack overpowered him so much. Patrick was not my favorite person." Never good, Pat's relationship with his father grew steadily worse in the years ahead.

Charles FitzSimons came to appreciate the subtlety of Ford's genius making *The Quiet Man*. The two men were standing on a bridge overlooking the railroad station at Ballyglunin, discussing an upcoming scene. "What a wonderful place to put the camera and catch the train coming in," FitzSimons remarked. Ford turned to him and said, "Charlie, when you talk to somebody, do you climb up on a ladder and look down at them. Or do you lie down on the ground and look up at them? Or do you look at them right between the eyes?" FitzSimons replied, "I look at them right between the eyes." Ford said, "That's how I shoot motion pictures. The camera will be on the platform watching the train come in." And that's the way the scene was shot.

FitzSimons located an old threshing machine about thirty miles from where Ford intended to film the scene in which Wayne throws O'Hara's dowry into a blacksmith's fire after defeating her brother in a fight. "I towed that thresher in overnight," FitzSimons said, "because I thought it would make a powerful image standing in the field." When Ford saw it, he immediately accepted the idea. "It was wonderful on the screen," FitzSimons declared.

Work in Ireland was finished on July 17, and the company returned to California. Ford spent August and September assembling the film, insisting that music for the picture should consist entirely of Irish folk songs. As editing on *The Quiet Man* neared completion, word spread that something special was happening; John Ford had created another masterpiece.

Herbert Yates still harbored doubts and preferred to call the picture "The Prize Fighter and the Colleen," since Wayne's character had been a boxer before returning to Ireland. But at the last minute even Yates realized that *The Quiet Man* would make money, and he agreed to mount a more extensive publicity campaign than any his studio had attempted before.

The film opened in New York City on August 21, 1952, to rave reviews. The *New York Times* declared it "as darlin' a picture as we've seen this year" and complimented Ford on his superb visual effects. The picture earned the director the last of his six Academy Awards and won a thunderous ovation, along with three awards, at the Venice Film Festival. "It was a night I do not ever expect to see again," Yates wrote from Venice. *The Quiet Man* proved the most acclaimed film Republic Pictures ever made and earned the studio an unprecedented income.

Ford thought he had made "the sexiest picture ever," presented "with honesty, good taste, and humor." He called *The Quiet Man* his "first love story" and was distressed when the film was not well received in Ireland. Irish critics resented the picture's stereotyped characters and many strongly objected to character actress May Craig's line "Here's a fine stick to beat the lovely lady." By contemporary standards *The Quiet Man* is blatantly sexist, even though Ireland in 1952 was a male-dominated society. Nevertheless the movie served as a tremendous boost to tourism.

"*The Quiet Man* is doing wonderful business here," Maureen O'Hara wrote Michael Killanin from the United States, "and it gives us all a warm feeling to see an Irish picture so successful." While the film captured Ford's dream of the Emerald Isle and its people, its story remained essentially American—an immigrant's return to the tranquility of his youth. "It's an American experience for an immigrant to yearn for his home and roots," Ford's grandson Dan remarked, "even though he may never have known that home."

Longing for an ancestral home was part of Ford's own story, for he wrote Killanin soon after returning to California: "Galway is in my blood and the only place I have found peace. I was all choked up at leaving our beloved Ireland. I was afraid I would burst into tears. It seemed like the finish of an epoch in my somewhat troubled life, or maybe it was a beginning." He was even then planning to set up an Irish film company with Killanin, to be called Four Province Productions. He talked to Maureen O'Hara about a part in a nationalistic picture he had in mind and "after a three-hour hysterical outburst," Ford wrote Killanin, "she agreed due to my persuasive powers and a swift kick in the arse." Nothing came of the project, but Ford and Killanin continued to discuss ideas for the future. "As a final warning," Ford wrote his Irish friend, "you must remember that in this day and age one doesn't get rich making films."

Ford and Merian Cooper were responsible for bringing O'Hara's brother to Hollywood, but after a few years Ford and Charlie FitzSimons had an argument and parted angrily. "Ford was very dictatorial, and he had made a statement which was untrue," FitzSimons said. "I guess I'm somewhat the same way, so I demanded an apology. Of course there was no way you could get an apology from John Ford, so I walked out. He never wanted to lose track of me, but he wouldn't come down off his pedestal." Several years passed, then one night Fitz-Simons heard a knock at his door. He answered to find Ford quite inebriated. "May I come in?" asked Ford. "I want to talk to an honest man." The two became close again and remained so until Ford's death. "He was suffering all that time," Fitz-Simons declared, "but his pride wouldn't let him give in. I think inside he was a sad man, as so many creative artists are. He wasn't able to enjoy his own genius, his own sensitivity, his own goodness. But he respected an honest man."

Ford invariably minimized his triumphs. "I'm pleased when I'm honored," he said, "I'm just not fooled by it. I don't think it's the measure of my success." He insisted that his Academy Awards didn't mean a thing to him. All that was important, he said, was to keep working, and that was important only "when you're actually doing it."

With *The Quiet Man* finished, Ford went to work on *What Price Glory* for 20th Century-Fox. He had staged the 1924 Maxwell Anderson–Laurence Stallings drama in 1949 at Grauman's Chinese Theater as a benefit for the Military Order of the Purple Heart. "I always wanted to direct a stage play," he said. "I thought it was quite easy. It was a one-set play, and after a short time I got the technique of it." George O'Brien assisted him, and the cast was loaded with stars. Pat O'Brien was Quirt, Ward Bond was Flagg, and Maureen O'Hara played Charmaine, with supporting roles taken by John Wayne, Gregory Peck, Oliver Hardy, Dobe Carey, Ed Begley, Forrest Tucker, William Lundigan, and James Lydon. "Even if people were miscast," said Carey, "if they had big names, Ford wanted them. Maureen was totally wrong for Charmaine; she was supposed to be a frumpy-looking French prostitute, and she looked so gorgeous." The production sold out every night and went on tour to San Francisco, Oakland, San Jose, Long Beach, and Pasadena, making a substantial sum for the Purple Heart.

What Darryl Zanuck had in mind for the film version was a musical, with James Cagney and Dan Dailey in the leading roles. "This is our only reason and justification for remaking this property," Zanuck wrote producer Sol Siegel from Paris. "We take an old classic and we give it a fresh musical treatment." The Fox production head was aware that *What Price Glory* would be an expensive undertaking and wanted the script loaded with comedy. In late September 1951 he hadn't decided who would direct the musical, but soon settled on Ford, who accepted since he needed money and welcomed payment up front, which he didn't receive from his own company.

Ford wanted O'Hara for Charmaine, but Zanuck insisted on Corinne Calvet, whom he had under contract. "I believe that Corinne Calvet is absolutely indispensable to this setup," wrote Zanuck. "With or without talent she was the hit of *On the Riviera*." Ford called Calvet "La Blonde" and was anything but cordial to her. "I soon found myself a pawn between two large egos," the actress said. "Ford was not a man who would let anyone make choices for him, and Zanuck was not one to back down from a decision." When Calvet appeared on the set, Ford looked her over, his cigar moving back and forth in his mouth, and said, "I saw your test. Very good. But of course it's a totally wrong interpretation of the part." With that he walked away.

Zanuck also cast young Robert Wagner, whom he was grooming for stardom, as the juvenile romantic interest in the picture, opposite Marisa Pavan. While Ford befriended handsome, young performers, he was consistently tough on them, and Wagner proved no exception. "I was just starting in the picture business," the actor said. "I was very eager, and having the opportunity to work with John Ford was quite a thrill. But he always had one guy that he'd pick on, and that was me. He was just tyrannical."

Wagner admitted that he was scared to death of Ford, who addressed him as "Boob" rather than Bob. The director called him over one day. "You want to be in this business, don't you?" Ford said to the nervous youth. "Yes, sir, Mr. Ford, I do," replied Wagner. Ford motioned to an actor playing a one-legged priest in the movie. "You see that guy over there?" Ford asked. "That's Barry Norton. Barry Norton played the part you're playing in the original *What Price Glory*. He was a big star. But he became king of the queens. That could happen to you." Wagner was so shattered that he bumped into a fellow as he turned to go. "Boob," Ford barked, "do you know who that was?" Wagner shook his head. "That was King Baggott," said Ford. "Do you know who King Baggott was, Boob?" Wagner shook his head again. "He used to make $27,500 a week, had a gold-lined swimming pool. Look at him. You could be with him. You could be doing what he's doing someday."

Wagner was mystified, not knowing what to make of this giant he'd respected from afar. "Whether he was trying to get me churned up or get something going in me, I don't know," the actor said later. "Maybe he was trying to get me angry instead of just being a complacent, good-looking kid who was walking through the part. Maybe he was trying to get me hot. But it was an interesting personality quirk."

Wagner was doing a scene in a trench one day when the director picked up a clod of dirt and appeared ready to throw it at him. The young actor was ready to tear into Ford, but John Wayne, who happened to be on the set that day, stopped him. "Take it easy," said Wayne, "don't get upset. That's just his way." Wagner grew even more confused when Ford chewed him out for not staying in camera range. "Boob, I couldn't see you," the director shouted. "If you can't see the camera, the camera can't see you." Wagner answered, "I thought I wasn't supposed to look at the camera, Mr. Ford." With two hundred extras present Ford raced toward the youth and knocked him to the ground. "I could have won the Academy Award for that moment," a mature Robert Wagner declared. "I was so startled. [James] Cagney picked me up. I didn't know what the hell had happened. Can you imagine being twenty-one years old and getting knocked on your ass by John Ford, the biggest picturemaker in the business at that time? I thought my career was at an end."

Wagner claimed that he never caught Ford's directorial sense and doubted that he would have survived the picture had it not been for cameraman Joseph MacDonald. The future star admired Ford's timing and his instinct for composition, but didn't feel he was an actor's director. "For me he was just a miserable son of a bitch," said Wagner.

Darryl Zanuck complained that MacDonald, who was shooting the film in color, got too artificial with his lighting. He also urged Ford to move along with the production when the director fell two days behind schedule. While Zanuck continued to voice concern over the photography, Ford grew uncomfortable with the musical aspects of the picture, which he admitted he knew nothing about. He resented the interference that came from the front office and complained that producer Sol Siegel was "butting in" and trying to "throw songs in the thing" that Ford claimed weren't any good to begin with. "There wasn't one catchy tune in the whole score," said Ford. "A quarter of the way through I got disgusted with it." Most of the songs were eventually eliminated, and Zanuck instructed Ford to play the drama straight.

The result was a mishmash. The picture became mainly a celebration of military camaraderie, with interesting battle sequences, slapdash humor, and poetic images of deserted villages and soldiers outlined against a multicolored sky. When the film was released in August 1952 reviews were mixed, but leaned toward the negative. *Time* called the adaptation "a soft-boiled movie version of the hard-boiled Anderson-Stallings war play of 1924," and said that Ford's rework had eliminated much of the play's "bawdy vitality and grim view of war."

What Price Glory had no sooner wrapped than Ford was aboard the *Araner* headed for Honolulu. His drinking between pictures had become even more problematic as his body grew less able to withstand the abuse. "He'd get so drunk that he wouldn't hear and couldn't even talk," said Charles Fitz-Simons. "He'd just mumble and you wouldn't know what he was talking about." But drinking remained one of the few ways Ford knew to relax. During the making of a picture he avoided liquor through sheer willpower. "He could control himself for the purity of the project," FitzSimons declared. "But he would finish a movie, and within two or three days he would go on a drunk that might last twenty days, where he'd end up helpless, lying in a bed, and have to be taken to a hospital. That was the great tragedy of his life."

Few doubted that Ford was well read and an authority on American history, especially on the Civil War, but most agreed he was anti-intellectual and liked to poke fun at the college educated, particularly those who took themselves seriously. Michael Wayne remembered Ford's putting a Phi Beta Kappa key, which he'd bought in a pawn shop, on his watch chain. Ford loved for people to notice the key and would then remark, "I got it at Vassar."

"If you walked into his bedroom, the shelves were lined with books," Charlie FitzSimons said. "The ceiling was stained with nicotine from the cigars and pipe smoke from Ford's reading in bed." Darcy O'Brien, who became a professor of literature and was impressed with Ford's knowledge of serious writers, felt that he surrounded himself with physical types to refresh him after prolonged exposure to books and the world of ideas. "He was intolerant of intellectual bullshit," said O'Brien, "and the word 'art' embarrassed him. Ford was a serious artist, but he was unbalanced, like all artists. That's the condition of being an artist."

In May 1952 Barbara Ford married Ken Curtis, who later won

fame as Festus on television's *Gunsmoke*. The wedding took place in Las Vegas. Although Ford was overprotective toward his daughter, he liked Curtis as much as he had disliked Robert Walker. Ford and Curtis had first worked together while his future son-in-law was singing with the Sons of the Pioneers. Aware that Barbara was in love with Curtis, Jack gave him as much camera exposure as he could. After the couple married, Ford bragged that Curtis was six feet tall, which was an exaggeration, but it was clear how happy he was with the match.

"Barb had a fixation on Western actors," said Jack's niece, Cecil de Prida. "She also had a fixation on other women's men." For a few years Barbara and Ken Curtis seemed like an ideal couple. Then Barbara started drinking heavily, and the marriage crumbled. "I've always felt that Barbara was very much like her father," Joanne Dru said. "She was just too vulnerable."

During the 1950s Ford's pessimistic outlook intensified; he fretted about Communists and beatniks and changes he didn't understand. His health was not good, and his brother Francis had developed cataracts. "I am terribly worried about Frank," Francis's wife wrote Jack in 1952. "He hasn't worked for over one year. Wish you could help him, he walks the floors constantly. I know he isn't too old to act." The next year Francis Ford died of cancer. "Frank had an easy passing and all his thoughts were about Ireland," Jack wrote Michael Killanin. "His last hours all he could speak was Irish."

Ford's brother-in-law Wingate Smith, known to Ford regulars as Unk, had his gallbladder removed in 1952, and Frank Nugent suffered a coronary. Ford visited the two men in the hospital and found them side by side. While he was waiting for the elevator, a nurse wheeled out Ward Bond, who had had his appendix taken out. The Ford stock company seemed to be falling apart.

Meanwhile the association with Herbert Yates had become strained, and Republic's bookkeeping system began to look suspicious. "Having acrimonious legal business complications with Yates," Ford cabled Michael Killanin. "Suing in process. Absolutely impossible for me personally to do business with him." The Republic mogul kept a spittoon by the desk in his office, which he aimed at more times than he hit. Ford claimed he spat in Technicolor and disliked him thoroughly. But the creative accounting Yates employed to tally box-office receipts on *The Quiet Man* led to rupture. Argosy's legal battle with Republic would drag on until 1956, when Yates agreed to pay Ford and Cooper $546,000 each. The director had one more movie to make for the studio under their three-picture deal; then he and Cooper planned to end the relationship.

Another of Ford's concerns during the early 1950s was that he was offered nothing but scripts he considered morally objectionable. For his final production at Republic, he decided on a remake of *Judge Priest*, called *The Sun Shines Bright*, based on three homespun stories by Irvin S. Cobb. Laurence Stallings wrote the screenplay, and the picture was shot in Kentucky, away from Yates's supervision, beginning on August 18, 1952. *The Sun Shines Bright* was everything films at that time weren't supposed to be. It was an unspectacular, unrealistic, lighthearted slice of Americana, made with no stars and a limited budget.

Ford loved the movie and later claimed it was his personal favorite. "It's a very simple story," he said, "the kind I like." He compared the picture to *Wagonmaster*, declaring, "I knew they weren't going to be smash hits—I did them for my own amusement." He told a reporter, "My own personal view is that a short story, like these, makes the best picture, better than a long novel which you have to cut." *The Sun Shines Bright* had a shooting schedule of twenty-four days. "The main thing we're up against today," said Ford, "is economy. We've got to concentrate and go like hell. Ten years ago we'd never shoot this fast."

The director eventually said that *The Sun Shines Bright* was the only picture of his that he liked to see over and over. "The only trouble was that when I left the studio, old man Yates didn't know what to do with it," said Ford. "The picture had comedy, drama, pathos, but he didn't understand it. . . . Yates fooled around with it after I left and almost ruined it." In New York the film opened not in downtown Manhattan, but in twenty neighborhood theaters. Most critics weren't particularly impressed, finding it saccharine and old-fashioned.

Times were changing, and Ford didn't seem to be keeping pace. In May 1952 Merian Cooper left Argosy to replace Mike Todd as head of production at Cinerama, ending the partnership with Ford. Both Cooper and Ford owned stock in Cinerama, but Ford seemed adrift.

That summer MGM asked him to direct a remake of *Red Dust*, which in 1932 had starred Clark Gable and Jean Harlow. Ford found the material trite, but a trip to Africa for location work appealed to him. *Mogambo,* as producer Sam Zimbalist called his updated version, was a big-budget production, and Gable was cast in his original role. Ford asked Charles Fitz-Simons to drive him to MGM for a conference, only to discover that he wasn't permitted to park in front of the administration building. He informed Metro's production head, Dore Schary, that he would prepare the movie from his office at Republic, which he did. He would be driven to MGM for lunch, but would immediately return to Republic, where he spent the afternoon working. "Ford kowtowed to nobody," FitzSimons said.

Ford wanted Maureen O'Hara for the Jean Harlow role in *Mogambo,* but Gable and Metro were intent on casting Ava Gardner. The studio won out, although O'Hara was considered. Ford succeeded in vetoing Deborah Kerr for the English woman, at which point studio executive Benny Thau suggested finding somebody new. Thau, Zimbalist, and Ford ran a test that 20th Century-Fox had made of a little-known actress who was thought to have promise. "The test was of a pretty girl who had a rather ordinary Irish accent and who looked drab and uninteresting," Dore Schary wrote, "but not to John Ford, who reminded us she was the lady who had played Gary Cooper's new wife in *High Noon.*" The actress—who was chosen for the part—was Grace Kelly, whom Ava Gardner remembered as "a great lady, and also great fun."

Mogambo was definitely Metro's picture, and Ford was quite aware of that fact. When screenwriter John Lee Mahin sent him a script, the director declined to attend a story conference, saying he'd shoot what he'd been handed. "But the things he added," Mahin remembered, "the little touches! The thing of the python. Then the thing of Kelly's walking in the rain, and Gable's going over and grabbing her and carrying her back in his arms in the rain. And the thing where Ava Gardner is out walking in the rain, hoping to be rescued and nobody rescues her. That and the confession and the leopard walking through the tent—those are priceless."

On October 17, 1952, Ford arrived in Nairobi, a town booming with Hollywood activity at the moment, since producers had been forced to take their cameras to exotic locations in response to growing competition from television. "Am at last in Kenya," Ford wrote Michael Killanin a week after his arrival, "which I must say is a fascinating place." He claimed that his crew worked right in the middle of the Mau Mau uprising, but they were never bothered.

Ford planned to start shooting the first week in November. The company lived in tents, but the heat and rain were oppressive. At times mud was so deep that moving equipment became impossible. By the end of the sixty-seven-day shooting schedule, Ford was feeling his age and yearning for home. He was not enthusiastic about the script, yet steeled himself to do the best he could with it. Sometimes a director "must hypnotize himself to be sympathetic toward the subject matter," he remarked. "One does one's job. The film of really personal interest is the exception."

At first Ford was cool toward Ava Gardner, quick to inform the Metro actress that he had wanted Maureen O'Hara in the part. "I can safely say that no picture in which I was ever involved got off to a worse start," Gardner wrote. "Jack Ford was in such a fury that he didn't know what to do." But after a few days Ford took Gardner aside and told her, "You're damn good. Just take it easy." From then on, they got along famously. "I never felt looser or more comfortable in a part before or since," the actress wrote, "and I was even allowed to improvise some of my dialogue." She agreed that Ford could be "one of the crustiest sons of bitches" ever to direct a film. "He could also be the meanest man on earth, thoroughly evil," she said, "but by the time the picture ended, I adored him."

The atmosphere on the set grew tense when Gardner's

husband, Frank Sinatra, arrived in Africa. Things became even more unsettled when the actress announced an impromptu trip to London. Ford and Gable worked well together, although the actor spent most of his free time in the company of Grace Kelly. "Grace wasn't pure at all," declared John Lee Mahin, "and she fell for Clark. They were in each other's beds."

Since *Mogambo* was an MGM-British production, interiors were shot at Elstree Studio, outside London. By the time postproduction was completed, Ford was exhausted and almost indifferent to the film, which he claimed had become an endurance contest. His vision had grown blurred, and when he had his eyes checked, London doctors discovered cataracts. Mary Ford joined her husband in Europe and on April 2, 1953, they boarded the *Andrea Doria* in Naples for the trip home. On the ship Jack's eyes got so bad that he spent most of his time in a darkened room, unable to read. "I know you will keep it confidential," he wrote Michael Killanin. "It is hard for me to say this, but the facts are briefly that I am afraid I am going blind."

In June he entered Good Samaritan Hospital in Los Angeles for removal of the cataracts. Although the operation proved successful, Ford's right eye remained sensitive to light the rest of his life. "My eyes are still bothering me terribly," he wrote Killanin on July 30, "just can't stand the light, although the doctor says that is a natural result of the operation and that I must be patient and allow plenty of time."

In October *Mogambo* opened at Radio City Music Hall, but was dismissed as another of Hollywood's safaris in Africa. Most of its interest centered around the performances of Clark Gable and Ava Gardner, since Gardner had never been better and Gable equaled his earlier performance.

While Ford was working in Africa news had arrived that *The Quiet Man* had won him his fourth Oscar as best director. John Wayne collected the award. While recuperating from his eye operation, Ford saw the picture on the big screen and was pleased with the final results. "Things that you didn't notice in the small screen popped out," he wrote Killanin, "and the characters seem so much more vital."

Yet Ford worried about his friend John Wayne, whose second marriage had ended amid scandal. "Don't ruin your life," Ford cautioned in a handwritten note in July 1953. He decided to fly down to Mexico for a visit with Wayne while the actor was making *Hondo*. Although John Farrow directed the picture, Wayne arranged for Ford to supervise some second-unit work. Wayne's leading lady, stage actress Geraldine Page, wasn't prepared for the Ford she met. "Mr. Ford affects army fatigues as a way of dress," she said, "with a hat cocked way over on one side, and he has a habit of having a very used handkerchief in his pocket, which he takes out and twists, and puts in the corner of his mouth and sucks on while he's talking. It gets wet with saliva about four inches down. He sits way down, and he has quite a big belly that sticks up, and he sort of pats himself. The visual image of him is so revolting that you have to remember the wonderful things he's done."

Unable to work for nearly a year after his eye operation, Ford was at loose ends. He visited his brother Pat in Maine, but sank into depression. He worried about the threat of communism and pulled more to the right politically. He revealed his conservative leanings to Michael Killanin: "Your letter received with the discouraging news that the Reds — to wit: one John Huston is seeking refuge in our lovely Ireland. This ain't good. He is not of the Right Wing."

Ford learned that a storm had struck Santa Barbara, where the *Araner* was moored, driving the yacht onto a sandbar and damaging its bottom. Worse still, the city of Los Angeles was enlarging the parking lot for the Hollywood Bowl and forcing owners to vacate the property needed. The Fords had no choice but to sell their Odin Street house, where they had lived for over thirty years. They bought a colonial mansion at 125 Copa de Oro Road in Bel Air, near the UCLA campus, a house once owned by Frank Lloyd and later by William Wyler. Ford insisted that his old den be recreated in the Bel Air home to house his massive library.

In March 1954 he began shooting *The Long Gray Line* and moved the company to West Point the following month. It was

Ford's first movie in CinemaScope, and he hated the wide-screen process. "You've never seen a painter use that kind of composition" he said. "Even the great murals weren't this huge tennis court. I like to see the people, and if you shoot them in wide screen, you're left with a lot of real estate on either side." He still believed the 1.85 ratio (the normal screen) was best and accepted the current fad only under pressure. *The Long Gray Line* was made for Columbia, whose boss, Harry Cohn, was among the more uncouth moguls in the business. But Ford found that Cohn operated with fairness; he simply spoke his mind in a loud voice.

The picture for Cohn was based loosely on the autobiography of Sergeant Martin Maher, an Irishman who spent fifty years at West Point as an athletic trainer. Ford wanted John Wayne for the lead, but drew Tyrone Power instead. Since Power played a man spanning several decades in age, the actor tried a number of props to make himself look older and decided on a corncob pipe for a later age. He mentioned the idea to Ford, only to have him call for silence on the set. "I would like to hear more from this thinking actor," Ford said, embarrassing Power before the crew. "John had to prove to himself and to the cast that everything came from him," screenwriter Nunnally Johnson said.

Ford succeeded in acquiring Maureen O'Hara for the film, but then proceeded to give her a difficult time. He was angry over a romance she was having in Mexico. After the director had harassed her on the set for a couple of weeks, O'Hara got mad. She announced that she'd had it, vowing that she'd never work with Ford again, but she did one more time.

Dobe Carey, who played Dwight Eisenhower as a cadet, made the mistake of partying one night with some buddies, since none of them was scheduled to work the next day. Ford found out they'd been drinking and left orders for them to be awakened early the next morning to shoot a scene he quickly made up. In the added sequence a group of cadets, played by the hung-over actors, receive swimming instructions beside an indoor pool. The actors arrived feeling terrible, and the hot, humid room merely exacerbated their misery. "I saw this horrible practical joke that Ford played on those guys," said Patrick Wayne, who played a part in the picture. "He liked to keep everybody on their toes."

Charlie FitzSimons recalled Ford's difficulty with his eyes during the making of *The Long Gray Line*. If Ford wanted to read something, he'd hold the page up to his covered eye, lift his eye patch, and read with that eye. "That meant that the 'good' eye was not capable of reading," said FitzSimons. "That must have been terrible for a man who spent his life reading. And it must have been terrible for a man to whom vision had been so important all his life."

Work on the picture wasn't easy for Ford, which in part explained his foul mood. He had contracted a virus in Honolulu before shooting began, and it seemed to be a recurring variety. He admitted to Michael Killanin that making *The Long Gray Line* was a trying experience — "three days up and one day in bed."

The picture was not a box office success, and critics branded it mawkish, even though they found its characters lovable and warm. Ford seemed uncertain about the glories of war, while his hero failed to succeed as he had wanted. The director's personal anguish was beginning to show in his work; the bitterness would become more manifest over the years ahead.

Ford's next project would push him to the brink. Before starting *The Long Gray Line* he had committed himself to the film version of the recent Broadway success *Mr. Roberts*, and he recognized that the picture carried the prestige he sorely needed. Since *Mr. Roberts* was a navy story, Ford appeared a logical choice to direct it. He was a navy man and the play was a comedy, which Ford considered his forte. Since the Pearl Harbor bombing, he had made fifteen films, ten of them dealing with war. Although Joshua Logan, who had directed the New York production and helped write the script, had hoped to direct the picture, producer Leland Hayward and agent Lew Wasserman talked him out of it. "Josh, you do want to make money out of *Roberts,* don't you?" Wasserman said. "I know a way of adding a million dollars to the gross. Let John

Ford direct it. He's got a reputation for being able to direct men. This is a man's story, and I think that he would be the ideal man to do it." Disheartened, Logan agreed.

Mr. Roberts reunited Ford and Henry Fonda, who had created the title role on Broadway. The two had worked together earlier with excellent results and had unlimited respect for one another. But Fonda had played Roberts for more than two years on the stage and had absorbed every nuance of the part, and was thus less amenable than usual to Ford's direction. The first indication of trouble appeared when Ford flew to New York to see *Mr. Roberts* on the stage. The management held reserved seats for him, and Fonda waited for Ford to come backstage after the performance, only to learn that Ford and his friends had returned to California without seeing the play. Fonda was flabbergasted. "You mean to tell me you didn't see it?" he asked Ford. "Do you expect me to sit through that homosexual play?" Ford replied.

Fonda was upset, and became more so when he discovered that Ford was rewriting the script, adding scenes that had little to do with the original play. "I am as busy as hell . . . trying to doctor *Mr. Roberts,*" Ford wrote Michael Killanin on June 4, 1954, "which has not been written to my satisfaction." Yet when Jack Warner decided Fonda was too old for the role and wanted to replace him with Marlon Brando, Ford said he wouldn't make the movie without him; the part belonged to Fonda.

Ford was to be paid $175,000 for the picture and assigned a shooting schedule of forty-five days. In mid-September the company flew to Honolulu, stayed overnight, then flew to Midway, where they were housed in naval installations. "While we were on Midway," Dobe Carey said, "I saw on the third or fourth day that things weren't going well. John Ford was not veering that much from the script, because he knew what a powerful story it is. But he was putting in pieces of business, and I felt that Henry didn't agree with that."

Carey was right; Fonda was furious. Ford began to mix the sailors' lines, giving them at random to various actors he liked. "Each sailor was a character of his own," Fonda said. "I knew what the timing on each scene was. Pappy was stacking one line on top of the other. There was no chance for the audience to laugh, and if they did laugh, they weren't going to hear the next line. Ford wanted to do it his way, and there was no way his way could work. There was only one way to do that play, and Josh Logan had done it."

William Powell, playing Doc, hadn't made a film in several years and was so nervous he developed facial tics and forgot lines. Powell's timing was off, and Ford's impatience made matters worse. James Cagney accepted the role of the captain thinking the picture would be a lark. He intended to sun on the beach and enjoy a vacation with his wife. "There was no plan for anything but having a little fun," said Cagney. "I played the Skipper because Jack Ford asked me to, but they kept delaying and delaying."

Jack Lemmon looked forward to playing the part of Pulver, which he considered one of the greatest comedy roles ever written. "I found that Ford gave less direction than any director I'd worked with," Lemmon declared. "I also began to learn through him that giving a lot of direction and saying a lot of words does not necessarily have anything to do with direction. Ford would maybe give one piece of direction in a three-page scene. But that one piece of direction he gave would open up a volume to you." Lemmon cited the example of Pulver's first encounter with the captain, who hasn't seen the ensign in nine months, despite their being on the same ship. Pulver explains to the captain that he's the laundry officer. "Spend most of your time in the laundry, I guess," the captain suggests, in an effort to explain why he's never laid eyes on the officer before. Pulver says yes, pointing to the laundry. Ford's one piece of direction was, "Do you really know where that laundry is?" It was the first scene Lemmon shot on the film. "That comment opened up a whole new world for me," the actor said. "That one thing gave me Pulver."

Often to the detriment of the original concept, Ford added his own brand of humor—a motorcycle racing off the pier, Pulver showing nurses around the ship and thinking dishwater is soup. The director wanted to make the humor more physical, add action, and take advantage of the location, but Fonda grew more antagonistic, objecting to what he termed "Ford's low-down Irish humor." The play held special meaning for the star, and he was convinced that the purity of the drama was being lost.

Leland Hayward was commuting back and forth between Hawaii and Midway, trying to keep peace. During a scene between Fonda and Powell, Powell had trouble with his lines and wanted another take. When Ford refused, Fonda became angry and at the end of the day stormed off to his room. A few minutes later Hayward came in and told the actor that Ford wanted to see him. Fonda and Hayward walked into Ford's quarters, finding him in a wicker chair. "I don't know how many words I got out," Fonda said, "but what I had to say was criticism. Ford rose out of his chair and knocked me over backwards. The chair knocked over a water pitcher, which scared the shit out of Leland. It was so embarrassing that I just walked out of the room. A half hour later Pappy came to apologize."

From then on their relationship was never the same. On almost every scene, Ford asked Fonda in a pointed way, "Is this right?" "So the relationship was gone," Fonda recalled, "and it's too bad. I've been sad about it the rest of my life." For a time the actor was bitter. "It had been a love story," said Fonda. "I'd done seven pictures for John Ford. I recognized all the sadistic, perverse things in this man, but he was pretty close to a genius. I'd seen him destroy people, and yet I would forgive him. He was always respectful of me, respected my talent, liked me as a person." Now that was gone.

By the time the company returned to Honolulu, Ford knew he had blown the picture. Breaking his own rule, he started drinking. At first it was only beer, but he surprised everyone by drinking openly, more each day. "It was as bad as it could be," Fonda remembered, "and he finally had to be dried out in a hospital." Ward Bond tried to keep the cameras rolling, but neither he nor Fonda could manage without a director at the helm. The picture was shut down while Ford pulled himself together. When filming resumed in Hawaii, Ford wasn't drinking, but was still in a bad way.

After the company returned to Hollywood, Dobe Carey arrived on the set one morning to have Ford say, "Look at me." Carey saw that the director's stomach was bloated. It was his gallbladder, which doctors said had to be removed. Ford would let only his own physician operate, which meant a delay of several days. He was taken off *Mr. Roberts* on October 15 and sent home.

On short notice Mervyn LeRoy replaced him, reverting to the play's original script as nearly as possible. LeRoy had been making *Strange Lady in Town* with Greer Garson, but the picture had temporarily shut down when its star became ill. "To be honest about it," Dobe Carey said, "Mervyn LeRoy didn't know anything about *Mr. Roberts.* He kept asking Henry Fonda what to do." A number of scenes that Ford had started on location were scheduled for completion in the studio, but now had to be reshot since LeRoy's style didn't match Ford's. The cinematic look that Ford wanted was lost, so the film became a disappointment to cameraman Winton Hoch. "They recreated the deck of the ship on a stage," Hoch said. "The sky was nailed onto the wall."

Joshua Logan eventually directed a few scenes. "I certainly don't look on John Ford as a legend," Logan said later. "I think he was a terrible man. He did some wonderful pictures, but he was a mean son of a bitch." To Logan, Ford's concept of *Mr. Roberts* was all wrong. The stage director was disgusted when he saw the movie, particularly objecting to the interpretation of the captain. Logan felt the captain had been turned into such a clown by Ford that he offered no threat. Critics and audiences, however, liked the film, finding it superior entertainment.

Ford had his gallbladder removed in late October and spent the remainder of 1954 recuperating. "He played like he was dying," recalled Michael Wayne, who visited Ford while he was sick. In December Jack, Mary, Barbara, and Ken Curtis went to Europe on a vacation, visiting London, Paris, and Rome. Ford gave an occasional interview, but in January 1955 was ordered by physicians to return home for complete rest.

With his career in shambles and on the threshold of disgrace,

Ford couldn't rest for long. In late January he and Frank Nugent started work on *The Searchers,* Ford's first Western in five years. "We are busy working on the script of *The Serachers,*" Ford wrote Michael Killanin in March. "It is a tough, arduous job as I want it to be good. I've been longing to do a Western for quite some time. It's good for my health, spirit, and morale and also good for the physical health of my numerous Feeney Peasantry, by whom I am surrounded."

Based on a novel by Alan Le May, *The Searchers* would prove Ford's visual masterpiece, his finest Western, and, many feel, the best film he ever made. The movie won a cult following that has outlasted any of his other pictures, and it demonstrates a psychological complexity the director had not achieved before and would never equal again. C. V. "Jock" Whitney put up the money for the project, and the movie saw a brief revival of Ford's partnership with Merian Cooper. *The Searchers* is a brutal story, its characters not the romantic figures the public had come to expect in Westerns. Ford felt the film called for a realistic look and chose the works of cowboy artist Charles M. Russell as his model.

Although *The Searchers* begins in Texas during 1868, Ford shot the picture mainly in Monument Valley. Never has the valley been photographed more magnificently. "For Ford, Monument Valley was not only a location," agent-producer Martin Jurow said, "it was his dream of the America he loved." This time the Navajo portrayed Comanche, with instructions from Ford relayed to them over a walkie-talkie through Lee Bradley. The company again was housed at the Gouldings' trading post and in nearby tents. "By then we knew how Ford wanted his room," Mike Goulding declared. "He wanted one double bed in his quarters, and he liked to have a refrigerator with different kinds of juices. He was a wonderful guest. So was John Wayne."

The role of Ethan Edwards in *The Searchers* proved one of Wayne's strongest characterizations. By 1955 Ford and Wayne had their signals worked out so well that they seemed to communicate by osmosis. Their relationship was sometimes abrasive, but was rooted in affection. Despite the director's political shift to the right, he still considered himself a Democrat, which placed him at odds with Wayne. Still, Ford would grin and say, "I love that damn Republican."

Sixteen-year-old Patrick Wayne played a young cavalry officer in the picture. Patrick was Ford's godson and his pet. "Someone was always in the barrel with John Ford," Pat Wayne confirmed. "Everyone had their turn. They were the brunt of his jokes or the object of his wrath—except me. I was the apple of his eye and could do no wrong. I was never criticized or reprimanded. I lived in fear of it, waiting for the other shoe to fall, but it never happened." Ford had initially thought that Duke's son Michael was his godson, then discovered his mistake. While Ford bragged on Patrick, his relationship with Michael grew progressively worse. The director rode Michael unmercifully and seemed to resent him.

In Monument Valley Ford and Patrick would perform parlor tricks for the company at night. Shooting had begun in June, when the days were long, and the crew worked until everyone was exhausted. "The main social event," Pat Wayne recalled, "was dinner, and dinners would last for two and a half to three hours because we'd sit around the table and talk. There was nothing else to do. Ford and I would do these parlor tricks that would amaze everybody, mostly card tricks or mental telepathy. Nobody could figure out how we did them. We would work as a team, but I would be his ploy. He taught me how to do them, and I picked them up fast. I think that was the reason he liked having me around. He wasn't crazy about kids generally. I always felt that I had a better relationship with him than he had with his own children."

The only negative experience Patrick had with Ford came over a game of gin rummy. Pat thought he was such a good gin rummy player that he'd let the old man win. They played a hand, and Ford won the game. Patrick assumed they'd play another, but Ford closed the deck and said, "From now on, stick to playing cards with little kids and Ward Bond."

Pat Wayne loved Monument Valley because he was there with his father. "All of that work for me at that age was special," he said, "because of my then four brothers and sisters, I was the only one working with Dad. I had my father to myself. I didn't have to compete for attention."

Young Wayne also enjoyed the location because he had an attractive friend his age working on the picture — Natalie Wood. "That really made it great," recalled Patrick, "so I wasn't completely dependent upon my father for my amusement. Natalie was super." Dobe Carey remembered how Wood developed a crush on Pat while they were making the film, but said the boy was too shy to reciprocate.

"*The Searchers* was extra special from the minute we started work on it," said Carey. "It was a different movie from anything I'd seen Ford do. From the first day of shooting it had a mood about it. Wayne was so powerful in that picture; he had really done his homework. He *became* Ethan Edwards. I think it was the greatest performance Duke ever gave."

Carey roomed with Ward Bond in Monument Valley, as he often did. Bond made a habit of walking around their quarters naked, hoping actress Vera Miles would notice him. Miles was rooming nearby with Olive Carey, but she paid no attention to the strutting actor. "Ward would say dirty things," Dobe Carey recalled, "because he thought the way to a woman's heart was to be as crude as possible."

Alan Le May's novel was so grim that Nugent and Ford added two comic characters: a top-hatted Texas ranger who also serves as a preacher (the Ward Bond part) and a fool of Shakespearean proportions named Mose Harper, played by Hank Worden. When Worden asked the director how he should interpret his part, Ford remarked, "Just play it naturally." The actor overheard Ford comment to John Wayne, "If the old son of a bitch will just play himself, he's stupid enough to be what I want." Old Mose spent most of the film looking for a rocking chair, but Worden said Ford improvised one of his best lines. Just before the Comanche cross a river to attack, Ford told Worden to look heavenward and say, "Oh, Lord, we thank thee for the blessings we are about to receive." It was a typical Ford touch.

Worden bunked in one of the tents below the Gouldings' post and claimed the food was better there than in the dining hall, where the stars ate. "Once in a while Ford and Duke and a few more would come down and eat with us," the actor recalled. "Duke would put his arm around me and say, 'Hank, you old son of a bitch.' That meant he liked me."

Jeff Hunter, who played Martin Pawley in the movie, also slept in one of the tents. Natalie Wood's future husband, Robert Wagner, had wanted Hunter's part, and realized what a great picture *The Searchers* was going to be. Wagner visited Ford in his office, hoping to be cast. "Boob," the director said as they talked, "you really want this part, don't you?" The young actor grew hopeful. "Yes, sir, Mr. Ford, I really do," he replied. "It's a great part." Ford led him on, then said, "Well, you're not going to get it. Jeff Hunter is." Wagner was devastated. "That was Ford's mean side," the actor later remarked.

Ford continued to be as hard on his friends as he was on anyone. "When will you learn to ride a horse" he growled at John Wayne, as the actor sat atop a gelding with his hand on the saddle horn. "You ride like a goddamn sissy." Ward Bond had a death in his family during filming and was absent a few days. When he returned to work, he was still shaken and didn't do a scene the way Ford wanted. "Get your damned mind off that funeral!" Ford yelled at him.

Since the company was in Monument Valley over Fourth of July, Ford arranged a celebration that included the three hundred Navajo who were working on the picture. The festivities involved food, fireworks, horse races, and other contests for the company's amusement. The wife of one of the Stanley brothers cooked, while her children clung to her skirt. Ford, wearing a purple neckerchief, delighted in growling and chasing a little Navajo girl around the wooden tables and back to her mother. When financier Jock Whitney visited the location, Ford ordered a mock fight between two stuntmen, along with horse falls.

Ken Curtis played Charlie McCorry in the picture, which was written as a straight part. Curtis and Jeff Hunter were competing for Vera Miles in the story, and Ford knew that Curtis would have to do something to make himself stand out, since he wasn't as good-looking as Hunter. One night Ford heard Curtis speaking in a country accent he had developed when he was with the Sons of the Pioneers. Ford told him to use the accent in the movie, claiming it would give his character a unique quality. Curtis did, and that marked the origin of his Festus characterization, used later on *Gunsmoke*. "The accent made the part," Curtis said. "Otherwise it would have been nothing."

Pat Ford was billed as associate producer on *The Searchers*, but the tension between Jack and his son became worse every time they worked together. Likewise Jack and his brother Eddie quarreled. Although Eddie O'Fearna continued to serve as Jack's assistant, he never visited his brother's home, insisting that he "wouldn't go into the son of a bitch's house." O'Fearna and Wingate Smith also feuded. "I liked parts of working with Jack," Smith later declared, "other parts I hated. I was going to quit after every picture."

"Nobody ever got close to John Ford," said Lefty Hough. "Not even his own brothers." As Ford grew older, he became more of a loner. When he was disturbed, he shut everybody out until he resolved whatever was bothering him. With *The Searchers* he knew that his career was on the line; another failure and he was through.

The director probed the movie's characters deeply, captured beauty and reality, improvised touches that were convincing and natural, and demonstrated his genius as never before. In time every frame of the picture would be dissected by film scholars. But Mike Goulding may have delivered the definitive critique, phrased simply but accurately. "I loved *The Searchers*," she said. "It was so complete."

The picture's final scene was shot late in the afternoon. The cast had rehearsed it two or three times, and all felt the importance of it. "Jack made you feel that every scene was one of the high spots of the movie," said Olive Carey, "even if it was walking through a door. That's why he got such great performances." But the last scene of *The Searchers* was special, and Carey became emotional while they filmed it. John Wayne returns from seven years of wandering, lets the other performers in the scene walk past him, then assumes a stance characteristic of Ollie's late husband, Harry. He holds the pose for a moment, before he turns and walks away. "Duke was the most graceful man I've ever seen," Olive declared, "and we knew the power of that scene. What a beautiful movie."

The buffalo-hunting scenes in the film were shot in Canada, while the snow scenes were filmed near Gunnison, Colorado. Interiors were photographed back in Burbank, since Warner Bros. released the picture. Toward the end of work in the studio, the camera quit suddenly in the middle of the dramatic scene in which Wayne tells Dobe Carey that he found Carey's girlfriend raped and killed by the Indians and buried her in his overcoat. Ford bawled out the operator, who looked perplexed and said, "The camera just stopped, Mr. Ford." Ward Bond had entered the soundstage and disconnected the camera by mistake to plug in his shaver.

The Searchers wrapped on August 16, 1955, after a shooting schedule of fifty-nine days. The company had worked in 115-degree temperatures, driving winds, and summer sandstorms, but they knew that Ford had photographed a masterpiece. The idealism of the director's earlier Americana had been replaced by anguish, while his Western hero had grown hard. Ethan Edwards is a frontiersman whose hatreds and obsessions border on insanity. The American dream had soured for Ford; *The Searchers* became a parody of the heroic quest.

Ford viewed the story as a tragedy, "the tragedy of the loner," he said. Ethan Edwards returns from the Civil War, after undisclosed adventures in Mexico, unable to accept or understand society. He cannot embrace family life and has allowed the woman he loves to marry his brother, even though she continues to love him. Ethan is hostile to civilization's rituals, easily becomes impatient and claustrophobic, and is doomed to remain a wanderer. He belongs neither to the white nor the Indian world, but remains a son of the frontier — masculine, repressed, celibate, brutalized. His very presence threatens to destroy the stability of his brother's family. The door of their cabin, which introduces and closes the film, is symbolic of the central conflict, family versus the eternal loner.

When his brother's family is massacred by Comanche and

their two daughters are abducted, Ethan's desire for revenge estranges him from society still further. With his mixed-blooded, adopted nephew, Martin Pawley, Ethan spends seven years looking for his niece Debbie, driven more by racial hatred and vengeance than a desire to rescue the kidnapped girl. When Ethan realizes that Debbie has come of age and become an Indian's squaw, his search turns destructive. Driven by psycho-sexual fears, Ethan is determined to kill the girl, who by mating with an Indian has ceased in his mind to be white. As the search continues, the similarities between Ethan and the Comanche chief who led the raid and captured Debbie become clear, since both are driven by a determination for revenge.

With every year Ethan's racism grows more fanatic, until the frontiersman is exposed as a maniac, his mind clogged with bigotry and sexual repression. He scalps the Comanche chief and attempts to carry out his threat to kill Debbie. In the end he relents for two reasons: through their journey together Ethan has come to accept Martin, himself one-quarter Indian, and to a degree surmounted his racism; and Ethan at last remembers that Debbie is the daughter of the woman he loved. In the original script Ethan lifts Debbie over his head and says, "You sure favor your mother." But in the film the line became, "Let's go home, Debbie."

In the final scene, the one that moved Olive Carey so deeply, Martin and Debbie are welcomed into the home of a neighboring family, but Ethan, the tragic outsider, stands framed in the doorway, then turns and walks away. The door shuts and the screen goes black, as it was in the beginning. "The tragic moment forces men to reveal themselves," said Ford at the time *The Searchers* was made. "What interests me are the consequences of a tragic moment—how the individual acts before a crucial fact, or in an exceptional circumstance. . . . I look before all else for simplicity, for the naked truth in the midst of rapid, even brutal action." The director captured basic truth in *The Searchers,* creating tensions so complex, so haunting, and so subliminal that critics have called the movie "the story of America."

No longer are the cavalry troops the knightly protectors of

an underdeveloped society, nor is there community on this frontier. Each family in *The Searchers* fights to hold its own homestead. Mrs. Jorgenson (the character portrayed by Olive Carey) understands that the settlers must learn to accept this rugged land on its own terms. To live by the rules she taught as a schoolmarm is to live in the past. Yet the film depicts neither the civilized order nor the wilderness in idealized terms. To live in harmony with the realities of this raw frontier necessitates compromise and change; there are no alternatives.

The Searchers would be Ford's last association with Merian Cooper, who decided to retire when the picture was finished and urged Ford to do the same. Ford considered the possibility, but work was his life. "Ford didn't have the domestic situation that Cooper had," Charles FitzSimons said. "Cooper had other involvements, a doting wife, and a son and daughter to be proud of, but for Ford there was nowhere else to go. He had to go on making movies." When Argosy Pictures dissolved in January 1956 he formed John Ford Productions, determined to continue on his own.

While waiting for his finest Western to hit the theaters, Ford made a trip to Ireland to talk with Michael Killanin about making movies there. He returned home to direct his first work for television, an episode for *Fireside Theatre* called "The Bamboo Cross," filmed in early November 1955 with actress Jane Wyman heading the cast. "Rookie of the Year" followed, a teleplay for *Screen Directors Playhouse,* featuring Patrick Wayne in the title role, and a supporting cast that included Vera Miles, Ward Bond, and John Wayne. Although television was considered by most Hollywood celebrities as slumming, Ford took the assignment seriously.

The Ford family spent the Christmas of 1955 in Hawaii, "on doctor's orders," Jack said. Then in January the reports on *The Searchers* started coming in. *"The Searchers!"* actor Kirk Douglas wrote Ford. "God, what a story!" Jack Warner previewed the film and said, "I got one helluva kick last night when I ran *The Searchers."* Three months later *Variety* wrote, "It's an exciting Western in the grand scale," and compared the film favorably to *Shane* (1953). The *Los Angeles Examiner* said, "Its scope is simply tremendous. Its motivation spine chillingly grim. Its setting the most starkly beautiful ever seen in a Western film." *The Searchers* proved the eleventh-biggest box office success of 1956. An acquaintance told Ford that he watched people's reactions as they watched the film. "The small-frys that usually wander around and cause trouble during the feature stayed glued to their seats," the friend said. *The Searchers* was hailed as a popular and critical success upon its release, but the greatest praise was yet to come. French director Jean-Luc Godard, a Marxist, was among the first to label the picture a masterpiece, and in time *The Searchers* earned Ford the respect of what would be termed "the New Hollywood."

CHAPTER 10

Decline

BY 1950 attendance at American movie theaters had declined over 25 percent from its postwar height, and cutbacks were soon evident throughout the Hollywood studios. Not only were budgets reduced, but studios began letting contract players go. The retrenchment affected everyone, from great stars to file clerks and janitors, as more films were made overseas where expenses were less. In 1957 only a third of MGM's soundstages were busy, and the once-glamorous studio was renting out half of its facilities to independent producers. The golden age of Hollywood was nearing an end, as nervousness gave way to panic and finally acceptance that tastes in entertainment had changed.

Although television was the immediate threat, Hollywood suffered a series of blows during the postwar decade that contributed to its decline. The death knell sounded in 1948, when by government decree the studios were divorced from their theaters on the premise that antitrust laws had been violated. The studios no longer had an assured market for their product, and one by one the old movie palaces disappeared. The purge by the House Un-American Activities Committee during the late 1940s and the subsequent blacklisting of supposed Communists and left-wing sympathizers also demoralized the industry. Badgered and bruised, the studios were in no condition to meet the competition from television.

John Ford sank into a similarly depressed state, happy only when he was working, but going for longer periods between projects. Ford and John Wayne continued to meet in each other's homes for poker games and drinking sessions, and Ford still enjoyed gatherings on board the *Araner*, where he and his select group drank, told stories, and sang Irish songs. "He loved it when some of us dropped over to see him," said Dobe Carey, for the truth was that Ford was a lonely man.

The director had grown more caustic over the years. His remarks were forthright, sometimes arrogant, and he responded best to frankness. A bulky man in later years, with thinning hair and a corrugated face, Ford often appeared impatient and out of sorts. He had no truck with Communist advocates, yet was no more tolerant of personal mannerisms that annoyed him. Part of his gruff exterior was the persona he had created to survive in Hollywood, but part was a deepening cynicism.

While his home on Copa de Oro Road was a Bel Air mansion, Ford developed a reputation as a miser. Darcy O'Brien remembered the director's being driven around town by his black chauffeur in the 1950s in the back seat of a Thunderbird, wearing his eye patch and looking dramatic. Yet when they traveled, Ford and his chauffeur stayed in the same hotel room, since Ford was too cheap to pay for separate quarters.

Outside of reading, Ford had no hobbies and no sustained diversions other than the *Araner*. His marriage provided indifferent companionship, and he treated Mary almost like hired help. "Mary, dinner!" he'd shout, and his dinner would appear. An ulcer forced Mary to quit drinking, but Jack's alcoholism persisted. "I like animals," he was fond of saying, "and then, after baseball, I like people." What he liked most was making movies, and despite the reverses in Hollywood, Ford remained a dedicated craftsman.

His record during the late 1950s was nothing remarkable. Ford, a man in his sixties, lacked the vitality he'd shown earlier, and he seemed out of step with the times. For years he had planned to form an Irish company with Michael Killanin, but even after Four Province Productions was established on paper, specific projects had been postponed. In 1953 Ford and Killanin had decided to activate their company with a small, noncommerical picture called *The Rising of the Moon*. "All portrait painters occasionally want to paint a miniature," the director said. The picture consisted of three segments, originally called "Three Leaves of a Shamrock," set in the Black and Tan period of Irish history (1921). Between other assignments

Ford worked on the script for the trilogy with Frank Nugent, got Tyrone Power enthusiastic about the movie, and wrote Killanin in March 1954, "for the sake of my artistic soul I long to get back to Ireland and make our simple little story."

After more postponements *The Rising of the Moon* was filmed in Ireland during the fall of 1955. Tyrone Power introduced the three stories, but the cast was entirely Irish. Ford had hoped to induce Maureen O'Hara to appear in the picture. "She's a greedy bitch," the director wrote Killanin, "and I wonder if she'd accept our terms. Of course her name on an Irish film has value." Ford wanted the picture to express the poetry of his parents' homeland, but he had reservations about the project even before it went before the cameras. He and Nugent had worked hard on the script, yet Ford was disappointed in the final draft. "It stops and just speaks and speaks and finally comes out as dialogue about matters of political and national character that I don't think any people in the world could understand, including the Irish," he wrote.

But Ford was intent on stimulating the Irish film industry. In the end he objected to Power's inclusion in the project, arguing that the presence of an American star destroyed the Irish flavor. To acquire the backing of a Hollywood studio, however, Power's participation was essential. Columbia planned to release the picture, then backed out when executives grew wary of the film's commercial value. Warner Bros. agreed to distribute it, although the salespeople there expressed reservations about its box-office appeal. Jack Warner wanted to make a number of changes, but Ford held his ground. "I'll fight to the last ditch before those bastards screw the picture up," he wrote Killanin.

The Rising of the Moon had its world premiere in Dublin on May 16, 1957, to an enthusiastic audience. "Even the Irish liked it," Killanin wired Jack Warner. "Now that Irish like it," Warner answered, "am sure rest of world will love it." They didn't. The film was banned in Belfast, while British and American critics dismissed it with faint phrase. When asked about the picture later, Ford said, "I made it just for fun and enjoyed it very much."

Since studio negotiations held up the release of *The Rising of the Moon*, *The Searchers* was followed on American screens by the rambunctious *The Wings of Eagles*, released in February 1957. *The Wings of Eagles* was a tribute to Ford's friend Spig Wead, a pioneer naval aviator who had written scripts for two of Ford's movies, *Air Mail* and *They Were Expendable*. Wead had turned to screenwriting after he fell down the stairs of his Santa Monica beach house, broke his back, and was left paralyzed. While Ford was working in Ireland MGM approached him about making *The Wings of Eagles,* and he accepted when the studio promised to team John Wayne and Maureen O'Hara.

From the outset the director had mixed feelings about the project. "I didn't want to do the picture because Spig was a great pal of mine," he said. "But I didn't want anyone else to make it." Wead was dead by the time the film was shot; Ford claimed, "He died in my arms." Ford hated the movie's title and applied pressure on MGM to change it, but said he "tried to tell the story as truthfully as possible." Wayne played Wead, whom the actor had admired as "a man with guts," while O'Hara played his troubled wife. The film includes impressive aerial stunts by movie flyer Paul Mantz, but the comedy sequences at the beginning rank among Ford's worst.

The Wings of Eagles was photographed amid the heat and humidity of Pensacola, Florida. The picture is interesting for Ward Bond's commendable depiction of Ford himself, complete with tinted glasses. "I didn't intend it that way," the director said later, "but Ward did. I woke up one morning and my good hat was gone, my pipe and everything else. They'd taken all the Academy Awards and put them in the office set." Bond captured Ford's authority, yet avoided self-glorification, proving himself a substantial actor.

"We had an explosive preview on—God Help Us—*Wings of Eagles*," Ford wrote John Wayne on December 26, 1956. "What a lousy title! The reaction of the powers that be—not [producer] Charlie Schnee—was that it had too many laughs. How the hell can a picture have too many laughs, I ask you?" But many of the film's laughs were misplaced, and its humor resembled the antics of the Keystone Cops. Still, preview cards gave a more positive report than the critics turned in when the picture opened at Radio City Music Hall in February.

Ford and his family spent the Christmas of 1956 in Honolulu aboard the *Araner*. They had "a terrific time," he said. "It was the best vacation we ever had." Ward Bond visited Hawaii at the same time, but as Ford explained in a letter to John Wayne, "he was pretty busy meeting incoming congressmen [and] palling around with top naval brass." Ford wrote Wayne that he was giving Bond to him as a Christmas gift. "You can have him," said Ford. "I must admit, though, that he gave a terrific performance in Hawaii. The only trouble was he kept switching his character. In the morning he would be the lazy, kindly old beachcomber, the ex-professor of literature at Harvard, Oxford, Heidelberg, etc. Then in the afternoon he would be a retired gentleman—the younger son of a noble family in England. In the evening he became just a sloppy, goddamned guttersnipe—big, boisterous—could lick anybody—his fly open, a good rich vocabulary of four-letter words, and an all-around pain in the ass."

In mid-January Ford was scheduled to collaborate with Frank Nugent on a script for *The Last Hurrah* for Harry Cohn at Columbia. The director liked the book by Edwin O'Conner, but had difficulties turning the novel into a satisfactory screenplay. Late in February, with script problems unsolved, Ford announced that the film would be postponed until the next year, since he could not cast the part of Frank Skeffington to his satisfaction. "I have been busy as hell!" he wrote Michael Killanin. "However, I enjoy work."

Ford had decided on Spencer Tracy for the role of Skeffington, but Tracy was unavailable until 1958. Ford determined to wait until he was. Working through Katharine Hepburn, the director talked Tracy into accepting the part, forcing further delay in production. "Future plans," Ford said, "have left me completely befuddled."

He bided his time as best he could, helping his two grandsons prepare for their confirmation. "As you went to the coronation of the last Hanovarian Queen," Ford wrote Michael Killanin in April, "you will get the idea when I tell you that this is of much greater magnitude. The grandmother, Mary, is acting as Hereditary Earl Marshall. My sisters, maiden and otherwise, are taking a strong firm hand. The mother and father are at odds about it. Timmy objects to wearing a red robe, complaining that 'I ain't no sissy.' I look back sadly on the days in Africa when I had to kick a wounded black panther into the pit, . . . or I think of the calm and the quiet and the love of one's fellow humans such as at the Normandy Landing. Ah, well!"

Ford sailed for England on May 10, 1957, after deciding to move ahead with *Gideon's Day* for Four Province Productions (released in the United States as *Gideon of Scotland Yard*). John Wayne and Wingate Smith traveled with him. They made the Savoy Hotel in London their headquarters, since Wayne, according to Ford, was "a film star and a great friend of the bartenders there." Michael Killanin, who produced *Gideon's Day*, thought the script was "pretty corny," but Ford was eager to get away from Hollywood and enthusiastic about filming a Scotland Yard story.

Jack Hawkins starred in the picture, which went before the cameras in September, and Ford worked well with a British crew. He wrote Mary from London that he had been "really busy," but was satisfied with the first week's work. Mary suggested that she join him, but Jack discouraged her. "I want you more than you need me," he wrote, "but let's keep something to look forward to. It's really dull here. Leave the hotel at 8 A.M., back at 7 P.M. . . . . Miss you terribly, but life's like that." Anna Lee, who was featured in the film, observed that Ford and Hawkins got along "tremendously well." She remembered that the director did get "rather irate" at the British technicians when they insisted on quitting at five o'clock. Michael Killanin discovered that his friend Jack Ford was in truth "something of a snob" and was greatly impressed by royalty. Killanin accepted Ford as a man of contradictions, although he admitted that he often found Ford's posturing humorous.

Columbia agreed to release the film, although executive Mike Frankovitch urged Ford not to make the picture too

British. Frankovitch later complained that the dialogue contained too many American expressions and wanted to change the title to *Gideon of Scotland Yard*. Since *The Last Hurrah* was also a Columbia production, the studio hierarchy found it advantageous to release Ford's British picture, although no one expected it to be successful with American audiences.

Gideon of Scotland Yard was not seen in the United States for almost two years. A bank robbery similar to the one in the picture gave *Gideon* free publicity, but most critics pointed out that Ford had wandered a long way off his accustomed beat with this British comedy-melodrama.

As soon as *Gideon's Day* wrapped in the fall of 1957 Ford began drinking a great deal. Killanin got him aboard a plane two days later, but the pilot put him off in Shannon, where he dried out. He returned to Los Angeles, came down with the flu twice, and on November 21 left for Honolulu. "I think that sunshine and swimming will do some good," Ford wrote Killanin. "I weighed myself today, and I lost 16 pounds on the picture. How many did you gain?"

Ford resumed work on *The Last Hurrah* early in 1958 and completed it on April 24. He had intended to make a controversial film, much as the book had been. But when Columbia boss Harry Cohn died a few days after production began, the studio's new executive team decided that the original concept was too daring and ordered the script diluted. "But there's still lots of good stuff left in," said Ford. "I think it makes you gulp in a couple of places."

The Last Hurrah was primarily a character study, patterned after James Michael Curley, former mayor of Boston and onetime governor of Massachusetts. For the only time in his career, Ford dealt with the Irish-American urban experience — and not in a flattering way. He found Spencer Tracy congenial to work with; the actor knew his lines and could do a scene in one take. "Tracy had what John Ford wanted," Martin Jurow said, "and Spencer wanted only directors who would get on with it. He didn't want a director to go into long explanations and talk endlessly about motivating forces."

Ford kept a portable dressing room next to his set, and

napped there during lunch. "When we'd call him," recalled
Wingate Smith, "the prop man would bring him a big dish of
ice cream. That's all he ate for lunch." Ford drank coffee most of
the day and smoked cigars cut in half. He looked rumpled and
appeared to have lost his energy.

Jurow, who spent hours with Ford during the shooting of
The Last Hurrah, detected a vanity in the director that became
disturbing. "He was an extremely sensitive man," said Jurow,
"and he was conscious of his physical ailments. So he retreated.
He always carried a handkerchief because there was saliva that
came from his mouth. He never looked into the camera because
his eyes were bad. He was no longer physically able to do the
pictures he wanted to do, yet he wanted to keep active."

Jurow felt that Ford was an unhappy man, in part because his
private life had not been rewarding, but also because he knew
he was not attractive to people physically. He had spent his
career working with beautiful people, striving for beauty, yet
was aware, particularly as he grew older, that he was not
attractive himself. Jurow thought that was the reason Ford
poked fun at beautiful people and bedeviled them. "He didn't
want anyone to see him privately," said Jurow. "He wanted to
be judged by the work he'd done. Yet in the latter part of his
life, he could no longer have the winds and the rain and the
terrible ordeals he'd gone through on location."

The initial cut of *The Last Hurrah* ran almost two and a half
hours, and Columbia insisted that the picture be shortened.
Critics found Ford's treatment of the final campaign of an
Irish-American political boss powerful, yet many judged his
approach old-fashioned. "Where has Mr. Ford been all these
years?" *Saturday Review* asked. Film scholar John Baxter later
claimed that *The Last Hurrah* was the beginning of a new phase
in Ford's career, one that concentrated on the destruction of
communities. Frank Skeffington, the son of immigrants, was
an old-style politician and an old-style Irishman, who'd raised
himself up from the slums. "But young Mr. Lincoln has
become old Mr. Skeffington and he dies," Jeffrey Richards
wrote in *Focus on Film*, "just as the hopes and the dreams have
died. The faceless, conscienceless organization men have won."

Alienated from the contemporary world, Ford withdrew into himself. Among strangers he feigned deafness to avoid questions he didn't want to answer. He spent hours alone in his bedroom, surrounded by his awards and medals. He came to look upon outsiders with suspicion. "The Admiral does not wish strangers, supervised or not, invading his privacy," Bea Benjamin, Ford's business manager, wrote to the skipper of the *Araner* in 1958. "He considers the *Araner* his home, and previously his private quarters were locked continuously unless he was on the ship. That is why I have said so many times to be careful who comes aboard. To him it is like strangers walking into his bedroom, and we must respect his wishes."

Relatives and acquaintances all seemed to want something from him. His brother Francis's widow, also named Mary, had taken a job at the *San Francisco Examiner*, but wrote Jack asking for money. "I wanted to just go away from Hollywood," she said. "Many tears I have shed for three years. . . . I am just trying my very best to stay Mary Ford. Will continue to work. I still get my pension, and it helps so much." Bea Benjamin answered her letter: "I shall be glad to call this to Mr. Ford's attention as soon as he becomes available. . . . In the meantime I trust you will find some way to work out your problems successfully."

Jack's daughter Barbara was again working and doing well as a film editor. "I get a big kick out of handling film," she wrote her father in 1957. Barbara was still a daddy's girl and the two of them spent hours talking shop. "My Aunt Barbara really loved to watch movies," Dan Ford maintained, "and she could discuss every cut and every scene. She was quite a student of film and loved to share my grandfather's life and be part of that atmosphere." But Barbara drank too much, and her marriage to Ken Curtis soon ran into trouble. When she drank she became nostalgic for the period right after the war, when she had accompanied Joanne Dru to Monument Valley. Family members tried to talk her into joining Alcoholics Anonymous, but she refused to go.

Meanwhile Jack's relationship with Pat grew worse. The two were fundamentally different in temperament. "My father didn't have the drive that my grandfather had," Dan Ford said, "nor was my father the kind of guy that my grandfather admired among men. He considered my father lazy. My father would have been better off if he'd not gotten into the picture business. I understand why he did; the opportunities seemed to be there. But there's no middle class in the picture business. There's an upper class and a lower class and nothing in between. You're either strong or you grovel."

After Patrick and his first wife separated, their two sons spent a great deal of time with their grandparents. Jack adored Danny, pampered the boy, and, without admitting it, tried to compensate for the rupture with Pat through his grandson. Privately Jack anguished over Patrick and felt responsible for his son's alcoholism, but never seemed able to reach out to him. "Ford so wanted his son to deliver," said Charles FitzSimons, "and the son didn't."

Far from the flamboyant Hollywood character he tried to appear, Ford was at heart a simple man. Despite his genius and an acquired sophistication, he remained Irish in his belief that a man's home should be his nest. His was less than that, and the estrangement within his family proved a source of torment. He knew that he had failed as a husband and as a father; the wounds were too deep to mend. "All of the career in the world couldn't make up for that," FitzSimons declared.

Yet Ford seemed surrounded by people—producers, agents, production managers, writers, and personal friends who came and went with regularity. He continued to give the impression of being a man in motion, always planning productions, conferring with studio executives, talking to his agent. But with the passing years much of the activity was a mirage. The subordinates circling the great man merely isolated him within a golden sphere that proved sterile with time.

During the summer of 1958 Ford started preparing *The Horse Soldiers*, a Civil War story based on Benjamin Henry Grierson's cavalry raid, for the Mirisch Company. Ford knew his Civil War history and thought that a Union cavalry brigade's six-hundred-dred-mile dash into Confederate territory to destroy a supply

center added up to "a pretty good horse yarn." He studied
Matthew Brady's photographs for ideas and worked closely
with cameraman William Clothier. "Ford is probably the greatest
authority on the Civil War I know," said Clothier.

But the epic ran into trouble from the start. Ford was
unhappy with John Lee Mahin's script and irritated by producer Martin Rackin. He wanted John Wayne and James Stewart for the leads, but when Stewart proved unavailable, William
Holden was cast instead. Holden and Ford did not get along,
and the actor, a heavy drinker, resented Ford's attempt to
enforce his mandate against liquor. Throughout the production Ford stayed in a vile mood, which got worse when Wayne
went on a drinking spree with his costar despite Ford's nag-
ging.

Patrick Ford, assistant to the producers, went to Louisiana
to scout locations a month before shooting was to begin. Pat
arrived in September, finding the country around Natchitoches lovely, but hot. He located an ideal river for the picture,
rail facilities but no train, splendid homes in the Creole tradition, plenty of horses and riders, cooperative citizens, and
adequate living facilities. "In many ways this is a foreign
country," Pat wrote his father. "Segregation is still complete,
but the Negroes seem to live with great dignity and in some
security. Louisiana is poor country for the most [part], with all
the land and industry in the hands of a few old families."

Ford complained about the budget the producers had arranged. "Two million-one above the line and no money to make
the picture," Ford wrote Michael Killanin. Wayne and Holden
received $750,000 each, plus 20 percent of the profits, while
the director rated only $200,000, as well as 10 percent of the
producers's share once box office receipts reached twice the
film's total expenditure before advertising costs. *The Horse
Soldiers* ended up costing around $5 million.

Shooting on the picture started in Louisiana on October 27,
1958. Holden refused to stay in Alexandria with the rest of the
company, taking better accommodations in Shreveport, where
he could drink without Ford's prying eye. Ford consented to
the change, but informed Holden, "If you're ever one second

late, there'll be hell to pay." The actor had his Thunderbird delivered to the location, and every day he drove back and forth to work, always showing up on time and knowing his lines.

Meanwhile Wayne took the brunt of Ford's wrath, to the point that Holden and Marty Rackin felt sorry for him. They concocted a scheme for Wayne to get away for a while. Rackin told Ford that he'd received word from the studio that Wayne's teeth weren't white enough in the early rushes, so Ford made arrangements for Wayne to go into Shreveport and have his teeth cleaned. Since Holden had a car, he offered to drive Wayne to the dentist, with Rackin tagging along to supervise. Wayne didn't realize that the trip was a ruse until Holden and Rackin pulled out a bottle of Wild Turkey in the dentist's office, whereupon the three of them got reeling drunk. Ford was furious when he found out.

Constance Towers played the female lead and remembered *The Horse Soldiers* as "the greatest experience I ever had making pictures." Ford worked with the actress a great deal and arranged for her to stay in a private home on location. The picture also marked the acting debut of tennis champion Althea Gibson (later a regular on television's *Trapper John, M.D.*), but Ford refused to take the black actress to Louisiana. "We're not going to subject you to that," he told her, "because you will have to eat differently and you'll have to live in a different hotel." For her scenes on location, he used a double.

The Horse Soldiers was photographed in color, which most cinematographers considered easier than working in black and white. Bill Clothier, Ford's cameraman on several of his later pictures, agreed that the director should probably have stopped working after *The Searchers*. "You can't let those last films mark the man," said Clothier. The cinematographer nonetheless found his association with Ford a revelation. "He knew more about photography than any other man who ever worked in the movies," Clothier declared. "He was a genius. He'd force me into situations where I'd have to sit up and take notice." Whether shooting interiors or exteriors, Ford was a master at composition. He seldom used dolly shots, although his approach changed from picture to picture. "I think it depended entirely upon the situation and what the Old Man had in mind," Clothier said, "and he never told you. In all the years I worked for him, he never told me anything as far as specific lighting instructions."

Ford watched Wayne like a hawk after the drinking excursion with Holden, so the actor didn't keep liquor in his room, knowing that Ford would wander in and snoop around. Since Bill Clothier always had a bottle in his room, Wayne would go down there for a drink or two after work. "It was a funny thing with Jack," Clothier remembered, "—socially you never wanted any part of him. He just wasn't that pleasant. He liked to play cards, but if you won, you were a no-good son of a bitch. He used to wear the same clothes day after day after day. He wore the same hat for twenty years!"

Clothier knew that his duty was to carry out the director's thinking. Ford would outline the first setup of the day the night before, so that Clothier would be ready to shoot when Ford arrived on the set. "I learned that you didn't walk up to Jack Ford when he was thinking about something and bother him," the cameraman said. "He had commonplace expressions he'd use all the time, like 'I guess I'll have to pull a rabbit out of my hat,' whenever a scene wasn't going well." But Clothier admired Ford's economy in filming, shooting only what he needed. Sometimes the cameraman would ask, "Do you want to get a closer shot in this scene?" Ford often answered, "If I do, they'll use it, and we don't need it." So the shot was never made.

As usual, Ford surrounded himself with "his people" on *The Horse Soldiers*—Lefty Hough as location manager, Wingate Smith as assistant director, Eddie O'Fearna as second assistant, and Meta Sterne as dialogue director, while the cast included Hoot Gibson, Anna Lee, Russell Simpson, Stan Jones, Ken Curtis, Hank Worden, Chuck Hayward, and Danny Borzage. When Hoot Gibson began drinking at the Alexandria Hotel, Ken Curtis tried to look after him. "Hoot got on one of his binges," Hank Worden recalled, "and Ken had a time with him." Gibson made only one more picture.

Worden remembered that Ford was unhappy with his son

throughout the shooting. "I don't know what the hell was wrong with Pat," said Worden, "but he got in the road where he shouldn't have been and got run over. Ford hated him for that." Stunt performers and extras worked in fear of what the director would do next. "He kept everybody on their toes," said stuntman Dean Smith. "You never knew whether you were going to get fired or what. He never let anybody know exactly what he was going to do. Ford was a lovable old character, but he was ornery, too."

Among the bit players Ford hired was forty-eight-year-old veteran stuntman Fred Kennedy. Halfway through the filming of *The Horse Soldiers*, Kennedy persuaded Ford to let him do a horse fall to earn extra money for Christmas. Although the stuntman had dissipated in recent years and was out of shape, the trick was one he had performed hundreds of times. Ford liked Kennedy, had used him in many pictures, and enjoyed kidding him. At first Ford told him that he was too overweight to double William Holden in the scene they were about to shoot, but when Kennedy persisted, Ford gave in. After the horse fall Constance Towers was to rush over and throw herself on the stuntman's body. When Ford called for action, Kennedy spurred his horse into action and rolled off on his mark. When he hit the ground, his head snapped back, and he lay in a contorted position. Towers ran to him, threw herself on his body, then pulled back in horror. Kennedy's neck had been broken, and he gasped for breath. Ford and a physician rushed to him and administered oxygen, but Kennedy was dead when he reached the parish hospital in Natchitoches.

Ford wanted to wrap the picture that same day and never regained interest in it. "We were all right there," Hank Worden said, "and I can remember Ford walking away, blaming himself for Kennedy's death." Ford couldn't put the tragedy out of his mind and began drinking. The script called for a bloody battle at the close of the film, but the director improvised a quick ending. "It was awful," said screenwriter John Lee Mahin. "Ford didn't shoot the battle at all. They charged across that damned bridge and not one guy fell off the saddle. I didn't know what the hell was the matter." Mahin wanted to redo the scene, but Holden refused. Marty Rackin finally said, "To hell with it."

The film's best sequence was one Ford added, based on an actual incident, in which boys from a military academy attempt to repel the invading army. The director used cadets from Jefferson Military College in Washington, Mississippi, and Jack Pennick spent a week drilling the boys. "That scene was absolutely marvelous," Mahin conceded. "We put it in the script, but that was Jack's."

After twenty-eight days on location, the company returned to Los Angeles. Kennedy's accident made finishing the picture an ordeal. John Wayne came home from Louisiana saddened by what had happened and disturbed about Ford. "Pappy just doesn't seem to care anymore," he told Pilar. "He looks and acts like a beaten man."

The Horse Soldiers was scheduled for nineteen days of shooting in the studio—interiors on the Goldwyn lot, exteriors at MGM. Wayne was haunted by the way Ford looked when they said good-bye on the final day of filming, and was certain the director would never work again. Apart from Kennedy's death, Ford was worried about his career. Currents of change were blowing through Hollywood, trends the veteran director had no capacity to understand. The mood of the country was shifting, as a more permissive attitude gained acceptance. The industry that John Ford helped shape was crumbling with the decline of the big studio system and the rise of independent producers. Times were uncertain, especially for the old guard, and Ford sensed that his time in the business was nearing an end.

The world premiere of *The Horse Soldiers* took place at the Strand Theatre in Shreveport on June 16, 1959. "I don't think I ever saw the picture," Ford said. While the film has distinguished moments, including magnificent images of cavalry riding across landscapes or silhouetted against the sky, it doesn't rank among the director's best efforts, and contains a bitterness that became typical of Ford's later movies. Critics, however, were kind. *Saturday Review* said the action scenes "tingle with an excitement all too rare upon the screen these days," while the *Hollywood Reporter* maintained, "*The Horse Soldiers* is packed with laughs, romance, and thrills." Financially the picture just about made its money back.

During the weeks before *The Horse Soldiers* opened Ford enjoyed a vacation in Honolulu and what he described as "a rather exciting tour of duty in the Orient." In Korea he met and spent three days with a designer's model named Heran, who harbored aspirations to a movie career. How physical their relationship became is a matter of conjecture, but Heran construed their time together as a grand romance. Over the next eight months she wrote Ford passionate letters, some of which he answered. "First, I would like to say that I love you," she wrote shortly after his return to California in June 1959. "The more I speak of this, the more I want to tell you that I love you so very much." She informed him that articles about his work had appeared in magazines since he'd left Korea. "Most every picture I'm with you," Heran wrote. "The rumors spread that I'll be going to Hollywood soon. . . . Whenever I receive your letter I forget everything."

A week later, Heran wrote again: "I want to be alone with you. . . . All I want to tell is how much I miss you. I just close my eyes and think and remember everything we shared and calm myself down. Darling, you brought me many things, happiness and others. I don't want to lose you, please don't go away from me. I want you to know that you are my life." When Ford failed to answer, she grew worried. "It has been over two weeks since I've received your letter," Heran wrote on June 29. "I love you, Jack, more than you can imagine. This secret love of mine for you just makes me sick."

Their correspondence continued through early February 1960, with Heran complaining often that she hadn't heard from her "darling Jack." "I suppose you are busy for the next picture," she wrote. "I am hoping that you are still thinking of me." Ford wrote Michael Killanin during this period: "I've had Asiatic Flu again . . . and this time really bad." He did respond to Heran's letters in January. "Your letter was welcome, darling," she replied on February 6. "I didn't know that you have traveled so many places. . . . Much things have changed in the movie industry of our country." With that, the affair—such as it was—seems to have been terminated.

Ford returned from his dalliance in Asia ready to plunge into work on *Sergeant Rutledge*. Originally entitled "Captain Buffalo," the film was an inexpensive Western. Jack liked the script by James Warner Bellah and Willis Goldbeck and welcomed a chance to return to Monument Valley. "No all-star cast, thank God," he wrote Michael Killanin, "just good actors."

The story focuses on the black Ninth Cavalry and specifically on a top sergeant idolized by the troopers. Rutledge possesses dignity, self-discipline, and a strong loyalty to the army, yet reveals his lack of faith in military justice for blacks when he is wrongly accused of raping a white woman and murdering her father. Afraid of the consequences, Rutledge deserts, but returns to his patrol when he encounters Indians preparing to attack. The picture was consistent with the contemporary civil rights movement, and Ford remained enthusiastic. "The colored soldier played a great role in our history," he said, "and I wanted to tell that story." But he also recognized that the theme of racism was harmonious with the time and held commercial possibilities. "I think he had a supportive concern for black people," Dan Ford maintained, "but his views were essentially conservative."

With fewer films being offered to him, John Ford was less interested in paying homage to the black cavalry than in making a picture that would score at the box office and earn him another job. Since Westerns still commanded a loyal following, his next four pictures were of that genre. Ford was established as a Western director, and that's what producers wanted him to make. Any Ford Western assured a profitable return.

Ford took Patrick, his two grandsons, and Wingate Smith with him to Monument Valley to scout locations for *Sergeant Rutledge*. "I remember going to Gouldings' and how wonderful it was," Dan Ford said. "I got a sense of that lifestyle and what it was like to be there with him. First of all, you got treated royally. The food they put out for breakfast was unbelievable—fried eggs, pork chops, and stacks of pancakes. It was all served family style, and the atmosphere was gregarious and warm." Dan recalled driving through the valley with his grand-father and Wingate Smith. "We'll set up here," the director would say. Jack mentioned that they'd have Indians riding along a ridge. Then he turned to Dan and said, "Of course, Indians never would have done that. They never exposed themselves like that. They'd ride under the ridge so you wouldn't see them, but it's a good shot." They went out to the valley's sand dunes. "We'll have to shoot this late in the day," said Ford, since he wanted long shadows of riders stretching across the sand.

Trucks, buses, and equipment arrived in Monument Valley on July 14, with shooting scheduled to begin two days later. Already Ford's interest in the picture had dwindled; even before filming started, he referred to *Sergeant Rutledge* as "just another job of work." Woody Strode, a former UCLA football and track star, played the title role, and although Strode was not a trained actor, Ford drew a solid performance from him. Warner Bros. had preferred an established black star—Harry Belafonte or Sidney Poitier—but Ford insisted that neither was tough enough. Since Strode hadn't ridden a horse in ten years, he spent four days at Hudkin's Ranch in Arizona training. Catering to conservative audiences, Ford was careful not to let his white actress, Constance Towers, touch Strode's skin dur-ing a scene in which she treated his wounds.

Still the silent picturemaker, Ford often gave direction while the camera was rolling. "Woody," he'd say, "unbutton the shirt. Now ease out of it." Since Strode was an inexperienced actor, the director would sometimes stand in front of the camera and play his scenes for him. If Strode didn't watch closely enough, Ford would grow angry, stomp his feet, even hit the former All-American with the butt of a rifle. "I thought the old bastard hated me," Strode wrote. But before the film was completed he realized that Ford was putting something good on the screen. "He knew how to pluck me like a harp," Strode said. "That old man not only directed me, he split my personality. I almost had a nervous breakdown doing *Sergeant Rutledge*, but it helped me become an actor."

The courtroom sequence in the picture was the most emotional moment of Strode's performing career. Ford got him drunk the night before the scene was filmed, convinced he would be more pliable in a weakened state. "John Ford was really smart," Strode declared. "He knew how to get the fire going, how to get all the emotions out of me. When he wanted to turn me on, boom, he'd just hit the switch. He was the roughest man I ever worked for, but he directed me so I was never afraid of being in front of a camera."

The two became friends. Strode thought that his relationship with Ford developed because he was "honest, strong, and crude. I reminded him of an earlier time in history," the former Rams player wrote, "a time he was in love with."

By the time *Sergeant Rutledge* was filmed, John Ford's powers as a director had diminished. Fred Kennedy's death had made him cautious about stunts, and horse falls in his later films were almost nonexistent. Nor were there the usual practical jokes and gags on his sets. Ford seemed subdued. "He had always been growly with us," said stuntman Chuck Roberson, "but now there was an edge of bitterness to him that seemed to dominate his personality." It was clear to Ford's close associates that he was getting old.

He seemed to be even more eccentric in his personal appearance. On location he'd take a bottle of suntan lotion, lift the hat he always wore, and pour lotion over his bald head. Then he'd take his handkerchief and wipe the lotion all around, until it dripped down his face and onto the collar of his shirt.

After ten days in Monument Valley the *Sergeant Rutledge* company returned in late July to California, where the picture was finished on studio sets. Principal photography was completed by mid-September, after forty-three days of shooting. Ford's fee for the picture was $250,000, paid over a five-year period.

The film previewed as "Captain Buffalo" on December 2 at the Crown Theatre in Pasadena. The consensus was that Ford still had few superiors in cinematic action, but that much of the picture seemed stage-bound. When *Sergeant Rutledge* was released in the spring of 1960 it was poorly received by both

black and white critics. Most reviewers expressed disappointment; *Films in Review* declared that Ford had apparently
directed *Sergeant Rutledge* "with his left hand."

From the viewpoint of black militants of the 1960s *Sergeant
Rutledge* was too little too late. Even those who maintained
that the film dealt frankly with racial prejudice did not feel that
it had probed deeply. Many held that it treated racism in a
synthetic way but defamed Native Americans while soothing
the relationship between blacks and whites. A young black
named Kirby Williams, however, wrote Ford: "I just saw your
movie *Sergeant Rutledge*. . . . [It] is, in my opinion, the most
significant Negro-theme movie that I have ever seen. If it were
up to me, I would have it shown in every classroom in America."

The director himself claimed to like the film. "It was the first
time we had ever shown the Negro as a hero," said Ford. "But
the picture was not successful because, I've heard, Warners sent
a couple of boys on bicycles out to sell it." Tame though
Sergeant Rutledge was as social comment, it did confront the
explosive issue of sex between whites and blacks.

After *Sergeant Rutledge* Ford went for several months without
another assignment. Feature films were on the decline, as the
Hollywood studios continued their retrenchment. "Hollywood today is a market for sex and horror," Ford remarked in
1959. "I don't want any part of that." But he didn't handle
unemployment well and grew depressed, spending most of his
time in bed. Sometimes he'd wear his pajamas all day. When he
came out of his bedroom, he'd simply pull his pants on over his
nightclothes, so he could quickly get back into bed. His beard
and fingernails grew long, while his teeth and hands became
yellow from nicotine.

Bored and dejected, Ford decided during the fall of 1959 to
visit Bracketville, Texas, where John Wayne was filming *The
Alamo* on Happy Shahan's ranch. "I hope to go to Texas," he
wrote Michael Killanin in September, "and cast a paternal eye
on Duke Wayne. This young and ambitious lad of fifty-six
years is writing, producing, acting, and directing *The Alamo*
with the excessive budget of five million bucks." Wayne had

begun planning the picture in 1946, and the project was dear to his heart. "My father had looked forward to that picture for a long, long time," said Patrick Wayne. "He ate, slept, and dreamed it, and nobody was going to take one frame of it away from him."

About a month into shooting the picture Ford showed up. He walked onto the set, plunked himself down in the director's chair, and interrupted the scene Wayne was filming. "Jesus Christ, Duke, that's not the way to do it," Ford barked. That evening Ford announced that he intended to vacation for a while in South Texas, and he spent the next day looking over Wayne's shoulder. Wayne had such respect for Ford that he didn't want to hurt his feelings, but neither did he plan to let his mentor direct his picture. "What the hell am I gonna do?" Wayne asked cameraman Bill Clothier.

Clothier loved Ford, too, and sympathized with Wayne's position. "Look," the cinematographer said, "I've got a big crew here, an extra first cameraman who's not doing a damn thing. Let's give the Old Man a second unit." Wayne thought that was a good idea, so Clothier assembled a crew—a cinematographer, a couple of operators, Michael Wayne as Ford's assistant, Ken Curtis, and some other actors Wayne wasn't using at the moment. Duke asked James Grant to write additional action sequences and turned those pages over to Ford, telling him that second-unit director Cliff Lyons would never be able to handle all the scenes needed. "Ford went out and shot stuff that couldn't possibly be used," Clothier recalled. "It had absolutely nothing to do with the picture we were making. I don't think we used three cuts that the Old Man did. But I would estimate that it cost Duke over $250,000 to give Ford that second unit."

"That was a rough position my father put me in," Michael Wayne admitted later, "to try to keep Ford happy. My father said, 'Look, let him do anything he wants, but don't let him talk to any of the principals.' So we did stuff with extras and stock shots, shots of the Mexican army charging and retreating. I worked with Ford every single day, and we had a lot of run-ins. I would never give him the principals, and he always wanted to do something with them. So I had rubs with Mr. Ford."

Ford was disappointed when most of his footage wasn't used, but there were a few shots that he directed, mainly of Mexican extras marching with bayonets, included in the film. Yet he remained convinced that Wayne couldn't finish the epic without him. "I've got to help Duke out with *The Alamo*," he wrote Killanin in February 1960. "This is a picture that actually cost $5,000,000. It's a helluva picture . . . a real spectacular . . . but, as I said, I've got to help him."

Despite Wayne's tact in dealing with a ticklish situation, *The Alamo* put a wedge between him and the Ford family. Patrick Ford had been hired to write the original script, at a time when Wayne's production unit was operating at Republic Studio. Patrick received a salary of $250 a week for ten weeks. "My concept was a semidocumentary, as historically accurate as possible," Pat said. Texas folklorist J. Frank Dobie had lent him a diary in return for Patrick's promise to write the truest account of the Alamo siege possible. Wayne stated later that Dobie had given him the key to his characterization of Davy Crockett. "Dobie once said that Crockett never ate on an empty stomach nor drank on a full," said Wayne. "That gave me an attitude of how to make a human being out of [one of] the great heroes." Patrick Ford contended that neither Wayne nor Herbert Yates lived up to his agreement of remaining historically accurate. Twenty-five years later, Pat was still angry: "I was to receive solo screenplay credit, be appointed associate producer, and receive fifteen thousand dollars from Wayne if he made the picture. I can only say that I hope Crockett and Bowie were more honest Western American heroes than Wayne proved to be in real life." In a letter to the archivist at Brigham Young University in 1980, Patrick Ford wrote, "For further details, I refer you to Budd Schulberg's *What Makes Sammy Run?*"

Meddlesome though John Ford may have been, his involvement with *The Alamo* seemed to give him a renewed outlook on life. In May 1960 he directed an episode of *Wagon Train* for television, as a personal favor to Ward Bond, who hosted the series. The segment was called "The Colter Craven Story," and Ford cast it with many of his own people: Frank McGrath, John Carradine, Ken Curtis, Anna Lee, Jack Pennick, Hank Worden, Good and Bad Chuck (Hayward and Roberson), and John Wayne (under the pseudonym Michael Morris) playing General William Tecumseh Sherman. Ford hated television, as most veteran filmmakers did, and grumbled that Bond had become a whore by starring in a weekly show, even though *Wagon Train* made the actor the star he'd always wanted to be. When Ford heard that Wayne would make a cameo appearance on Bond's program, he snapped, "I taught him better than that. I've given up on Bond, the big, ugly, stupid gorilla, but I thought Duke had more intelligence." Yet Ford couldn't resist the challenge when Bond said, "Why don't you come over and direct this thing for us? Show them how it's done."

He took the assignment seriously, prepared it thoroughly, and finished work every day by 3:30 or 4:00. "The shit hit the fan up at the front office," said Ace Holmes, who worked on the project. Television executives weren't used to such knowledge and efficiency. They were used to directors who worked on a different script every week and complained they were hard put to complete the episode in time for airing.

In June Ford began a feature film for Columbia entitled *Two Rode Together*. Based on the novel *Comanche Captives* by Will Cook, the script was so grim Ford almost turned it down. "I didn't like the story," he declared, but he liked the idea of working with James Stewart and Richard Widmark and was eager to stay busy. Even before shooting began Ford said, "Good God, this is a lousy script." By the time the picture was finished he pronounced it "the worse piece of crap I've done in twenty years."

Ford noted with disgust that the committee system of production had taken over in Hollywood, and making *Two Rode Together* substantiated his worst fears about a collective approach. Aware that he must cooperate to assure future employment, he yielded to studio pressures far more than he would have a few years earlier. But he had begun to fear that he couldn't live up to his own reputation; he was competing with his previous triumphs with diminished strength, and his depression deepened.

Budgetary considerations limited *Two Rode Together* even further. Ford decided to film most of the picture in South Texas, using sets that Wayne's crew had built for *The Alamo*, including an old San Antonio street. The director left for Bracketville on October 15, 1960, taking along veterans of his stock company. "John had all of these old-timers, like Mae Marsh and Ruth Clifford, some of whom were actually boarded out at the Motion Picture Home," actress Anna Lee said. "He would give them little parts to play, sometimes just one line or so. I don't think I had more than six lines in *Two Rode Together*, which was like a dress extra. But he liked to have us around."

"I felt that Ford didn't like actors who talked too much," said James Stewart, who headed the cast. Sometimes the director would interrupt a scene to say, "Everybody's talking too much. You must have different scripts than I do." His actors would watch while Ford cut out eight or ten lines from a four- or five-minute scene. "If you can't do it without relying on the spoken word," he told them, "you're not doing it visually, and that's what I intend to do." Stewart became convinced that the director was right. "In motion pictures the visual is much more important than the vocal," the actor said. "Ford always claimed that the best things in American films happen by accident. He was a great believer in the spontaneous. Yet he'd spend an hour getting the wind at the right force, so that it blew the sand in the background just right."

Stewart and Widmark shared a long scene sitting on a log beside a river, in which their dialogue seemed almost improvised. The sequence was shot early one morning, and the two actors were going over their lines when Ford arrived on the set, grouchier than usual. He walked into the river and signaled for his camera crew to follow. "He didn't have to put the camera in the river," said Stewart, "but I think he did it because it meant that all the crew had to walk out in the river up to their waists. It was terribly cold, but he was like that." They finished the scene in one take.

Stewart proved to be Ford's kind of actor — sensitive, natural, delivering dialogue as if it were everyday speech. "James Stewart is a lion underneath the skin of a lamb," said actress Linda Cristal, who was featured in the film. "He is just monumental. When the camera came close, you could see the caliber of his emotions in his eyes, and you knew what a genius this man was. He was such an honorable gentleman, so kind, so helpful, so easy."

Widmark was more reserved, less open when it came to feelings. An excellent actor, he seemed free to express whatever emotions were needed for the camera, but shrank into himself once the scene was over. In mornings, particularly, he could be downright short-tempered. "Nobody sits with Widmark in the morning," character actor Andy Devine declared.

Shirley Jones, *Two Rode Together*'s female lead, claimed that she felt like an outsider on the picture. "Ford's stock company knew him so well," she said, "and knew the way he worked. For me it was a different way of working, and I was in shock." Jones maintained that there was no real script on the film; Ford simply improvised dialogue as they went along. "He'd have a writer sitting on the set typing pages," she recalled. "I'd arrive in makeup and in costume, and Ford would say, 'Here are your pages. Look at them and get on the set.' That's the way he worked. I couldn't believe it."

Jones came from the musical theater and viewed Ford as the ultimate movie director. "If he could have made a film without actors," she said, "he would have loved to do that. He let you know that in no uncertain terms. It was difficult for me, because I was accustomed to stage directors who would sit down and talk to you about the part. Ford just made beautiful motion pictures. He'd say, 'You walk to the left and stand there and stare. If you can cry, cry. If you can't, damn it, I'll give you something to make you cry.' That was John Ford."

Linda Cristal, on the other hand, worked comfortably with Ford. Cristal had made movies in Latin America and met Ford on the set of *The Alamo*. He decided to cast her in *Two Rode Together* as a young Mexican woman captured by the Comanche. "Ford was a very cerebral man," Cristal said, "with a great ego. But because of his talent one didn't resent that." The director suggested a hand movement that Cristal thought seemed mechanical and forced, since it didn't correspond with what she was thinking. "But when I saw it on the screen," she said, "the feeling that Ford wanted was there."

When she met Ford, the Latin American actress didn't realize how important a director he was, or what a genius he was. "I just thought, 'What a nice old man,'" she said. "I couldn't understand why everybody was so afraid of him." But she quickly learned why Ford was so revered. Not only was he knowledgable and clever, he understood human emotions. "When he came to the set, he was ready," said Cristal. "He'd done his homework and knew exactly what he wanted to see on that film. He wanted to play every part, and he played the heavens by rearranging the clouds in the sky. He would sometimes wait a whole day for a certain sunset or a certain cloud formation." The actress had occasion to observe Ford's sarcastic side, yet recognized it as defensiveness. "With me," she said, "his defenses came down. There was sweetness and tenderness; he was gentlemanly."

Ford brought Navajo from Monument Valley to play the Comanche in *Two Rode Together*, except for Stone Calf, who was played by Woody Strode. The director got into an argument with executives at Columbia over casting a black actor as an Indian chief. "But, in costume," said Strode, "I looked so much like an Indian that the studio bosses couldn't argue."

Andy Devine worked on the picture during the time the Indians were in Bracketville. Remembering what a prankster Ford had been, Devine went to the wardrobe manager, got a wig and a squaw's outfit, and began mingling with the Indians. Ford recognized the actor and began maneuvering him toward the camera. Devine was experienced enough to know that once he was established in camera range, he'd have to stay in the scene until it was finished, possibly the rest of the day, which was what Ford had in mind. "I knew what he was doing," the actor said, "so I took my wig off." The company enjoyed a good laugh.

The moment a day's work was over, Ford disappeared. He

didn't socialize during the making of the picture and went to
bed early. He seemed listless and bored. Despite the constant
movement of the characters from town to fort to Indian camp,
the landscape in the film is rarely shown. There is little of the
director's customary visual splendor, and the actors seem
cramped. "*Two Rode Together* didn't look like a Ford film,"
declared Dobe Carey. Ford himself said, "The old enthusiasm
has gone, maybe."

On November 13, while the company was working near
Bracketville, Ward Bond died in Dallas of a heart attack. He
had stopped off to watch a football game before flying south to
visit Ford's company. Ford heard the news from Ken Curtis,
who was crying. As Chuck Roberson remembered it, "The Old
Man hung his head for a minute, and when he looked up again,
I could see tears trickling down from beneath his dark glasses.
He had lost a friend of nearly thirty years." Ford shut down the
picture and flew home to make arrangements for Bond's funeral at the Field Photo Farm.

Bond's death was a devastating blow to Ford, as it was for
John Wayne. Ford posted a uniformed guard at Bond's flag-
draped coffin in the chapel at the Field Photo Farm. Wayne
gave the eulogy with tears in his eyes and his voice choking
with emotion. "Ward Bond was a great big, ugly, wonderful
guy," said Ford, who loved him more than he could admit.

Much of the remainder of *Two Rode Together* was filmed at
the Columbia ranch, but Ford had lost interest. He didn't
enjoy the picture, and while it is almost a remake of *The
Searchers*, the film is by far the most cynical Western the
director had made. Community is no longer viewed as a
potential vehicle for good, but rather as the cause of evil and
pain. *Two Rode Together* lacks the subliminal element of *The
Searchers* and contains little of the action and dramatic value of
the earlier picture. Clearly the director's heart was not in his
work, and critics were quick to point that out.

Saddened by the death of Ward Bond, disgusted with the
current movie business, and sickened by what he considered
the breakdown of American society, Ford flew to Honolulu in
late November to spend the holidays aboard the *Araner*. In

Hawaii he began drinking and spent almost three weeks in an alcoholic haze. When alcoholic dehydration became evident, Mary convinced him to check into Queen's Hospital in Honolulu.

By mid-January 1961 Ford was back in Los Angeles preparing *The Man Who Shot Liberty Valance*. He was determined to have John Wayne in the picture, although Wayne's fee by then was far more than was budgeted. Ford phoned Wayne, but convinced himself that the actor was avoiding his calls. In April he received a note from Wayne: "I don't know who you heard over the phone when you called my home, but it was certainly not I. . . . I talk to every Tom, Dick, and Harry who calls. I certainly would not be too tired to talk to a man whom I consider my best friend—that I have a feeling of blood kinship with." Ford still remained peevish.

The Man Who Shot Liberty Valance would be Ford's last great film. He insisted on shooting it in black and white, wanting a dark, anachronistic look, since the picture incorporated his diminishing faith in American values. No longer did he feel like celebrating the course of civilization, which he accepted, but did not necessarily see as progress. "For a change, no locations," Ford wrote Wayne in July 1961. "All to be shot on the lot." The director wanted a claustrophobic feel and photographed all but three days inside the Paramount studio.

The starting date was postponed until September 5, with everything through October 20 scheduled to be shot on a soundstage. Pat Ford served as his father's executive assistant, and the script was written by James Warner Bellah and Willis Goldbeck. At first Ford was enthusiastic about the project, but his interest faded even before shooting began. He worked fast and with an attitide that bordered on indifference, trimming corners whenever possible.

He seemed angry at Wayne, perhaps because of his treatment on the set of *The Alamo*. Whatever the reason, Ford was unusually hard on Wayne, and bawled him out in front of the company. One day, with fifty people on the set, Ford was talking between takes, with Wayne seated on a box next to him.

Wayne made a suggestion and Ford exploded, "Jesus Christ, here I take you out of eight-day Westerns, I put you in big movies, and you give me a stupid suggestion like that!"

Jimmy Stewart remembered a great deal of tension on the picture, but felt it was beneficial. "People didn't know exactly what was going to happen next," he said, "and that's the way Ford wanted it. He tried to set up a competitive spirit among the actors and used that effectively." Stewart saw the director's "planned improvisation" as part of his genius. "He hated talk," the actor said, "but the way he got the story up on the screen was pretty much a reflection of his own character."

Lee Marvin, cast as Liberty Valance, among the screen's most flamboyant villains, had fun playing the role. "Of course it was a dangerous kind of character," said Marvin, "wide open." Actor Edmond O'Brien claimed that he couldn't wait to get to work every morning while he was making *Liberty Valance*. "In all the years, I have never enjoyed an acting experience so much," he wrote Ford.

Ken Murray, also in the film, remembered the experience less fondly. "Ford was a monster on the set," he said. "He was an ogre; I was scared of him." The performer's part called for him to fight one of the bit players, and Ford told him, "Do it. Hit him!" So Murray hit the fellow, who recoiled from the blow and fell down. Ford yelled, "Cut." The director walked over to Murray, called the felled extra over, and said, "Now listen, Ken, it's near Christmas. When a stuntman plays a part, he gets more money. But he doesn't get more money if you hit him like a pansy. We don't pay him for that. Whether or not you want this fellow to have money for his kids for Christmas is up to you. But if you want him to have it, hit him. For Christ's sake, hit him, and let's get on with the scene!" On the next take, Murray practically knocked the fellow through the scenery. "Cut!" Ford yelled, a smile wrinkling his jowly face.

Woody Strode played Pompey, the black man who works for Tom Doniphon, Wayne's character in the picture. To needle Wayne, Ford would point to Strode and say, "Duke, there's the real football player." Ford teased Wayne about the fact that both he and Strode had been in the service during World War

II, while Wayne hadn't. Wayne became furious, and it was
evident that Ford was pushing their relationship to the brink.

Toward the end of the picture, Ford had grown bored and
began to slough off even more. He clearly was tired. He had
wanted to shoot *Liberty Valance* in black and white partly
because of the gunfight at night between Marvin and Stewart,
where Wayne actually does the killing. "That was the key to the
whole film," cameraman Bill Clothier said, "and Ford didn't
want that in color. Of course, he was right because black and
white looks more like night."

As *Liberty Valance* opens, Tom Doniphon, the frontier hero,
lies dead; his coffin establishes the spirit of the film. Senator
Ransom Stoddard, who reputedly shot the gunman Liberty
Valance, has returned to Shinbone with his wife, Hallie, to
bury Tom. They arrive by train (the Western symbol of progress) to find the landscape tamed and the frontier town they
once knew orderly and depersonalized. While the town's violent past was horrendous, its tepid present seems sterile. The
film's dialectic is encapsulated in the image of a cactus rose,
symbol of the contradiction between desert and garden. Stoddard, a man of books and compassion, has led the frontier
toward civilization through his successful political career, while
Tom (the actual slayer of Valance) had begun to act as wild as
Liberty had, tossing chairs around, breaking glass, and creating havoc, an anachronism amid changing times.

Ford mourned the passing of the mythic frontier, as he
lamented the corrosive forces of progress. By the time he made
The Man Who Shot Liberty Valance the iron horse for him had
become an iron monster, yet he remained convinced that
change could not be stopped, no matter how much cultural
dislocation resulted. Tom Doniphon, whose fast gun epito-
mizes the Old West, appears to have lived a meaningless life.
He lies dead in a pine box in a cluttered stable—a pauper at the
end of his life, his boots stolen by an avaricious undertaker. Yet
Tom had known that his world was coming to an end. He
allowed Stoddard to take credit for killing Valance so that a
new order could emerge, and willingly accepted anonymity for
himself.

Since the conquest of the wilderness had been founded on myth, the progress achieved rests on shaky ground. At the end of the film, as Stoddard and his wife leave Shinbone, Hallie looks out the train window at the grassy plains and remarks wistfully, "Look at it. It was once a wilderness. Now it's a garden." Ford suggests that the Old West and its values survive in the legends its heroes helped create. To have exposed what the frontier symbolizes as fraud would have destroyed its meaning in history, and the public wouldn't have accepted the truth anyway. Therefore, the newspaper editor says in the fadeout, "When the legend becomes fact, print the legend."

In *The Man Who Shot Liberty Valance* Ford confronted the losses of the past — his personal and professional losses, as well as broad historical sacrifices. The picture makes a melancholy and troubling statement, yet one consistent with the dark side of Ford's romanticism. Toward the end he questioned the mythology he had himself invented over four and a half decades of filmmaking. While Ford admired Tom Doniphon and regretted the passing of frontier individualism, he saw value in Ransom Stoddard as a modern and more flexible male who could wash dishes and wear an apron without losing his masculinity.

Liberty Valance wrapped on November 7, 1961, and had its preview on February 2, 1962, in Riverside, California. "Reminds me of silent movies," one viewer wrote on a preview card. "Everything exaggerated but refreshing and also funny." But when the picture was released in April, the critical response was mostly negative. "John Ford's *The Man Who Shot Liberty Valance* is a parody of Mr. Ford's best work," Brendan Gill wrote in the *New Yorker*. *Variety* dismissed the film as "Model A 'Ford,'" calling the director "the screen's past master of the sagebrush idiom." Later the picture received serious attention from film scholars and enjoyed far more positive acclaim.

When asked if his view of the West was becoming increasingly sad, Ford answered, "Possibly. I don't know; I'm not a psychologist. Maybe I'm getting older." *The Man Who Shot Liberty Valance* would be his last complete Western with John

Wayne. Despite recent tension between them, both knew that their association, personally and professionally, had been unique and shared regret over the changes that had taken place in their industry. "Those were great days," Wayne said. "You're not supposed to look back, but it's pretty hard not to when there were guys like Ward and Jack. You don't meet them everyday."

CHAPTER II

Despair

BY the early 1960s Ford had become despondent about Hollywood and about American society. The movie business, he felt, was no longer run by experienced filmmakers, but by Madison Avenue and Wall Street financiers who rejected scripts without abundant sex and violence. "Talk about moral bankruptcy!" Ford declared in 1962. "Our ancestors would be bloody ashamed if they could see us today." Yet he wanted to keep working. "Directing's like dope addiction," he said. "It's something you can't leave." But his Hollywood dream had turned to ashes.

In his late sixties Ford was more than ever the hardnosed, crotchety Irishman. He was also lonely. John Wayne was absorbed in his own projects and family, Ward Bond was dead, and most of the old crowd had scattered. Ford's estrangement from his son neared the breaking point, and Barbara had become a chronic alcoholic. Vacationing in Europe with Mary, Jack had fallen down stairs in Paris and injured his back. But it was the pain of living that seemed greatest.

Film offers slowed to a trickle, in part because an aging director had difficulty securing insurance. With his health failing, companies considered Ford too large a risk; should he become ill and unable to finish a picture, producers would be in a bad way.

When interviewed by reporters or film critics, Ford enjoyed playing the curmudgeon, assuming the pose of an old-fashioned action director trying to make a living. "He liked to reduce things to gags and anecdotes and Ward Bond stunts," Dan Ford said. "I don't think he was capable of telling his own story."

Ford liked watching other people's movies on television, and Dan remembered his grandfather close to tears when they saw

The Wizard of Oz together. "Boy, that was a hell of a picture," he said at the end. According to his grandson, Ford's favorite American filmmakers were "Frank Capra, Frank Capra, and Frank Capra." The renowned director of *Mr. Smith Goes to Washington* visited Ford in his home a number of times and talked about movies; Ford in turn was moved by Capra's book *The Name above the Title*.

During lulls between pictures Ford mainly drank. "He'd start off with a little beer and wine and he'd be fine," Dan Ford recalled. "A few beers and then he was really funny, he was a delight. But he didn't stop; he just kept going. He'd work up to where he'd get really obnoxious, and my father and brother and I would get out of there. When he got to the hard stuff, look out." Ford feared that he was finished in the picture business. "I remember he told my Aunt Barbara once that he was concerned that he was losing it," Ford's grandson said, "and didn't have the stamina to work anymore. My father claimed he was taking steroids, because he felt they would give him strength. It could well be true. He was concerned with being macho and keeping his strength and being able to work."

Ford was invited by the Metropolitan Opera to stage Puccini's *The Girl of the Golden West*, which was slated to open the Met's season in the fall of 1961. He declined, saying he thought it "a lousy opera"; he claimed that had he been offered *La Bohème*, he might have accepted. In all likelihood he would have felt confined directing singers, particularly with the limited facilities at the old Metropolitan Opera House.

What Ford did accept was a segment of the $14 million Cinerama production in preparation at MGM called *How the West Was Won*. The sweeping story was divided among three veteran directors—John Ford, George Marshall, and Henry Hathaway. While Hathaway was assigned the bulk of the picture, Ford was given the Civil War section, which centered around the battle of Shiloh. The film boasted an all-star cast, but the Cinerama process was its real star. Ford hated Cinerama even more than he did CinemaScope, since images on the curved screen became distorted. As he put it, "the audience moves instead of the picture." In Ford's section of *How the West Was Won* the pace slows and the human dimension deepens. "I have seen it on the screen," the director said, "and was pleased to find it touching and strong. It is more or less a true situation."

In the Ford sequence, a youth goes off to the Civil War, experiences the horrors of Shiloh, returns home to find his mother dead, and heads west. George Peppard, who played the young man, found Ford "caustic, intelligent, an absolute autocrat." Yet the director's attitude toward Peppard was friendly, "as though I were his son," the actor remembered. "When I went onto the set, I'd sit down next to him and we'd talk. In some mysterious way we were simpatico." To Peppard, "the difference between John Ford and other directors is the difference between Gulliver and the little people who tied him down."

Most of Ford's portion of *How the West Was Won* was shot near Paducah, Kentucky, and involved scenes with Carroll Baker and Andy Devine. "It was a warm sequence," Peppard maintained, "and Ford shot it that way. Most young actors, when they finish a take, will look at the director to see if they've given what he wanted. It's something you do when you're working closely with a director and trust him. Ford was absolutely trustworthy, and his eye for detail was exceptional." While he demanded intelligent acting from players, most of his attention was taken up with adjusting positions. "He never really said anything to me except positive things," Peppard recalled. "He wasn't much interested in the internals of acting. He expected us to be prepared and to deliver. He would listen carefully to a scene and had an ear for the truth."

The young actor observed that Ford was distant in most relationships and saw his cruel side, too. When Andy Devine failed to deliver a scene the way the director wanted it, Ford was scathing in his criticism. "Everybody was shifting feet with embarrassment," Peppard remembered.

Devine had worked with Ford enough by then to understand his ways; later the actor characterized Ford as "a wonderful, sentimental old man." While the company was filming in Kentucky, Ford called Devine aside and said, "You're not working this afternoon. Would you do me a favor?" The actor replied that he'd be happy to be of service. "Will you take my driver," Ford asked, "go by a floral shop, get some flowers, put them on Irvin Cobb's grave, and say a prayer for both of us?" (Irvin S. Cobb was the Kentucky writer responsible for *Judge Priest* and a favorite author of Ford's.) Devine knew that Ford would never have taken the flowers to the graveyard himself for fear somebody might see him. "He was a softie in a lot of ways," the actor declared, "and still you couldn't figure him out. But I think anybody who was around him was like a little kid with his father. He'd tell you to do something, and you'd think, 'What am I doing this for?' You did it because to have known John Ford, and worked for him, was to have loved him."

George Peppard had a night scene with cavalry troops beside a stream that ran blood because of the battle that day. Since it was a somber scene, Ford called Danny Borzage over with his accordion. "To my astonishment," said Peppard, "he sent me off with this accordion player, who played me sad music of the time. I was puzzled. I'd had a lot of training as an actor, and I thought I was ready to do the scene." Ford, ever the silent picturemaker, had another method for getting actors into the mood he wanted.

Jimmy Stewart played Peppard's father in the movie, although he didn't work with Ford on the picture. While the crew was in Kentucky, Stewart came to Ford's set to watch him shoot the scene in which Peppard leaves home to fight in the war. There were townspeople standing around, including a boy with a mongrel dog. After a tender farewell between Peppard and Carroll Baker, who played his mother, the actor rides away in a wagon with Andy Devine. As he did so, the dog darted after the wagon. The boy chased after his dog, whereupon Ford practically tackled the boy before he entered camera range. "It made a wonderful end to the scene," Stewart recalled. "The kid's parents were there, and they came up and apologized for the dog." Ford told them the dog had made the scene and that it was one of the finest touches he'd ever seen. "Those little pieces are what movies are made up of," said Stewart. "They certainly aren't made of sustained performances like in the theater, because that would be an impossibility."

Although the Cinerama lens was peculiar, taking an actor from a three-quarter figure to nearly a full close-up within a single step forward, Ford used it effectively. "I watched him compose a shot," Peppard said, "that included all the foreground action, with five actors moving about, and culminated in a steamboat coming around the bend almost three-quarters of a mile away. Ford composed shots in his mind with an astonishing ease. All of this had to be timed so that the foreground action and the steamboat matched."

John Wayne appeared briefly in Ford's portion of *How the West Was Won*, again playing William Tecumseh Sherman, opposite the Ulysses S. Grant of Henry Morgan. Since Wayne's part was small, Ford took delight in introducing him to Peppard. "Duke," he said with a smile, "I want you to meet the star of the picture." In their scene together Ford had Wayne and Morgan chewing cigars and spitting to an extent that Henry Hathaway, the film's principal director, considered inordinate. "The only segment I didn't change in the picture," said Hathaway, "was John Ford's, and I should have. It was terrible. But I didn't want it to get around Hollywood that I was making something of Ford's over again."

Everybody worked on *How the West Was Won* for half-salary or less, since a percentage of the profits went toward a new wing on St. John's Hospital. The star-studded, giant-screen saga was supposed to lure audiences away from their television sets and back into movie theaters, but the results were disappointing. "*How the West Was Won* is not the best Western ever made," *Life* magazine declared when the picture opened in the spring of 1961, "but it surely is the biggest and gaudiest."

Film scholars later isolated Ford's fifteen-minute segment with kinder words, pointing out that when he takes charge, the mood of the picture changes from light adventure to heart-rending nostalgia. Rather than affirming strength, Ford's accent is on mortality, brutally expressed in the aftermath of Shiloh. "The conclusion of the battle is one of Ford's most evocative passages," wrote John Baxter, "reminiscent of Whitman's descriptions of lamp-lit hospitals and men dying in torment."

During the fall of 1962 Ford directed a television episode for *Alcoa Premiere* entitled "Flashing Spikes," featuring James Stewart and Patrick Wayne. The show, a baseball story, was shot in five days. "I was never a baseball player," said Pat Wayne. "I was football and track, so I never played baseball in grammar school or Little League." Young Wayne had a scene where he was to hit the ball, with the camera positioned directly in front of him and Ford seated beside it. "I didn't know how to hit a baseball," said Wayne, "but I did and hit Ford right in the family jewels. I couldn't believe I was in that situation."

Since his son was in the show, Ford talked Duke Wayne into appearing in a cameo role, playing the umpire and billed as Marion Morrison. Cameraman William Clothier remembered Ford's quarreling with the television producer. "Ford wanted cigars," said Clothier, "but we couldn't use cigars [on camera] because a cigarette company might sponsor the show."

The director's last film with John Wayne, *Donovan's Reef*, was completed in 1963. It was a sad experience for everyone concerned. Ford had hired Wayne's friend James Edward Grant to write the script, but he hated what Grant turned in. Ford then asked Frank Nugent to do a revision. "The result was what you saw on the screen," Bill Clothier said. "I suppose you've got to blame the Old Man for that. It was just plain bad judgment."

The picture was intended as a light comedy, but Ford seemed to have lost his gift for making audiences laugh. *Donovan's Reef* focuses on characters who have chosen to stay on a Polynesian island rather than return to the America they fought for during World War II. Even a proper Bostonian, ready to condemn their way of life when she arrives, ends up joining them. The humor that surfaces above the picture's melancholy strain is heavy-handed and slapstick.

Lee Marvin, who costarred with Wayne in the film, remembered Ford's personal privacy, a trait Marvin thought "all authoritarians have." But the actor related to the director's robust humor. "That kind of fun, locker room, jockstrap talk," said Marvin, "is really a lot of flexing, getting the war drums going to get the juices flowing." Unfortunately it seems overdone in the movie.

Wayne watched over Ford during the making of the picture, acting almost as his assistant. "Duke loved John Ford," said Cesar Romero, who was in the cast, "and he had great respect for him. But Ford was a crochety old man by that time. He wasn't much fun to work with. He was just a gruff old Irishman." As the production wore on, it became clear Ford was not well. Wayne admitted to his costars that Ford's thinking wasn't as sharp as it had been.

Romero recalled how Ford gave Dorothy Lamour a particularly hard time while shooting *Donovan's Reef.* He was brusque with her and impatient, although Lamour finally stood up to him. "Look, Mr. Ford," the former Paramount star said, "I didn't ask for this part. You asked for me. I've made a lot of money for this studio in years past, and I don't have to take this treatment from you or anyone." She started to leave the set, but Ford called her back.

Lamour had been excited about working with the director again, since *The Hurricane* had been one of her most successful pictures. She and Mary Ford had enjoyed a long friendship, so when the costume designer decided Lamour should wear muumuus in *Donovan's Reef,* Jack sent her home to try on some of Mary's. "I found one that was perfect," the actress declared, "so that eliminated wardrobe fittings."

Lamour's relationship with the director reached a crisis when she complimented Lee Marvin on a scene, only to have Ford call her down in front of the company. He was the director, he told her, and would decide whether a scene was good or bad. Lamour was thoroughly embarrassed. Five minutes later Ford walked into her dressing room and apologized, putting his arms around her. "That man could charm the apples right out of the tree," the star said. "Angry and indignant as I was, he won me over and soon we both were crying and laughing."

Donovan's Reef was a limited success, praised more in retrospect than at the time it was released. "Only an ancient hermit would believe that the director John Ford and his writers . . . were serious," the *New York Times* maintained. "Mr. Ford has been involved with movies for 45 years, and his associates, including his principals, are no tyros either, so they cannot be blamed for using what would be film clichés in less practiced hands."

Idle for several months early in 1963, Ford grew restless. His former assistant Andrew McLaglen was making *McLintock* at the time in Arizona. McLaglen's picture featured Ford's favorite performers, John Wayne and Maureen O'Hara, and was being photographed by his cameraman, Bill Clothier. Ford was hurt that McLaglen hadn't consulted with him about the film, but when his protege fell ill, Ford was invited to take over the direction for a few days. Stefanie Powers, just beginning her career, remembered that the cast showed up one morning in costume and makeup only to be told, "Andy's not here. He's sick. Pappy's coming." Powers was so inexperienced she didn't know who Pappy was, but recalled how everybody stood expectantly on a plateau at the Green Ranch, where the picture was being shot. Finally a cloud of dust appeared in the lowlands beneath them. Ford had flown into Tucson and was driven directly to McLaglen's location. "I swear," said Powers, "it must have taken him half an hour to get up to us." There was silence as the crowd watched, mesmerized by the tail of dust from the approaching car. "It arrived in a whoosh of smoke," Powers declared. "The door opened and out stepped Ford, with his hat, the patch, the glasses, the red bandana, the stained old safari jacket. It was like a caricature. I promise you, he pushed Duke aside and pushed Maureen aside, pushed everybody aside, and walked over to Bill Clothier, put his hand on him and said, 'Let's get to work, Bill.' I will never forget that day, because it was so unbelievably dramatic. Every move that man made was so absurdly dramatic. There was never anything about John Ford that was normal or human."

The aging director guarded his human side more than ever, hiding his problems as best he could. In April Jack spelled out the family's economic situation to Pat, insisting that Mary was a spendthrift. "She spent over seven thousand dollars on Barbara's clothes alone last year," Jack said. He went on to mention that one day between 10:30 A.M. and noon his wife had paid six hundred dollars for a car for Danny, sixty dollars for a Hertz rental car, and over one hundred dollars for a new coat to wear to ball games. "She keeps talking about the enormous holdings I have in A. T. and T.," Jack wrote his son, urging that this information be kept confidental. "Actually the bank holds the stock for loans to pay income tax over the years. She has been told over and over, but refuses to believe it, or doesn't want to believe it. . . . She spends more than our annual income — [on] silly things."

Jack said he had considered divorce, but remained "a strong believer in the marriage vow." Whenever he mentioned expenses to Mary, she became hysterical and talked about "separate maintenance," accusing him of keeping another woman. "Perhaps I should turn everything over to her and go to Europe on a tax dodge stint," he said. "Maybe I could leave a comfortable estate that way. (No! I'm not pessimistic — just Irish.) Of course, she'd piss everything away in a year."

He had suggested turning the *Araner* over to the navy, but claimed Mary wouldn't hear of it. "The *Araner* to her is a status symbol," Ford wrote his son. "She hates the boat — won't use it, but refuses to give it up. . . . It's crippling us." He ended by saying how he hated to criticize Mary, since he loved her dearly. "Ten years ago it would have been so simple! Now — take heart. After all, I've not much time left," reminding his son that he would turn seventy the next year. "I'm really leveling with you, Pat," he wrote. "You must believe me. . . . But it's necessary at long last to inform you of our situation. Thank God we're Irish. I always feel better and fight harder when the odds are against one."

Ford was trying to get *Cheyenne Autumn* before the cameras. It was to be a joint venture with producer Bernard Smith, whom Ford had recently accepted as a partner. At his age the director found that making motion pictures became more difficult with time, and he needed someone to supervise production details while he concentrated on creative matters. But Warner Bros. had temporarily reneged on their agreement with Ford-Smith Productions to release *Cheyenne Autumn*. "Too much money — not enough 'stars,'" he explained to his son. "We have no other offers or interest in the property. Same story—so I'm not working, and no prospects in sight." Within three months, the situation had changed. "Right now I am working on a very big picture, *Cheyenne Autumn*, the Indian side of the West," Ford wrote Michael Killanin in July 1963. "This, I think, will be a welcome [change from] the movies and TVs of the past. It will be a costly picture and entail much physical labor."

Inspired by Mari Sandoz's book about the heroic flight in 1878 of three hundred Northern Cheyenne from a reservation in Oklahoma back to their ancestral lands near the Yellowstone River, *Cheyenne Autumn* was Ford's final Western. Based on a true story, it portrayed a tragic people at the mercy of a heartless majority—a theme in harmony with the rising Native American rights movement. "I've long wanted to do a story that tells the truth about them [the Indians]," said Ford, "and not just a picture in which they're chased by the cavalry." *Cheyenne Autumn* took a viewpoint opposite that of the James Warner Bellah Westerns. Rather than glorifying an expanding American empire, as Bellah ("the American Kipling") had done, *Cheyenne Autumn* concentrates on the victims of Anglo-American expansion. In that regard it was a forerunner of New West history. The Cheyenne faced starvation, disease, and death on the fifteen-hundred-mile return to their homeland, pursued along the way by the cavalry, with only eighty of them surviving. "I've killed more Indians than Custer," said Ford. "This is their side."

The director's association with the Navajo had sensitized him to Native American cultures, and he was sympathetic to their side. "They are a very dignified people," Ford remarked about the Indians with whom he had worked through the years. "I liked the story," he said when *Cheyenne Autumn* went into production, "and caught Jack Warner in a weak moment. He agreed to let me do it." Warner assigned Ford a budget of $5.1 million and agreed the film could be shot mostly in Monument Valley and around Moab. Ford was ecstatic: "Every time I make a Western, they say, 'There goes senile old John Ford out West again,' but I just don't give a damn."

Preparation on the film began in the West Hollywood offices that Ford's company shared with Batjak Productions, John Wayne's company. Although Ford took liberties with Sandoz's book, he remained sensitive to the story, yet helped screenwriter James R. Webb shape it into a big outdoor drama. He seemed sharp as a tack socially, but there was little question that his powers as a director had diminished. Physically debilitated, he moved slower, and the hardships of working on location took their toll. When rumors circulated that *Cheyenne Autumn* would be Jack's last Western, Patrick Ford denied the charge. "Hell!" said Pat, "he'll be making Westerns a couple of years after he's dead."

Ford looked forward to being back in Monument Valley with the Gouldings and his cowboys and Indians. *Cheyenne Autumn* would be the seventh film he had made there, and it would be his last, except for a documentary made shortly before his death. Prices at the Gouldings' lodge had swollen to twenty dollars a bed in 1963, but meals were still enormous, and the bulk of the company was housed in trailers on the flat below the trading post.

Cheyenne Autumn rescued the Navajo from another recession. Ford would again be working with Lee and Frank Bradley, Many Mules, and the Stanley brothers, as well as thirty-six Navajo extras on horseback and twenty-seven on foot, all playing Cheyenne. The highway into Monument Valley had been paved and the reservation had changed in other ways that seemed less positive. "The young squaws [are] wearing tight Capri pants and modern hairdresses," camera assistant Jack Woods wrote in October. "The bright velveteen skirts and blouses and the jewelry are getting to be a scarce item in some places, as civilization encroaches by way of paved roads. They even have a stop sign where Goulding's side road meets the highway."

Shooting on the picture began on October 1, 1963, with the company scheduled to work in Monument Valley throughout the month. Days at first were warm, but evenings were cool. "The trailer camp is superb with big sixty-foot trailers arranged in rows, with running water, electricity, and even movies in the mess hall at night," Jack Woods reported. "It's a typical Ford company with no levity and yessir and nosir! We never know when he's nice or will blow his top, but it's sure good to be back in Monument with the old Master with a capital M!"

Ford was delighted to be away from the tumult of Hollywood. "If there were more concern with what the public wants and less with what the critics want, Hollywood wouldn't be in the awful fix it's in right now," he told reporters. In his opinion Westerns were still vital to the industry. "They're not cheap or easy to make," said Ford. "They have to be done on location, which is damned hard work, the most expensive and most difficult form of moviemaking."

Cheyenne Autumn would have its ludicrous aspects, beginning with the director's casting of Ricardo Montalban, Dolores Del Rio, Sal Mineo, Gilbert Roland, and Victor Jory in Native American roles. Montalban, a Latin aristocrat, found working with Ford difficult and objected to his badgering. Uncomfortable with the director's approach, the actor told Patrick Wayne, "I'm putting my complete trust in him because he's absolutely leaving no margin for anything. He's telling me exactly how to play this part. He's not accepting anything but what he wants." Montalban came to recognize that, despite Ford's opinionated, demanding attitude, he had "a poetic eye with the camera" that was impossible to match.

Richard Widmark, who played a demoralized cavalry officer in the picture, and Karl Malden, cast as a Teutonic prison commandant, also experienced frustrations working with Ford. The director would sometimes come on the set and ask them how they felt a scene should be played. They'd offer suggestions, only to have him shoot it a different way, making fun of the ideas they'd expressed. The actors concluded that he was trying to rattle them, intending to break their will. Still, after *Cheyenne Autumn* wrapped, Widmark wrote Ford: "I enjoyed working with you on this picture more than anything I've ever done. I wish it could have gone on forever."

Carroll Baker became the director's pet, and she clearly adored him. "While we were on location," Baker said, "I always ate lunch and dinner by his side. He used to watch my plate and never allowed me dessert or bread and butter or potatoes. I was a slim 118 pounds, but Pappy didn't want me to gain even an ounce in my face." Ford had initially wanted to portray Baker's role, a Quaker schoolteacher, as a middle-aged spinster, since that interpretation would have been more realistic. "But you couldn't do that," said Ford, "you had to have a young, beautiful girl." Movies in 1963 still emphasized romance over realism.

Sal Mineo spent most evenings at Goulding's Lodge in his room playing records on a phonograph he'd brought along, usually jazz records, which he played fairly loudly. One night Ford entered his room and asked the young actor why he couldn't play his records more quietly. "Well, you see, sir," Mineo answered, "this kind of music has to be played at that volume. Otherwise one can't derive complete satisfaction from it." Ford took out his knife, opened it, and laid it on the table beside the phonograph. "Can you play it a little softer?" he said. "Yes, sir, I can play it very soft!" replied Mineo. Ford picked up the knife and closed it. "That's what I thought," he said and walked out.

"Uncle Jack got bored with *Cheyenne Autumn*," Dobe Carey declared. "I could see it happening." With his sight and hearing failing, Ford was no longer operating at full capacity. "He had passed his peak and was beginning to lose touch with the way he used to direct pictures," said Carey. "He still had the talent with the camera, but not how to tell the story. He couldn't keep it all in his mind. When he needed help, he didn't know whom to turn to for it. Nobody would offer any, because he would bawl them out. When he needed help, there was nobody around."

As the weeks in Monument Valley wore on, Ford sometimes opted to shoot scenes right in front of Goulding's Lodge, since that took less effort. "I think the same thing happened on *Cheyenne Autumn* that happened on a number of the Old Man's later films," Bill Clothier said. "He just got tired and lost interest. You could see his energy flagging. After a while he just wanted to wrap the picture up."

The weather presented problems during the weeks on location. Skies were overcast much of the time, so the light was often flat and dull. Since the production had fallen behind schedule, winter began to set in. "We have had an epidemic of flu," Jack Woods wrote from Monument Valley on November 4, "both intestinal and the kind that makes you feel like you were hit by a horse truck. Four Indian infants died in the local hospital, and the entire crew, including the actors, have had it at one time or another."

The huge servings of food caused the company "to cut extra notches in our belts," said Woods, but socializing after dinner fell to a minimum. Ford usually stayed at the table just long enough to smoke half a cigar, chatting with actors as he did. Then he'd nudge his son. "I'm going to call Mother," he'd say to Patrick, and the two of them would leave the dining hall together. "Jack wasn't feeling good on *Cheyenne Autumn*," Wingate Smith recalled. "He was sloughing." George O'Brien, who, forty years before, had starred in *The Iron Horse*, noticed that the director was staying in bed more.

Ford tried to keep up appearances. He'd arrive on the set a little past 8:30 A.M., driven there in Harry Goulding's jeep station wagon. Danny Borzage would walk to the side of the road as the jeep drew near and begin playing "Bringing in the Sheaves" on his accordion. He would continue until the vehicle came to a stop; as Ford walked toward the set, a hush fell over the company. With shooting ready to start, Lee and Frank Bradley lifted their bullhorns and shouted instructions to the Navajo.

Chuck Roberson recalled that there were not many stunts used in *Cheyenne Autumn*, although stunt performers frequently dressed and made up to look like Indians. Even with his wranglers Ford seemed more short-tempered than usual. Carroll Baker in one scene was to drive a wagon into a river, but before she did, Ford wanted to make sure the crossing was safe. "Can Carroll go in the river with the wagon?" he asked a wrangler. "Well, when I went in—" the fellow started to explain. "Don't give me the story of your life," Ford snapped, "just answer the question."

From Monument Valley the company moved up to Moab for another thirteen days of filming, staying there in various motels. They were working in Moab when John F. Kennedy was assassinated on November 22. Devastated, Ford closed the production for two days. He remarked to a friend that it was not until Kennedy, a fellow Irishman, had been elected president in 1960 that he truly felt like a first-class citizen.

In December Ford spent nine days shooting near Gunnison, Colorado, and planned to move on up into Canada. He insisted that he needed at least a foot of snow for *Cheyenne Autumn*'s snow scenes. He had found only six inches on the ground in Colorado and prepared to wait for more, while his company sat idle. Within a few days word came from the studio: "Shoot it or else come home." Furious, Ford went to his room and started drinking. "That's when the whole thing fell apart," said Ben Johnson, who was working on a Ford film for the first time in eleven years. "They sent another director up there to finish the job."

By Christmas the company was back in Hollywood, with twenty-one days of work left in the studio. Plagued by a cold, Ford was sullen and withdrawn, functioning mechanically. Scenes with James Stewart and Edward G. Robinson, who had replaced Spencer Tracy as Carl Schurz, were shot at Warner Bros. *My Fair Lady* and *Cheyenne Autumn* were the only films in production there at the time, and the studio's empty sound-stages seemed like tombs. "It's just no fun anymore," said Ford.

The director made a practice of finishing up the day's shooting around 2:30 every afternoon. A Warner executive soon informed him that the company was expected to work until at least 4:00. The next morning the cast and crew were on the set by 8:30 ready to begin, but at 9:00 Ford still hadn't shown up. Someone called his house at 9:30, but the maid said that Ford had left a long time before. At 10:30 his limousine arrived at the soundstage, and he got out. "The funniest thing happened," he said. "I've had the same goddamn chauffeur for twenty-five years, and this morning he got lost!" The next day Ford appeared at 8:30 and quit at 2:30 with no more complaints.

When *Cheyenne Autumn* wrapped in January 1964, the director kissed cinematographer William Clothier on the cheek and told him, "This is the best-photographed picture I ever made in my life." While it contains some majestic photography, much of the picture seems lackluster, particularly by Ford standards. When a viewer commented that *Cheyenne Autumn* looked like a silent movie, Ford was quick to reply, "It's still a silent medium."

Exhausted from making a huge Western, Ford went to work with editor Otho Lovering on assembling it. Publicly he remained enthusiastic about *Cheyenne Autumn*, but privately he knew the picture was not the masterwork he'd hoped for. He objected to the score, claiming that the music was more appropriate for cossacks than Indians.

A print was screened at Warner Bros. on June 23. "Even though all present seemed to like the picture," a studio memo read, "there was a definite feeling of length. Therefore, Mr. Warner has decided to make certain eliminations and trims." Ford locked himself in a cutting room and took out twenty minutes of his original version, hoping to give the movie added verve.

When the picture was released in the fall, most critics weren't impressed. "*Cheyenne Autumn* is a rambling episodic account," said *Variety*. Stanley Kauffmann, reviewing for *New Republic*, found the cast "beyond disbelief." *Cheyenne Autumn*, he wrote, is "a pallid and straitened version of the best Ford, with no new visual ideas and, what is perhaps worse, fumbling use of the old ones." *Newsweek*'s assessment was even harsher: "Ford has apparently forgotten everything he ever knew, about actors, about cameras, about Indians, and about the West. The performances by Edward G. Robinson, Carroll Baker, Karl Malden, and the rest are uniformly terrible. Sal Mineo, the worst of all, walks with a pelvic lead, as if he were playing the first Cheyenne female impersonator."

When author Mari Sandoz saw the film, she was "terribly disappointed." The picture's release was the occasion for a four-day premiere in Cheyenne, Wyoming, but the director didn't attend. The movie was selected as the outstanding

Western of 1964 by the Cowboy Hall of Fame, but the general appraisal was that the Old Master had lost his touch. "There was nothing you could learn from a thing like that," screenwriter Nunnally Johnson said after seeing *Cheyenne Autumn*. "It was pure trash to me, just great crowds of people riding across the screen."

Ford defended his film, but his words sounded synthetic. "In most Westerns you never really get to see the Indians," he said. "They're off on a cliff somewhere, they come riding down on the stagecoach, they bite the dust, and that's it. I wanted to make a picture in which the audience not only met the Indian face to face, but got to know and admire him."

The picture had unquestionably turned the cavalry story around, giving what hope there was to a minority culture at the mercy of an inhumane majority. The Indians are no longer the savage enemies of an advancing civilization; they are the tragic heroes, the dispossessed. The cavalry has become the pawn of a remote and vindictive government, while Ford appears to have lost faith in the individual's capacity to right society's wrongs. Secretary of the Interior Schurz fears that his benevolence toward the Indians will give his political opponents "the false move they are waiting for." Society's leaders have become powerless, in contrast to Ford's lifelong hero, Abraham Lincoln, in whose framed portrait Schurz's face is reflected. But the Cheyenne are doomed to defeat, too. The Indians not only face starvation and annihilation, but they splinter from within.

The Dodge City sequence stands as a controversial and confusing interlude. Ford claimed he added the episode for comic relief, a light touch after the intermission, in what otherwise was a tragic story. Others have viewed the insert as Ford's reflection on the degeneracy of the Old West, a counterpoint to the plight of the Native Americans. Wyatt Earp, the idealized western hero in *My Darling Clementine*, has become a parody, a threat to decent values. At best the Earp depicted in *Cheyenne Autumn* is a middle-aged buffoon, with Doc Holliday as his sidekick; at worst the gambler is a selfish cynic and decadent capitalist, caring only for his poker game. "*Cheyenne Autumn* shows us how the formerly tragic and heroic figures of

the winning of the West have become crafty, tired old men,"
Jeffrey Richards wrote, "playing cards and resting on their
laurels. Someone once said that all great events in history are
played twice, first as tragedy and then as farce. Perhaps the
same can be said of Ford's films." The director later admitted
that the Dodge City sequence "screwed up the rhythm of the
picture" and that originally there had been a great deal more of
it. But as it is the interlude reduces heroism to clowning.

During the weeks the *Cheyenne Autumn* company was filming in Monument Valley, future director Peter Bogdanovich
spent hours with Ford, gathering insights into the old master's
work habits for an article to be published in *Esquire*. The
aspiring filmmaker sent Ford a draft of the piece before his
subject returned to Hollywood. "I think your article is nau-
seating," Ford wrote Bogdanovich. "I dislike immensely your
portrait of the senile, illiterate, drunken director. . . . I had
several people in the troupe read your article. They were
horrified. They consider it a violation of privacy and that you
transgressed the laws of hospitality. I hope you don't submit it.
To sum it all up, I think it is cheap." Yet Ford respected
Bogdanovich, in part because the ambitious film student
talked to him as a picturemaker rather than as a reporter or an
academic. At Bogdanovich's request Ford helped talk Ben
Johnson into playing Sam the Lion in *The Last Picture Show*
(1971), for which the former wrangler won an Academy Award
as best supporting actor. "Bogdanovich did a wonderful job of
capturing Ford in my grandfather's own larger-than-life terms,"
Dan Ford said of the *Esquire* piece. "It's almost caricature, but
it's how Ford wanted it."

In July 1964, before *Cheyenne Autumn* opened, Ford flew to
Ireland to make another picture with Michael Killanin. Based
on the early life of Irish playwright Sean O'Casey, the film—
Young Cassidy—starred Rod Taylor, Julie Christie, and Maggie
Smith. Tired and in poor health, Ford nonetheless approached
the project with optimism. "You know there's no such thing as
a good script," the director had commented a few months
earlier. "I've never seen one." Then he corrected himself. "Yes, I
have. I've seen *one*. This O'Casey thing I'm going to do next,

based on his autobiography. It's the first script I've ever read that I can just go over and shoot."

He worked on the picture in Dublin less than a week before he reportedly became ill with strep throat. Ford later claimed that he had decided the script wouldn't work after all, but Killanin described how his heart sank when he discovered two grocery bags full of Scotch bottles in Ford's living quarters. Killanin knew then that Ford was finished so far as *Young Cassidy* was concerned. The badly debilitated director left Dublin by chartered plane for London on August 4, en route to Los Angeles. The O'Casey picture was finished by director-cinematographer Jack Cardiff, who followed Ford's design.

Ford spent August and September in Hawaii aboard the *Araner*, but the depression he suffered in Ireland failed to lift. His hearing had become so bad that people had to shout to be heard, and he shouted back. His personality seemed even more forbidding, while his memories were coated with bitterness. He had lost weight and walked with a limp.

The Ford marriage had reached its nadir, with Jack and Mary living in different sections of the same house. Their son's relationship with Bernard Smith had become so strained during the making of *Cheyenne Autumn* that the producer refused to work with Patrick again. When Pat, remarried and with a baby daughter, asked his parents for money in 1965, Jack was outraged; they never reconciled.

Although *Cheyenne Autumn* opened amid a blaze of publicity, its reception left Ford shaken. Outwardly he was too tough to admit defeat, but he realized that he couldn't work much longer. In November 1964 he moved into offices at MGM, filling the walls with pictures of the West, the sea, and actors he had known. Surrounded by his mementos, he looked like a relic from another time and place, some inelegant character out of the Old West. In his study at home was a war bonnet, supposedly from the battle of Little Big Horn, along with a pair of gloves that, according to Ford, had been worn by Buffalo Bill Cody in his Wild West show. Increasingly he seemed to be living in the past.

Ford wrote Michael Killanin on November 30 that he had

gained thirty pounds and was feeling better than when they were last together. "The swimming, sleeping, and eating in Honolulu did me a lot of good," he reported. But his three-year-old grandchild had left her roller skates beside his bed, and he stepped on one and broke a bone in his left hand. Also, his brother Patrick had died in Portland the week before. "The sad part of it is that he, a fluent Irish speaker, was the only one of the family that never got back to Spiddal," Ford wrote. Killanin arranged for a mass to be said for Patrick in Spiddal's church.

The new year found Ford at Metro, preparing to film *Chinese Finale,* later renamed *Seven Women.* Jack thought a picture about women would be a good change for him, and he professed to like the story. He wanted Katharine Hepburn for the role of the spirited doctor, but considered Jennifer Jones when Hepburn proved unavailable. Eventually Patricia Neal was cast. Soon the director ran into interference from the studio and began leaving most of the details to his partner, Bernard Smith. Even before shooting started it was clear that *Seven Women* would be a studio production. Since Ford was merely an employee, he became indifferent. He quickly realized that it wasn't his kind of picture, but intended to fulfill his commitment. "Let's do the goddamn thing," he told Wingate Smith. "It's no good, but let's do it and get the hell out."

Ford started shooting *Seven Women* in February 1965, a week after his seventy-first birthday. A special luncheon was held for him at MGM, attended by studio executives and the Hollywood press corps, but gloom pervaded the affair. Although Ford had Wingate Smith, Anna Lee, and Woody Strode on the picture, his old support system wasn't there. He found himself, a man's director, working with a cast of women, most of them strangers, and filming a story that dealt with missionaries in China and repressed lesbianism. Ford acknowledged "the disintegration of everything he had believed in," but *Seven Women* seemed to symbolize for him the decay of traditional values, becoming almost a mockery of civilization.

Patricia Neal was cast as a worldly medical missionary who

sacrificed herself to the ravages of a Mongol barbarian. Ford and Neal got along well, but three days after filming began the star suffered a stroke that left her paralyzed and unable to speak. She was replaced by Anne Bancroft, and her scenes were reshot. Ford complained that he had difficulty getting Bancroft to expand her performance and maintained that she was "the mistress of monotone."

Although surrounded by women and Chinese extras, Ford remained on his best behavior, "very courteous and polite," according to Anna Lee. Lee said no one in the company sensed how ill their director was. "The only problems he had were with the writers," she declared. "The writers were living in Paris and sending their lines to Ford by wire. Jack was incensed. Every morning we would come in, sit down at a long table, and Meta Sterne would be there to take notes. Jack would lift up his eye patch and begin looking at the pages he'd just received. Then very deliberately he would take them and tear them into shreds. 'Now,' he'd ask, 'what are we going to say?'"

Ford gave Eddie Albert and Mike Mazurki a tougher time on the picture than he did his actresses. "He had a knack for putting everyone on the defensive," Albert recalled. "If you were five minutes late, he'd see you come in the door and let you know. He always wanted to be one up on you and made sure we all knew he was in charge. Little by little most of us tended to become cautious. If you stuck your neck out, he'd cut you down. And he knew how to do it." The actor said that Ford worked fast and feared nothing. "He was a giant," Albert said, "but *Seven Women* was not his best."

Neal's condition hung over the picture, since her very existence was at stake. Rumors circulated, while the actress remained in a coma and the cast and crew worried. Ford tried to keep their spirits up by telling them jokes and talking more than usual, but the ruse was transparent. Those who knew him recognized that he didn't give a damn about the picture. Before long even the electricians were asking, "What the hell is Ford making this shit for?"

"He wasn't Ford," Wingate Smith said. "I saw that he was drinking too much and couldn't get off of it. He couldn't stand what was happening." By the end of the picture Ford was almost an automaton, sensing scenes more than seeing them. When *Seven Women* wrapped on April 21, he knew the time had come to quit the business altogether.

Although the picture has its moments, *Seven Women* was a hollow valedictory for Hollywood's most illustrious director. It was an ironic conclusion for a filmmaker who had largely worked in a masculine world. Gossips supposed that Ford resented his label as a director of cowboy movies and decided at last to prove his versatility. But despite its outrageousness, *Seven Women* seems dated. Robin Wood observed in *Film Comment* that Ford's direction of Margaret Leighton looked as if somebody had explained to him what a lesbian was five minutes before the scene was shot and he hadn't recovered from the shock.

While the picture fared reasonably well in England and France, it opened in New York at a Forty-second Street theater on the bottom half of a double bill with *The Money Trap*. *Variety* found *Seven Women* "a run-of-the-mill story," while *Cue* said the film went "hopelessly wrong" and resulted in an "old-fashioned mess."

Ford never announced his retirement, but the offers for work stopped coming. "We don't make pictures anymore in Hollywood," he said in 1965. "Madison Avenue and Wall Street make the films." Months passed, and it became clear that studio executives had all but forgotten John Ford. "This town is terrible," declared writer-director Burt Kennedy. "If you make a bad picture like *Seven Women* at his age, the studios are off of you. I always said Ford was so rough when he was younger, because he was getting even for what was going to happen when they dumped him. In Hollywood you haven't got the luxury of failure."

Once *Seven Women* was completed, Ford flew to Honolulu to rest on the *Araner*. He knew that the picture was a disaster and drank to forget. "I had seen him drunk before," wrote Dan Ford, "but never so depressed." With work no longer a wedge, Jack and Mary began quarreling more. He insisted that she cut back on expenditures and threatened to sell the house in Bel Air. She pointed out that they were worth approximately $1.7 million in blue-chip stocks and were well off. The tension between them became such that when Jack wanted to hang the portrait of Lincoln used in *Cheyenne Autumn* on their den wall, Mary insisted that one of Robert E. Lee be hung opposite it.

Ford handled the strife by becoming more reclusive, spending greater amounts of time in bed, shut up in his room with his books and television set. He seemed determined to barricade himself from a world that offered him no work and endless pain. He was stunned when he learned that John Wayne had lung cancer. Wayne worried about his mentor's state of mind and had delayed telling him the truth. Once he knew, Ford spent hours with Pilar Wayne at Good Samaritan Hospital, talking about the old times. "He is like a son to me," Ford said, his voice quaking. Pilar recalled how shocked she was at Ford's bleary eyes and rumpled appearance. "We both knew the glory days were gone," she wrote. "The Ford bunch had ceased to exist."

In February 1965 Ford was invested with the jewel and cape of a Knight of Malta, the highest honor granted by the Pope to a Catholic layperson. Since completing *Seven Women* Ford had shown renewed interest in the navy and went to sea with the USS *Columbia* for a few weeks in 1966. On May 2 he wrote Michael Killanin, "You may now call me fatso. From 139 leaving Dublin, I am now 192—pounds, that is." His excessive drinking continued, as Ford attempted to forget the career that was over.

When he discussed contemporary Hollywood, his remarks were always negative. "You've got to go through a series of commands now, and you never know who the hell reads the scripts anymore," he said. "You can't get an okay here for a script. It's got to go back to New York and through a president and a board of directors and bankers and everybody else." Ford claimed in 1967 that he had read and turned down nineteen scripts. "All of them are lousy!" he wrote Killanin. "Sex, sex, sex. As a Roman I was nauseated."

Ford became ill in Honolulu in May 1967 and was again admitted to Queen's Hospital. The next month his grandson

Tim returned from Vietnam, just as Dan shipped out with the navy. "We hope and pray," Ford wrote Killanin. The boys' father had accepted a position with the local school system, working with disturbed children, but Jack saw little of his son.

After Barbara and Ken Curtis divorced, Barb's alcoholism got out of control. She would call Andy McLaglen or George O'Brien at two or three o'clock in the morning, drunk and upset. O'Brien tried to mediate between Barbara and her parents, but other friends grew disgusted with her and hung up when she called in the middle of the night. "After Barbara and I got divorced," said Curtis, "I stayed completely away. I don't know if Jack would have used me in a picture or not. That was a painful time, and it was just easier to stay away." In later years Barbara talked about Curtis with affection, but never mentioned Robert Walker.

Ford would occasionally venture out to visit a friend's set. He showed up unannounced one day where Andrew McLaglen was working. "That was a funny feeling and a little bit of a shock," McLaglen said, "because I hadn't seen much of him. All of a sudden I saw that he was an old man. He just became old fast. He talked in a loud voice, and right in the middle of a take he dropped his watch. He was a cantankerous old bastard and probably did it on purpose." Wingate Smith felt that Ford still planned to make another picture. "God bless him," said Smith. "Maybe it was a good thing for him to think that."

By 1968 Ford was lecturing at various colleges. "It's fun," he wrote Michael Killanin, "and I use the same speech at each place, so it's easy." Dan Ford had returned from Vietnam, decorated seven times, which pleased his grandfather more than it did Dan. Friends dropped by Jack's house to sit and talk with him, but he mainly read and watched old movies on television, particularly budget Westerns.

When asked if he kept up with the current picture business, Ford's answer was usually profane. A reporter inquired if he had seen *Midnight Cowboy*. "Especially not that!" Ford exploded. "I don't like porn—these easy, liberal movies. A lot of junk. I don't know where they're going. They don't either." As the years passed, his awareness of contemporary Hollywood shrank. "My wife never sees pictures," Ford told an inter-viewer. "She only goes out at night to Anaheim to see the Angels play."

Ford's brother Eddie O'Fearna died in 1969, sending him into another depression. In May he saw Vietnam himself when he went on a tour of duty with the navy. "Horrible!" he wrote upon his return. "Got shot down. Typical Feeney luck. I have only a splinter fracture, but I'm able to walk or hobble a bit." Whatever reservations he may have had about the war, Ford was appalled by antiwar demonstrators' desecrations of the American flag and wouldn't tolerate derision of the nation's leadership in his presence.

When Merian Cooper and his wife visited the Connemara coast early in 1970, Cooper wrote Ford that the various places where *The Quiet Man* had been filmed were still pointed out to tourists. (Over twenty years later they remained tourist attrac-tions.) Ford continued to keep an office in Beverly Hills, but most of his appointments were with journalists and film scholars. Motion picture historian Joseph McBride met with him a number of times and reported that talking to Ford "was like squatting beside the chuck wagon with one of the Earp brothers for a chaw and a swig of coffee from a tin cup."

In March 1970 Ford sold the *Araner*, whose upkeep had become a financial drain. Later in the year he was involved in an automobile accident in which he broke a rib and cracked three more. His pessimism about America's destiny reached new depths, while his surly disposition grew even more acri-monious.

On July 6 Jack and Mary celebrated their Golden Anniversa-ry in the John Ford Chapel at the Motion Picture Home. When Ford was asked the secret of their marital success, he answered, "Keeping your mouth shut." In recent months their relation-ship had actually improved. It became increasingly clear that the aging couple needed one another, even though they spent most of their time in separate rooms.

The Fords' chauffeur died in October. "He passed away in my arms Tuesday morning," Ford wrote Katharine Hepburn. "We had services in a black mortuary. I'll write later . . . now

I'm not up to it." In May 1971 Mary's doctor determined that she was in the early stages of Parkinson's disease.

That August Ford attended the Venice Film Festival, where he was presented with the Grand Lion Award. Although he didn't feel well, he tried to exhibit a sense of humor in public. Dan Ford had recently taken a job in film production, so when a friend asked him what his grandson was doing, Jack replied, "He's playing piano in a whorehouse." The friend look puzzled. Jack gave a mischievous smile and said, "Well, you didn't want me to admit he's a producer, did you?"

A few months later Ford told his doctor that he suffered abdominal pains and asked what could be causing them. The physician feared he might have cancer, and exploratory surgery was ordered. The doctors found a massive, inoperable malignancy. Beyond question the cancer was terminal. "He is improving day by day," Mary wrote Michael Killanin on October 30, 1971, "but an operation as serious as his takes time and much rest." Olive Carey stopped by to visit Ford once he was out of the hospital. They talked for a while, but the change in him was so tremendous that when Ollie got back in her car she couldn't stop crying.

Accepting his fate, Jack and Mary decided to sell their Bel Air house and in 1972 moved to Palm Desert, where he would be near the Eisenhower Hospital, well-known for its cancer treatment. They bought a five-bedroom, desert home on Old Prospector Trail from Robert Wagner's sister. "His business manager arranged the purchase," said Wagner. "It was an incongruous kind of house for them. It was a Spanish-style home that maybe Zane Grey would have owned, but not John Ford." The house had two wings off a central living room. Jack took one wing, Mary took the other.

Honors and accolades continued to pour in. Ronald Reagan, then governor of California, said, "John Ford can bring out in actors as many curves and bends as we have in federal highways." Richard Nixon awarded the director the Presidential Medal of Freedom, the nation's highest civilian honor, but Ford was more pleased when he was made a rear admiral in the

U.S. Navy. In October 1972, before the Fords moved to Palm Desert, the Screen Directors Guild honored Jack with an evening of appreciation, during which *How Green Was My Valley* was shown. Ford, quite feeble, looked like a dying man as he was escorted in. After the screening the celebrants adjourned to the Guild's boardroom for drinks, songs, laughter, and tears before Ford was helped to his car. "It was at once a sad time and a merry time," screenwriter Philip Dunne recalled, "like an Irish wake, which in a way is just what it was."

On March 31, 1973, the American Film Institute presented Ford with its first Lifetime Achievement Award. Although he had avoided such ceremonies throughout his life, he appeared at the Beverly Hills Hilton, looking shrunken and frail, but maintaining a dignified presence. John Wayne pushed the director's wheelchair to the platform so he could receive his citation. Dorris Bowdon, who had made three successful pictures with Ford, wept as she watched the ceremony on television. "You could see that his mouth was dry," Bowdon said, "for he had to lick his lips constantly. I knew that he was on his way out and hadn't much longer to live."

Friends visited Ford in Palm Desert as he grew weaker. Robert Parrish, who had worked with him as a film editor and had been part of the Field Photographic Unit, came from London to see him. A nurse met Parrish at the door, informing him that he could stay five minutes and no longer. The former editor discovered Ford propped up in bed. A small statue of the Virgin Mary and some burning candles were in the bedroom, and a black saddle was mounted on a sawhorse at the foot of the bed. Ford was wearing the familiar patch over his left eye, and looked astonishingly thin. When he stood up, his legs were like matchsticks. A plastic bucket, half full of cigar butts, sat beside him; occasionally he attempted to rummage out one he liked. Since Mary was sick, too, Barbara was on hand to look after them.

Aware that time was running out, Ford avoided doctors so far as possible, but seemed happy to receive friends. Katharine Hepburn visited him and was surprised at his docile disposition. "Now you're so sweet to everyone," she told him. "This is not your true self." They spent hours ruminating over his life and career, with Hepburn doing most of the talking. Ford listened, then remarked how much he'd learned about himself from their conversation. "I took life as it came along," he said. There was a pause before he added, "You're a remarkable woman, Kate."

Peter Bogdanovich came to Palm Desert and was shocked to discover that Ford seemed to have shrunk by half. His hair was gone, his face like a skull. Gaunt though he was, the pugnacious spirit surfaced from time to time. When William Wyler dropped by, the two laughed about how they'd alternated making *Three Godfathers* through the years. When Wyler was ready to leave, Ford said, "By the way, it's your turn to do *Three Godfathers* again."

He was exceptionally weak the last time Patrick Wayne saw his godfather alive, but Ford rallied when young Wayne walked in. Patrick knew that he held a special place in Ford's heart, but was shocked when the dying man whispered, "Become a priest, become a priest." The last words Ben Johnson heard from Ford were, "Ben, don't forget to stay real." Johnson made that advice his credo.

Until the final two weeks, Ford refused painkillers. His bedroom had large windows that looked onto the desert, but the draperies were seldom open. He wanted them closed, even though the room was dank and smelled, despite air-conditioning. "His eyes became more clouded," Dan Ford said, "the look behind them more distant."

Director Howard Hawks lived in Palm Springs at the time. Although many found Hawks an austere man, he and Ford had been close friends, and he often came to visit. The last time was three days before Ford died. When Hawks was ready to go, Ford said, "Good-bye, Howard." The visitor started out of the room. "Howard," Ford called after him, "I mean *really* good-bye." Hawks turned and gave his friend a somber look. "Really good-bye, Jack?" he said, walking back to the bed. "Really good-bye," Ford answered. They shook hands, and Hawks left.

The next day Ford said he wanted to see John Wayne, so the actor flew to Palm Springs the following morning. As he left

Ford's side, Wayne was sad and depressed, and later said it was like losing his father again. Barbara Ford's friend Joanne Dru had been with Ford a few hours earlier. "Papa wanted to see me," Dru recalled, "but he wouldn't let me comfort him. I was crying so I had to leave the room."

On Friday, August 31, 1973, John Ford received the last rites of the Roman Catholic Church. For six hours Woody Strode sat at the side of Ford's bed, holding his hand until he slipped into a coma. Ford died peacefully at 6:00 P.M. "His sister and I took an American flag and draped him in it," Strode wrote. "We got some brandy, toasted him, and broke the glasses in the fireplace."

A requiem mass was held for the seventy-nine-year-old director on September 5, at the Church of the Blessed Sacrament in Hollywood. Interment followed at Holy Cross Cemetery in Culver City. Ford was laid to rest with military honors in a rolling green near the graves of his brothers Francis and Edward, his coffin covered with the tattered flag from his headquarters during the Battle of Midway. A navy rifle squad fired a salute; a bugler blew taps.

Iron Eyes Cody arrived for the service in full tribal regalia. On a hilltop overlooking Ford's grave, silhouetted against the afternoon sky, were two distant figures, a woman and a child, standing between two oak trees. The woman was actress Anna Lee. "It was poetically fitting that the archetypal grieving widow of the Ford stock company should be the only member of his troupe watching him being committed to the earth," declared Joseph McBride, who attended the funeral.

After the family, the military honor guard, and the great names from Hollywood's golden era had left the cemetery, only a handful of people and five grave diggers remained. As Ford's coffin was lowered into the grave, one of the grave diggers lost his grip and took a pratfall into a bouquet of flowers. "A bit of Fordian comedy," one observer commented, as the director's body descended to its final resting place.

"It was a beautiful death," Jack's sister Josephine told mourners. If the funeral lacked the master's touch, it was close enough to reflect his presence. Michael Killanin arranged a mass for his friend in the church at Spiddal, and there were those who felt that Ford should have been buried in Monument Valley. Few doubted that his likes would ever be seen in Hollywood again. "I miss him," writer James Warner Bellah said. "He was a son of a bitch, but I miss him." It was a eulogy after Ford's heart—honest, direct, full of sentiment.

Ford's will excluded his son, Patrick, from sharing the estate, most of which went to Mary. Upon her death half was to be divided between Dan and Tim, and the rest put into a trust fund for Barbara. Mary later filed a $4.1 million lawsuit against the executors of her husband's estate, claiming that they had mismanaged his affairs before and after his death. Much of the director's memorabilia and personal effects were sold at public auction. Barbara lived with Mary in Palm Desert until her mother's death from respiratory failure in 1979. Barbara died of cancer in 1985, Patrick a year later.

John Ford's career spanned Hollywood's formative years and its decades of maturation. He was of a pioneering breed, a man who talked with action. Probably no American director's work has endured the passage of time more gracefully than his. Not only did Ford enjoy unprecedented success in his lifetime, directing possibly twice the number of successful pictures that any of his rivals did, but he has been written about more than any director in Hollywood history. A matchless storyteller, Ford by any standards ranks high among the cinema's major filmmakers, a popular artist who expressed contemporary American ideals. Steven Spielberg, Martin Scorsese, and Peter Bogdanovich all have been Ford admirers, as have Ingmar Bergman and Jean-Luc Godard, and he remains a legend among current moviemakers. "I think my grandfather would have loved *Dances with Wolves*," Dan Ford said, "especially the dignity, the respect, and the humor that Kevin Costner attributed to the Indians in that film."

Ford's cinematic instincts, his insights into human nature, and his craftsmanship were unparalleled, representing old Hollywood at its best. "The power of Ford burns through," Stanley Kauffmann wrote in 1986, "a power that makes us a part of lives far from our own and makes our own lives more vivid." No artist could want for more. "Pappy was a painter with a camera," John Wayne declared shortly after the director's death, "a rock of strength for his friends and acquaintances. Many will miss him; I most of all." Wayne's words are almost pure Ford, for a feeling of life's slipping away is pervasive in the director's work; happiness seems to exist only in the past, and loved ones are loved best in memory. While John Ford adored America and elevated its creation myth to epic proportions, he remained thoroughly Irish in his attitudes and neuroses. The blend shaped his genius, but Ford's Irish viewpoint permeates his sagas of the American frontier, adding melancholy and poetic tension that came from his anguished life.

For those who knew him best, Ford was an enigma, at times seeming like two completely different men. Most acquaintances understood that the tough, ruthless, sarcastic curmudgeon they observed on a set or read about in interviews was not the true John Ford. The real Ford was gentle, sensitive, and kind, yet he feared his tenderness and protected himself even with those he trusted most. "There were so many sides to him that people never saw," Ford's friend Frank Baker said. "There was a man in my estimation; he had the touch of greatness."

Baker had known Jack and his brother Francis since the early days in Hollywood, and remembered the last time he saw Ford. The director had come to visit at the Motion Picture Home and by then was confined to a wheelchair. "I guess this is it," Ford told Baker as he was leaving. "I'd like you to know that you're one of the few people I ever respected. You never crawled on your belly to me."

Ford admired toughness and demanded strength and honesty from others, yet he could sustain neither toughness nor honesty himself. Afraid of impulses he lacked the capacity to understand and accept, he postured—hiding an artist's soul within a demon's facade. His was a lonely route, separated as he was from loved ones and himself, but out of the pain came creativity and the substance of art.

Filmography

Films are listed in chronological order within each year

FEATURE FILMS

1917

The Tornado. Universal. Screenplay: Jack Ford. Cast: Jack Ford, Jean Hathaway, John Duffy, Pete Gerald, Elsie Thornton, Duke Worne.

The Scrapper. Universal. Screenplay: Jack Ford. Camera: Ben Reynolds. Cast: Jack Ford, Louise Granville, Duke Worne, Martha Hayes, Jean Hathaway.

The Soul Herder. Universal. Screenplay: George Hively. Camera: Ben Reynolds. Cast: Harry Carey, Jean Hersholt, Elizabeth James, Molly Malone, Fritzi Ridgeway, Duke Lee, Vester Pegg, Bill Gettinger, Hoot Gibson.

Cheyenne's Pal. Universal. Screenplay: Charles J. Wilson, Jr., from a story by Jack Ford. Camera: Friend F. Baker. Cast: Harry Carey, Jim Corey, Gertrude Aster, Vester Pegg, Steve Pimento, Bill Gettinger, Hoot Gibson, Ed Jones.

Straight Shooting. Universal. Screenplay: George Hively. Camera: George Scott. Cast: Harry Carey, Molly Malone, Duke Lee, Vester Pegg, Hoot Gibson, George Berrell, Ted Brooks, Milt Brown.

The Secret Man. Universal. Screenplay: George Hively. Camera: Ben Reynolds. Cast: Harry Carey, Morris Foster, Elizabeth Jones, Vester Pegg, Elizabeth Sterling, Bill Gettinger, Steve Clemente, Hoot Gibson.

A Marked Man. Universal. Screenplay: George Hively, from a story by John Ford. Camera: John W. Brown. Cast: Harry Carey, Molly Malone, Harry Rattenbury, Vester Pegg, Anna Townsend, Bill Gettinger, Hoot Gibson.

Bucking Broadway. Universal. Producer: Harry Carey. Screenplay: George Hively. Camera: John W. Brown. Cast: Harry Carey, Molly Malone, L. M. Wells, Vester Pegg.

1918

The Phantom Riders. Universal. Producer: Harry Carey. Screenplay:

George Hively. Camera: John W. Brown. Cast: Harry Carey, Molly Malone, Buck Conners, Vester Pegg, Bill Gettinger, Jim Corey.

Wild Women. Universal. Producer: Harry Carey. Screenplay: George Hively. Camera: John W. Brown. Cast: Harry Carey, Molly Malone, Martha Maddox, Vester Pegg, Ed "Pardner" Jones, E. Van Beaver, W. Taylor.

Thieves' Gold. Universal. Screenplay: George Hively. Camera: John W. Brown. Cast: Harry Carey, Molly Malone, L. M. Wells, Vester Pegg, John Cook, Harry Tenbrook, M. K. Wilson, Martha Maddox.

The Scarlet Drop. Universal. Screenplay: George Hively. Camera: Ben Reynolds. Cast: Harry Carey, Molly Malone, Vester Pegg, M. K. Wilson, Betty Schade, Martha Maddox, Steve Clemente.

Hell Bent. Universal. Screenplay: John Ford, Harry Carey. Camera: Ben Reynolds. Cast: Harry Carey, Neva Gerber, Duke Lee, Vester Pegg, Joseph Harris, M. K. Wilson, Steve Clemente.

A Woman's Fool. Universal. Screenplay: George Hively. Camera: Ben Reynolds. Cast: Harry Carey, Betty Schade, Roy Clark, Molly Malone.

Three Mounted Men. Universal. Screenplay: Eugene B. Lewis. Camera: John W. Brown. Cast: Harry Carey, Joe Harris, Neva Gerber, Harry Carter, Anna Townsend.

1919

Roped. Universal. Screenplay: Eugene B. Lewis. Camera: John W. Brown. Cast: Harry Carey, Neva Gerber, Molly McConnell, J. Farrell McDonald, Arthur Shirley.

The Fighting Brothers. Universal. Screenplay: George Hively. Camera: John W. Brown. Cast: Pete Morrison, Hoot Gibson, Yvette Mitchell, Jack Woods, Duke Lee.

A Fight for Love. Universal. Screenplay: Eugene B. Lewis. Camera: John W. Brown. Cast: Harry Carey, Joe Harris, Neva Gerber, Mark Fenton, J. Farrell McDonald, Princess Neola Mae, Chief Big Tree.

By Indian Post. Universal. Screenplay: H. Tipton Steck. Cast: Pete Morrison, Duke Lee, Magda Lane, Ed "Pardner" Jones, Jack Woods, Harley Chambers, Hoot Gibson, Jack Walters, Otto Myers, Jim Moore.

The Rustlers. Universal. Screenplay: George Hively. Camera: John W. Brown. Cast: Pete Morrison, Helen Gibson, Jack Woods, Hoot Gibson.

Bare Fists. Universal. Screenplay: Eugene B. Lewis. Camera: John W. Brown. Cast: Harry Carey, Molly McConnell, Joseph Girard, Howard Ensteadt, Betty Schade, Vester Pegg, Joe Harris, Anna Mae Walthall.

Gun Law. Universal. Screenplay: H. Tipton Steck. Camera: John W. Brown. Cast: Pete Morrison, Hoot Gibson, Helen Gibson, Jack Woods, Otto Myers, Ed Jones, H. Chambers.

The Gun Packer. Universal. Screenplay: Karl R. Coolidge, from a story

by John Ford and Harry Carey. Camera: John W. Brown. Cast: Ed
Jones, Pete Morrison, Magda Lane, Jack Woods, Hoot Gibson,
Jack Walters, Duke Lee, Howard Ensteadt.

Riders of Vengeance. Universal. Producer: P. A. Powers. Screenplay:
John Ford, Harry Carey. Camera: John W. Brown. Cast: Harry
Carey, Seena Owen, Joe Harris, J. Farrell McDonald, Jennie Lee,
Glita Lee, Alfred Allen, Betty Schade, Vester Pegg, M. K. Wilson.

The Last Outlaw. Universal. Screenplay: H. Tipton Steck. Camera:
John W. Brown. Cast: Ed "Pardner" Jones, Richard Cumming,
Lucille Hutton, Jack Walters, Billie Hutton.

The Outcasts of Poker Flat. Universal. Producer: P. A. Powers.
Screenplay: H. Tipton Steck. Camera: John W. Brown. Cast:
Harry Carey, Cullen Landis, Gloria Hope, J. Farrell McDonald,
Charles H. Mailes, Victor Potel, Joe Harris, Duke R. Lee, Vester
Pegg.

The Ace of the Saddle. Universal. Producer: P. A. Powers. Screenplay:
George Hively. Camera: John W. Brown. Cast: Harry Carey, Joe
Harris, Duke R. Lee, Peggy Pearce, Jack Walters, Vester Pegg, Zoe
Ray, Howard Ensteadt, Ed "Pardner" Jones, William Cartwright.

The Rider of the Law. Universal. Producer: P. A. Powers. Screenplay: H.
Tipton Steck. Camera: John W. Brown. Cast: Harry Carey, Gloria
Hope, Vester Pegg, Theodore Brooks, Joe Harris, Jack Woods,
Duke R. Lee, Claire Anderson, Jennie Lee.

A Gun Fightin' Gentleman. Universal. Producer: P. A. Powers. Screen-
play: Hal Hoadley, from a story by John Ford and Harry Carey.
Camera: John W. Brown. Cast: Harry Carey, J. Barney Sherry,
Kathleen O'Conner, Lydia Yeamans Titus, Harry von Meter, Duke
R. Lee, Joe Harris, Johnny Cooke, Ted Brooks.

Marked Men. Universal. Producer: P. A. Powers. Screenplay: H. Tip-
ton Steck. Camera: John W. Brown. Cast: Harry Carey, J. Farrell
McDonald, Joe Harris, Winifred Westover, Ted Brooks, Charles
Lemoyne, David Kirby.

1920

The Prince of Avenue A. Universal. Screenplay: Charles J. Wilson, Jr.
Camera: John W. Brown. Cast: James J. "Gentleman Jim" Corbett,
Mary Warren, Harry Northrup, Cora Drew, Richard Cummings,
Frederik Vroom, Mark Fenton, George Vanderlip, Johnny Cooke,
Lydia Yeamans Titus, George Fisher.

The Girl in No. 29. Universal. Screenplay: Philip J. Hurn. Camera: John
W. Brown. Cast: Frank Mayo, Harry Hilliard, Claire Anderson,
Elinor Fair, Bull Montana, Ray Ripley, Robert Boulder.

Hitchin' Posts. Universal. Screenplay: George C. Hull. Camera: Ben-
jamin Kline. Cast: Frank Mayo, Beatrice Burnham, Joe Harris, J.
Farrell McDonald, Mark Fenton, Dagmar Godowsky, Duke R.
Lee, C. E. Anderson, M. Biddulph.

Just Pals. Fox. Screenplay: Paul Schofield. Camera: George Schneiderman. Cast: Buck Jones, Helen Ferguson, George E. Stone, Duke

R. Lee, William Buckley, Edwin Booth Tilton, Eunice Murdock Moore, Burt Apling, Slim Padgett, Pedro Leone, Ida Tenbrook, John J. Cooke.

1921

The Big Punch. Fox. Screenplay: John Ford, Jules Furthman. Camera: Jack B. Good. Cast: Buck Jones, Barbara Bedford, George Siegmann, Jack Curtis, Jennie Lee, Jack McDonald, Al Freemont, Edgar Jones, Irene Hunt, Eleanor Gilmore.

The Freeze Out. Universal. Screenplay: George C. Hull. Camera: Harry C. Fowler. Cast: Harry Carey, Helen Ferguson, Joe Harris, Charles Lemoyne, J. Farrell McDonald, Lydia Yeamans Titus.

The Wallop. Universal. Screenplay: George C. Hull. Camera: Harry C. Fowler. Cast: Harry Carey, Joe Harris, Charles Lemoyne, J. Farrell McDonald, Mignonne Golden, Bill Gettinger, Noble Johnson, C. E. Anderson, Mark Fenton.

Desperate Trails. Universal. Screenplay: Elliott J. Clawson. Camera: Harry C. Fowler, Robert DeGrasse. Cast: Harry Carey, Irene Rich, George F. Stone, Helen Field, Barbara La Marr, George Siegmann, Charles Insley, Ed Coxen.

Action. Universal. Screenplay: Harvey Gates. Camera: John W. Brown. Cast: Hoot Gibson, Francis Ford, J. Farrell McDonald, Buck Conners, Byron Munson, Clara Horton, William R. Daly, Charles Newton, Jim Corey, Ed "Pardner" Jones, Dorothea Wolburt.

Sure Fire. Universal. Screenplay: George C. Hull. Camera: Virgil G. Miller. Cast: Hoot Gibson, Molly Malone, Reeves "Breezy" Eason, Jr., Harry Carter, Murdock MacQuarrie, Fritzi Brunette, George Fisher, Charles Newton, Jack Woods, Jack Walters, Joe Harris, Steve Clemente, Mary Philbin.

Jackie. Fox. Screenplay: Dorothy Yost. Camera: George Schneiderman. Cast: Shirley Mason, William Scott, Harry Carter, George E. Stone, Elsie Bambrick, John Cooke.

1922

Little Miss Smiles. Fox. Screenplay: Dorothy Yost. Camera: David Abel. Cast: Shirley Mason, Gaston Glass, George Williams, Martha Franklin, Arthur Rankin, Baby Blumfield, Richard Lapan, Alfred Testa, Sidney D'Albrook.

The Village Blacksmith. Fox. Screenplay: Paul H. Sloane. Camera: George Schneiderman. Cast: William Walling, Virginia True Boardman, Virginia Valli, David Butler, Gordon Griffith, Ida Nan McKenzie, George Hackthorne, Pat Moore, Tully Marshall, Caroline Rankin, Ralph Yeardsley, Henri de la Garrique, Francis Ford, Bessie Love, Helen Field, Mark Fenton, Lon Poff, Cordelia Callahan, Eddie Gribbon, Lucile Hutton.

1923

The Face on the Barroom Floor. Fox. Screenplay: Eugene B. Lewis, G. Marion Burton. Camera: George Schneiderman. Cast: Henry B. Walthall, Ruth Clifford, Walter Emerson, Alma Bennett, Norval McGregor, Michael Dark, Gus Saville.

Three Jumps Ahead. Fox. Screenplay: John Ford. Camera: Daniel B. Clark. Cast: Tom Mix, Alma Bennett, Virginia True Boardman, Edward Piel, Joe E. Girard, Francis Ford, Margaret Joslin, Henry Todd, Buster Gardner.

Cameo Kirby. Fox. Screenplay: Robert N. Lee. Camera: George Schneiderman. Cast: John Gilbert, Gertrude Olmstead, Alan Hale, William E. Lawrence, Jean Arthur, Richard Tucker, Phillips Smalley, Jack McDonald, Eugenie Ford.

North of Hudson Bay. Fox. Screenplay: Jules Furthman. Camera: Daniel B. Clark. Cast: Tom Mix, Kathleen Key, Jennie Lee, Frank Campeau, Eugene Pallette, Will Walling, Frank Leigh, Fred Kohler.

Hoodman Blind. Fox. Screenplay: Charles Kenyon. Camera: George Schneiderman. Cast: David Butler, Gladys Hulette, Regina Connelly, Frank Campeau, Marc MacDermott, Trilby Clark, Eddie Gribbon, Jack Walters.

1924

The Iron Horse. Fox. Screenplay: Charles Kenyon. Camera: George Schneiderman, Burnett Guffey. Cast: George O'Brien, Madge Bellamy, Judge Charles Edward Bull, William Walling, Fred Kohler, Cyril Chadwick, Gladys Hulette, James Marcus, Francis Powers, J. Farrell McDonald, James Welch, Colin Chase, Walter Rogers, Jack O'Brien, George Waggner, John Padjan, Charles O'Malley, Charles Newton, Delbert Mann, Chief Big Tree, Chief White Spear, Edward Piel, James Gordon, Winston Miller, Peggy Cartwright, Thomas Durant, Stanhope Wheatcroft, Frances Teague, Dan Borzage.

The Hearts of Oak. Fox. Screenplay: Charles Kenyon. Camera: George Schneiderman. Cast: Hobart Bosworth, Pauline Starke, Theodore von Eltz, James Gordon, Francis Powers, Jennie Lee, Francis Ford.

1925

Lightnin'. Fox. Screenplay: Frances Marion. Camera: Joseph H. August. Cast: Jay Hunt, Madge Bellamy, Edythe Chapman, Wallace McDonald, J. Farrell McDonald, Ethel Clayton, Richard Travers, James Marcus, Otis Harlan, Brandon Hurst, Peter Mazutis.

Kentucky Pride. Fox. Screenplay: Dorothy Yost. Camera: George Schneiderman. Cast: Henry B. Walthall, J. Farrell McDonald, Gertrude Astor, Malcolm Waite, Belle Stoddard, Winston Miller, Peaches Jackson.

The Fighting Heart. Fox. Screenplay: Lillie Hayward. Camera: Joseph

H. August. Cast: George O'Brien, Billie Dove, J. Farrell McDonald, Diana Miller, Victor McLaglen, Bert Woodruff, James Marcus, Lynn Cowan, Harvey Clark, Hank Mann, Francis Ford, Francis Powers, Hazel Howell, Edward Piel.

Thank You. Fox. Producer: John Golden. Screenplay: Frances Marion. Camera: George Schneiderman. Cast: George O'Brien, Jacqueline Logan, Alec Francis, J. Farrell McDonald, Cyril Chadwick, Edith Bostwick, Vivian Ogden, James Neill, Billy Rinaldi, Maurice Murphy, Robert Milasch, George Fawcett, Marion Harlan, Ida Moore, Frankie Bailey.

1926

The Shamrock Handicap. Fox. Screenplay: John Stone. Camera: George Schneiderman. Cast: Janet Gaynor, Leslie Fenton, J. Farrell McDonald, Louis Payne, Claire McDowell, Willard Louis, Andy Clark, George Harris, Ely Reynolds, Thomas Delmar, Brandon Hurst.

Three Bad Men. Fox. Screenplay: John Ford, John Stone. Camera: George Schneiderman, Cast: George O'Brien, Olive Borden, J. Farrell McDonald, Tom Santschi, Frank Campeau, Lou Tellegen, George Harris, Jay Hunt, Priscilla Bonner, Otis Harlan, Walter Perry, Grace Gordon, Alec B. Francis, George Irving, Phyllis Haver, Vester Pegg, Bud Osborne.

The Blue Eagle. Fox. Screenplay: L. G. Rigby. Camera: George Schneiderman. Cast: George O'Brien, Janet Gaynor, William Russell, Robert Edeson, David Butler, Phillip Ford, Ralph Sipperly, Margaret Livingston, Jerry Madden, Harry Tenbrook, Lew Short.

1927

Upstream. Fox. Screenplay: Randall H. Faye. Camera: Charles G. Clarke. Cast: Nancy Nash, Earle Foxe, Grant Withers, Raymond Hitchcock, Lydia Yeamans Titus, Emile Chautard, Ted McNamara, Sammy Cohen, Francis Ford, Judy King, Lillian Worth, Jane Winton, Harry Bailey, Ely Reynolds.

1928

Mother Machree. Fox. Screenplay: Gertrude Orr. Camera: Chester Lyons. Cast: Belle Bennett, Neil Hamilton, Philippe De Lacy, Pat Somerset, Victor McLaglen, Ted McNamara, John MacSweeney, Eulalie Jensen, Constance Howard, Ethel Clayton, William Platt, Jacques Rollens, Rodney Hildebrand, Joyce Wirard, Robert Parrish.

Four Sons. Fox. Screenplay: Philip Klein. Camera: George Schneiderman, Charles G. Clarke. Cast: Margaret Mann, James Hall, Charles Morton, George Meeker, Francis X. Bushman, Jr., June Collyer, Albert Gran, Earle Foxe, Frank Reicher, Jack Pennick, Archduke Leopold of Austria, Hughie Mack, Wendell Franklin, Auguste

Tollaire, Ruth Mix, Robert Parrish, Michael Mark, L. J. O'Conner, Ferdinand Schumann-Heink, Capt. John Porters, Carl Boheme, Constant Franke, Hans Furberg, Tibor von Janny, Stanley Blystone, Lt. George Blagoi.

Hangman's House. Fox. Screenplay: Marion Orth, Willard Mack. Camera: George Schneiderman. Cast: Victor McLaglen, Hobart Bosworth, June Collyer, Larry Kent, Earle Foxe, Eric Mayne, Joseph Burke, Belle Stoddard, John Wayne.

Napoleon's Barber. Fox. Screenplay: Arthur Caesar. Camera: George Schneiderman. Cast: Otto Matiesen, Frank Reicher, Natalie Golitzin, Helen Ware, Philippe De Lacy, Russell Powell, D'Arcy Corrigan, Michael Mark, Buddy Roosevelt, Ervin Renard, Joe Waddell, Youcca-Troubetzkoy, Henry Herbert.

Riley The Cop. Fox. Screenplay: James Gruen, Fred Stanley. Camera: Charles G. Clarke. Cast: J. Farrell McDonald, Louise Fazenda, Nancy Drexel, David Rollins, Harry Schultz, Billy Bevan, Tom Wilson, Otto H. Fries, Mildred Boyd, Ferdinand Schumann-Heink, Del Henderson, Russell Powell, Mike Donlin, Robert Parrish.

1929

Strong Boy. Fox. Screenplay: James K. McGuinness, Andrew Bennison, John McLain. Camera: Joseph H. August. Cast: Victor McLaglen, Leatrice Joy, Clyde Cook, Slim Summerville, Kent Sanderson, Tom Wilson, Jack Pennick, Eulalie Jensen, David Torrence, J. Farrell McDonald, Delores Johnson, Douglas Scott, Robert Ryan.

The Black Watch. Fox. Screenplay: James K. McGuinness, John Stone. Camera: Joseph H. August. Cast: Victor McLaglen, Myrna Loy, Roy D'Arcy, Pat Somerset, David Rollins, Mitchell Lewis, Walter Long, David Percy Lumsden Hare, Cyril Chadwick, David Torrence, Francis Ford, Claude King, Frederick Sullivan, Joseph Diskay, Richard Travers, Joyzelle.

Salute. Fox. Screenplay: James K. McGuinness. Camera: Joseph H. August. Cast: George O'Brien, Helen Chandler, Stepin' Fetchit, William Janney, Frank Albertson, Joyce Compton, Cliff Dempsey, Lunsden Hare, David Butler, Rex Bell, John Breeden, Ward Bond, John Wayne.

1930

Men Without Women. Fox. Screenplay: Dudley Nichols. Camera: Joseph H. August. Cast: Kenneth MacKenna, Frank Albertson, Paul Page, Pat Somerset, Walter McGrail, Stuart Erwin, Warren Hymer, J. Farrell McDonald, Roy Stewart, Warner Richmond, Harry Tenbrook, Ben Hendricks, Jr., George Le Guere, Charles Gerard, John Wayne, Robert Parrish.

Born Reckless. Fox. Screenplay: Dudley Nichols. Camera: George Schneiderman. Cast: Edmund Lowe, Catherine Dale Owen, Lee Tracy,

Marguerite Churchill, Warren Hymer, Pat Somerset, William Harrigan, Frank Albertson, Ferike Boros, J. Farrell McDonald, Paul Porcasi, Eddie Gribbon, Mike Donlin, Ben Bard, Paul Page, Joe Brown, Jack Pennick, Ward Bond, Roy Stewart, Yola D'Avril.

Up the River. Fox. Screenplay: Maurine Watkins. Camera: Joseph H. August. Cast: Spencer Tracy, Warren Hymer, Humphrey Bogart, Claire Luce, Joan Lawes, Sharon Lynn, George McFarlane, Gaylord Pendleton, Morgan Wallace, William Collier, Sr., Robert E. O'Connor, Louise MacIntosh, Edythe Chapman, Johnny Walker, Noel Francis, Mildred Vincent, Wilbur Mack, Goodee Montgomery, Althea Henley, Carol Wines, Adele Windsor, Richard Keene, Elizabeth and Helen Keating, Robert Burns, John Swor, Pat Somerset, Joe Brown, Harvey Clark, Black and Blue, Morgan Wallace, Robert Parrish.

1931

Seas Beneath. Fox. Screenplay: Dudley Nichols. Camera: Joseph H. August. Cast: George O'Brien, Marion Lessing, Warren Hymer, William Collier, Sr., John Loder, Walter C. "Judge" Kelly, Walter McGrail, Henry Victor, Mona Maris, Larry Kent, Gaylord Pendleton, Nat Pendleton, Harry Tenbrook, Terry Ray, Hans Furberg, Ferdinand Schumann-Heink, Francis Ford, Kurt Furberg, Ben Hall, Harry Weil, Maurice Murphy.

The Brat. Fox. Screenplay: Sonya Levien, S. N. Behrman, Maude Fulton. Camera: Joseph H. August. Cast: Sally O'Neil, Alan Dinehart, Frank Albertson, Virginia Cherrill, June Collyer, J. Farrell McDonald, William Collier, Sr., Margaret Mann, Albert Gran, Mary Forbes, Louise MacIntosh.

Arrowsmith. Goldwyn–United Artists. Producer: Samuel Goldwyn. Screenplay: Sidney Howard. Camera: Ray June. Cast: Ronald Colman, Helen Hayes, A. E. Anson, Richard Bennett, Claude King, Beulah Bondi, Myrna Loy, Russell Hopton, De Witt Jennings, John Qualen, Adele Watson, Lumsden Hare, Bert Roach, Charlotte Henry, Clarence Brooks, Walter Downing, David Landau, James Marcus, Alec B. Francis, Sidney McGrey, Florence Britton, Bobby Watson.

1932

Air Mail. Universal. Producer: Carl Laemmle, Jr. Screenplay: Dale Van Every, Lt. Comdr. Frank W. Wead. Camera: Karl Freund. Cast: Pat O'Brien, Ralph Bellamy, Gloria Stuart, Lillian Bond, Russell Hopton, Slim Summerville, Frank Albertson, Leslie Fenton, David Landau, Tom Corrigan, William Daly, Hans Furberg, Lew Kelly, Frank Beal, Francis Ford, James Donlan, Louise MacIntosh, Katherine Perry, Beth Milton, Edmund Burns, Charles de la Montte, Lt. Pat Davis, Jim Thorpe, Enrico Caruso, Jr., Billy Thorpe, Alene Carroll, Jack Pennick.

Flesh. Metro-Goldwyn-Mayer. Screenplay: Leonard Praskins, Edgar Allen Woolf. Camera: Árthur Edeson. Cast: Wallace Beery, Karen Morley, Ricardo Cortez, Jean Hersholt, John Miljan, Vince Barnett, Herman Bing, Geta Meyer, Ed Brophy, Ward Bond, Nat Pendleton.

1933

Pilgrimage. Fox. Screenplay: Philip Klein, Barry Connors, Camera: George Schneiderman. Cast: Henrietta Grosman, Heather Angel, Norman Foster, Marian Nixon, Maurice Murphy, Lucille Laverne, Charle Grapewin, Hedda Hopper, Robert Warwick, Betty Blythe, Francis Ford, Louise Carter, Jay Ward, Francis Rich, Adele Watson.

Dr. Bull. Fox. Screenplay: Paul Green. Camera: George Schneiderman. Cast: Will Rogers, Marian Nixon, Berton Churchill, Louise Dresser, Howard Lally, Rochelle Hudson, Vera Allen, Tempe Pigotte, Elizabeth Patterson, Ralph Morgan, Andy Devine, Nora Cecil, Patsy O'Byrne, Effie Ellsler, Veda Buckland, Helen Freeman, Robert Parrish.

1934

The Lost Patrol. RKO Radio. Producer: Merian C. Cooper. Screenplay: Dudley Nichols, Garrett Fort. Camera: Harold Wenstrom. Cast: Victor McLaglen, Boris Karloff, Wallace Ford, Reginald Denny, J. M. Kerrigan, Billy Bevan, Alan Hale, Brandon Hurst, Douglas Walton, Sammy Stein, Howard Wilson, Neville Clark, Paul Hanson, Francis Ford.

The World Moves On. Fox. Producer: Winfield Sheehan. Screenplay: Reginald C. Berkeley. Camera: George Schneiderman. Cast: Madeleine Carroll, Franchot Tone, Lumsden Hare, Raul Roulien, Reginald Denny, Siegfried Rumann, Louise Dresser, Stepin' Fetchit, Dudley Diggs, Frank Melton, Brenda Fowler, Russell Simpson, Walter McGrail, Marcelle Corday, Charles Bastin, Barry Norton, George Irving, Ferdinand Schumann-Heink, Georgette Rhodes, Claude King, Ivan Simpson, Frank Moran, Jack Pennick, Francis Ford, Torbin Mayer.

Judge Priest. Fox. Producer: Sol Wurtzel. Screenplay: Dudley Nichols, Lamar Trotti. Camera: George Schneiderman. Cast: Will Rogers, Henry B. Walthall, Tom Brown, Anita Louise, Rochelle Hudson, Berton Churchill, David Landau, Brenda Fowler, Hattie McDaniel, Stepin' Fetchit, Frank Melton, Roger Imhof, Charley Grapewin, Francis Ford, Paul McAllister, Matt McHugh, Hy Meyer, Louis Mason, Robert Parrish.

1935

The Whole Town's Talking. Columbia. Producer: Lester Cowan. Screen-

play: Jo Swerling. Camera: Joseph H. August. Cast: Edward G.
Robinson, Jean Arthur, Wallace Ford, Arthur Byron, Arthur Hohl,
Donald Meek, Paul Harvey, Edward Brophy, J. Farrell McDonald,
Etienne Girardot, James Donlan, John Wray, Effie Ellsler, Robert
Emmett O'Connor, Joseph Sawyer, Francis Ford, Robert Parrish.

The Informer. RKO Radio. Screenplay: Dudley Nichols. Camera: Jo-
seph H. August. Cast: Victor McLaglen, Heather Angel, Preston
Foster, Margot Grahame, Wallace Ford, Una O'Connor, J. M.
Kerrigan, Joseph Sawyer, Neil Fitzgerald, Donald Meek, D'Arcy
Corrigan, Leo McCabe, Gaylord Pendleton, Francis Ford, May
Boley, Grizelda Harvey, Dennis O'Dea, Jack Mulhall, Robert
Parrish, Clyde Cook, Barlowe Borland, Frank Moran, Arthur
McLaglen.

Steamboat Round The Bend. 20th Century-Fox. Producer: Sol M.
Wurtzel. Screenplay: Dudley Nichols, Lamar Trotti. Camera:
George Schneiderman. Cast: Will Rogers, Anne Shirley, Eugene
Pallette, John McGuire, Berton Churchill, Stepin' Fetchit, Francis
Ford, Irvin S. Cobb, Roger Imhof, Raymond Hatton, Hobart
Bosworth, Louis Mason, Charles B. Middleton, Si Jenks, Jack
Pennick.

1936

The Prisoner of Shark Island. 20th Century-Fox. Producer: Darryl F.
Zanuck. Screenplay: Nunnally Johnson. Camera: Bert Glennon.
Cast: Warner Baxter, Gloria Stuart, Claude Gillingwater, Arthur
Byron, O. P. Heggie, Harry Carey, Francis Ford, John Carradine,
Frank McGlynn, Sr., Douglas Wood, Joyce Kay, Fred Kohler, Jr.,
Francis McDonald, John McGuire, Ernest Whitman, Paul Fix,
Frank Shannon, Leila McIntyre, Etta McDaniel, Arthur Loft, Paul
McVey, Maurice Murphy, Jack Pennick, J. M. Kerrigan, Whitney
Bourne, Robert Parrish.

Mary of Scotland. RKO Radio. Producer: Pandro S. Berman. Screenplay: Dudley Nichols. Camera: Joseph H. August. Cast: Katharine Hepburn, Fredric March, Florence Eldridge, Douglas Walton, John Carradine, Monte Blue, Jean Fenwick, Robert Barrat,
Gavin Muir, Ian Keith, Moroni Olson, Donald Crisp, William
Stack, Molly Lamont, Walter Byron, Ralph Forbes, Alan Mowbray, Frieda Inescort, David Torrence, Anita Colby, Lionel Bel-
more, Doris Lloyd, Bobby Watson, Lionel Pape, Ivan Simpson,
Murray Kinnell, Lawrence Grant, Nigel DeBrulier, Barlowe Borland, Alec Craig, Mary Gordon, Wilfred Lucas, Leonard Mudie,
Brandon Hurst, D'Arcy Corrigan, Frank Baker, Cyril McLaglen,
Robert Warwick, Earle Foxe, Wyndham Standing, Gaston Glass,
Neil Fitzgerald, Paul McAllister.

The Plough and the Stars. RKO Radio. Screenplay: Dudley Nichols.
Camera: Joseph H. August. Cast: Barbara Stanwyck, Preston
Foster, Barry Fitzgerald, Dennis O'Dea, Eileen Crowe, Arthur
Shields, Erin O'Brien Moore, Brandon Hurst, F. J. McCormick,

Una O'Connor, Moroni Olsen, J. M. Kerrigan, Neil Fitzgerald, Bonita Granville, Cyril McLaglen, Robert Homans, Mary Gordon, Mary Quinn, Lionel Pape, Michael Fitzmaurice, Gaylord Pendleton, Doris Lloyd, D'Arcy Corrigan, Wesley Barry.

1937

Wee Willie Winkie. 20th Century-Fox. Producer: Darryl F. Zanuck. Screenplay: Ernest Pascal, Julian Josephson. Camera: Arthur Miller. Cast: Shirley Temple, Victor McLaglen, C. Aubrey Smith, June Lang, Michael Whalen, Cesar Romero, Constance Collier, Douglas Scott, Gavin Muir, Willie Fung, Brandon Hurst, Lionel Pape, Clyde Cook, Lauri Beatty, Lionel Braham, Mary Forbes, Cyril McLaglen, Pat Somerset, Hector Sarno.

The Hurricane. Goldwyn–United Artists. Producer: Samuel Goldwyn. Screenplay: Dudley Nichols. Camera: Bert Glennon. Cast: Dorothy Lamour, Jon Hall, Mary Astor, C. Aubrey Smith, Thomas Mitchell, Raymond Massey, John Carradine, Jerome Cowan, Al Kikume, Kuulei DeClercq, Layne Tom, Jr., Mamo Clark, Movita Castenada, Reri, Francis Kaai, Pauline Steele, Flora Hayes, Mary Shaw, Spencer Charters, Roger Drake, Inez Courtney, Paul Strader.

1938

Four Men and a Prayer. 20th Century-Fox. Producer: Darryl F. Zanuck. Screenplay: Richard Sherman, Sonya Levien, Walter Ferris. Camera: Ernest Palmer. Cast: Loretta Young, Richard Greene, George Sanders, David Niven, William Henry, C. Aubrey Smith, J. Edward Bromberg, Alan Hale, John Carradine, Reginald Denny, Berton Churchill, Claude King, John Sutton, Barry Fitzgerald, Cecil Cunningham, Frank Baker, Frank Dawson, Lina Basquette, William Stack, Harry Hayden, Winter Hall, Will Stanton, John Spacey, C. Montague Shaw, Lionel Pape, Brandon Hurst.

Submarine Patrol. 20th Century-Fox. Producer: Darryl F. Zanuck. Screenplay: Rian James, Darrell Ware, Jack Yellen. Camera: Arthur Miller. Cast: Richard Greene, Nancy Kelly, Preston Foster, George Bancroft, Slim Summerville, Joan Valerie, John Carradine, Warren Hymer, Henry Armetta, Douglas Fowley, J. Farrell McDonald, Dick Hogan, Maxie Rosenbloom, Ward Bond, Robert Lowery, Charles Tannen, George E. Stone, Moroni Olsen, Jack Pennick, Elisha Cook, Jr., Harry Strang, Charles Trowbridge, Victor Varconi, Murray Alper, E. E. Clive.

1939

Stagecoach. United Artists. Producer: Walter Wanger. Screenplay: Dudley Nichols. Camera: Bert Glennon. Cast: John Wayne, Claire Trevor, John Carradine, Thomas Mitchell, Andy Devine, Donald Meek, Louise Platt, Tim Holt, George Bancroft, Berton Churchill, Tom Tyler, Chris Pin Martin, Elvira Rios, Francis Ford, Marga Daighton, Kent Odell, Yakima Canutt, Chief Big Tree, Harry Tenbrook, Jack Pennick, Paul McVey, Cornelius Keefe, Florence Lake, Louis Mason, Brenda Fowler, Walter McGrail, Joseph Rickson, Vester Pegg, William Hoffer, Bryant Washburn, Nora Cecil, Helen Gibson, Dorothy Annleby, Buddy Roosevelt, Bill Cody, Chief White Horse, Duke Lee, Mary Kathleen Walker, Ed Brady, Steve Clemente, Theodore Larch, Fritzi Brunette, Leonard Trainor, Chris Phillips, Tex Driscoll, Teddy Billings, John Eckert, Al Lee, Jack Mohr, Patsy Doyle, Wiggie Blowne, Margaret Smith.

Young Mr. Lincoln. 20th Century-Fox. Producer: Kenneth Macgowan. Screenplay: Lamar Trotti. Camera: Bert Glennon. Cast: Henry Fonda, Alice Brady, Marjorie Weaver, Dorris Bowdon, Eddie Collins, Pauline Moore, Richard Cromwell, Ward Bond, Donald Meek, Spencer Charters, Eddie Quillan, Judith Dickens, Milburn Stone, Cliff Clark, Robert Lowery, Charles Tannen, Francis Ford, Fred Kohler, Jr., Kay Linaker, Russell Simpson, Charles Halton, Edwin Maxwell, Robert Homans, Jack Kelly, Dicky Jones, Harry Tyler, Louis Mason, Jack Pennick, Steven Randall, Clarence Wilson, Elizabeth Jones.

Drums Along the Mohawk. 20th Century-Fox. Producer: Raymond Griffith. Screenplay: Lamar Trotti, Sonya Levien. Camera: Bert Glennon, Ray Rennahan. Cast: Claudette Colbert, Henry Fonda, Edna May Oliver, Eddie Collins, John Carradine, Dorris Bowdon, Jessie Ralph, Arthur Shields, Robert Lowery, Roger Imhof, Francis Ford, Ward Bond, Kay Linaker, Russell Simpson, Chief Big Tree, Spencer Charters, Arthur Aylsworth, Si Jenks, Jack Pennick, Charles Tannen, Paul McVey, Elizabeth Jones, Lionel Pape, Clarence Wilson, Edwin Maxwell, Clara Blandick, Beulah Hall Jones, Robert Greig, Mae Marsh.

1940

The Grapes of Wrath. 20th Century-Fox. Producer: Darryl F. Zanuck. Screenplay: Nunnally Johnson. Camera: Gregg Toland. Cast: Henry Fonda, Jane Darwell, John Carradine, Charley Grapewin, Dorris Bowdon, Russell Simpson, O. Z. Whitehead, John Qualen, Eddie Quillan, Zeffie Tilbury, Frank Sully, Frank Darien, Darryl Hickman, Shirley Mills, Grant Mitchell, Ward Bond, Frank Faylen, Joe Sawyer, Harry Tyler, Charles B. Middleton, John Arledge, Hollis Jewell, Paul Guilfoyle, Charles D. Brown, Roger Imhof, William Pawley, Arthur Aylsworth, Charles Tannen, Selmar Jackson, Eddie C. Waller, David Hughes, Cliff Clark, Adrian Morris, Robert Homans, Irving Bacon, Kitty McHugh, Mae Marsh, Francis Ford, Jack Pennick.

The Long Voyage Home. United Artists. Producer: Walter Wanger. Screenplay: Dudley Nichols. Camera: Gregg Toland. Cast: Thomas Mitchell, John Wayne, Ian Hunter, Barry Fitzgerald, Wilfred Lawson, Mildred Natwick, John Qualen, Ward Bond, Joe Sawyer,

Arthur Shields, J. M. Kerrigan, David Hughes, Billy Bevan, Cyril McLaglen, Robert E. Perry, Jack Pennick, Constantin Frenke, Constantin Romanoff, Danny Borzage, Harry Tenbrook, Douglas Walton, Raphaela Ottiano, Carmen Morales, Carmen d'Antonio, Harry Woods, Edgar "Blue" Washington, Lionel Pape, Jane Crowley, Maureen Roden-Ryan.

1941

Tobacco Road. 20th Century-Fox. Producer: Darryl F. Zanuck. Screenplay: Nunnally Johnson. Camera: Arthur C. Miller. Cast: Charley Grapewin, Marjorie Rambeau, Gene Tierney, William Tracy, Elizabeth Patterson, Dana Andrews, Slim Summerville, Ward Bond, Grant Mitchell, Zeffie Tilbury, Russell Simpson, Spencer Charters, Irving Bacon, Harry Tyler, George Chandler, Charles Halton, Jack Pennick, Dorothy Adams, Francis Ford.

How Green Was My Valley. 20th Century-Fox. Producer: Darryl F. Zanuck. Screenplay: Philip Dunne. Camera: Arthur C. Miller. Cast: Walter Pidgeon, Maureen O'Hara, Donald Crisp, Anna Lee, Roddy McDowall, John Loder, Sara Allgood, Barry Fitzgerald, Patrick Knowles, the Welsh Singers, Morton Lowery, Arthur Shields, Ann Todd, Frederick Worlock, Richard Fraser, Evan S. Evans, James Monks, Rhys Williams, Lionel Pape, Ethel Griffes, Marten Lamont, Mae Marsh, Louis Jean Heydt, Denis Hoey, Tudor Williams, Clifford Severn, Eve March.

1945

They Were Expendable. Metro-Goldwyn-Mayer. Producer: John Ford. Screenplay: Frank W. Wead. Camera: Joseph H. August. Cast: Robert Montgomery, John Wayne, Donna Reed, Jack Holt, Ward Bond, Louis Jean Heydt, Marshall Thompson, Russell Simpson, Leon Ames, Paul Langton, Arthur Walsh, Donald Curtis, Cameron Mitchell, Jeff York, Murray Alper, Harry Tenbrook, Jack Pennick, Charles Trowbridge, Robert Barrat, Bruce Kellogg, Tim Murdock, Vernon Steele, Alex Havier, Eve March, Pedro de Cordoba, Trina Lowe, Pacita Tod-Tod, William B. Davidson, Robert Emmett O'Conner, Max Ong, Bill Wilkerson, John Carlyle, Phillip Ahn, Betty Blythe, Kermit Maynard, Stubby Kruger, Sammy Stein, Michael Kirby, Blake Edwards, Wallace Ford, Tom Tyler.

1946

My Darling Clementine. 20th Century-Fox. Producer: Samuel G. Engel. Screenplay: Samuel G. Engel, Winston Miller. Camera: Joseph P. MacDonald. Cast: Henry Fonda, Linda Darnell, Victor Mature, Walter Brennan, Tim Holt, Ward Bond, Cathy Downs, Alan Mowbray, John Ireland, Grant Withers, Roy Roberts, Jane Darwell, Russell Simpson, Francis Ford, J. Farrell McDonald,

Don Garner, Ben Hall, Arthur Walsh, Jack Pennick, Robert Adler, Louis Mercier, Mickey Simpson, Fred Libby, Harry Woods, Charles Stevens, William B. Davidson, Earle Foxe, Aleth "Speed" Hansen, Danny Borzage, Frank Conlan, Don Barclay, Mae Marsh.

1947

The Fugitive. Argosy Pictures–RKO Radio. Producers: John Ford, Merian C. Cooper. Screenplay: Dudley Nichols. Camera: Gabriel Figueroa. Cast: Henry Fonda, Dolores Del Rio, Pedro Armendariz, Ward Bond, Leo Carrillo, J. Carroll Naish, Robert Armstrong, John Qualen, Fortunio Bonanova, Chris Pin Martin, Miguel Inclan, Fernando Fernandez, Jose I. Torvay, Melchor Ferrer.

1948

Fort Apache. Argosy Pictures–RKO Radio. Producers: John Ford, Merian C. Cooper. Screenplay: Frank S. Nugent. Camera: Archie Stout, William Clothier. Cast: John Wayne, Henry Fonda, Shirley Temple, John Agar, Ward Bond, George O'Brien, Victor McLaglen, Pedro Armendariz, Anna Lee, Irene Rich, Guy Kibbee, Grant Withers, Miguel Inclan, Jack Pennick, Mae Marsh, Dick Foran, Frank Ferguson, Francis Ford, Ray Hyke, Movita Castenada, Hank Worden, Harry Tenbrook, Mary Gordon.
Three Godfathers. Argosy Pictures–Metro-Goldwyn-Mayer. Producers: John Ford, Merian C. Cooper. Screenplay: Laurence Stallings, Frank S. Nugent. Camera: Winton C. Hoch, Charles P. Boyle. Cast: John Wayne, Pedro Armendariz, Harry Carey, Jr., Ward Bond, Mildred Natwick, Charles Halton, Jane Darwell, Mae Marsh, Guy Kibbee, Dorothy Ford, Ben Johnson, Michael Dugan, Don Summers, Fred Libby, Hank Worden, Jack Pennick, Francis Ford, Ruth Clifford.

1949

She Wore a Yellow Ribbon. Argosy Pictures–RKO Radio. Producers: John Ford, Merian C. Cooper. Screenplay: Frank S. Nugent, Laurence Stallings. Camera: Winton C. Hoch, Charles P. Boyle. Cast: John Wayne, Joanne Dru, John Agar, Ben Johnson, Harry Carey, Jr., Victor McLaglen, Mildred Natwick, George O'Brien, Arthur Shields, Francis Ford, Harry Woods, Chief Big Tree, Noble Johnson, Cliff Lyons, Tom Tyler, Michael Dugan, Mickey Simpson, Fred Graham, Frank McGrath, Don Summers, Fred Libby, Jack Pennick, Billy Jones, Bill Gettinger, Fred Kennedy, Rudy Bowman, Post Park, Ray Hyke, Lee Bradley, Chief Sky Eagle, Dan White.

1950

When Willie Comes Marching Home. 20th Century-Fox. Producer:

Fred Kohlmar. Screenplay: Mary Anita Loos, Richard Sale. Camera: Leo Tover. Cast: Dan Dailey, Corinne Calvet, Colleen Townsend, William Demarest, James Lydon, Lloyd Corrigan, Evelyn Varden, Kenny Williams, Lee Clark, Charles Halton, Mae Marsh, Jack Pennick, Mickey Simpson, Frank Pershing, Don Summers, Gil Herman, Peter Ortiz, Luis Alberni, John Shulick, Clarke Gordon, Robin Hughes, Cecil Weston, Harry Tenbrook, Russ Clark, George Spaulding, James Eagle, Harry Strang, George Magrill, Hank Worden, John McKee, Larry Keating, Dan Riss, Robert Einer, Russ Conway, Whit Bissell, Ann Codee, Ray Hyke, Gene Collins, James Flavin, David McMahon, Charles Trowbridge, Kenneth Tobey, Maj. Sam Harris, Alberto Morin, Louis Mercier, Paul Harvey, James Waters, Ken Lynch.

Wagon Master. Argosy Pictures–RKO Radio. Producers: John Ford, Merian C. Cooper. Screenplay: Frank S. Nugent, Patrick Ford. Camera: Bert Glennon, Archie Stout. Cast: Ben Johnson, Harry Carey, Jr., Joanne Dru, Ward Bond, Charles Kemper, Alan Mowbray, Jane Darwell, Ruth Clifford, Russell Simpson, Kathleen O'Malley, James Arness, Fred Libby, Hank Worden, Mickey Simpson, Francis Ford, Cliff Lyons, Don Summers, Movita Castenada, Jim Thorpe, Chuck Hayward.

Rio Grande. Argosy Pictures–Republic. Producers: John Ford, Merian C. Cooper. Screenplay: James K. McGuinness. Camera: Bert Glennon, Archie Stout. Cast: John Wayne, Maureen O'Hara, Ben Johnson, Claude Jarman, Jr., Harry Carey, Jr., Chill Wills, J. Carroll Naish, Victor McLaglen, Grant Withers, Peter Ortiz, Steve Pendleton, Karolyn Grimes, Alberto Morin, Stan Jones, Fred Kennedy, Jack Pennick, Patrick Wayne, Chuck Roberson, the Sons of the Pioneers (Ken Curtis, Hugh Farr, Karl Farr, Lloyd Perryman, Shug Fisher, Tommy Doss).

1952

What Price Glory. 20th Century-Fox. Producer: Sol C. Siegel. Screenplay: Phoebe and Henry Ephron. Camera: Joseph MacDonald. Cast: James Cagney, Corinne Calvet, Dan Dailey, William Demarest, Craig Hill, Robert Wagner, Marisa Pavan, Casey Adams, James Gleason, Wally Vernon, Henry Letondal, Fred Libby, Ray Hyke, Paul Fix, James Lilburn, Henry Morgan, Danny Borzage, Bill Henry, Henry "Bomber" Kulkovich, Jack Pennick, Ann Codee, Stanley Johnson, Tom Tyler, Olga Andre, Barry Norton, Luis Alberni, Torben Meyer, Alfred Zeisler, George Bruggeman, Scott Forbes, Sean McClory, Charles FitzSimons, Louis Mercier, Mickey Simpson, Peter Ortiz, Paul Guilfoyle.

The Quiet Man. Argosy Pictures–Republic. Producers: John Ford, Merian C. Cooper. Screenplay: Frank S. Nugent. Camera: Winton C. Hoch. Cast: John Wayne, Maureen O'Hara, Barry Fitzgerald, Ward Bond, Victor McLaglen, Mildred Natwick, Francis Ford, Eileen Crowe, May Craig, Arthur Shields, Charles FitzSimons,

Sean McClory, James Lilburn, Jack McGowran, Ken Curtis, Mae Marsh, Harry Tenbrook, Maj. Sam Harris, Joseph O'Dea, Eric Gorman, Kevin Lawless, Paddy O'Donnell, Webb Overlander, Hank Worden, Harry Tyler, Don Hatswell, David H. Hughes, Douglas Evans, Jack Roper, Al Murphy, Patrick Wayne, Antonia Wayne, Melinda Wayne, Michael Wayne, Pat O'Malley, Bob Perry.

1953

The Sun Shines Bright. Argosy Pictures–Republic. Producers: John Ford, Merian C. Cooper. Screenplay: Laurence Stallings. Camera: Archie Stout. Cast: Charles Winninger, Arleen Whelan, John Russell, Stepin' Fetchit, Russell Simpson, Ludwig Stossel, Francis Ford, Paul Hurst, Mitchell Lewis, Grant Withers, Milburn Stone, Dorothy Jordan, Elzie Emanuel, Henry O'Neill, Slim Pickens, James Kirkwood, Mae Marsh, Jane Darwell, Ernest Whitman, Trevor Bardette, Hal Baylor, Eve March, Clarence Muse, Jack Pennick, Ken Williams, Patrick Wayne.

Mogambo. Metro-Goldwyn-Mayer. Producer: Sam Zimbalist. Screenplay: John Lee Mahin. Camera: Robert Surtees, Fredrick A. Young. Cast: Clark Gable, Ava Gardner, Grace Kelly, Donald Sinden, Philip Stainton, Eric Pohlmann, Laurence Naismith, Dennis O'Dea, Asa Etula, Wagenia Tribe of Belgian Congo, Samburu Tribe of Kenya Colony, Bahaya Tribe of Tanganyika, M'Beti Tribe of French Equatorial Africa.

1955

The Long Gray Line. Rota Productions–Columbia. Producer: Robert Arthur. Screenplay: Edward Hope. Camera: Charles Lawton, Jr. Cast: Tyrone Power, Maureen O'Hara, Robert Francis, Donald Crisp, Ward Bond, Betsy Palmer, Phil Carey, William Leslie, Harry Carey, Jr., Patrick Wayne, Sean McClory, Peter Graves, Milburn Stone, Erin O'Brien-Moore, Walter D. Ehlers, Don Barclay, Martin Milner, Chuck Courtney, Willis Bouchey, Jack Pennick.

Mister Roberts. Orange Productions–Warner Bros. Directors: John Ford, Mervyn LeRoy. Producer: Leland Hayward. Screenplay: Frank S. Nugent, Joshua Logan. Camera: Winton C. Hoch. Cast: Henry Fonda, James Cagney, Jack Lemmon, William Powell, Ward Bond, Betsy Palmer, Phil Carey, Nick Adams, Harry Carey, Jr., Ken Curtis, Frank Aletter, Fritz Ford, Buck Kartalian, William Henry, William Hudson, Stubby Kruger, Harry Tenbrook, Perry Lopez, Robert Roark, Patrick Wayne, Tige Andrews, Jim Moloney, Denny Niles, Francis Conner, Shug Fisher, Danny Borzage, Jim Murphy, Kathleen O'Malley, Maura Murphy, Mimi Doyle, Jeanne Murry-Vanderbilt, Lonnie Pierce, Martin Milner, Gregory Walcott, James Flavin, Jack Pennick, Duke Kahanamoku.

1956

The Searchers. Warner Bros. Producers: Merian C. Cooper, C. V. Whitney. Screenplay: Frank S. Nugent. Camera: Winton C. Hoch. Cast: John Wayne, Jeffrey Hunter, Vera Miles, Ward Bond, Natalie Wood, John Qualen, Olive Carey, Henry Brandon, Ken Curtis, Harry Carey, Jr., Antonio Moreno, Hank Worden, Lana Wood, Walter Coy, Dorothy Jordan, Pippa Scott, Patrick Wayne, Beulah Archuletta, Jack Pennick, Peter Mamakos, Bill Steele, Cliff Lyons, Chuck Roberson, Mae Marsh, Danny Borzage, Billy Cartledge, Chuck Hayward, Slim Hightower, Fred Kennedy, Frank McGrath, Dale van Sickle, Henry Wills, Terry Wilson, Away Luna, Billy Yellow, Bob Many Mules, Exactly Sonnie Betsuie, Feather Hat, Jr., Harry Black Horse, Jack Tin Horn, Many Mules Son, Percy Shooting Star, Pete Grey Eyes, Pipe Line Begishe, Smile White Sheep.

1957

The Wings of Eagles. Metro-Goldwyn-Mayer. Producer: Charles Schnee. Screenplay: Frank Fenton, William Wister Haines. Camera: Paul C. Vogel. Cast: John Wayne, Maureen O'Hara, Dan Dailey, Ward Bond, Ken Curtis, Edmund Lowe, Kenneth Tobey, James Todd, Barry Kelley, Sig Ruman, Henry O'Neill, Willis Bouchey, Dorothy Jordan, Peter Ortiz, Louis Jean Heydt, Tige Andrews, Danny Borzage, William Tracy, Harlan Warde, Jack Pennick, Bill Henry, Alberto Morin, Mimi Gibson, Evelyn Rudie, Charles Trowbridge, Mae Marsh, Janet Lake, Fred Graham, Stuart Holmes, Olive Carey, Maj. Sam Harris, May McEvoy, William Paul Lowery, Chuck Roberson, Cliff Lyons, Veda Ann Borg, Christopher James.
The Rising of the Moon. Four Province Productions–Warner Bros. Producer: Michael Killanin. Screenplay: Frank S. Nugent. Camera: Robert Krasker. Cast: Tyrone Power, Noel Purcell, Cyril Cusack, Jack McGowran, Eric Gorman, John Cowley, Jimmy O'Dea, Tony Quinn, Paul Farrell, J. G. Devlin, Michael Trubshawe, Anita Sharp Bolster, Maureen Porter, Godfrey Quigley, Harold Goldblatt, Maureen O'Connell, May Craig, Michael O'Duffy, Ann Dalton, Kevin Casey, Dennis O'Dea, Eileen Crowe, Maurice Good, Frank Lawton, Edward Lexy, Donal Donnelly, Joseph O'Dea, Dennis Brennan, David Marlowe, Dennis Franks, Doreen Madden, Maureen Cusack, Maureen Delaney, Martin Thornton, John Horan, Joe Hone, John Comeford, Mafra McDonagh, and members of the Abbey Theater Company.

1958

The Last Hurrah. Columbia. Producer: John Ford. Screenplay: Frank S. Nugent. Camera: Charles Lawton, Jr. Cast: Spencer Tracy,

Jeffrey Hunter, Dianne Foster, Pat O'Brien, Basil Rathbone, Donald Crisp, James Gleason, Edward Brophy, John Carradine, Willis Bouchey, Basil Ruysdael, Ricardo Cortez, Wallace Ford, Frank McHugh, Anna Lee, Jane Darwell, Frank Albertson, Charles FitzSimons, Carleton Young, Bob Sweeney, Edmund Lowe, William Leslie, Ken Curtis, O. Z. Whitehead, Arthur Walsh, Helen Westcott, Ruth Warren, Mimi Doyle, Danny Borzage, James Flavin, William Forrest, Frank Sully, Charlie Sullivan, Ruth Clifford, Jack Pennick, Richard Deacon, Harry Tenbrook, Eve March, Bill Henry, James Waters.

1959

Gideon of Scotland Yard (Gideon's Day). Columbia British Productions–Columbia. Producer: Michael Killanin. Screenplay. T. E. B. Clarke. Camera: Frederick A. Young. Cast: Jack Hawkins, Dianne Foster, Anna Massey, Cyril Cusack, Andrew Ray, James Hayter, Ronald Howard, Howard Marion-Crawford, Laurence Naismith, Derek Bond, Griselda Harvey, Frank Lawton, Anna Lee, John Loder, Doreen Madden, Miles Malleson, Marjorie Rhodes, Michael Shepley, Michael Trubshawe, Jack Watling, Hermione Bell, Donal Donnelly, Billie Whitelaw, Malcolm Ranson, Mavis Ranson, Francis Crowdy, David Aylmer, Brian Smith, Barry Keegan, Maureen Potter, Henry Longhurst, Charles Maunsell, Stuart Saunders, Dervis Ward, Joan Ingram, Nigel Fitzgerald, Robert Raglan, John Warwick, John Le Mesurier, Peter Godsell, Robert Bruce, Alan Rolfe, Derek Prentice, Alastair Hunter, Helen Goss, Susan Richmond, Raymond Rollett, Lucy Griffiths, Mary Donevan, O'Donovan Shiell, Bart Allison, Michael O'Duffy, Diana Chesney, David Storm, Gordon Harris.

The Horse Soldiers. Mirisch Company–United Artists. Producers/Screenplay: John Lee Mahin, Martin Rackin. Camera: William H. Clothier. Cast: John Wayne, William Holden, Constance Towers, Althea Gibson, Hoot Gibson, Anna Lee, Russell Simpson, Stan Jones, Carleton Young, Basil Ruysdael, Willis Bouchey, Ken Curtis, O. Z. Whitehead, Judson Pratt, Denver Pyle, Strother Martin, Hank Worden, Walter Reed, Jack Pennick, Fred Graham, Chuck Hayward, Charles Seel, Stuart Holmes, Maj. Sam Harris, Richard Cutting, Bing Russell, William Forrest, William Leslie, Bill Henry, Ron Hagherty, Danny Borzage, Fred Kennedy.

1960

Sergeant Rutledge. Ford Productions–Warner Bros. Producers: Patrick Ford, Willis Goldbeck. Screenplay: Willis Goldbeck, James Warner Bellah. Camera: Bert Glennon. Cast: Jeffrey Hunter, Constance Towers, Woody Strode, Billie Burke, Juano Hernandez, Willis Bouchey, Carleton Young, Judson Pratt, Bill Henry, Walter Reed,

Chuck Hayward, Mae Marsh, Fred Libby, Toby Richards, Jan Styne, Cliff Lyons, Charles Seel, Jack Pennick, Hank Worden, Chuck Roberson, Eva Novak, Estelle Winwood, Shug Fisher.

1961

Two Rode Together. Ford–Shpetner Productions–Columbia. Producer: Stan Shpetner. Screenplay: Frank S. Nugent. Camera: Charles Lawton, Jr. Cast: James Stewart, Richard Widmark, Shirley Jones, Linda Cristal, Andy Devine, John McIntire, Paul Birch, Willis Bouchey, Henry Brandon, Harry Carey, Jr., Ken Curtis, Olive Carey, Chet Douglas, Annelle Hayes, David Kent, Anna Lee, Jeanette Nolan, John Qualen, Ford Rainey, Woody Strode, O. Z. Whitehead, Cliff Lyons, Mae Marsh, Frank Baker, Ruth Clifford, Ted Knight, Maj. Sam Harris, Jack Pennick, Chuck Roberson, Danny Borzage, Bill Henry, Chuck Hayward, Edward Brophy.

1962

The Man Who Shot Liberty Valance. Ford Productions–Paramount. Producer: Willis Goldbeck. Screenplay: Willis Goldbeck, James Warner Bellah. Camera: William H. Clothier. Cast: James Stewart, John Wayne, Vera Miles, Lee Marvin, Edmond O'Brien, Andy Devine, Ken Murray, John Carradine, Jeanette Nolan, John Qualen, Willis Bouchey, Carleton Young, Woody Strode, Denver Pyle, Strother Martin, Lee Van Cleef, Robert F. Simon, O. Z. Whitehead, Paul Birch, Joseph Hoover, Jack Pennick, Anna Lee, Charles Seel, Shug Fisher, Earle Hodgins, Stuart Holmes, Dorothy Phillips, Buddy Roosevelt, Gertrude Astor, Eva Novak, Slim Talbot, Monty Montana, Bill Henry, John B. Whiteford, Helen Gibson, Maj. Sam Harris.
How the West Was Won. Cinerama–Metro-Goldwyn-Mayer. Directors: John Ford, George Marshall, Henry Hathaway. Producer: Bernard Smith. Screenplay: James R. Webb. Camera (Ford sequence): Joseph La Shelle. Cast (Ford sequence): John Wayne, George Peppard, Carroll Baker, Henry Morgan, Andy Devine, Russ Tamblyn, Willis Bouchey, Claude Johnson, Raymond Massey.

1963

Donovan's Reef. Ford Productions–Paramount. Producer: John Ford. Screenplay: Frank S. Nugent, James Edward Grant. Camera: William H. Clothier. Cast: John Wayne, Lee Marvin, Elizabeth Allen, Jack Warden, Cesar Romero, Dorothy Lamour, Jacqueline Malouf, Mike Mazurki, Marcel Dalio, Jon Fong, Cheryline Lee, Tim Stafford, Carmen Estrabeau, Yvonne Peattie, Frank Baker, Edgar Buchanan, Patrick Wayne, Charles Seel, Chuck Roberson, Mae Marsh, Maj. Sam Harris, Dick Foran, Cliff Lyons.

1964

Cheyenne Autumn. Ford–Smith Productions–Warner Bros. Producer: Bernard Smith. Screenplay: James R. Webb. Camera: William H. Clothier. Cast: Richard Widmark, Carroll Baker, James Stewart, Edward G. Robinson, Karl Malden, Sal Mineo, Dolores Del Rio, Ricardo Montalban, Gilbert Roland, Arthur Kennedy, Patrick Wayne, Elizabeth Allen, John Carradine, Victor Jory, Mike Mazurki, George O'Brien, Sean McClory, Judson Pratt, Carmen D'Antonio, Ken Curtis, Walter Baldwin, Shug Fisher, Nancy Hsueh, Chuck Roberson, Harry Carey, Jr., Ben Johnson, Jimmy O'Hara, Chuck Hayward, Lee Bradley, Frank Bradley, Walter Reed, Willis Bouchey, Carleton Young, Denver Pyle, John Qualen, Nanomba "Moonbeam" Morton, Danny Borzage, Dean Smith, David H. Miller, Bing Russell.

1965

Young Cassidy. Sextant Films–Metro-Goldwyn-Mayer. Directors: John Ford, Jack Cardiff. Producers: Robert D. Graff, Robert Emmett Ginna. Screenplay: John Whiting. Camera: Ted Scaife. Cast: Rod Taylor, Maggie Smith, Julie Christie, Flora Robson, Sian Phillips, Michael Redgrave, Dame Edith Evans, Jack MacGowran, T. P. McKenna, Julie Ross, Robin Sumner, Philip O'Flynn, Pauline Delaney, Arthur O'Sullivan, Tom Irwin, John Cowley, William Foley, John Franklyn, Harry Brogan, James Fitzgerald, Donal Donnelly, Harold Goldblatt, Ronald Ibbs, May Craig, May Cluskey, Tom Irwin, Shivaun O'Casey, and members of the Abbey Theatre.

1966

Seven Women. Ford–Smith Productions–Metro-Goldwyn-Mayer. Producer: Bernard Smith. Screenplay: Janet Green, John McCormick. Camera: Joseph LaShelle. Cast: Anne Bancroft, Sue Lyon, Margaret Leighton, Flora Robson, Mildred Dunnock, Betty Field, Anna Lee, Eddie Albert, Mike Mazurki, Woody Strode, Jane Chang, Hans William Lee, H. W. Gim, Irene Tsu.

DOCUMENTARIES

1941

Sex Hygiene. Audio Productions–U.S. Army. Producer: Darryl F. Zanuck. Camera: George Barnes. Cast: Charles Trowbridge.

1942

The Battle of Midway. U.S. Navy–20th Century-Fox. Camera: Lt.

Comdr. John Ford, U.S.N.R., Jack McKenzie. Narrative writers: John Ford, Dudley Nichols, James Kevin McGuiness. Narrators: Henry Fonda, Jane Darwell, Donald Crisp.
Torpedo Squadron. U.S. Navy.

1943

December 7th. U.S. Navy. Directors: Lt. Gregg Toland, U.S.N.R., Lt. Comdr. John Ford, U.S.N.R. Camera: Gregg Toland.
We Sail at Midnight. Crown Film Unit–U.S. Navy. Narrative writer: Clifford Odets.

1951

This Is Korea! U.S. Navy–Republic. Narrators: John Ireland et al.

1955

The Red, White, and Blue Line. U.S. Treasury Department–Columbia Pictures. Screenplay: Edward Hope. Camera: Charles Lawton, Jr. Narrator: Ward Bond.

1957

The Growler Story. U.S. Navy. Producer: Mark Armistead. Camera: Pacific Fleet Combat Camera Group. Narrator: Dan Dailey. Cast: Ward Bond, Ken Curtis, and navy personnel, wives, and children.

1959

Korea. U.S. Defense Department. Producers: John Ford, U.S.N.R., Capt. George O'Brien, U.S.N. (Retd.). Cast: Capt. George O'Brien.

TELEVISION SHOWS

1955

"The Bamboo Cross." Lewman Ltd.–Revue; episode for *Fireside Theatre.* Producer: William Asher. Screenplay: Laurence Stallings. Camera: John MacBurnie. Cast: Jane Wyman, Betty Lynn, Soo Yong, Jim Hong, Judy Wong, Don Summers, Kurt Katch, Pat O'Malley, Frank Baker.
"Rookie of the Year." Hal Roach Studios; episode for *Screen Directors Playhouse.* Cast: Patrick Wayne, Vera Miles, Ward Bond, James Gleason, Willis Bouchey, John Wayne.

1960

"The Colter Craven Story." Revue Productions; episode for *Wagon*

Train. Producer: Howard Christie. Screenplay: Tony Paulson. Camera: Benjamin N. Kline. Cast: Ward Bond, Carleton Young, Frank McGrath, Terry Wilson, John Carradine, Chuck Hayward, Ken Curtis, Anna Lee, Cliff Lyons, Paul Birch, Annelle Hayes, Willis Bouchey, Mae Marsh, Jack Pennick, Hank Worden, Charles Seel, Bill Henry, Chuck Roberson, Dennis Rush, Harry Tenbrook, Beulah Blaze, Lon Chaney, Jr., John Wayne.

1962

"Flashing Spikes." Avista Productions–Revue; episode for *Alcoa Premiere.* Screenplay: Jameson Brewer. Camera: William H. Clothier. Cast: James Stewart, Jack Warden, Patrick Wayne, Edgar Buchanan, Tige Andrews, Carleton Young, Willis Bouchey, Don Drysdale, Stephanie Hill, Charles Seel, Bing Russell, Harry Carey, Jr., Vin Scully, Walter Reed, Sally Hughes, Larry Blake, Charles Morton, Cy Malis, Bill Henry, John Wayne, Art Passarella, Vern Stephens, Ralph Volkie, Earl Gilpin, Bud Harden, Whitney Campbell.

Bibliographical Essay

THE beginning point for any serious study of the life and work of John Ford is the voluminous John Ford Collection in the Lilly Library at Indiana University in Bloomington, which consists of correspondence, scripts and production materials, legal documents, financial records, photographs, and interviews taped by Dan Ford, some of which have been transcribed. The interviews beneficial to this study were those with Mark Armistead, James Warner Bellah, Bea Benjamin, Katherine Cliffton Bryant, Harry Carey, Jr., Olive Golden Carey, William Clothier, Ken Curtis, Cecil de Prida, Joanne Dru, Philip Dunne, Allan Dwan, Josephine Feeney, Henry Fonda, Barbara Nugent Ford, Mary Ford, Phil Ford, Chuck Hayward, Katharine Hepburn, Winton Hoch, Frank Hotaling, Ace Holmes, Lefty Hough, Ben Johnson, Nunnally Johnson, Anna Lee, John Lee Mahin, Lee Marvin, Roddy McDowall, George O'Brien, Robert Parrish, Wingate Smith, James Stewart, John Wayne, Albert Wedemeyer, and Terry Wilson. Included in the twenty-one cassettes containing discussion with John Ford is a revealing conversation between Ford and Katharine Hepburn, recorded late in the director's life. Of major importance, too, are several issues of *The Iron Horse* location newsletter and the log of the *Araner*, Ford's yacht.

Expressly for this book, I interviewed Eddie Albert (Los Angeles, 1991), James Bellah, Jr. (Los Angeles, 1991), Dorris Bowdon (Los Angeles, 1991), Linda Cristal (Los Angeles, 1991), Joanne Dru (Los Angeles, 1991), Charles FitzSimons (Los Angeles, 1991), Dan Ford (Los Angeles, 1991), Gene Fowler, Jr. (Los Angeles, 1991), Mike Goulding (Monument Valley, 1991), Ben Johnson (Mesa, Ariz., 1992), Martin Jurow (Dallas, 1992), Don MacWilliams (Portland, Maine, 1991), Andrew McLaglen (San Juan Island, Wash., 1992), Mary McPhillips (Portland, Maine, 1991), Winston Miller (Los Angeles, 1991), Darcy O'Brien (Tulsa, Okla., 1992), Robert Parrish (Bridgehampton, N.Y., 1991), George Peppard (Los Angeles, 1991), Stefanie Powers (Dallas, 1991), Robert Wagner (Dallas, 1991), Michael Wayne (Los Angeles, 1991), Patrick Wayne (Los Angeles, 1991), Hank Worden (Los Angeles, 1991), and Billy Yellow (Monument Valley, 1991, translated by Evelyn Nelson). A tape of each is now available in the Southern Methodist University Oral History Collection, housed in the DeGolyer Library.

Other oral histories in the SMU collection containing Ford material include interviews with Leon Ames (Corona Del Mar, Calif., 1983), Pandro S. Berman (Los Angeles, 1978), Budd Boetticher (Ramona,

Calif., 1988), Donald Curtis (Dallas, 1988), Dan Dailey (Dallas, 1974, interviewed by Sally Cullum), Edward Dmytryk (Austin, Tex., 1979), Philip Dunne (Los Angeles, 1983), Bonita Granville (Los Angeles, 1976), Henry Hathaway (Los Angeles, 1983), Helen Hayes (Nyack, N.Y., 1979), John Ireland (Montecito, Calif., 1990), Shirley Jones (Los Angeles, 1984), Gene Kelly (Dallas, 1974), Burt Kennedy (Los Angeles, 1987), Hubie Kerns (Los Angeles, 1989), Otto Lang (Los Angeles, 1981), Anna Lee (Los Angeles, 1981), Mary Anita Loos (Los Angeles, 1990), James Lydon (Los Angeles, 1989), Ken Murray (Los Angeles, 1981), Mildred Natwick (New York City, 1979), Pat O'Brien (Dallas, 1975), Gil Perkins (Los Angeles, 1986), Cesar Romero (Dallas, 1979), Vincent Sherman (Los Angeles, 1981), Joseph Silver (Los Angeles, 1982), Dean Smith (Dallas, 1979), James Stewart (Dallas, 1989), Milburn Stone (Rancho Santa Fe, Calif., 1976), Marshall Thompson (Los Angeles, 1980), Henry Wilcoxon (Los Angeles, 1983), and William Wyler (Los Angeles, 1979). Dale Evans (Fort Worth, 1982), Peggy Stewart (Los Angeles, 1985), and Linda Stirling (Los Angeles, 1992) provide vivid recollections of Republic Studios under Herbert J. Yates in their interviews. Unless otherwise stipulated all of these sessions were conducted by the author. My conversations with John E. Feeney (Spiddal, Ireland, 1991), Michael and Sheila Killanin (Dublin, 1991), Kay Naughton (Galway, Ireland, 1991), and Claire Trevor (New York City, 1992) were not recorded; quotations from these sources are from my notes.

Relevant interviews in the Mayer Library of the American Film Institute are those with Pandro S. Berman (1972), Philip Dunne (1970–71), Allan Dwan (1969), Ted French (1972), Hoot Gibson (1961), Nunnally Johnson (1968–69), Henry King (1970–71), Ann Little (1971), Barbara McLean (1970–71), Virgil Miller (1971), Edna Rush (1972), and Irvin Willat (1971).

The Columbia Oral History Collection contains interviews with Gilbert M. "Broncho Billy" Anderson (1958), Dana Andrews (1958), Pandro S. Berman (1971), Walter Brennan (1971), James Cagney (1958), Andy Devine (1971), Henry Fonda (1959), Bonita Granville (1959), Henry Hathaway (1971), Howard Hawks (1971), George "Gabby" Hayes (1959), Ben Hecht (1959), Nunnally Johnson (1971), Jack Lemmon (1959), Joshua Logan (1980), Roddy McDowall (1959), Geraldine Page (1959), George Seaton (1958), James Stewart (1971), Eddie Sutherland (1959), and John Wayne (1971).

Taped interviews belonging to the Arizona Historical Society include sessions with Yakima Canutt, William Clothier, William Holden, Ann Little, James Pratt, and John Wayne, all dating from 1970.

A longer oral history with Yakima Canutt was conducted in 1977 by Louis McMahon for the Directors Guild of America, a copy of which resides in the Margaret Herrick Library at the Motion Pictures Academy of Arts and Sciences. Film historian Scott Eyman shared with the author copies of interviews he had recorded with John Carradine and William Clothier, and Selden West contributed observations from her research on Spencer Tracy.

Other manuscript collections essential to this study include the records of Argosy Productions; the Harry Carey and Harry Carey, Jr., papers at Brigham Young University; the David O. Selznick papers in the Humanities Research Center at the University of Texas at Austin; the Pandro S. Berman, Joseph McBride, Winston Miller, Walter Mirisch, and Walter Wanger papers at the Wisconsin Center for Film and Theater Research; George O'Brien's scrapbooks and diary for 1931, in the possession of his son, Darcy O'Brien (Tulsa, Okla.); and the Ford correspondence of Michael Killanin (Dublin).

Vital have been the production files of Metro-Goldwyn-Mayer, 20th Century-Fox, and Warner Bros. in the Doheny Library at the University of Southern California, which contain scripts, memos, and schedules related to the making of Ford films. Clipping folders in the Herrick Library of the Motion Picture Academy, the Maine Historical Society, the Portland Public Library, and the University of Maine also proved useful.

Of the extensive printed material on the director, Dan Ford's *Pappy: The Life of John Ford* (Englewood Cliffs, N.J.: Prentice-Hall, 1979) and Andrew Sinclair's *John Ford* (New York: Dial, 1979) serve as introductions to his life and career. Other major studies of Ford are headed by Lindsay Anderson's *About John Ford* (New York: McGraw-Hill, 1981), John Baxter's *The Cinema of John Ford* (New York: A. S. Barnes, 1971), Tag Gallagher's *John Ford: The Man and His Films* (Berkeley: University of California Press, 1986), Joseph McBride and Michael Wilmington's *John Ford* (New York: DaCapo, 1975), J. A. Place's *The Western Films of John Ford* (Secaucus, N.J.: Citadel, 1974), Andrew Sarris's *The John Ford Movie Mystery* (Bloomington: Indiana University Press, 1975), and Peter Stowell's *John Ford* (Boston: Twayne, 1986). Joseph W. Reed's *Three American Originals* (Middletown, Conn.: Wesleyan University Press, 1984) is an interesting comparision of John Ford, Charles Ives, and William Faulkner.

The longest published interview with the director is Peter Bogdanovich's *John Ford* (Berkeley: University of California Press, 1978). Shorter ones are "An Interview with John Ford," *Focus!* (October 1969), 3–4; Mark Haggard, "Ford in Person," *Focus on Film* (Spring 1971), 31–37; Burt Kennedy, "A Talk with John Ford," *Action!* 3 (September-October 1968), 6–9; Bill Libby, "The Old Wrangler Rides Again," *Cosmopolitan* (March 1964), 13–21; George J. Mitchell, "Ford on Ford," *Films in Review* 15 (June-July 1964), 323–32; and "One More Hurrah" in Walter Wagner's *You Must Remember This* (New York: Putnam's, 1975), 55–65. Jay Leyda, ed., *Voices of Film Experience* (New York: Macmillan, 1977) and Andrew Sarris, *Interviews with Film Directors* (Indianapolis: Bobbs-Merrill, 1967) also offer comments from Ford.

Articles of importance include "John Ford Gives Us Another Great Example of Screen Art," *The Film Spectator* 9 (February 15, 1930), 5–6; "John Ford: The Quiet Man from Portland," *Maine Life* (July 1976), 56–59; Richard A. Blake, "John Ford: A Sense of Worth," *America* 129 (October 6, 1973), 243–44; Peter Bogdanovich, "The Autumn of John Ford," *Esquire* 61 (April 1964), 102–7, 144–45; Ron Chernow, "John

Ford: The Last Frontiersman," *Ramparts* 12 (April 1974), 45–48; David Coursen, "John Ford: Assessing the Reassessment," *Film Quarterly* 29 (Spring 1976), 58–60; Emanuel Eisenberg, "John Ford: Fighting Irish," *New Theatre* 3 (April 1936) 7, 42; Kirk Ellis, "On the Warpath: John Ford and the Indians," *Journal of Popular Film and Television* 8, no. 2, 34–41; Peter Ericsson, "John Ford," *Sequence* (Winter 1947), 18–25; William K. Everson, "Forgotten Ford," *Focus on Film* (Spring 1971), 13–19 and "John Ford Goes to War — Against VD," *Film Fan Monthly* (May 1971), 14–18; Michael Goodwin, "John Ford: A Poet Who Shot Great Movies," *Moving Image* 1 (December 1981) 59–63; Grady Johnson, "John Ford: Maker of Hollywood Stars," *Coronet* 35 (December, 1953), 133–40; Stanley Kauffmann, "The Unquiet Man," *The New Republic* (August 11, 1986), 24–28; Douglas McVay, "The Five Worlds of John Ford," *Films and Filming* 8 (June 1962), 14–17, 53; William T. Murphy, "John Ford and the Wartime Documentary," *Film and History* 6 (February 1976), 1–8; Frank S. Nugent, "Hollywood's Favorite Rebel," *Reader's Digest* 55 (October 1949), 53–57; Janey Place, "A Family in a Ford," *Film Comment* 12 (September-October 1976) 46–51; Jeffrey Richards, "Ford's Lost World," *Focus on Film* (Spring 1971), 20–30; Lane Roth, "Frontier Families: John Ford, Sergio Leone," *American Classic Screen* 5 (July–August 1981), 36–38, 42; Charles Silver, "The Apprenticeship of John Ford," *American Film* 1 (May 1976), 62–67; H. Peter Stowell, "John Ford's Literary Sources: From Realism to Romance," *Literature/Film Quarterly* 5 (Spring 1977), 164–73; and Robin Wood, "Shall We Gather at the River?: The Late Films of John Ford," *Film Comment* 7 (Fall 1971), 8–17.

Worthwhile, but of secondary value, are Noel Berggren, "Arsenic and Old Directors," *Esquire* 77 (April 1972), 132–35; Frank Daugherty, "John Ford Wants It Real," *Christian Science Monitor* (June 21, 1941), 5; "Down with Rebecca," *Newsweek* 70 (September 22, 1958), 104–7; Caryn James, "History, Justice and Heroism in the Films of John Ford," *New York Times* (January 26, 1990); Arthur Knight, "Watch the Fords Go By," *Saturday Review* 35 (August 23, 1952), 28–29; Geoffrey O'Brien, "John Ford Superstar," *Village Voice* 31 (October 21, 1986), 41–43; "Old Master," *Time* 102 (September 17, 1973), 58; Seymour Peck, "The Autumn of John Ford," *New York Times Magazine* (November 29, 1964), 124–29; Pete Rainer, "John Ford, 1895–1973," *National Review* 26 (March 1, 1974), 264–65; Richard Schickel, "Good Days, Good Years," *Harper's* 241 (October 1970), 44–50; and Colin Young, "The Old Dependables," *Film Quarterly* 13 (Fall 1959), 2–17.

Doctoral dissertations worth consulting include Michael N. Budd, "A Critical Analysis of Western Films Directed by John Ford from *Stagecoach* to *Cheyenne Autumn*" (University of Iowa, 1975); William C. Howze, "The Influence of Western Painting and Genre Painting on the Films of John Ford," (University of Texas at Austin, 1986); and Peter Robert Lehman, "John Ford and the Auteur Theory," (University of Wisconsin, 1978).

Olive Carey talks about John Ford in Cork Millner, *Santa Barbara Celebrities: Conversations from the American Riviera* (Santa Barbara,

Calif.: Santa Barbara Press, 1986); Philip Dunne in Patrick McGilligan, *Backstory* (Berkeley: University of California Press, 1986); Henry Fonda in "Fonda on Ford," *Sight and Sound* 42 (Spring 1973), 85; Howard Hawks in Joseph McBride, *Hawks on Hawks* (Berkeley: University of California Press, 1982); Arthur C. Miller in Charles Higham, *Hollywood Cameraman* (Bloomington: Indiana University Press, 1970); George O'Brien in Leonard Maltin, "FFM Interviews George O'Brien," *Film Fan Monthly* (May 1971), 19–27; and Maureen O'Hara in "Sitting Pretty: Interview by Roddy McDowall," *Premiere* 4 (July 1991), 62–67.

Among the autobiographies with Ford material are Mary Astor, *A Life on Film* (New York: Delacorte, 1971); Carroll Baker, *Baby Doll: An Autobiography* (New York: Arbor House, 1983); Ralph Bellamy, *When the Smoke Hit the Fan* (Garden City, N.Y.: Doubleday, 1979); Shirley Temple Black, *Child Star* (New York: McGraw-Hill, 1988); Corinne Calvet, *Has Corinne Been a Good Girl?* (New York: St. Martin's, 1983); Yakima Canutt with Oliver Drake, *Stunt Man* (New York: Walker, 1979); Frank Capra, *The Name Above the Title* (New York: Macmillan, 1971); Iron Eyes Cody with Collin Perry, *Iron Eyes: My Life as a Hollywood Indian* (New York: Everest House, 1982); Edward Dmytryk, *It's a Hell of a Life But Not a Bad Living* (New York: Times Books, 1978); Philip Dunne, *Take Two: A Life in Movies and Politics* (New York: McGraw-Hill, 1980); Henry Fonda with Howard Teichmann, *Fonda: My Life* (New York: New American Library, 1981); Ava Gardner, *Ava: My Story* (New York: Bantam, 1990); Katharine Hepburn, *Me: Stories of My Life* (New York: Knopf, 1991); Elia Kazan, *A Life* (New York: Knopf, 1988); Slim Keith with Annette Tapert, *Slim: Memories of a Rich and Imperfect Life* (New York: Simon and Schuster, 1990); Dorothy Lamour with Dick McInnes, *My Side of the Road* (Englewood Cliffs, N.J.: Prentice-Hall, 1980); Mervyn LeRoy with Dick Kleiner, *Mervyn Le-Roy: Take One* (New York: Hawthorn, 1974); Myrna Loy and James Kotsilibas, *Myrna Loy: Being and Becoming* (New York: Knopf, 1987); Tim McCoy with Ronald McCoy, *Tim McCoy Remembers the West* (Lincoln: University of Nebraska Press, 1988); Raymond Massey, *A Hundred Different Lives* (Boston: Little, Brown, 1979); Arthur C. Miller and Fred J. Balshofer, *One Reel a Week* (Berkeley: University of California Press, 1967); Patricia Neal, *As I Am: An Autobiography* (New York: Simon and Schuster, 1988); David Niven, *The Moon's a Balloon* (New York: Putnam's, 1972); Pat O'Brien, *The Wind at My Back* (Garden City, N.Y.: Doubleday, 1964); Robert Parrish, *Growing Up in Hollywood* (New York: Harcourt Brace Jovanovich, 1976); Chuck Roberson with Bodie Thoene, *The Fall Guy* (North Vancouver, B.C.: Hancock House, 1980); Edward G. Robinson with Leonard Spigelgass, *All My Yesterdays* (New York: Hawthorn, 1973); Dore Schary, *Heyday: An Autobiography* (Boston: Little, Brown, 1979); Woody Strode and Sam Young, *Goal Dust: An Autobiography* (Lanham, Md.: Madison, 1990); Gene Tierney with Mickey Herskowitz, *Self-Portrait* (New York: Wyden, 1979); and Pilar Wayne with Alex Thorleifson, *John Wayne: My Life with the Duke* (New York: McGraw-Hill, 1987). References to Ford's association with David Selznick are to be found in

Rudy Behlmer, ed., *Memo from David O. Selznick* (New York: Viking, 1972).

Books and articles on specific Ford films include David Bordwell, "The Man Who Shot Liberty Valance," *Film Comment* 7 (Fall 1971), 18–20; Nick Browne, "The Spectator-in-the-Text: The Rhetoric of *Stagecoach*," *Film Quarterly* 29 (Winter 1975), 26–38; Stuart Byron, "*The Searchers*: Cult Movie of the New Hollywood," *New York* 12 (March 5, 1979), 45–48; David F. Coursen, "John Ford's Wilderness: *The Man Who Shot Liberty Valance*," *Sight and Sound* 47 (Autumn 1978), 237–41; Philip Dunne, "*How Green Was My Valley*": *The Screenplay for the John Ford Directed Film* (Santa Barbara, Calif.: Santa Teresa, 1990); Bert Glennon, "Photographing *Rio Grande*," *International Photographer* (September 1950), 4–5; Robert Lyons, ed., "*My Darling Clementine*": *John Ford, Director* (New Brunswick, N.J.: Rutgers University Press, 1984), and Gerry McKnee, *In the Footsteps of "The Quiet Man"* (Edinburgh: Mainstream, 1990). Quotations from reviews of Ford films came from the *New York Times*, *Los Angeles Times*, *Variety*, *Hollywood Reporter*, *Saturday Review*, *New Republic*, *Films in Review*, *Newsweek*, *Life*, *Family Circle*, and *Cue*.

On Monument Valley, the Navajo, and reservation trading posts, the Norman D. Nevills papers at the University of Utah and Mike Goulding's oral history with Gary Topping for the Utah State Historical Society (September 6, 1989) stand as basic primary sources. Books include Garrick and Roberta Glenn Bailey's *A History of the Navajos: The Reservation Years* (Santa Fe, N.M.: School of American Research Press, 1986), Richard E. Klinck's *Land of Room Enough and Time Enough* (Salt Lake City: Peregrine Smith, 1984), Frank McNitt's *The Indian Traders* (Norman: University of Oklahoma Press, 1962), and Samuel Moon's *Tall Sheep: Harry Goulding, Monument Valley Trader* (Norman: University of Oklahoma Press, 1992).

Of the articles on the Gouldings' trading post, Monument Valley, and movie location work in the area, the following proved helpful: Raymond Carlson, "Guest Book in the Valley," *Arizona Highways* 32 (April 1956), 2–3; Neil M. Clark, "Desert Trader," *Saturday Evening Post* 209 (March 29, 1947), 36–37, 110–17; Carlo Gaberscek, "*The Vanishing American*: In Monument Valley Before Ford," *Griffithiana* (October 1989), 140–49; Richard L. Gilbert, Jr., "Harry Goulding," *Point West* 5 (October 1963), 24–27; Barry Goldwater, "On Hoskinini's Trail," *Arizona* (October 3, 1971), 18–23; Harry Goulding with Joyce R. Muench, "When Tombstone Came to Monument Valley," *The Desert Magazine* 11 (October 1948), 6–10; Randall Henderson, "Navajo Gods Guard the Silver of Pish-la-ki," *The Desert Magazine* 14 (December 1950), 5–7 and "With Harry Goulding in Mystery Valley," *The Desert Magazine* 20 (August 1957), 4–7; Charles Kelly, "Graveyard of the Gods," *The Desert Magazine* 1 (July 1938), 4–6; Bill Knyvett, "A Man, His Monuments, His Mission," *Desert* 33 (May 1970), 22–25; Todd McCarthy, "John Ford and Monument Valley," *American Film* 3 (May 1978) 10–16; Allen C. Reed, "John Ford Makes Another Movie Classic in Monument Valley," *Arizona Highways* 32 (April 1956), 4–11; and Susan Bayer Ward, "Mike

Goulding's Treasure House in Monument Valley," *Arizona Highways* 67 (September 1991), 30–34.

Robert Wooster's *Soldiers, Sutlers, and Settlers: Garrison Life on the Texas Frontier* (College Station: Texas A & M University, 1987) provides historical background for understanding Ford's cavalry pictures, whereas Henry Nash Smith's *Virgin Land* (Cambridge, Mass.: Harvard University Press, 1950) remains the classic study of the American West as myth and symbol.

Among the analytical books on Western films are Gretchen M. Bataille and Charles L. P. Silet, eds., *The Pretend Indians: Images of Native Americans in the Movies* (Ames: Iowa State University Press, 1980); Kevin Brownlow, *The War, the West, and the Wilderness* (New York: Knopf, 1979); John G. Cawelti, *The Six-Gun Mystique* (Bowling Green, Ohio: Bowling Green University Press, 1971); George N. Fenin and William K. Everson, *The Western* (New York: Bonanza, 1962); Ralph E. and Natasha A. Friar, *The Only Good Indian . . . The Hollywood Gospel* (New York: Drama Book Specialists, 1972); Philip French, *Westerns: Aspects of a Movie Genre* (New York: Oxford University Press, 1977); John H. Lenihan, *Showdown: Confronting Modern America in the Western Film* (Urbana: University of Illinois Press, 1980); Kim Newman, *Wild West Movies* (London: Bloomsbury, 1990); William T. Pilkington and Don Graham, *Western Movies* (Albuquerque: University of New Mexico Press, 1979); Wayne Michael Sarf, *God Bless You, Buffalo Bill* (Rutherford, N.J.: Fairleigh Dickinson University Press, 1983); and Jon Tuska, *The American West in Film* (Westport, Conn.: Greenwood, 1985).

More specific items on the making of early Hollywood Westerns are Diana Serra Cary, *The Hollywood Posse* (Boston: Houghton Mifflin, 1975); William S. Hart, *My Life East and West* (Boston: Houghton Mifflin, 1929); Howard Karren, "Rancho Deluxe," *Premiere* (Winter 1991), 40–41; and John H. Nicholas, *Tom Mix: Riding Up to Glory* (Oklahoma City: Persimmon Hill, 1980).

The Wyatt Earp correspondence with William S. Hart in the Hart papers at the Los Angeles County Museum of Natural History is of primary interest, supplemented by Glenn G. Boyer, ed., *I Married Wyatt Earp: The Recollections of Joseph Sarah Marcus Earp* (Tucson: University of Arizona Press, 1976).

Relevant general works on film and Hollywood are Andre Bazin, *What Is Cinema?* (Berkeley: University of California Press, 1971); Kingsley Canham, *The Hollywood Professionals* (London: Tantivy, 1973); Molly Haskell, *From Reverence to Rape* (New York: Holt, Rinehart and Winston, 1974); Garson Kanin, *Hollywood* (New York: Viking, 1974); Kenneth Macgowan, *Behind the Screen* (New York: Delacorte, 1965); Joan Mellen, *Big Bad Wolves: Masculinity in the American Film* (New York: Pantheon, 1977); Bill Nichols, "Style, Grammar, and the Movies," *Film Quarterly* 28 (Spring 1975), 33–49; Gertrude Samuels, "The Director—Hollywood's Leading Man," *New York Times Magazine* (October 26, 1952), 22–23; Budd Schulberg, *Moving Pictures: Memories of a Hollywood Prince* (New York: Stein and Day, 1981); and Aubrey Solomon, "A Corporate and Financial History of the 20th Century-Fox Studio" (photocopy, 1979, Mayer Library, American Film Institute).

Nancy Scheper-Hughes, *Saints, Scholars, and Schizophrenics: Mental Illness in Rural Ireland* (Berkeley: University of California Press, 1979) is a perceptive dissection of the rural Irish personality by an anthropologist. Valuable also are Conrad M. Arensberg, *The Irish Countryman* (Gloucester, Mass.: Peter Smith, 1959); Oscar Handlin, *Boston's Immigrant's* (New York: Atheneum, 1972); John Duffy Ibson, *Will the World Break Your Heart?* (New York: Garland, 1990); James H. Mundy, *Hard Times, Hard Men: Maine and the Irish, 1830–1860* (Scarborough, Maine.: Harp, 1990); and William V. Shannon, *The American Irish* (New York: Macmillan, 1963). Joseph M. Curran's *Hibernian Green on the Silver Screen: The Irish and American Movies* (New York: Greenwood, 1989) treats Ford's films intelligently and at length.

Joseph Campbell with Bill Moyers, *The Power of Myth* (New York: Doubleday, 1988) is an engaging introduction to the role of myth in world cultures, whereas M. Owen Lee, *Wagner's Ring: Turning the Sky Round* (New York: Summit, 1990) serves as a model for studies of myth aimed at a wide readership.

Index